Making a Game Demo

From Concept to Demo Gold

Chad Walker, Eric Walker, and Jani Kajala

Wordware Publishing, Inc.

Library of Congress Cataloging-in-Publication Data

Walker, Chad Gregory, 1976-.
    Making a game demo : from concept to demo gold / by Chad Walker, Eric Walker, and Jani Kajala.
      p. cm.
    Includes index.
    ISBN 1-55622-048-0 (pbk., companion cd-rom)
    1. Computer games--Programming. 2. Computer games--Design. 3. Computer graphics.
    I. Walker, Eric, 1970-. II. Kajala, Jani. III. Title.
    QA76.76.C672W324 2005
    794.8'1526--dc22
                                   2005009711
                                      CIP

ISBN-13: 978-1-55622-048-0
ISBN-10: 1-55622-048-0
10 9 8 7 6 5 4 3 2 1
0505

All inquiries for volume purchases of this book should be addressed to Wordware Publishing, Inc., at the above address. Telephone inquiries may be made by calling:

(972) 423-0090

Contents

Contents

Contents

Contents

Part 3 — Game Programming

Contents

Foreword

I get e-mails from aspiring game developers almost every day asking me what they should do to get into game development and how to get publishers interested in them. The answer is always the same: Make a demo! A resume full of the right buzzwords is all well and good, but new development groups are always better off by showing a demo of what they can do.

I interview people for positions a lot. I'm very critical of a person's resume because it shows the level of organizational and communicative skills of the individual. Having years of experience in the industry is a big plus and having shipped successful titles is an even bigger plus. But the biggest plus is when I can see an impressive demo — it's worth so much more. It indicates the person is very serious about showing his or her skills and getting a job.

Another trait that I value highly is when a person works on improving skills on his or her own time. Several times I've talked with someone who could easily reach "the next level" simply by putting in some effort during off-hours. Doing this shows an individual's strong drive for success. And why wouldn't I want to hire someone with a drive like that?

You know what the most impressive demo is? A complete game that's polished — with a menu system, scores, installer, etc. The last 10% of putting together a game is the hardest and anyone who can show me an entire game they've finished — it's golden. This book is all about showing you how to put together the most impressive presentation you can — and get the job or deal that you want!

— John Romero

Acknowledgments

This project is bigger than any one person. The idea of creating a book with so much art and code for the public is simply amazing. To be sure everyone is mentioned, we want to list the great group of people who helped make this book come to life.

Eric and I would like to thank the following:

Number one, we thank God for all His love and blessings.

To our family — Greg and Juanita Walker (our parents) and sister Sheila and brother Dario and their super-sweet girl Sofia.

To my (Chad) adoring and compassionate wife, Chelsea, whose patience allowed me to disappear for six months while working on this book.

To my (Eric) loving wife, Maria, may the chapters in our life be more exciting than this book (he he). Thank you for the future you let me live in and the present you hold me to.

I want to thank Wes, the greatest editor ever, for keeping things going and running so smoothly from start to finish.

I also want to thank a handful of people who wrote chapters in the book and created some outstanding art, sound, and music for you to have and enjoy:

Professor David March — Thanks for writing the entire chapter on animation and for being such great support through the duration of the book.

Nathan Howard — Thanks to a superb friend for creating all the great SFX noises and sounds for the demo.

Giuseppe — Special thanks to my most excellent friend, owner of Twelve Interactive - Crotone, Italy (www.twelvegames.com).

Tommaso Pau — The man behind the music (www.kitchenprod.com).

Tim Evans — Excellent work on the evil Worker Bot.

Matt Manchester — Thanks for taking the time to model and write about vehicle creation! Check him out at www.modelforge.com.

Juan Martinez and Michael Little — Thanks for your excellent scripts and additions to 3D Studio MAX. Way to go, guys!

The Guildhall at SMU — A special thanks goes out to everyone who works and contributes at the Guildhall for their continued dedication and commitment to the gaming community and to raising the bar and producing top-notch talent for the industry. Also, a big thanks for giving graciously of their motion capture system and animation data.

Jani would like to say a big thank you to the following people:

Chad Walker — For asking me into this project. It has been great to work with you!

Everyone at Pixelgene, Ltd. — For giving me time to work on this. Especially, thanks to Fernando Herrera for his constructive discussions and support.

Acknowledgments

Walker Boys Studio, Saurav Mohapatra (Etvig Interactive), Mikko Heilimo (Pixelgene), and Fredrik Svensson (Mindforce) — For your most welcome Ka3D engine feedback and testing.

Jeff Royle (ATI) and Keith Galocy (NVidia) — Thank you for supporting my engine development.

Erin Palmroth, Tuomas Kähkönen, Kirsi Uimi, Mikko Kodisoja, and Mika Tammenkoski — For your long-time friendship, which I highly value. (Erin and Kirsi: Among many other things, you happen to be also two of the best writers I know.)

Finally, thanks to my family for endless support — My parents, Tarja and Pentti Kajala, and sister Jenni, brother Kai, and their families. And last and most importantly my darling Ichinkhorloo Ganbold, who had to bear the extra stress of having me write this book.

Eric and Chad Walker, Jani Kajala

Introduction

Welcome, reader! Have you ever wanted to make your own computer game? Do you find yourself playing games constantly? Does the thought of having your very own characters running around in a world you create excite you? If you have answered yes to these questions, then you have certainly picked up the right book! *Making a Game Demo* is the first of its kind. With a straightforward and structured approach we will guide you from A to Z through the entire process of creating game demos. The combination of art, level design, scripting, and programming makes this book an invaluable purchase for the beginner all the way through to the professional in the gaming industry. The authors have worked on many of the hottest titles to ever hit the store shelves and want to share with you more than 30 combined years of experience in the business.

A certain phrase from the Guildhall at SMU comes to mind, "Stop playing games and start making them!" This is a noteworthy thought especially if you're holding this book in your hands and reading it right now. You must have a passion and desire in developing your own games, and with *Making a Game Demo*, you are on your way.

Making a Game Demo is jam-packed with everything you will need to create your very own game demo or full-fledged AAA game. The book is divided into three parts, providing a quick and organized means to find what you need. Part 1, "Game Design," walks you through writing your first design document and the level design document, and then helps you capture the perfect look and feel of your game with an art style guide. From there it's on to the art assets and level design of the game in Part 2, "Art Creation," where you will learn all about 3D Studio MAX, Photoshop, and most importantly, how to use them to their fullest when it comes to creating the best art on the market today. With the art complete, it's time to take on the task of game programming in Part 3. With well-written tutorials and solid programming elements, we'll have you creating everything from the simple "Hello, 3D World" to finite state machines and very robust code. Every tutorial will take you step by step toward understanding the full complexity of the Ka3D engine and provide you with working examples so you can see exactly how it is done. With a built-in scripting language, particle editor, and shader system, we will have you up to speed in no time writing intuitive cameras, intelligent AI (artificial intelligence), normal mapping, cartoon rendering effects, dynamic lighting, and much more.

The main purpose and design of this book is to show you how it's done. Rather than spending pages talking about the theory of other games or hard-core design or interviews, what we talk about is how to create a game demo! We spend our pages and your time working on practical applications, real-world solutions to problems we come across, and much more while creating a game demo.

The features and tutorials of the book are simply too numerous to list in this introduction. *Making a Game Demo* covers multiple topics and no matter how well laid out, it will take some time to get through everything, so without further hesitation let's take our first steps into creating a game demo.

> **Note:**
>
> Don't forget to pace yourself daily with this book. I would suggest setting aside two to three hours each day, begin and complete every exercise, and never lose focus on the end goal. If you can do that, then your game demo is that much closer to being realized.

We wish you the best of luck with this endeavor and hope to see some great work from you soon. For technical issues, max questions, a great community, and more, visit us at www.Ka3d.com. We're only a click away. :-)

Part 1

Game Design

In the beginning, every project starts off with an idea. This idea is built upon and expanded to generate thoughts and designs until finally there is so much that you are forced to write it all down. The idea is the cornerstone of the game design. In the chapters ahead we walk through brainstorming the ideas, making sense of what you have written, and conceptualizing the game. All these steps make up what I call the game design documents (GDD). These documents are often considered "living documents," meaning they are continually revised until the game is finished and out the door heading to the publisher (and

sometimes even after). Revising the documents will continue to keep things on the edge. Remember, this doesn't mean you don't need a solid game design to start with; it means that working with a team and getting feedback from focus studies and playtesters can often cause the designer to change his/her mind about certain features, gameplay aspects, characters, etc.

In Chapter 1 we are going to look at one way of coming up with a game idea. Typically, I take a different approach each time I come up with an idea. For me it really depends on the overall theme, whether it's a third-person, FPS, RTS,

RPG, puzzle game, etc. The two main rules I stick with while creating any and every type of game are "gameplay" and "storyline." I believe if you take the story first and write it out, you will find yourself not sticking to any one "theme." The story truly dictates the direction, feel, look, gameplay...everything.

Let's brainstorm some ideas and see what we can come up with!

Chapter 1

Brainstorming Ideas

A quick story to get us going…. There once was a group of intelligent and creative people who ran a company. (I realize this may sound untrue, but it did happen. ☺) Every so often when they got together in a meeting, they would discuss their next set of ideas that would keep the company innovative and a step ahead. What makes this story interesting is how they went about discussing their ideas. The staff would sit around a table and have the secretary take notes while they talked. They all agreed to say nothing negative or pick at any idea. The point of an open forum with no criticism ensured forward, positive thinking, which stimulated everyone in the meeting to their peak performance. The goal was not to delve into any one idea but to generate as many creative ideas as possible. Afterward, they would take the notes and begin refining the great ideas and throwing out the bad ideas until they came up with a list of things that could work.

In the same way, except for the secretary, we came up with the following list of options for our first game demo. Let's check out all the great ideas and even those few funny, not so good ideas.

In brainstorming the first demo we randomly thought of topics and genres that could work for a fun action-packed game as well as themes, gameplay styles, and environments.

- Third-person action adventure game
- FPS shooter
- RTS strategy with a twist of third-person

- Horror style (Resident Evil)
- RPG quest/adventure
- War strategy
- Puzzle game
- Side scroller
- Two-person fighter style
- Period style game (civil war, Indian, medieval, imperialistic, pirates, etc.)
- Cartoon style
- Racing game
- Sporting event
- Mystery/detective style
- Submarine
- Paper dolls
- Raindrops
- Hero male/female
- Team play
- Superheroes
- Regular hero
- Story-driven shoot 'em up
- Realistic style
- Comic style
- Epic stories
- Genetic research
- The girl-next-door scenario
- Aliens
- Doomsday
- Apocalyptic
- Fairy/dream-like
- Underground world
- Girl spy, CIA, FBI, etc.
- Winter scene
- Forest worlds
- Lava worlds
- Dragons and creatures

- Fantasy
- Space age and sci-fi
- Modern-day Rambo
- Vigilante
- Cop
- Secrets
- Animal game style
- Hunting
- Mobsters
- Twists and turns for plots
- Multiple storylines
- Friendship
- Big bosses for fights
- Robots and wires
- Animation driven
- Combo moves
- Demo levels — show off tech and art
- Kung fu adventure
- Comedy
- Tech-like
- Take over the world
- Find a lost treasure

- Robots
- Hidden treasure
- Sci-fi
- Adventure
- Action
- Combo moves
- Third-person action adventure game
- Story-driven
- Tech-like
- Friendship
- Realistic style
- Genetic research
- Hero male

Okay, above is a partial list of the ideas we came up with. Once you have brainstormed the initial ideas, take a highlighter and mark the ones that are the coolest. Below is the list we selected.

The Word List

- Female FBI agent
- Cartoon style
- Lava world
- Mobsters
- Secrets
- Comedy
- Epic
- Twists and turns for plots
- Multiple storylines
- Big boss fight

The Sentence Structure

Now, we need to see about fitting them together into a cohesive storyline or a run-on sentence. Remember, we are still brainstorming here. It's okay if your English isn't perfect and/or your sentence structures are not chiseled down. We want thoughts and ideas to flow at this point.

"The first demo idea will be a **cartoon style, third-person action adventure** game. A **techy** or **sci-fi male hero** will begin his **adventure** in a world by itself in the universe. Being a messup, he leaves to fix a wrong starting in a **lava world** fighting **robots** and **big bosses**. The character will have weapons, **combo moves**, and jumping moves…lots of **action**, but will stick to a very **story-driven** idea consisting of **comedy** and **hidden treasures** or **tech-like** objects. To make it more grandiose, the hero's story will be of **epic** proportions as he attempts to save the universe from total destruction."

And while we are at it, let's use the rest of the words to create another game idea.

"The second idea we could work on revolves around an undercover **female FBI agent** who is caught up in a **mobster** shoot-out. Her initial assumption is that the local mob boss wants her dead, but she has no idea that most of the story doesn't involve her. By writing a **story-driven**, **realistic style** adventure game, the female character will become thrown into **twists and turns**. Her adventures will result in **multiple storylines** about **genetic research** and former FBI agents while making new **friendships** and discovering her family's past **secrets**."

■ ■ ■

Excellent! A handful of words and a couple sentences later and we have the makings of some fun games.

The first brainstorming session is over! We have managed to pull out some great ideas through our word list and sentence structures. It's time to take these thoughts and expand them into full-fledged game design documents.

Design Documentation

The design document is at the heart of any game. The name "design" implies the "creation" and "documentation" of some-thing — in this case the game demo project. With our brainstorming ideas still fresh in our minds we should go ahead and set up a solid design document for the cartoon game. If you have never designed a game before, don't worry — we are going to go step by step through each portion of the documentation. A design document can take anywhere from a solid two weeks to three months to complete; however, since we are just writing a document for a demo, it will be much easier and less time consuming. When creating a demo design document we want to include a brief history of the characters, the general storyline, and an outline of the major events, and then focus in on the details of the level being created.

> **Note:**
>
> The demo should be a vertical slice of the game at some point at which it is the most engrossing and fun to play. We don't want the slice to be the part where the hero sleeps for three hours and the players only get to watch him snore. It needs to be action packed, enveloping gameplay and a com-pelling enough storyline to want more.

The Design Document

Why is a design document important? The design document is like the who, what, where, when, and how of games. It tells us "who" our audience is, our characters, our villains, our purpose, etc. The "what" lets us know the technical side of our game like code, scripting, and a cool feature list. The "where" tells us about the environments, settings, and levels. The "when" and "how" of the design document describe the gameplay aspects and events that occur throughout the course of the game.

The game design document is probably the largest and most in-depth portion of the design process. I have attempted to keep things simple and divided into basic sections so that when you read through it you will be able to tell the pattern as well as the direction you could take when designing your own document. Also, remember that there is a blank design document in the Templates folder on the companion CD. This should be an excellent starter for you as well.

The second and possibly more important reason behind writing a design document is that it allows you to clearly express your ideas through a written means for friends, co-workers, and publishers. Without docu-ments like this, everyone else will assume you have an overactive imagination. But with this document on hand, you can prove

to them that you really do have an overactive imagination.

In this chapter we are looking at the elements of a design document. Each company
I have worked for has created design documents differently, so I figure it's best to
follow that trend. The name "Design Document" is the heading for all the documents
in the game. This places the examples at
the top of our hierarchy and keeps them
organized and simple. Oftentimes, design
documents are overworked and complicated. Remember, if you can't make it
sound simple, then chances are you don't
know what you're talking about or you don't
have a clear enough understanding of the
project.

> **Note:**
>
> Take your time with the design phase. The
> design is *key* to a successful game. So sit
> back, read over the chapter, and really take
> in what you study. You need to be able to
> apply the same practices to your own docu-
> ments when you get ready to create a game.

To reiterate once more: Our main objective
is to keep things *simple* when writing the
design document. If it takes specialized programs, years of practice, and the ability to
stand on one hand, then there's a good
chance we are making things too difficult
for ourselves and our team. We will stick
with a straightforward design and carry that
through with everything else, so that you
can easily implement this style of design
into your own work.

> **Note:**
>
> Instead of touching up the design docu-
> ments to make them fit perfectly with the
> actual demo created, I have left them in the
> original format so you can read through and
> see what we did have time to accomplish as
> well as the things that didn't get imple-
> mented with the actual demo. If you were
> handing this off to a publisher to review, I
> would suggest cutting it down to what is in
> the demo and then having a side notation of
> "wish list" items that you would like to
> implement with more time and funding.

Vision Statement (One-liner)

The vision statement, or one-liner as I like
to call it, is simply that. When writing the
vision statement you want a short, one-line
sentence that sums up the entire scope of
the game. By writing this one-liner, you
sum up what it is you are trying to accomplish with the game and thereby force
everyone to remain focused on that idea. If
someone were to ask you what makes your
game fun or why someone would want to
play your game, the underlying answer
would revolve around the vision statement.

For the Zax demo we came up with this
vision statement:

> **"Destroying and exploring
> is the name of the game"**

Sounds simple, right? When I think about
games, two design elements come to mind
first. Most game players love destroying
objects and blowing up levels and enemies,
so the first word I chose was "destroying."
(Also note that the verb form gives the
effect that it's happening now.) In cartoon-
style games there is a huge draw in exploration, since "exploring" gives the
impression of something grander or larger
than life. Everyone wants to know what's
around the corner or on the other side of
the mountain. So by using these two words

in our vision statement, we secure the basic parameters and visualization of the Zax demo.

Note:

There's a good chance the vision statement won't just jump out at you in the beginning of the project. Once you begin to flesh out the idea it becomes easier to associate a one-liner with the game project. So if it doesn't just come to you, give it some time. (Not too much time though.)

Prelude

The second thing we are going to look at is the "prelude" to the Zax demo. Any story, whether short or long, should always have a history to it. If you create a character and don't know where it came from, then chances are you won't know where to take it or how to take it through the rest of the story. The following is the first part of the Zax demo, which is a simple example of creating a history for the characters and storyline.

Note:

Remember the prelude basically answers the who, what, where, when, and how of Zax's history.

Zax's Adventure Storyline

Prelude to the Zax demo...

Jask, the home planet of Zax's people, is full of happiness, joy, and peace. This world hasn't known war for more than two centuries. The planet Jask retains a large army, of which our young upstart hero, Zax, is a member. The army is used mostly for formal ceremonies, parades, and the occasional fundraiser.

Zax of course is one of the few who has an itching desire for more. He wants what his ancestors had — adventure, excitement, and exploration. On his days off Zax decides to explore the books of old. These ancient books were written during the war times of his people. They tell tales of heroes, murders, justices, great losses, and sacrifices. All these things begin to entice Zax to learn more of his past. He hears the ancient times calling out to him.

One day while browsing books, Zax bumped a shelf and an old, dusty manuscript fell from the top shelf and opened to a special page in front of Zax. His interest was piqued after he read the story of **Lexus the Lifebreaker**, the leader of all that is evil in the universe.

So, after a bit of research, he found out that the people of Jask are alone in the universe. Centuries ago, in order for his people to escape utter defeat by the hand of Lexus, they created a device that sent them into another realm. At first the warriors wanted to go back and help their friends who were left fighting to finish Lexus off, but the majority of the civilians were tired of fighting. They wanted peace at least once before they died. They figured their children could deal with it when the time came. So their king, weary and of old age, gave in to just that. They used the excuse that they would rebuild and make a large enough army to stop Lexus and then they would go back and join the rest of the universe in the battle.

Time went on, peace prospered, and the people adjusted well to one another. They soon found themselves delighting in the fact that they were alone. Years go by and it becomes official: They're staying put. The machines that got them there were stored away. The armies for most of the planet were disassembled and sent home. They became farmers and workers, husbands, and fathers.

That was good for the time, but Zax is ready for more. He wants to go back so he pursues a different course of action and goes to see the king. Zax informs the king of all that was going on, unaware of the king's position, and asks him to rectify the situation. The king enlightens Zax of the kings of the past. Each king before him continued to pass down an emblem as it were. It's the eye of Lexus. The story goes that a brave soldier dear to all the people struck the mighty beast Lexus and cut loose an eye before being dashed to oblivion. So long as the eye still lives, Lexus is alive. Each king decided not to go back until the eye was dead; then they would return. The eye of Lexus sees all that is around him and his anger for Zax's people continues to burn to this day.

The king said, "So, I made the same decision my ancestors made. I will keep our people safe and in peace until Lexus is no more." The news of all this, of course, didn't sit well with Zax. He felt as if his people weren't living in peace but in fear, and it grieved him deeply. So, he sought out the secrets and the hiding places around the land. Soon, he discovered the hidden pathway leading to the ancient temples where the Teleport pods were stored away. Zax managed to get inside the temples and that's where things begin...

Note: The next portion of the story is designed around the few moments before the actual demo takes place.

The Teleport pods are all stored in a high-tech room where Zax attempts to quietly sneak in and look around to see if any of the equipment still works. Standing on a control panel area, he pushes what he assumes is the light switch. All the pods activate. They begin glowing and then poof, they are all gone except for one. The pit of his stomach turns and the alarms scream out as he's stuck holding the trigger.

The catch here is that each pod is a one-way ticket to the next pod. The last pod is a straight portal to their home world, which naturally opens the link to Lexus and his tormented universe. Zax is too worried at this point to think straight and figures he'd better do something really quick.

Zax decides to jump into the light from the glowing portal, but before he makes another move the king runs in and falls to the floor as his legs give way. "So, it is true. The portal in the sky is from the pods. They have been reactivated." Looking directly at Zax, the king solemnly cries, "What have you done? What have you done, Zax? Already the sky is opening up. If we don't get to the last portal in time the doorway will soon grow and envelop our planet and take us back. Right now it's only small enough for a bird to come through, but who knows what terrible sin could enter our world...and given time armies could flood the planet."

Zax looks at the king sorrowfully and says, "Sire, I must go then and try to fix the wrong I've done."

The king responds with compassion, "Go then with speed. I will wait for you on this side. I will gather our troops and prepare for battle. Take this with you. It will help you to find the other pods." The king tosses him a tracking device.

Zax leaps into the bright beam and teleports away. He takes with him the tracking device and courage, which will lead him to adventures more grand than all his people have ever known.

Game Synopsis

The game synopsis is basically a short summary or a few paragraphs of what the game is all about. Think about it like a press release that gives readers just enough information to know what the idea is all about yet builds up enough curiosity to make them want more. Let's give it a try.

The universe has fallen into times of darkness where shadows steal the daylight and evil rules the night. Twelve pods scattered around all creation breathe life into centuries of tyranny and destruction. Zax must seek out the twelve pods to close the portal between his home planet and Lord Lexus before it is too late.

Using a third-person follow camera, the player uses Zax's unique abilities of strength, agility, and humor to navigate through fascinating worlds full of adventure and never-ending excitement.

Zax, our overzealous soldier and a young hero in the making, is confronted with more than just thoughts and dreams but with a reality that he must save his planet and the universe from the dreaded Lord Lexus. The quest for battle and adventure comes at a high price, one which Zax will have to face as he fights his way through dozens of frightening creatures and nonstop destruction.

Will one light in all the darkness be enough to change the tides of war?

That wraps up the brief history of Zax and his people as well as the synopsis of the storyline. Now we are ready to create the full "demo" game design document in all its detail and glory.

Zax Game Design Document

Cinematic 1
Opening Sequence

For the opening of the game we've decided to keep it nice and simple, since it is a demo and our budget is zero bucks. A paper style scroll from the book that Zax discovers lays open. Words scroll by, giving the history of what has happened up to this point and why our "hero in the making" is traveling the universe. Along with the words will be a set of pictures (comic style) that highlight the main portions of the story.

Storyboard 1
A detailed version of the scroll paper fills up the screen as pictures fade in and words begin moving across it.

Note: Work up the .avi inside Flash MX.

Act 1 — Leaky Looney's Lava Pit

Summary

The hot, sulfury smells of volcanic ash fill the hollow environment into which Zax teleports. Zax's confidence is all he has to go by. This baked land will test his ability to reason, to shoot, and even to survive. Large pipes and conduits run across the lava below, creating a mirrored range of obstacles and "floating" land masses. Zax must help the Bots of Lava Land and defeat the tyrant Leaky Looney in order to open the door to a Lava Suit and begin his quest. Once Zax gets the Lava Suit, he will be able to jump off the volcanic rock and continue his search for the Teleport pods in the pool of lava waiting below.

Load Screen Image
Level_1_Lava_Pit_1

Objectives
Learn player controls
Explore the environment
Talk with the Worker Bots and find a way to help them
Collect all the Glow Coins
Reopen the passageway to the mine
Dodge lava bombs
Defeat Leaky Looney
Get the Lava Suit and dive off into the lava below

Special Gameplay
Search for clues — Zax must search around for clues when the player first begins.
Secondary firing — Zax will have to find the grenade launcher in order to blow apart the rocks.
Lava bombs — Zax won't be able to stay in one spot too long. Lava bombs will be flung into the air by Leaky Looney.

Upgrades
Laser gun
Grenade launcher
Light pads

Environment Sounds
Ambient lava sounds
Lava bubbling
Heat crackling
Steam pipes hissing

NPC
Worker Bot

Enemies
Worker Bot
Wobbles

Boss
Leaky Looney

Extra Challenges
Must keep all the Worker Bots alive, even the crazy ones that want to kill Zax.

Scene 1 — A New Beginning

The game starts with a cut scene, an establishing shot of the Teleport pad. The camera pans by slowly behind the Teleport pad as a bright bluish-colored beam emerges from the center of it. At this point Zax fades slowly into the level.

Onscreen Text: *Leaky Looney's Lava Pit*

The sulfuric ash fills the air with a mysterious evil.

a1s1_teleport_01.wav
<<Effects Sound>>
(Beaming noise should be the first sound you hear)

As the bright blue and white lights fade out, a hero steps forth from the mechanical device. Unsure of what to expect, Zax quickly surveys the area around him.

Sounds from below become evidence of life in the fiery volcanic pit. Zax's attention is drawn downward toward the voices and clanks.

a1s1_Worker_Bot1_01.wav
<< Worker Bot 1>>
**(Worker Bots are all communicating with one another
as they zip around digging aimlessly)**
BEeP....ziippp zipp.....burrrrrirpp......clank.clank.ca...

a1s1_Worker_Bot2_01.wav
<<Worker Bot 2>>
(Darker-colored Bot begins beeping wildly then walks madly away)
Riiiiiinggg....zzzzappppp.l...liiiiii..tiiiiickkkkkkk..taa.

a1s1_Zax_01.wav
<<Zax>>
(Thinking to himself)
Hmm...Robots with attitudes...now that's a scary thought.

Cut Scene — The camera begins panning to the side of Zax as he looks toward the sign that says, "Looney's Lava Pit."

a1s1_Zax_02.wav
<<Zax>>
(Talking to himself once again)
Looney's Lava Pit...
(A slight pause as he thinks, then says)
Maybe someone down there has seen my Teleporter.

Zax heads down the slope of the rocky hillside and begins to gesture as though to say something to one of the Worker Bots.

The green-eyed glowing Bot stops its senseless walking and stares at Zax. It mumbles a few words, then proceeds to tell him about their cave-in. They need Zax's help to get the grenades located on the side of the volcano.

a1s1_Worker_Bot1_02.wav
<<Worker Bot 1>>
(Tired and out of it)
beeeezzzzzz....ickk...?....blink??

a1s1_Zax_03.wav
<<Zax>>
(Cautious yet warming)
Uh...hello....um...I come in peace?..?
(Smiles after he speaks)

a1s1_Worker_Bot1_03.wav
<<Worker Bot 1>>
(A bit more focused, Bot 1 stares directly at Zax)
Tiiii....ziip...zipp.....du....op...burrrrrrrrrrrr....toip...tieeeep........clafffic...soop.

Onscreen Text: *Ah, welcome to Leaky Looney's Lava Pit. I am Worker Bot 1. Our mining shaft caved in from a rock slide a few days ago. We need to get back to work before we short circuit and Leaky Looney finds replacements. There are some grenades across the way but we cannot get to them. Maybe you can reach them? I know if you jump on the red button pad over there, it will activate the generator and can help you get to them.*

Zax realizes that they need help and figures that if he does this, there's a good chance that they will help him find his Teleporter. It's worth taking a chance on.

a1s1_Zax_04.wav
<<Zax>>
(Willingly he agrees with the Bot)
Sounds like something I can help you with. I'll be right back with the grenades.

Scene 2 — Activation

Zax jogs toward the generator button and jumps onto it. Things get interesting now. All the supply ports on this side of the level light up and begin generating their specified items. Zax is taken aback for a moment by this because he wasn't aware that technology like this existed. But with every price of achievement, there comes a higher price of restitution. The Wobbles become active as well. In the beginning they simply laid dormant like junk, but because of the activation, they are alive and start cleaning the level of everything. Zax will be slightly sidetracked because he wants to investigate the new objects that appear around the level.

To ensure that he gets the Laser Gun when the supply ports become active, we need a cut scene of the weapon on the hilltop.

Cut Scene — Camera pans up toward the supply port at the top of the hill. Visible in the bright light is the Laser Gun.

a1s2_Zax_05.wav
<<Zax>>
(That coolness effect seeing awesome technology)
Whoa. Now that is cool.

Zax begins making his way up toward the Laser Gun just as one of the Wobbles decides he needs to be cleaned up and off the volcano. Zax leaps out of the way and continues toward the weapon. Once Zax acquires it, he begins to take notice of all the Glow Coins in the area. He decides to walk toward one. As he gets closer, the Glow Coin vanishes with a "cling" noise.

When Zax collects the first Glow Coin an onscreen text will appear.

Onscreen Text: *You have just collected a Glow Coin. There are many Glow Coins located around the level. If you collect all the Glow Coins, you can deposit them at the coin station to activate the bridge.*

With the Glow Coins located all over the map, Zax now has two objectives. Since he is at the top of the hill, he makes his first daring leap to the small lava rock. From there Zax works his way over to the tilt pad, which he finds himself using to leap high into the air. At this point Zax might be able to see the glowing boot located above him. Zax decides to jump to the rock and collect the Boot.

When Zax collects the Boot an onscreen text message will come up explaining how to use it.

Onscreen Text: *You have upgraded your jump boots. Now when you jump, you can press the jump button once more to soar twice as high.*

Zax realizes he needs to get his priorities straight. He leaps back down and jumps on the moving pad, then carefully jumps to each of the moving pads. After a planned and skillful jump, Zax reaches the side of the volcano where he recovers several Glow Coins and the Secondary Ammo.

a1s2_Grenade _Pickup_01.wav
<<Effects Sound>>

The grenade pickup sound activates, letting Zax know he's picked up the ammo

Zax is now armed and dangerous.

Onscreen Text: *You now have Grenades! In order to launch the Grenades press the secondary fire button.*

Note: This is secondary ammunition, meaning Zax has to have the Laser Gun in order to use the Grenades. If he doesn't have the gun by this point, we need an onscreen text saying, "You have the secondary ammunition, but you still need the Laser Gun in order to use the Grenades."

Scene 3 — Blow Up

Jumping back to the mainland, Zax finds his way over to the cave-in and blows apart all the rocks and debris.

All of this happens in real time. No cut scenes should be needed. The Worker Bots that went mad become a bit more civilized. They come up to Zax and thank him for his help.

a1s3_ Worker_Bot1_04.wav
<<Worker Bot 1 and 2>>
(Excited)
Yiiippppp.....zzzzz...yiiiiiieeee...txxzzz..t

Onscreen Text: *You did it! Thank you so much! As a reward, we want to give you this.*

Cut Scene — Camera zooms in and rotates around the light pads that the Worker Bots give Zax.

a1s3_ Worker_Bot1_05.wav
<<Worker Bot 1>>
(Explains what the light pads do)
Ysheepii.....brrrtt...liiittzz...chiiieep..t

Onscreen Text: *The lights are connected to your shoulder pads. Simply press the Activate light button and the pads will light up any dark place you have to go into.*

a1s3_Zax_06.wav
<<Zax>>
(Thankfully responds)
Thanks, Bot 1. I have a feeling I'll need these real soon.

Zax decides to run into the mining shaft and explore a bit. The mine is extremely dark so he turns on his lights and has a look around. Running down the mining shaft, Zax has to maneuver around until he makes his way to the center of the volcano. Zax had noticed from the opening above that there was a Glow Coin in the mining shaft and makes his way down to it. Collecting the final Coin, Zax is met with a message on the screen.

Onscreen Text: *You have all the Glow Coins. Congratulations!*

a1s3_Glow_Coins_Collected_01.wav
<<Effects Sound>>
(Collecting all the coins)

Scene 4 — Angry Looney

With all the Coins collected, Zax makes his way back up the mining shaft and out to the orange daylight that exists. As he leaves the comforts of the mining shaft a terrible noise is heard all across the volcano.

a1s4_Loony_01.wav
<<Looney>>
(Putting fear into one's heart)
Arrrrrrriiiiiiiiieeeeeeeeeee

a1s4_Loony_02.wav
<<Looney>>
(Very irritated)
Who has disturbed my slumber!?
(Breathing in)
It doesn't matter! You will all pay the price!

That's when you hear the noise. The sound of a large bomb whizzing by Zax's head and crushing into the ground behind him, smashing one of the Worker Bots (should be slightly humorous). It's a lava bomb! Zax is now challenged with not only the Wobbles cleaning up the new messes (lava bombs), but he's plagued by lava bombs that are homed into wherever he is. Zax has to stay on the move.

With the new twist, Zax decides it's time to activate the bridge and get on with the show.

Zax deposits the Glow Coins and activates the bridge. The bridge begins humming and then slowly moves toward Zax. The lava bombs continue to pelt the ground, forcing Zax to move around until the bridge gets to him.

a1s4_Bridge_Moving_01.wav
<<Effects Sound>>
(Humming noise with a slight sound of an engine)

Unfortunately, Looney is a good aim with the lava bombs and takes out the bridge motors. The bridge stops about halfway. The engine slows to a hum, then dies out. With smoke drifting upward, Zax decides his only option is to leap across to the bridge with his jump boots. Executing a flawless jump, Zax glides across the chasm to find himself on a new portion of the level.

Scene 5 — Boss Fight

Zax is given a bit of a breather as Looney becomes tired and stops tossing lava bombs. The metal expands across the full side of the volcano, weaving in and out with platforms and pipe work. Zax's first objective is to get the Generator up and running so that the moving pads will start up. Zax figures it will be easy and jumps on one of the generator buttons, then steps off. The moment he steps off a counter begins at five seconds, giving him only a short time to press the adjacent button. Once pressed, the Generator begins to spin in the distance and the lights and pads come to life.

Zax makes his way to each of the supply ports and refills on health, ammo, and an extra life. He then navigates up the lift pad and to the top of the volcano.

Cut Scene — Camera is low to the ground, panning by Zax's legs from behind. You can see a shape rising up from the lava in front of him. (This should definitely be "spooky.")

a1s5_ lava_bubble_01.wav
<<Effect Noise>>
(Bubbling noise from lava)

Cut Scene — Close in on Leaky Looney as he spouts at Zax. Looney is upset and prepared to battle anyone at this point. (No one messes with his volcano and gets away with it.)

a1s5_ Looney_03.wav
<<Looney>>
(Shouting angrily)
Sooo, you've come to hurt Looney? Master has told me many things of thissss.

a1s5_Zax_07.wav
<<Zax>>
(Taken off guard)
Master? Where does your loyalty lie?

a1s5_ Looney_04.wav
<<Looney>>
(Talking with contempt in his voice)
Lord Lexus...Ahh, so you really are from the other realm...sssss...I remember when your people ran from the face of destruction. They left the fate of the world in the hands of broken promises and liessss. Herhh..haaher.

Cut Scene — Over the shoulder of Looney showing Zax getting upset.

a1s5_Zax_08.wav
<<Zax>>
(Defensive response)
You know nothing about my people!

a1s5_ Looney_05.wav
<<Looney>>
(Shouting angrily)
Fine, have it your way then. I will burn you alive, the same way I did to all your kind that got in my master's way!

The fight begins. Zax shoots several "test" shots to find out if there are any weak points on the creature. The eyes and the underside of Looney are quite soft and glow each time they are hit. The rest of Looney is protected with a hard protective shell. Looney immediately starts throwing lava bombs at Zax. Hopefully he can hit the wooden crates behind Zax. Initially, the only things Zax will be able to shoot at are the eyes. Once Looney's health is worked halfway down, he loses eyesight and goes mad crazy! Looney begins jumping into the air and doing his spin attack move and splash attack move. Finally, Zax finishes him off by shooting out the underbelly while dodging the lava splashes and spin attacks.

Looney dies and sinks deep into the lava. (Or possibly off the side into the metal grate below.)

Cut Scene — Camera pans down, showing the door in Section 1 opening up to reveal the "Lava Suit."

Realizing what's down there, Zax hurries along the side of the volcano and gets to the Lava Suit.

Cut Scene — Body shot camera view of Zax playing his victory animation.

Optional
Cut Scene — Worker Bots congratulate Zax and thank him for freeing them of the evil tyrant Looney.

With the lava helmet on Zax's head, he jumps off the side of the rock into the fiery lava below.
Load Level 2

Act 2 — End of Demo

Summary
The end of the demo changes up a bit. Instead of Zax going into the lava with a cut scene, we see Zax fall to a *Star Trek* holodeck.

a2s1_Zax_01.wav
<<Zax>>
(Irritated by joke)
Very funny guys…now put me back in the game.
I was just about to save the world and get the girl.

a2s1_Zax_02.wav
(Slight pause, then he looks at the screen)
What do you mean that's it? What, I fight one boss and finito, I'm done?
You've gotta be kidding me. What about the toy line, the cartoon shows…
you said there would be a movie deal! I should have seen it comin'.

a2s1_Zax_03.wav
**(Walks back and forth for a moment…
he comes to the realization as he takes a breath)**
I feel so used…

Onscreen Text: *to be continued…maybe.* ☺

Zax's voice fades off into the background while the screen fades to black. Load the Credit Screen and begin playing the theme music.
Any button now will take the player back to the Start menu.

The End

So there you have it. The basic elements and layout for an entire game are shown here. There is one point I want to bring out that hasn't been directly discussed all through the design document, which is the order of writing. The gameplay is set up to allow the player the choice of direction and goals. For instance, the player could attempt to get all the Glow Coins before ever getting the weapons or vice versa. The main point is that the design document was written with objectives completed in certain steps, which fortunately doesn't have to happen in that order since the gameplay is open to variations. Just remember that whether the design is linear or not, you still need to write a basic order of how things could occur. After playtesting you may find a need to update the order, change the objective goals, or simply keep it the same.

> **Note:**
>
> By maintaining a "linear" undertone we have allowed the player to assume full control of Zax, yet we (designers) still keep the player focused and directed. This subtle degree of management allows the designer and the player to have a great time and never feel as though one side is impeding the other.

Is It Alive or Dead?

That's right, don't think that once you have the game design document (GDD) complete that you will never see any changes made to it. What we have is a living document that will hopefully grow and produce tenfold through the process.

For example…

If technology changes halfway through the development cycle, there's a good chance things may need updating to keep current with newer features and technology. Additional characters and level expansions could present an added challenge when it comes to making the project larger in scope. The opposite could happen as well, which would mean scaling down the project, causing changes to the storyline and gameplay that might not have been considered before.

Updates and revisions will always be a part of the design process. If you are like me and enjoy going back through the docs to revise and update information, that's wonderful! But if you don't enjoy the task, be sure to give it to someone else on the team who does. One of the quickest ways to lose interest in any project is to do something you don't take pleasure in. Surround yourself with a variety of people who have talents different than yours. This will let everyone have an important role within the team and allow skill sets to grow and become refined.

Cinematic Script/ Storyboard/Screenplay

The cinematic scripts, storyboards, and scenes are placed together for these docs. I usually write the script in a format similar to a screenplay. The actual dialog parts (reserved for voiceovers) will have prefixes and color text to offset them as well as cut scenes, visual text on screen, and much more, similar to the GDD we just wrote. When scenes get complicated and need further details to depict what's going on we'll use storyboards. Also, storyboards are used to lay out the cinematic scenes, which could be anything from the opening movie or a cut scene in game to the victory screens and advertisements.

We wanted to design something that was easy to set up and still fun enough to enjoy watching a couple of times over. Check out Intro_2.max at \Tutorials\Art_Tutorials\ Zax_Intro_Cinematic.

Zax Opening Cinematic

Description: Opening sequence fades in as Zax is walking across the screen, possibly humming to himself. Zax begins walking down the hallway and then a button noise sounds and a beam of bright light enters the world. The noise is the button press and Zax realizes that it's time to start up the demo again.

Game Options

The final portion of the GDD documents the characters, combat system, weapons, interface screens, controls, interactions, and more. This part of the document is meant to establish a solid foundation for the actual game aspects and gameplay issues that take place in the demo.

Note:

The document may begin to appear difficult and complex, but if you use the blank template provided, it will be more like filling in the blanks versus coming up with everything from scratch.

Let's start the list off with the hero character and go through his special movements, combat abilities, and weapon arsenal. Then we will approach the controls overview for the character and identify the enemy characteristics and behaviors. We will wrap up the document with the language, interactions, and interface screens.

The Hero

Name: Zax Steel

Description: Zax is the young upstart whose desire to be fearless and brave leads his world to near destruction. Being an orphan, Zax grew up with the knowledge of his people's rich and exciting history as his only source of the past. Unknown to Zax, his great-great-grandfather was the brave soldier who cut the eye from Lexus during the final days of battle. That same blood and heroism flows through Zax's veins as well. With adventure knocking on his door, Zax waits for the opportunity to shine and prove himself a mighty warrior with no fear.

We know that Zax will have the basic walk and run elements, but what else does the character do? Think of these as the complex movements Zax will have throughout the demo.

Special Movements and Navigation

Jump — Zax's mechanical suit allows him to jump slightly higher than a normal person, which gives him advantages over tough obstacles.

Double Jump — After obtaining the Booster Boots, Zax will be able to jump twice as high as before.

Bounce Dodge — Dodges allow Zax to jump swiftly to the side or around enemies and obstacles by leaping sideways onto his shoulder pads and bouncing off of them.

Edge Pull-up — When Zax can't jump high enough, he grabs for whatever is close at hand and pulls himself up.

Fall — Zax may be able to jump extra high and leap tall buildings, but he has a limit to how far he can fall. (A considerable distance can certainly send him to the doctor.)

Sneak — Since Zax isn't always aware of the surroundings, he finds sneaking around can definitely help out.

Block — Amazingly, Zax is not always on the offensive. Occasionally he feels the need to block and protect himself.

These are the basic special movements for the demo. As you can most likely predict, the full game design would cover additional movements like tightrope walk, ledge walk, crawl, tunnel slide, climb, drive, swing, rail slide, swim, jet pack, and more.

The next sets of Zax's motions are the melee combat and projectile weapons. This section focuses on the abilities that Zax has or will have during the game.

Melee Combat

Fist Attack — When Zax is out of ammunition, it's time to use his fists. Zax's multi combo moves will prove very effective against many foes. He will also use his weapon as a blunt object to fight with if needed.

Kick Attack — Zax takes advantage of his boots when in close combat. Having a multi combo move with kicks as well proves to settle any disagreements.

Jumping Attack — With the proper boots on Zax's feet, he can jump high into the air and come down like a two ton rock.

Actor Object Attack — Zax can use nearly everything in the world to his advantage. Most of the objects are either breakable or physics oriented.

Projectile Weapons

The guns listed below are Zax's arsenal of weaponry. Zax can pick up a weapon and use it instantly and with his extra storage ability on his back, he can carry his arsenal with him as he travels.

Auto-Pickup and Discard — Zax will automatically pick up weapons, ammo, health, etc., and will determine if he needs them or has enough at the time. Also, when he gets done with certain items, he'll go ahead and discard them to free up more inventory room.

Beam Blasters — Zax has two beams that he can shoot out from his right wrist. They do minimal damage but will never run empty.

Laser Gun — This gun will get off several rounds a second with above average accuracy. It can normally load a 60-round energy cartridge.

Grenade Launcher — The Grenade Launcher has an excellent range of up to 60 yards on an angle. It holds six rounds and has a slow reload time but has an excellent widespread range on impact.

Just like with the special moves, this section only lists a handful of potential abilities and weapons that Zax will obtain during the full game.

Acquired Abilities: These abilities are learned during gameplay. For instance, if Zax had to jump to a pole and swing inside a window, the player would receive onscreen text explaining how to do just that. Currently for the demo there are no planned acquired abilities.

Special Items and Supplies: Special weapons and supplies are the added bonuses for being Zax. During his adventures and wanderings, he will come across many obstacles that require different items. These are the items that Zax will acquire and use through Level 1.

   Tracking Device — The tracking device works similar to a map except that it only shows a beep and not the actual level. (He'll get that map style finder during the game.)

   Light Pads — Zax will get two light pads that attach to his shoulder pads and provide him with quick, easy access to light anywhere he travels.

   Lava Suit — The Lava Suit allows Zax to swim in the lava only. It's extremely heavy so his standard movements are slowed quite a bit. Also, this will not work for the water unless you want him to walk on the ocean bottom.

   Double Jump Boots — When Zax is wearing these boots he is able to jump two times as high in the air by pressing the jump button twice.

   Coin Holder — Zax will be able to "magically" collect the Glow Coins on his adventure. They will simply disappear, then add to his counter on the HUD.

Method of Deletion: Once Zax's health runs down, he will die and the player will have the choice of whether or not to continue.

Behavior: Zax's typical behavior is quick and responsive. He doesn't like waiting around in one place for too long, especially when it's new. Also, Zax has the ability to help the player out in game. If the player passes by something of importance, Zax will stare at it while walking by and sometimes make comments to make sure you stop and look.

Weapon Stats: Zax's weapons need a bit of configuring so that everyone will know the details of each weapon. Be sure when you work out the weapon stats to your game that you document all the revisions made each time changes occur.

Weapon	ROF (per sec)	Damage	Ammo
Beam Blasters	15 per sec	5-12	Limitless
Laser Gun	3 per sec	15-19	60
Grenade Launcher	2 sec	0-38	6

The weapon stats are very simple for this demo. Remember, if you want to create a more complex system you can use many of the following ideas to advance the structure.

Weapon type — blunt object, range weapon, spell, and special powers

Ammo — bullets, rockets, liquid, ice, electricity, smoke, etc.

Ammo definitions — range, speed, rate of fire, damage points, duration, amount, capacity, cost, reload time, recovery rate, and spell cast time/cost/delay/recovery/effect

Damage type/description — percentage, value, armor, defend, block, shooting, spell resistance, movement, etc.

The cast of characters as a rule are placed below the hero(s) section. We want to ensure that all the characters remain relatively close at hand for quick reference, so keeping them together maintains that organization. You can use either a list or a table to document the character information and description.

Enemy and NPC Characters

Name: *Character name*

Description: *Verbal description of the character.*

Special Movements and Navigation: *A list of any unique movement or characteristic in terms of animation.*

Melee Combat: *Point system and list of Melee combat moves. This should include the hit point range as well.*

Projectile Weapons: *Point system and list of Projectile weapons available to the character. Make reference to the weapon being used for quick lookup.*

Acquired Abilities: *Can and does the NPC or enemy learn from its actions? One example could be if you asked an NPC a question and if the NPC remembers the question and responds differently or not.*

Special Items and Supplies: *Objects the character possesses while alive or after it is killed.*

Method of Deletion: *States how the character is deleted from the game. This can be very in depth depending on the complexity of deletion. If you have simple characters with a single health it would track that and then describe whether it fades away or stays on screen, while a boss character would describe where and what each hit point value is worth and tactics used during play depending on the health value.*

Note: *Once the characters die, they (determining on who they are and importance in the level) will eventually fade out to nothing to reduce the high count of polygons and textures being rendered. The other characters will be replaced with lower poly count versions of themselves and remain on the screen.*

Behavior: *Think characteristics, movement, and attitude.*

Weapon Stats: *Describes what weapons are used by the character during the game.*

The second option is to use a table style system. Check out the next example to see if that's more your approach.

Character Type					
Character Name					
Character Description					
Health Properties					
The health properties affect all behaviors and abilities.					
Health (Starting level)	(1-100)	Melee Resistance	%	Speed and Agility (Dependent on health)	% from original
Recovery Rate	%	Projectile Resistance	%	Intelligence and Behavior	% from original
Armor Pickup	%	Powers Resistance	%	Marksmanship	% from original
Special Health Powers	%	Other Resistance	%	Difficulty Level	% from original
Behavior Properties					
The numbering system here creates the uniqueness (AI) of each character and affects all properties.					
Anger	(1-10)	Courage	(1-10)	Intelligence	(1-10)	Loyalty	(1-10)

Vision Properties				
The visual acuity of characters contributes to their intelligence and abilities.				
Visual Acuity (Starting level)	(1-100)	Environment disturbances (Fog, rain, time of day, etc.)	%	Current Health	%

Marksmanship Properties				
Dependent on health, vision, and skill.				
Aim Quality (Starting level)	(1-100)	Environment and fog distance (Vision)	%	Current Health	%

Melee Abilities				
Attack 1 Name				
Attack 1 Description				
Damage Amount	(1-100)	Rate of Attack	Per sec	Distance/Accuracy	%
Cost Amount	% or #	Damage Effect Type	Name	Percent of Use	%

Projectile Weapon				
Weapon 1 Name				
Weapon 1 Description				
Damage Amount	(1-100)	Rate of Fire	Per sec	Distance/Accuracy (Takes into account the Marksmanship %)	%
Cost Amount	% or #	Damage Effect Range	Name	Percent of Use (Randomness of use)	%

Character Statistics

The characters that Zax interacts with are referred to as NPC and enemy characters. Their behavior is based on a series of statistics listed below.

Ranging from 0 to 10, base statistics are the unmodified or "true" statistics. They are indicated by their full names. Dynamic stats (changed statistics) represent the current value of that stat modified by the situation and environment. They are indicated by three-letter abbreviations. Over time, dynamic stats revert to their base values.

Combat Stats

Marksmanship (MAR)

Every attack is modified by MAR. The higher the value, the closer the attack is to its intended target. At negative values, bullets miss entirely or hits deflect harmlessly. Base marksmanship is a fixed value that does not change. Depending on the circumstances and environment, the actual MAR value decreases over time. Starting at 50% of the fog distance, a character's MAR loses points until — at full fog distance — MAR is 0. After the fog calculation, MAR is further reduced based on the percentage of the character's current health. Melee attacks succeed or fail based on the actual location of the two combatants.

Vision (VIS)

Every character has a certain visual acuity that determines how much light is required for them to see. Each point of VIS represents 10% of the total light. A character with VIS 4 can see the hero only if the light hitting him is at 40% intensity or more. (Ambient light and spot-lights are combined for this calculation.)

Health (HIT)

Every character has a starting Health and Hit Point status. HIT is simply a counter that either adds to or subtracts from the total number. Normal characters have about 100 HIT to begin with.

Behavior Stats

Characters choose what to do based on a variety of events and conditions. By setting up a personality-based behavior, characters are able to react and interact on their own without scripted events. We can simply place a bunch of enemies into an area and let them sort out their own behaviors. Some scenes require specific custom scripting, but in many cases, the enemies will simply work on their own.

Anger (ANG)

High anger levels overwhelm most other behavior. For a loyal character, seeing a friend slain increases ANG. Receiving minor wounds and other events also increase anger. Anger equates roughly to aggression. Up to a certain point, increasing ANG increases the accuracy and damage of a character's attack. Beyond that point, a Rage state activates in which accuracy decreases. In that Rage state, the character does not react to damage. The more enraged he is, the less time he spends flinching from damage.

A totally enraged character will charge at Zax, never breaking stride. They still take damage and die as usual, but they don't play their damage animation fully. A good example of rage would be the end sequence with Leaky Looney, whose rage becomes so evident that nothing stops him.

Courage (COU)

The decision to attack or flee comes from COU. COU decreases as HIT declines. Simply witnessing some circumstances can cause COU to decline. A character with low Loyalty and low Courage can result in fear. For example, seeing a friend get captured or knocked out can cause a character to flee.

Intelligence (INT)

The ability to make complex decisions is based on INT. Built into the engine are certain actions that characters can take. Some actions require a higher intelligence to perform, and not all characters will have that ability.

Loyalty (LOY)

Characters have loyalty to certain types of characters, usually of the same type. A loyal character will stay in a fight despite his fear if his friends need help. Characters with a fierce Loyalty to their cause will fight to the death. If fear exceeds Loyalty, then that character will flee.

Languages

Characters in the game speak their own native languages. The characters will talk with you verbally in their language but text will reveal the actual message. The only localization of the game occurs in the text subtitles and Zax's dialog.

Interactions

With Characters

Zax can apply several hit and kick moves that act upon all of the characters in the game. When a character falls over, based on the direction of the impact, it can strike other characters and set actors, causing the appropriate reactions. An example of this would be if Zax were to kick a character onto a wooden crate. If the character's hit point was higher than the crate, it would break into pieces as the character fell into it.

With Set Actors

Most pieces of the environment are interactive. Special break-away wall pieces, rocks, crates, lights, and other pieces of the environment can be broken by nearly every move Zax knows, including explosive and other special types of damage. Many of the items have at least one intermediate state of damage before it completely shatters or crumbles, allowing the player to know whether or not it can be destroyed.

Falling and exploding debris damages characters that get in the way as well. Zax can use this as a weapon sometimes when enemies get close enough to the action.

Difficulty Levels

By default, the game begins at normal difficulty. The player chooses when he starts the game whether he wants to change that mode to easy or hard. These settings affect the enemies' strength, resilience, and intelligence. In hard mode, enemies are faster and do more damage and resist damage better. They're also smarter, meaning they'll use advanced tactics more often. The opposite holds true for easy mode.

Replay

Once the player has won the game, he/she can restart the game, retaining the stats from the previous game and optionally setting the difficulty to a higher level. Other rewards and "Easter eggs" could be hidden throughout the game on subsequent plays to allow replayability.

Camera Effects

Camera distance behind the character varies based on the environment. The default camera setup will be introduced at the start of the level and then the user can choose to move the view around. Tighter environments require tighter cameras, while some open scene environments will pull back further to open up the area. This could also be dependent on the controller or keyboard style that was chosen.

Controls Overview

The control scheme for the demo was created for use with the mouse and keyboard. In order to be assured that everyone could play on the PC, we decided to keep the joysticks and pads out of the equation for now. If you develop for the Xbox, PS2, or GameCube, then it's guaranteed you will need to include the mapping and button configurations in this portion of the document.

Default Controls Overview

Look/turn
Mouselook
Left and Right turn the camera. Up and Down rotate the camera up and down a slight degree from home. Preferences can be set in menu if player prefers different styles.
(**Optional**: This may also use the pivot left and right animations for Zax. When the camera reaches a certain angle, the animations will rotate Zax along with the camera position.)
Movement — Sneak, Walk, Run, and Strafe
WASD
WASD is full run only (unless modified with Shift). Up is forward. Down is back. Left/Right rotate to the left and right.
"Mouselook" Analog Stick 2 Mouse
Strafe Left — "A" key
Zax will strafe or move to the left side while still looking forward.
Strafe Left Dodge — "A" key (double tap)
Double tap will cause Zax to jump and bounce/roll off his shoulder pad to the left.
Strafe Right — "D" key
Zax will strafe or move to the right side while still looking forward.
Strafe Right Dodge — "D" key (double tap)

Double tap will cause Zax to jump and bounce/roll off his shoulder pad to the right.

Sneak — Ctrl key

By pressing the Ctrl key, Zax will crouch over and sneak around. Pressing the Ctrl key again will resume his normal movements.

Action — Mouse 1

Zax attacks an enemy. Optional: Punches and/or shoots.

Action — Mouse 2

Action button two. Controls the secondary weapons and/or kicking.

Note: To use the Grenade throw, tap the button to throw a grenade. The distance thrown is based on the angle of the camera. Zax can "cook" the grenade by holding the button for a few seconds so it goes off very close to when it hits.

Jump and Double Jump — Spacebar

Jump

Zax can jump in any direction, so even if he's sidestepping, Zax will jump in that direction while facing forward. The longer the button is pressed, the farther he will jump up to a max distance. The player can also steer in the air using the WASD keys.

Double Jump

Double Jump becomes active once Zax is in the air. There is only a 1-second window, which allows the player to press the Spacebar again, sending Zax twice as high into the air.

Reload — "R" key

When Zax needs to reload a weapon or change out clips, press the R key.

Conversation and Action — "E" key

Speaking with NPCs. When in appropriate locations (in front of a door or NPC), Zax performs actions such as opening doors, pulling levers, flipping switches, and talking to people.

Taunt — "Q" key

Zax has a lot of extra energy inside him and occasionally needs to vent. By pressing Q, you give Zax the opportunity to do just that.

Block — "Z" key

Zax occasionally needs to defend himself. Using the Z key, Zax is able to decrease the amount of hit point value a Melee attack does to him. Projectile weapons still cause the same amount of damage.

Scroll Weapon Modes — F and V key and middle mouse wheel

Two different options are available for scrolling through the weapons. Using F and V you scroll the list of available weapons, or use the number keys to go directly to a weapon. Also, we can (if time allows) have the weapon options fade in and scroll through them.

Menu Start — Esc

Menu

The Menu presents a list of commands including: Resume, Save, Load, Options, and Exit. It also lists a brief set of current goals that Zax has to accomplish and other useful information.

PC Alternative Controls

Typically, games provide the player with multiple control configurations, so I've included an additional control scheme that could be included in the demo.

Always Run — Check box in options or Caps Lock

Run/Walk — Left Shift

Look Up — Mouse move down (Invert)
Look Down — Mouse move up (Invert)
Melee Attack — Ctrl or Right Mouse Button (RMB)
Gun Attack — Enter or Left Mouse Button (LMB)
Jump — Spacebar
Forward — Up Arrow
Backward — Down Arrow
Turn Left — Left Arrow
Turn Right — Right Arrow
Next Weapon Mode —] or Mwheel Up
Previous Weapon Mode — [or Mwheel Down
Action 1 — Ctrl
Action 2 — Shift
Objectives/Target List — F1
Save Game — F2
Load Game — F3
Controls Screen — Esc
Quicksave — F5
Screenshot — F11
Pause Game — Pause

You can configure several different control schemes in case of a left-handed player or a player prefers the inverted movement. By having several variations set up, you allow the player a smoother transition to your game.

Start Menu

The Start menu is presented at the beginning of the game. The options listed below represent each form of play and actions that the player can choose from. Also, pressing the Esc key pauses the game and brings up a similar menu of useful information for the player.

Menu choices:

Resume
Objectives
New Game
Load
Options
Credits
Exit

Start Menu

This screen refers to the first menu screen (not the in-game menu). Navigation within the menu is a simple act of moving the highlight via the mouse. The LMB accepts the choice.

Continue

Finds newest saved game and loads it automatically. (This only shows up if a saved game is present.)

New Game

Brings up a new selection screen. This will set up the Difficulty level and Player information before the game begins.

Difficulty Selection (Easy, Medium, Hard)

Note: The Difficulty selection is not implemented in the demo version.

Player Name
Starts a new game using the settings set in place.
Load
Brings player to the load screen to choose a file. Current files can be saved on hard drive.
Options
The player is presented with the Options sub-menu:
    Controls
    Cycle control schemes (there needs to be at least three different button configurations)
    Choose mouse, keyboard, or both
    Choose whether left/right is strafe or turn
    Check box for inverse look (like aviation controls)
    Check box for auto-center camera
    Slider for mouse sensitivity
    Gameplay
    Check box for showing weapons on body
    Slider for camera agility (Gives player options as to how the camera will follow Zax.)
    Slider for ammo vs. quality preference (ammo===[]===quality)
    Check box for special FX (High, Medium, Low, Off)
    Check box for shadows (Real-time, Spot, None)
    Drop-down menu for screen resolution
    Slider for character speech (This will allow the option to decrease or increase the verbal speech from characters.)
    Slider for music (Music from the game can be turned up or down. Also, you have the option to load your own music into the game while you play.)
    Button for having the computer check the performance level and determine the best performance and playability level to choose.

In-Game Menu (Pause)

Hitting Esc during the game freezes the action and the camera pivots slowly around Zax. Zax will then randomly cycle through idle states. A menu is overlaid, which displays the following:
Resume — Returns player to current game
Objectives — Brings up objective list
Save — Allows the player to save the game at any point during play
Load — Brings player to load screen
Options — Lists options available during gameplay
Quit — Brings player to Start menu
Skip Scene — This only comes up during a cinematic. Choosing this skips to the end of the scene.

That's a lot of information to soak up. I hope you made it through and with at least half of the information put to memory.

So, we have "properly" dissected our hero character and the additional characters as well as set up standards for control schemes, interfaces, and weaponry. Now we need to keep the fire burning and work on the level design document so that all our newly created characters will have a wonderfully inspired world to run around in.

Level Design Document

The level design document (LDD) is at the heart of gameplay and environmental design. Within this document you should find yourself working on a walk-through (point list), level designs, and gameplay aspects. Here, we discuss the walk-through and level maps.

Note:

Characters are great, but remember that three-quarters of the playing screen is made up of backgrounds, level work, lighting, and creative environments. Remember, most people playing either a first-person or third-person soon look past the gun or char-acter because it's always there, but the environment they run around in is constantly changing and always new and exciting. Let's be sure to make it memorable, as well.

Walk-Through

A walk-through document describes every step involved in the game. Oftentimes I'll think of a game and say things like, "Yeah, we'll make him jump over here and bounce off this then dive into there and...." Well, enough talk. We need a bullet point list or a numbered list of everything and every action that occurs in the game. If you can't write down the list, then you had better rethink your story. The walk-through in the document will start when you double-click the Zax Demo.exe and plot out every step the character should and could make while playing the game. If completed properly, this will provide the scripters and level designers with everything needed to lay out each level in the project.

The walk-through for the Zax demo uses a bullet list. Typically, if you are creating a complex level it's a better idea to use a numbering system so that you can quickly locate that number on the level map and vice versa. Be sure to keep your sentences fairly short. They need to read easily and fast so that anyone can comprehend the game in a matter of minutes.

Walk-Through of Zax Demo

We catch up to our hero Zax teleporting into Leaky Looney's Lava Pit. Not certain what to expect here, Zax decides to investigate the mysterious orange and yellow glow from the level. Smoke (sulfur) and ash fill the sky as the player runs Zax through an exhilarating and mind-boggling environment.

Starting the Demo — Double-click the Zax Demo.exe icon to begin the Zax demo.

Intro Screens — Time to plug everyone and the engine screen.

WBS

KA3D Engine

Start Screen —

Idea for Menu Screen

3D background (Probably a camera set in the level cut down in size to increase load time speed.)

The user interface POD will appear from the bottom of the screen and then a blue particle beam is produced. Text is then displayed on it, possibly in a static form.

The background will have the sulfur particles and lava flow to keep the movement going. Red orangish lava mixed with a cool blue particle beam should make a very nice mix.

The screen will stay the same for all options until "Play" is pressed.

Options on the Start Screen

Play — Begins the demo

Practice — Test/sandbox level where you get to try out Zax's moves and abilities. *(Developer side)*

Options — Sound, video, controller, mouse, joystick setup, etc.

Save/Load — Save a game during play or at locations and load a saved game

Website — Quick access to developer web site

Exit — Stop the play and exit to Windows

When the player chooses **Play**, the **Load screen** appears while **Level 1** loads.

Level 1 — Leaky Looney's Lava Pit

Cut Scene — Zax beams in — Player will start on **Player Start** location identified on the map key.

Objective 1

Zax will explore the area and find that the Glow Coins are needed to access the bridge in **Objective 3**. A text message will state, "That is a Glow Coin! You need to collect all of them before the bridge will activate." So he begins collecting the Coins. Zax immediately realizes that as he walks on the surface of the volcano, his metal shoes are smoking from the heat of the surface.

None of the Base Stations (things that project the weapon, ammo, or health) will be active. (They'll glow, but they won't have items showing.) Zax will have to push the big **Red Button** to activate the **Twirling Generator**, which will spin around with particles glowing in the back for the exhaust.

Cut Scene — Once the **Twirling Generator** is active, it will **Trigger** the **Base Stations** to light up and begin the particle effects.

Base Stations in **Objective Area 1** will now be operational and displaying the **Weapon (Laser Gun), Health, and Ammo**. Use a camera pan and pull out to show the changes taking effect.

From a Worker Bot, he will learn that he must blow apart the rocks to help them continue mining for Looney.

Cut Scene — Camera will rotate from the rocks and Zax to looking at the Secondary Ammo.

Some of the robots will become agitated at not being able to get into the mine and their green eyes will turn red in the heat of the moment. Unfortunately, Zax cannot kill too many without losing one of his objectives, which is to keep the Worker Bots alive.

Zax must make his way across the moving pads to collect the **Secondary Ammo**, which is used to blow up the rocks.

In the center of the Tilt pad is a Jump pad (circle shape). When Zax makes it to the end he will be propelled upward toward a platform. On the top of it will be Jump Boots. These Jump Boots will propel Zax farther distances without the use of all the lift pads.

He will jump down from there to the Generator Arm, where he will get his Secondary Ammo.

Objective 2

Once Zax has his **Laser Gun** and **Secondary Ammo**, a text screen will pop up to indicate that he has a new firing weapon and tell him how to use it. Zax will use his **Secondary Ammo** in his **Laser Gun** to help the Worker Bot get into the cave. Once the rocks are blown away it will reveal a new portion of the level that contains the last two Glow Coins.

The Worker Bots rejoice and give him **lights** for the sides of his armor as a reward. The lights become a button option to turn the two lights on and off. (The mining cave will be extremely dark, which is also why the robots have lights on top of their heads.) He will now be able to see his way down the tunnel to retrieve the final Glow Coins.

Cut Scene — Zax made too much noise blowing the rocks apart and angered Looney the boss. Because of this, when Zax comes back out of the tunnel, Looney is now tossing huge lava bombs down from the top of the volcano. (*Basically it will be targeting Zax throughout the rest of the level. Zax will constantly have to move, which will make some parts of the level very tough.*)

Zax will make his way to the bridge to complete Objective 2.

Objective 3

When player makes his way to the Yellow Pad, the **Bridge** will be activated and begin coming out. Also, all the lights on the Bridge Platform will light up. There is a catch; Looney is still throwing **lava bombs** at you. So Zax must continue running around and away from the bombs until the bridge gets to him.

Learns a new move — No cut scene, just part of gameplay — a few of the **lava bombs** hit the bridge and stop it about halfway. A text message pops on the screen, "Double tap your **Jump Button** to have Zax do a **Double Jump** in the air." This will allow him to jump all the way across to the bridge. (*This will later be changed to finding the Jump Boots, which allow him to jump extra high.*)

Objective 4

In order for Zax to continue on his journey he must activate the second **Twirling Generator** by pressing two **Push Buttons**. The fun part of Objective 4 is that Zax must press the two buttons within 5 seconds of each other. Otherwise, each button resets itself. A **Timer** is displayed to show how long Zax has before the button resets itself.

Remember, this is still while dodging the **lava bombs** from Leaky Looney.

Objective 5

Rest and collect. Zax has gone through a bunch in the last two objectives, so before he meets up with the Boss, he will have a chance to stock up on **Ammo** *(Primary and Secondary)* and **Health.**

The **lava bombs** will still be coming down but not as fierce. Sort of like Looney is losing interest and taking a break as well.

The player will make his way over to the **Lift Pad** and meet the Boss.

Cut Scene — Camera will pan around both characters before they begin fighting.

Objective 6

Zax will fight **Boss Looney** and defeat him by shooting his eyes and underbelly. Once defeated, the **Glass Door** in Area 1 will open, revealing a **Lava Suit**, which will allow Zax to swim in the lava below.

Cut Scene — **Looney** will fall off the volcano and be sucked up partway into the Metal Gate. (Or will simply sink down into the lava.)

Objective 7

Zax will slide down from the top of the volcano and retrieve his **Lava Suit**.

Zax needs to jump off the volcano. The **Lava Suit** will just be an attachment like his **Weapon**.

That's the end of it. Once he jumps off, we cut to a new level, which has some humorous dialog in it as discussed in the game design document.

Level Maps

Accompanying the walk-through docs are the level maps. These maps are the visual portions of the game. They help us to see where and what happens in the game before we spend hours and hours developing the real environment models. A top-down view of the levels and a key of all the events in the game are created for this section in order for everyone to have a quick reference guide to what happens. Included with the level maps are a handful of conceptual illustrations, which further define the look of the levels. In Figures 2-1 through 2-3 we have the designs and concepts for Leaky Looney's Lava Pit.

Figure 2-1: Lava Map

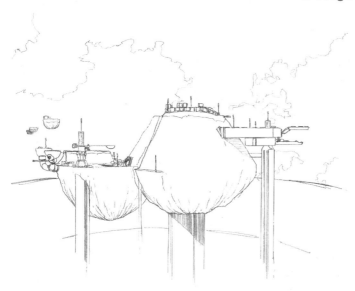

Figure 2-2: Concept 1 of Lava Map

Figure 2-3: Concept 2 of Lava Map

The illustrations are excellent examples of the level, which truly help further develop the look of Leaky Looney's Lava Pit.

Note:

The level images are also found in the art style guide, discussed next.

Art Style Guide

In order to keep everything organized and in easy to find places, we are taking the majority of the art for the game and placing it here inside the art style guide. That means everything from character lineups, font style, title, exterior, interior world colors and mood, SFX power designs, the color palette for characters, screen mockups, UI, and HUD pieces to about anything else that would be art in the game.

The demo art style guide is simplified compared to a full-fledged guide because we are only creating one level and a handful of objects. When creating a full style guide, be prepared to spend about two weeks up to a month on just the conceptual design of the game. The following list provides examples from the art style guide for the Zax demo. To see the full guide, go to \Templates\Documents\Design_Document\Art_Style_Guide. The examples and explanations below will help you understand the sections and issues involved in writing and illustrating an art style guide.

Note:

Remember, the art style guide is set up to help you illustrate your ideas to designers, publishers, developers, venture capitalists, and the sort. This is as much a living document as any other part of the design doc. Be prepared to make changes artistically at any point to help ensure the success of the demo.

Characters

The characters section lists all actors involved in the game or game demo. The main purpose for the character list is to provide a working design of the characters and also a lineup, which depicts the height ratio between characters. See Figure 2-4.

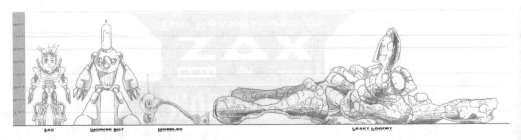

Figure 2-4: Character lineup

Note:

The character lineup doesn't have to be detailed. If you are not the greatest of artists, simply use silhouettes to define the height of each character. Be sure to place a measurement stick in the lineup.

The first character should normally be the Hero in the game. It's best to introduce the main characters so that the reader will know who's most important. Here's a quick list of the order in which you should have the characters.

- Hero
- Supporting cast
- Boss characters
- Enemies
- Nonplayer characters

Zax

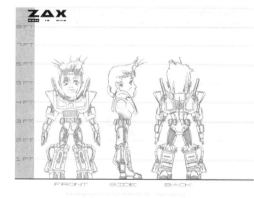

Figure 2-5: Zax character sheet

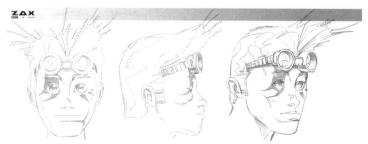

Figure 2-6: Zax face designs

Along with the full body stance, it's good to include a few face shots with different expressions and angles. See Figure 2-6.

Note:

The conceptual designs typically illustrate a couple of points. First is the front, back, and side view sketch, which lets everyone know that you have more than ideas floating around in your head. With these three views we now have a solid idea of what the character looks like. The next sketch would be an action pose, showing off some particular move or attitude the character would demonstrate during the game. Finally, you want to create a color guide of one of the pieces already created or a new one.

Within the character section, be sure that you spend time detailing the characters conceptually first. It is much more time efficient to change ideas at this stage than after the character is in the game with all its animations and attitude.

Levels and Environments

The levels and environments section defines the look and feel of the worlds defined in the game. This section is actually one of the more important aspects to the art style guide. "Why?" you might ask yourself. The reason it is so important is because of real estate. Think about when you play a game — the majority (70 to 80%) of the screen shows the environments. That means that a good 70% of the game's look and feel is defined with the levels.

We need to create a set of images that help define the look of the Lava level as well as color comps that give us the mood and feeling surrounding the level.

If all the levels and environments in a game are defined properly, then you won't have the inconsistencies that could arise. Also, a final thought before we look at some examples: An average level takes anywhere from three weeks to two months to create. If you begin creating the level with no more than a rough sketch of a top view, you run the risk of having some major problems and hang-ups four weeks down the road. Conceptualizing the levels prior to the 3D models is a must when working in a team environment where time plays a large factor in production.

Let's take a look at how the Looney Lava level was created.

Level 1 Leaky Looney's Lava Pit

The first step in conceptualizing a level is to draw a detailed top view of the environment, keeping in mind the dimensions and proportions of everything. Check out Figure 2-7.

The first thing you probably notice is that it's on graph paper. (I've included a digital piece of graph paper on the companion CD for you to use.) Having preset grid lines to follow will help your straight lines be straight and give you a better sense of proportion and scale.

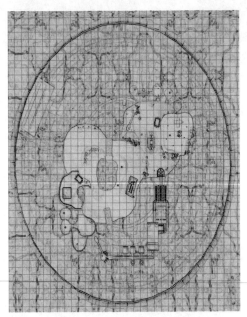

Figure 2-7: Top view of Looney's Lava level

As the "designer" it's our job to lay out where and when things will happen. We need to have and define the following:

- Level key
- Objectives and locations
- Cut scenes and locations
- Health, weapons, coins, ammo, extra lives, etc., placement
- Moving pads, doors, and elevator-style objects
- Player and enemy start points and spawn points
- Trigger points and definitions
- End point/level change

The list is a small sample of the actions and events that could be defined in your level. For the Zax demo this is essentially all we need.

In Figure 2-8, the map has been generated from the concept design above. This
map is highly detailed for purposes of giving
you an idea of what can be done. Take note
of all the level key items listed. Everything
on the map is color coded as well, so be
sure to look at Level_1_Looney_Lava_
Map_01.bmp found in the \Art_Tutorials\
Art_Asset_Guide folder.

Figure 2-8: Detailed map of events and objectives

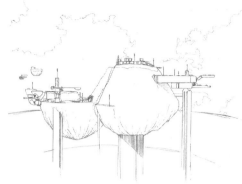

Figure 2-9: Environment concept 1

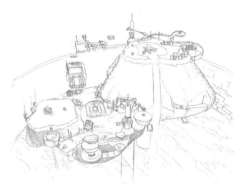

Figure 2-10: Environment concept 2

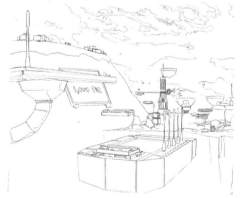

Figure 2-11: Environment concept 3

The top view is pretty tight, so we can
now extrapolate some perspective views
from it to begin establishing a look and feel
for the actual level. In Figures 2-9 through
2-11 you can see a few examples of what
the level could look like if it were kept close
to these illustrations.

Weapons

The weapons section provides an in-depth
look at the weapons, stats, and ammo in the
game. Be sure to place the detailed concepts in this area as well as some
information about each weapon for quick
reference.

Under each weapon type you can include
the ammo type/definition, damage
type/description parameters and endless
other options here. Feel free to continue
thinking of ways to reinvent weapons in a
game. Some of Zax's weapons are listed
below and illustrated in Figure 2-12.

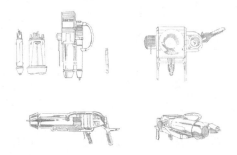

Figure 2-12: Weapon — Laser Gun and ammo

Weapon	ROF (per sec)	Damage	Ammo
Beam Blasters	15 per sec	5-12	Limitless
Laser Gun	3 per sec	15-19	60
Grenade Launcher	2 sec	0-38	6

So, what weapon should be listed first? The
best option here is to list the first weapon
the player has or collects, then follow it up
in the order of collection.

Collectibles and Power Ups

In the collectibles and power ups section
we have all the objects in the level that the
player will use. I am grouping all of the following together:

- Health
- Extra life
- Coins
- Keys
- Item triggers
- Outfits
- Accessories
- Boot types
- Power up items
- Objective items

Basically, if you can collect or interact with
an item in the level, then it goes under this
heading. However, if you plan on making a
game where there are 45 different health
items, then they would certainly be worthy
of their own section.

The collectibles and power ups do not have to be defined in this section. But to make things easier in terms of quickly looking up properties and descriptions, we'll place a bit of information next to each item. See Figure 2-13.

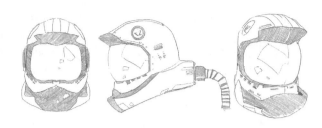

Figure 2-13: Lava Suit

Object type: Collectible

Object description: The Lava Suit is the final item to collect in the Lava level. It gives Zax the ability to swim in the lava after he puts it on.

Trigger event: Cut scene — Camera panning around Zax as he holds the Lava Suit up.

Sound: No

Animated: No

Amount +/−: 0

Health +/−: Resistant to lava and fire

As I stated before, this is simply a short list to help the reader know what each item does and whether it has an effect on anything else.

World Objects

World objects include everything from rocks to 50-ton doors. Each object created for the game should be documented in this section before it is modeled and textured. In addition to the pictures there needs to be an explanation of the object type, description, whether it's breakable, its physics, and its method of deletion if applicable.

Note:

The more you document now, the less thinking is involved later. ☺

The following is an example of a World object.

Crate

The crate object is designed to add filler to the level as well as to hide collectibles and power ups. See Figure 2-14.

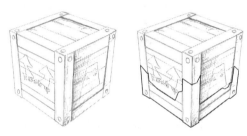

Figure 2-14: Crate

Object type: Crate

Object description: The crate is an object that will have physics and have the ability to break into multiple pieces.

Collision: Yes

Breakable: It will consist of about 25 broken pieces and one base piece.

Physics: Box type

Door: No

Animated: No

Trigger: No

Sound: Box_Broken.wav and Box_Tumble.wav

The list is one option to help give everyone a general idea of what each object does in the game.

The concept shows the crate in the standard views as well as a depiction of the breakable pieces.

Note:

For the artist, things like breakables or crates are extremely easy to understand, but you have to remember this is not just for the artists. The art style guide is meant to be handed out to anyone to help give a clearer understanding of "everything" the game is about. That means the "artistic" and "non-artistic" individual will be able to get a complete grasp of the project.

User Interface and HUD Screens

The user interface and HUD screens are two of the main components of any game. Why do I say that? Think about it this way: Other than the hero character, you will see the UI and HUD pieces more often and for longer periods of time than any other art created for the game. With that in mind, you want to create a layout and design that will be both intuitive and exciting for the player to see and use over and over again.

In Figure 2-15, you can see that the Options screen is small enough to fit in the center of the screen and still leave parts of the level visible. In addition, there is no text. This optional display is left open so that text can be placed programmatically. Notice the options below it that describe what does what.

Figure 2-15: Options selection interface screen

UI Title: Options screen

UI Description: This UI is available at any point before (from the Start menu) or during the game (by pressing the Pause button). It is used to select options and preferences.

UI Option 1: Return to game — returns player to game

UI Option 2: Video — ability to change graphic settings

UI Option 3: Sound — change music, on-screen dialog, effects noise, etc.

UI Option 4: Controller — ability to load, save, or change the controller scheme

UI Option 5: Objectives — point list of objectives accomplished and pending

UI Option 6: Map — view of the level map if available

UI Option 7: Save — ability to save the game at any point

UI Option 8: Restart level — start over at the beginning of the level with original settings

UI Option 9: Quit — end game

Effects

The effects section identifies the look of a particle or special effect during gameplay. It also includes things such as muzzle flashes, explosions, sparks, bullet trails, and teleporting beams. The main purpose behind this is to have an idea of the look you want to achieve with the particle editor.

We will look at the Steam particle to find the basic look and description of an effect. See Figure 2-16.

Figure 2-16: Steam particles

Effect Name: Steam

Effect Type: Particle — Single image file

Effect Description: The steam particle will spew out from holes in the metal pipes. Its pattern is very random and fast. Since the lava is continually flowing the steam will not diminish at any point.

Effect Health +/–: 0

2D/3D Animation: none

Note:

Once again, this is the type of section that requires attention before jumping into effects. Having an idea of the color, shape, and behavior of the effect will allow you more time to be certain that it's correctly defined.

Font Style

The fonts are key to keeping everything together. If the look and style of the fonts accurately depict the game, then you are heading in the right direction. You should stick to a maximum of three or four font styles. Figure 2-17 shows the three fonts that were chosen for the Zax demo.

Figure 2-17: Fonts

These fonts give a modern, technical appearance with an underline of cartoon playfulness. Each font is strong enough to stand on its own and complements the others.

Color Guide

The look and feel of any game comes down to what colors are being used. In the art style guide it's best to work up a couple of colored illustrations (preferably the environmental pieces you sketched earlier). These pieces will help everyone on the team understand what it is the game is supposed to look and feel like.

In Figure 2-18, I have created simple color swatches showing off the basic colors that we want to use for this level and characters. I've taken a picture shown earlier and colored it using Photoshop. See Figure 2-19.

Note:

The images for this book are also provided in color on the companion CD. The design document file on the CD also shows the color swatches.

Figure 2-19: Color comp

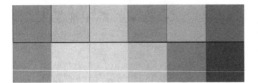

Figure 2-18: Color swatches

Remember, the swatches of colors define the look and feel of the game.

Note:

Take your time with this section. The colors you choose determine the look and feel of all the levels after it. If you go in creating a game with no color guide, there's a good chance you'll end the game the same way and it will show. Trust me on this one — I know from past experience.

That's it! We have developed the entire art asset guide. Be sure to check out the document for the Zax demo to get a good look at the process. With the art guide created, it provides the artist with lots to do, but not in any great order. Let's create an art asset document next. This document will provide lists and order to all the art being created.

Art Asset Document

An art asset document contains a list of every object, character, weapon, etc., created for the entire game. This will best serve the lead artist in keeping track of how things are progressing for the art staff. Notice that the following table is not highly detailed in terms of texture names, animation lists, etc. The lead needs a document like this one that keeps a step back from the details and still shows the progress being made. Along with an art asset document is a broken down version for each artist to use,

which we will call the artist task list. This list is a bit more detailed and gives the artist a personal checklist of things to do.

So how did things look for the Zax demo? Let's check out the art asset document during one phase of the development cycle. (The following example lists only a few items.) The complete document can be found at \Game_Demos\Zax_Demo\Documents\Art_Asset_List.

	Zax Art Asset Document			
	Last Updated 06-23-04			
MS 01				
	Item	**Dept**	**Person**	**Status**
[ ]	Build MS 01 map	ART	CW-01	75
[ ]	Create Volcano	ART	CW-01	80
[ ]	Create Floating Rocks	ART	CW-01	90
[ ]	Create Mining Shaft and Entrance	ART	CW-01	70
[ ]	Assemble final "Clean" build of MS01	ART	CW-01	90
[ ]	**Character — Zax (Hero)**			
[ ]	Create Zax Hero Model	ART	CW-01	100
[ ]	Create Zax Hero Texture	ART	CW-01	100
[ ]	Animate Zax Hero Model	ART	EW-02	100
[ ]	Implement Zax Hero	Prog	JK-03	100
[ ]	**Character — Wobbles**			
[ ]	Create Wobbles Model	ART	CW-01	90
[ ]	Create Wobbles Texture	ART	CW-01	70
[ ]	Animate Wobbles Model	ART	EW-02	95
[ ]	Implement Wobbles	Prog	JK-03	95
[ ]	**Character — Looney Lava**			
[ ]	Create Looney Lava Model	ART	CW-01	95
[ ]	Create Looney Lava Texture	ART	CW-01	95
[ ]	Animate Looney Lava Model	ART	EW-02	95
[ ]	Implement Looney Lava	Prog	JK-03	95
[ ]	**Moving Objects — Jump Pads**			
[ ]	Create Jump Pads Model	ART	CW-01	90
[ ]	Create Jump Pads Texture	ART	CW-01	90
[ ]	Implement Jump Pads	Prog	JK-03	0

In the Zax art asset table we have five different columns. The first column is for a check box. The next column lists the items. This includes every piece of art made for the game. Notice each major item has rows below them. They are as follows:

Model — The model refers to the actual model, UVW map, and high poly model.

Texture — The texture row includes the diffuse (base) map, specular level, specular color, bump/normal map, alpha map, and reflection map.

Animation — States whether or not the item has animations.

Implement — Programmer/artist collaboration. It's an excellent idea to include a simple status report so that the artist knows whether or not certain features or items have been implemented and if the code side of a model or animation is troublesome.

As you can see, it's not incredibly detailed. For the purpose of an art asset list we want to keep the size small and limit the complexities. Anyone should be able to look at it and know the general idea of what is going on.

The next step down is to create an artist task list, which has a bit more information. Typically, the lead artist has a highly detailed list of everything involved. Work on demos demand a bit of a switch for responsibilities.

We want everyone on the art team creating art assets, and if the lead is given too much paperwork, it will never happen. The artist task list makes each artist responsible for his/her work. See the following example artist task list.

Approved	Item	Artist	Timeframe	Information	Status	Date
	Zax Artist Task List					
	Last Updated 09-10-04					
MS 01						
Approved	Item	Artist	Timeframe	Information	Status	Date
Art Director	Object name	Name/ Num	Total=xx	Poly or Size	%	Completion
[ ]	Character — Zax (Hero)		5 days			
[ ]	Zax Model					6/12/2004
[x]	Low Polygon Model	CW-01	2 days	4442	90	
[ ]	Gore Parts			na		
[ ]	High Polygon Model	CW-01	1 day	19680	40	
[ ]	Zax Hero Texture					6/14/2004
[ ]	Diffuse map	CW-01	4 hours	1024x1024	100	
[ ]	Specular Level map	CW-01	30 minutes	1024x1024	100	
[ ]	Specular Color map	CW-01	10 minutes	1024x1024	100	
[ ]	Bump/Normal map	CW-01	20 minutes	1024x1024	100	
[ ]	Alpha map	CW-01	5 minutes	1024x1024	100	
[ ]	Reflection map	CW-01	5 minutes	1024x1024	100	
[ ]	Zax Rig and Physique	CW-01	3 hours	na	100	6/12/2004
[ ]	Animate — Animation doc	EW-01	na	na	95	7/1/2004

Let's take a moment to go through each of these columns.

Approved — Art lead checks off completion of work

Item — Name of "official" object for the game and details of item

Artist — Name of artist working on project

Timeframe — Estimated length of time for an item to be completed

Information — Restrictions (size, poly count, etc.)

Status — Percentage complete at current time

Date — When the model was completed and approved

The last thing we want to discuss is the Item column, which gives a detailed breakdown of what is expected in each model. The list should always be detailed in order to give an artist all the proper information. Be sure that each step is taken into account and identified, allowing for anyone to jump on board and know what's going on.

Sounds and SFX

The sound document is a document listing all the necessary voiceovers, FX sounds, character sounds, and music tracks for the entire game. It includes the timing length, description, and name for each sound. The sample sound task list is located in \Templates\Documents\Design_Document\Sound _Task_List.

Approved	Sound Files	Description	Time Length	Status
[ ]	**In Game Sounds**			
	Environments			
[ ]	Level 1 Looney Lava			
[ ]	ambient1	Background noise — air	5 secs	100
[ ]	ambient2	Eerie cave-like sound	10 secs	50
[ ]	lava flow	Thick waterlike sound running	2 secs	0
[ ]	lava pop	Bubble pop	1 sec	100
[ ]	humming noise	Something hot giving it a noise	1 sec	80
	Etc...			

Project Dates and Milestones

Project dates and milestones are included in the design document. In order to have everything within reach we will keep them here. When you begin writing your project dates it's best to only detail out the first two weeks to a month. After that you should write a high-level projection for month to month dates. Things could change or switch on you pretty fast and it is better that you spend your energies working on the actual demo.

Your milestones for the project will be set up on a month to month basis. Companies will have internal and external milestones, which keep them on a strict schedule — for the most part. Milestones should detail what the team plans to accomplish from the start to the end of the project.

Note:

If you have to place an image in multiple spots throughout the document, then you are making things complicated and repetitive. Things should typically be mentioned only once to keep everything simple. No one wants to read the same thing over and over again...no one wants to read the same thing over and over again...no one...had you that time.

Postmortem

At the end of the project it comes time to work up a document on things that went right and things that went wrong. Typically, you want to generate comments from everyone who worked on the game. Remember, this is not a time to start complaining about particular people, but more about the particulars of what happened. The questions below are not only for the post-mortem, but should also be asked during the project from the beginning through to the end.

Question examples:

- Do you remember why you were making this game and did it work?
- Was there enough communication between everyone involved in the project?
- Do I still have a compelling storyline?
- Did the software and hardware sustain the needs of everyone?
- Is there more to it than just the art and programming?
- If it were built for the Atari system would it still be a fun game?
- Does it have replayability or a one-time storyline?
- Are the characters really worth getting to know?
- Was the pipeline smooth or problematic?
- Is there a prologue to the story? Have we thought about the history of the story and a possible future?
- Is the game designed around a story or just attempted to make gameplay and story points every so often?
- What have I learned from this so far?
- What things went right?
- What things went wrong?

Naturally, this list has just a few of the potential questions that could be asked. What you want to start looking for are areas that appear to slow the process down and create frustration and tension among the team.

Remember once again that we want to keep things simple. Just stick to the points that will help the team improve on the next project, meaning learn from what went right and what went wrong.

The Wrap-Up

We covered a lot in the previous pages, so I want to be sure that we list the appropriate order in which each document will appear in the final design documentation as well as a short explanation. They are as follows:

Design Documentation

Title Page — The title page for the project (art piece)

Table of Contents — A concise list of the items listed below

Game Design Document

Gameplay Synopsis — This should include the vision statement, the history of the characters, the short story (a few sentences), and the long story (a paragraph) behind the game idea.

Storyline — The storyline requires detailed documentation of everything that occurs in the game along with the script, narrative, and .wav file settings.

Cinematic Scripts and Storyboards — The cinematic section covers the opening sequences, advertisements, and the sort.

Game Options — Technical information such as controller schemes, special character movements, menu options, and character stats

Level Design Document

Walk-Through — The walk-through, or point list, is provided to assist the level designers and scripters with the gameplay.

Level Maps — The level maps are designed to give an easy point of reference and layout to the environments.

Art Style Guide

The art style guide contains all the art designs and concepts for the game.

Technical Design Document

The technical design document lists features, programming aspects, and current engine specs and designs.

Art Asset List

This lists all the art in the game (objects, characters, animations, levels, etc.).

Sound Asset List

This sound document lists everything needed to complete the theme music, backgrounds, FX, and miscellaneous sounds.

Programming Asset List

All programming tasks are listed here.

Projects, Dates, and Milestones

This contains internal records for the projected dates and schedules.

Postmortem

This document should not be completed until after the game demo is concluded. Remember, it's the wrap-up to how the whole project went.

The documents are divided into four separate categories: game design, level design, art style guide, and technical design. The main reason for organizing the documents this way is to provide the reader with the most important information first. The gameplay synopsis provides a first-time reader the general storyline along with the vision statement and other basic information. Next, we tackle the full game design and storyline in the game design documents. Following right along, we have the level design documents. These include the walk-through, which provides the reader with a quick and clear understanding of the entire game demo, and level maps that detail the first look and feel of the levels. The art style guide comes into play next, illustrating all the finer points in the game. The last few sections of the document are the task lists and technical docs, which represent the true work involved in creating the demo. The design document largely remains quite simplistic, yet still provides all the necessary paperwork and detailed information to run a project successfully.

Be sure to print the documents out and place them together in a professional three-ring binder. That should do it. Remember, not everyone is a great note taker or designer. When it comes to creating documents, be certain to nominate a person on your team who enjoys this kind of work to ensure quality and direction throughout the project.

> **Note:**
>
> Blank templates of each document described have been included in the ...\Templates folder on the companion CD for you to use when writing a design document.

■ ■ ■

Working on a design document is a great experience and one that I hope you have fun laboring on in the late hours of the night. Giving life to characters and adding plot twists and new features to a game can be an enjoyable experience. Remember to take a break at least once a day and always stay true to the vision statement so you will never get off course.

Chapter 3

Gameplay and Design Basics

Game design is a process of developing an idea with a start, middle, and end. During this process, there is typically gameplay, which is the creation of objectives, strategies, missions, puzzles, actions, and adventure. Is it possible to have a great game design and no gameplay? Or what about lots of gameplay but no game design? I would have to say the answer is yes to both. However, as each idea goes hand in hand with the other, they are equally needed for complete success. In this chapter we are going to take a look at some elements of gameplay, game design, and ideas that will generate thoughts and hopefully assist you with good habits and techniques for your next project.

Game Blueprints

A common phrase among gamers (and developers) is, "Well, there was a great story to begin with, and then about halfway through it was sort of there, and then toward the end, it felt like they gave up on solid game design and storylines and just tossed stuff together to finish it off." Does that sound familiar? There are many factors that contribute but, yes, that is oftentimes the case. Projects are underbudgeted, deadlines creep up too fast, team dynamics fall apart, designers quit, QA becomes a joke, and numerous other things contribute to the lack of quality in the final product.

So what we want to do is learn from other people's experiences and build on them toward perfection. Let's start off by figuring out what can be done to ensure that the storyline and game design remain the highest priority from start to finish.

Vision Statement

What's this doing here again? Haven't we already covered it in Chapter 2? Yes, we have talked about the vision statement; however, it is important enough that it takes first place here. The vision statement should be in the forefront of your thoughts. If this one sentence stays true throughout the project, then you have accomplished the difficult task of remaining focused and following through.

Scope

Scope is the size of a project from start to finish. The scope deals with the timeframe, the amount of art assets being generated, programming tasks involved, and game design. When crafting the design, it's easy to create something so grand and huge that even a team of 200 would have difficulty completing it on time. The scope of your project should be reviewed by many individuals (programmers, artists, producers, and designers) before starting anything. Programmers may tell you that your five coolest features will take them three years to create, while the artists may say they need to ramp up to a team of 70 if they hope to get it done in a two-year timeframe. All of this, of course, comes right after the producer tells you that the budget is being cut in half. On the other hand, the scope could be so small that all sides are requesting more material and ideas. So where do you find the balance? Practice and experience.

These two words are key to successfully scoping a project. If someone were to ask you how long it takes to roof a house and how much it would cost, do you know the answer? Now, if you had been roofing for a month, you would probably have a good idea of time and general knowledge of what you've been practicing on. But would you know the finer details? An experienced roofer might know to ask questions first, before giving any answer. For example, "What's the square footage of the roof?", "What's the pitch (angle) of the roof?", "Is it a tear-off and if so how many layers?", "Comp, wood, tar?" As you can tell, what appears to be an easy question on the surface opens up to a much larger and more complicated answer underneath.

When working on the scope of the game, it takes practice going through the process, learning from your experiences, and building on them until you gain the know-how and understanding necessary to make perfectly scoped projects. Sometimes to find a good balance (if you are a first-time designer), you take what you have created and cut it in half. From there, work on cutting at least another third of the ideas. At that point, you should have a well-refined document for a game demo. If you can complete that portion of the game and have everyone still together and friends, then there's an excellent chance of developing an entire game.

> **Tip:**
>
> A great way to understand how other companies deal with scope issues is to see what they ended up with at the conclusion of a game. Count the number of features, characters, animations, texture sets, levels, cut scenes, cinematics, objectives, etc., to find out what they were capable of doing in an "x" year timeframe with a team of "x" number of people. The same can also be done for game demos that companies produce.

The last part of scope that I want to discuss is individual timing. The only way to know how long it takes to model a 5,000-polygon character is to have the artist keep track of the hours. The same can be said for level designers working up environment models or trigger systems and programmers keeping track of their time writing code, scripting, and even creating tools. If you have a timetable with your team's capabilities and speed, you will be able to scope the project within the timeframe provided, ensuring a much better projection and scale. It also increases personal accountability within a team, which helps things to run smoother.

Questions, Questions, and More Questions

When writing a game design, you want to look at the scope of the project but also beyond it to the larger picture: "What is my full intent in creating this game?" Currently, there are no movies, cartoons, children's books, board games, or previous versions of the idea on the market. There's no cereal box, toy line, or clothing line for this game — so why make it? Excellent question! Before you begin a project, give some consideration to the above questions. Is it your goal to have all those things as well? Are you anticipating having a video game and that's it? Are you ready to contend with the rest of the marketplace? Are you prepared to push a new idea through the long and dark tunnel to success?

Tip:

If you are truly passionate about your idea, then the people on your team will see the idea in the same light you see it in. I believe that everyone out there has at least one great idea. Too often though, we find ourselves "attempting" to put something together — and that's where the great idea falls short. The correct and proper implementation of the idea is where it's all at.

I've posed a few questions below that should help you out when thinking about a new game concept. If you can answer these questions, then there's a great chance the rest of the documentation will be a breeze (that's the optimist in me).

Game Time

- What is the theme of the game?
- What is the game trying to accomplish?
- What are the genre/mood/emotional aspects of the game? Why are they important?
- What makes this game different?
- What platform(s) will it be on?
- Who is the audience? (Gender, age, race, etc.)
- If it were built for the Atari system would it still be a fun game?
- Does it have replayability or a one-time storyline?
- Are the characters really worth getting to know?
- Single player, multiplayer, or massive multiplayer online?
- Is there a prologue to the story? Have we thought about the history of the characters and a possible future?
- Is there going to be a continuation of the story (Parts I, II, III, IV, V, etc.)?

Personal Questions

- Why you, why now, and why this project?
- Who is involved in the project and what are their skills and abilities?
- Do you want funding and/or a publisher at some point?
- Is there a studio or is distribution primarily over the Internet?
- What do you expect out of this venture?
- Will you see it through to completion?
- Have you signed contracts between all parties involved?
- Are you going to incorporate?
- Will you attempt to retain all rights to the intellectual property and creation?
- Is everyone committed to seeing the project through to the set goal?
- Advertising, marketing, selling — can you do it or do you need some help?

Many of these questions can be difficult to answer at first. Some of them you might not even have an answer for just yet. Just remember, the more of these questions you knock out of the way at the beginning, the greater your chance of success at the end.

> **Note:**
>
> You need a clear understanding of what you are trying to accomplish before you begin, and you definitely need to write it down on paper and even tell a friend and especially your teammates. By verbally stating your goals and writing them down, you put yourself into a contract of sorts. This is and can continue to be a good self-motivating factor for you while working.

Now that we know why we are creating this game and where we plan on taking it in the future, we can begin studying gameplay elements and figure out which ones will be worth adding to our game projects.

Gameplay Elements

The general idea behind gameplay is dividing the game into sections and parts using the following elements. Each of the elements listed provides some insight into gameplay styles.

- **Maze** — Mazes are excellent forms of linear gameplay and fun because you start with an entrance and have to work your way to the exit. Even on paper the scheme works out extremely well.
- **Puzzle** — A riddle, crossword puzzle, matching up shapes or objects, and even a murder mystery are ideal for puzzles. The idea of thinking about something and solving a question

makes for outstanding gameplay. Allowing the player to think through situations and events increases the involvement and realism for the player.

- **Action** — Action allows events to occur in the game that quicken the pace and timing of things. An action could be anything from a player shooting an enemy to opening a door or even NPCs talking among themselves. Each event, whether small or large, produces movement, expectations, and a realization that more goes on than just walking around.
- **Exploration** — The idea of exploring a dark cave in the middle of the jungle or

a burned out plane in the desert produces the sense of exploring. Searching
the unknown with the sense of danger
mixed in creates an excellent form of
gameplay.

- **Emotion** — Imagine becoming so
involved in a character's life that making decisions could hurt, help, or
endanger the character. In a movie or
comic book you are merely the reader,
not a participant, but in a computer
game you are allowed to make choices
that can affect the outcome of the story
and characters involved. A simple list
could include emotions like fear, happiness, regret, despair, confusion, anger,
laughter, and tension, to name a few.

- **Learn** — Educational and historical
games are excellent examples of games
that make teaching and learning part of
gameplay. But remember, every game
does some form of teaching/learning
because the player has to learn the
control scheme, storyline, and rules.

- **Defend** — The desire to defend is
almost instinctive. Imagine the player
having to defend a village from a horde
of evil creatures. The sense of being
the underdog is typically exciting for
people.

- **Hide and Seek** — Both hiding and
seeking produce very pointed and
direct gameplay elements. Giving a
player reasons to find items or hide
them allows him to feel a sense of purpose and direction.

- **Collect** — Finding one object is great,
but what about collecting an entire set
of items or a particular number of
coins. The act of collecting gives
empowerment and reason to the player
as well.

- **Dodge** — A basic yet very useful
gameplay feature is the act of dodging.
In the old 2D side scroller games, the
player would oftentimes have to move
the character or vehicle up and down to
dodge oncoming objects. The same can
be implemented in 3D as well.

Most of these basic elements can be found
in games made on the Atari and PC years
ago. The idea of being able to play with simple art and basic colors on a monitor is
incredibly amazing. The majority of gamers
enjoyed and still enjoy playing similar
games that are now on cell phones and
mobiles. The following games from the
Atari and early PC age seem to stand out.
What others can you think of that contained
a very strong gameplay aspect?

- Pac-Man
- Breakout
- Joust
- Dig-Dug
- Asteroids
- Driver
- Montezuma's Revenge
- Pong
- Defender
- Pit Stop
- Load Runner

Each game focuses on one or two elements.
Try your hand at picking out which primary
elements are used with the above games.
See if you can figure out what makes them
great and then use those basic elements in
a level or objective design.

Note:

The process of studying a game and picking
it apart can also be thought of as decons-
tructing a game.

After reading through the above list, you
should begin to get a picture of what type of

information needs to be in the design documents. "Gameplay" helps dictate the design as well as the storyline in a game. Now that we know some characteristics of gameplay, we should see whether or not it fits in with the visual and audible aspects of game creation.

Gameplay Is Visual and Audible

Gameplay is not something you can take one piece from and run with for an entire game. The parts of gameplay make up the full complexity, and by taking one part away you can leave it broken. Let's take a look at some of the aspects on the art and sound side that help maintain and add to the gameplay.

Screen Size and Space

How do you create space and feeling? Have you ever considered the fact that you have a square frame around the scene (the monitor)? Whether it's a rectangle or a square, you are left with just that. In the world of comics, you get to change the "panel" to fit the mood. For instance, if a part of the story was meant to be scary and intense, a comic book panel would typically be extremely vertical while keeping the horizontal portions very tight. Now, your first thought

might be, well that's nice that you can do that in comics, but how does that help me out? In games, we simply have to improvise to create those very same effects and visuals. In Figure 3-1, you can see the example of the vertical box and a few "improvised" versions.

Notice how the boxes and city walls close in the gaps and provide a center area similar to the vertical box. The image on the left shows how closing in a space can create tension, especially with another person in the scene. The middle image depicts an entrance that blocks out the sides and top, focusing on just the center area, while the right image is the same except for the top portion. You can see the sky in this image and have the impression of something coming down from above. Also, when you begin cutting up space like this in games you touch on the ideas of positive and negative spaces.

Figure 3-1: Direction and size of space

Positive and Negative Space in Games

Having visual positive and negative spaces in a moving game might appear a difficult task. If the screen is constantly moving about, how do you control the space?

Just because you have a moving screen you should not forget the importance of design and layout. The idea of cutting the screen visibly into pieces and attempting to light the scene to help distinguish layers and depth is one very important way to create and sustain the atmosphere and mood.

> **Note:**
>
> A great homework assignment is to play some games and take notes and screen shots every time you recognize positive and negative spaces being used properly and improperly. Deconstruct what was done and attempt to understand why certain aspects were created that way.

Gameplay in Art

So how does art truly play a part in actual gameplay? Once again we are faced with a tough question. In the previous sections we looked at elements of gameplay such as puzzles and actions that take place in the game and saw that even using square blocks of color was enough years ago. The idea that art can contribute to the actual gameplay aspect needs to find a place in some of these gameplay elements. Let's look at a couple of them to find out if it's possible.

Emotion

The emotional state of being is always changing and always different. The situations and environment surrounding a player help create the person's perception and attitude. Before we go further let's list some more of those basic emotional states we can use.

- Surprise
- Excitement
- Frustration
- Grief
- Suspense
- Tension
- Anger
- Denial
- Fear
- Laughter
- Happiness
- Hopelessness
- Cluelessness

Think of an illustration (painting or photo) that contains some of these elements in context visually. Frank Frazetta is an ideal example of someone who sets up scenes with emotions and storylines. A painting of any degree of complexity will generate a number of emotions that subsequently contribute to gameplay. Everything from the layout to the color scheme helps add a layer of "play."

Let's set up an emotion. You, the player, walk up to a door that is torn to shreds, the squeaky metal hinges loosely support the frame, and blood drips from the busted handle. What emotion are we trying to convey? My first guess would be suspense, fear, and/or tension. Since emotion is an element of gameplay, the artist has to create and force that element through with visual representations. If the dilapidated door were 25 feet in size with busted wooden planks scarred with teeth marks, pieces of which lay scattered around, artistically you have created a gameplay element.

By causing the player to have an emotional reaction to a situation or event, you also fashion the stage for even further gameplay elements. From the visual images, the player would be confronted with multiple gameplay elements such as puzzle, action, emotion, and exploration. As the designer you would then have the choice of which element to use next and walk the character through the next stage in the journey.

> **Note:**
>
> Remember, there are bad element combinations. For instance, if you decided to go with the "learning" element right after setting up a scary scene, it would completely go against everything that was done up to this point. You don't want to "break" the mood with something so drastically different. What if a happy clown walked out and told a joke, then walked away? Yes, it could work if the game was designed with humor in mind, but otherwise that would break the mood and effect as well.

Another thought to keep in mind are the characters. If your player were to fight a character that stood 50 feet tall, you could easily produce an element of fear, strategy, and action. Flip the idea around and make the hero player 50 feet tall. What type of elements would change and what kind of impact would it have on the rest of the game?

Maze

Mazes are another potential for artistic gameplay. Suppose you're playing a first-person shooter and as you explore a world you find yourself running through a maze. Artistically, you can create an excellent gameplay feature or possibly ruin it by doing a few different steps. A maze is created by having walls of various sizes and lengths. If the player were to go through a maze with all the walls being of the same length and height as well as color and texture, then the maze would get incredibly boring and confusing. So, by making sure that certain sections of the maze were different in either geometry or color, the player would be able to rely on the art aspects to help maintain a solid and fun gameplay experience.

Puzzles

Puzzles are big questions and lingering mysteries waiting to be solved. Artistically, art puzzles contribute to the visual gameplay aspects of a game. Imagine having to solve a puzzle in game with three square blocks of varying colors. If one represents a lamp and the other two represent cars, how would you be able to tell other than color? The addition of detailed geometry and modeling contributes directly to gameplay in that it also helps maintain that sense of illusion.

> **Note:**
>
> Gameplay is also about keeping a player's attention and focus on the game and inside the monitor. By placing objects that don't belong in a world, you can literally destroy any hope of maintaining their focus or interest.

It definitely looks like art makes a difference in gameplay. The visual representation can affect major gameplay decisions and elements, which means we have to give them thought when designing our games.

Sound

Note:

You remember the hearing tests given in school. You would wear a headset and they would test your hearing by randomly pushing a button that generated a beep in your left ear, right ear, or both ears simultaneously. The noise would cause thought, reaction, emotion, and decision making.

In the original Atari games, the sound coming from the television set was not in Dolby 5.1 surround sound. Just the opposite; it was usually from a small speaker on the TV and simplified to the max. The wonderful thing was, at the time it hit the spot. The sound matched with the visuals and the gameplay kept you hooked. The question is, did and does sound directly contribute to gameplay? The answer is very much "Yes." Similar to the art side of things, sound has the ability to create emotion, which affects all the elements of gameplay.

If you were running through a world and heard a sick moaning noise come from the right side of the screen, there's an excellent chance you would look in that direction. The sound in this case directs the player in movement and objective.

Since one of the gameplay elements is "learning," we can use sound to coincide with its properties. Some games have trainers at the beginning of the level to teach you about your character, controller schemes, and abilities. These trainers take advantage of sound and communicate to the player verbally, allowing you to learn.

I certainly think that sound plays an important role in gameplay and will continue to play a larger role in the whole scheme of things.

With both sound and art working for us in game design and gameplay, we need to allow those aspects to develop our designs and help build the project.

■ ■ ■

We have covered only a small portion of gameplay and the elements that make it up that I consider some of the essentials. I would love to continue writing on this subject, but we still have an entire demo to create. So go grab some coffee or whatever keeps you awake and join me back here for Chapter 4, "Getting Set Up."

Part 2

Art Creation

We are finally here! My favorite part of game creation, the art content! The design documents are written, the art style guide has been hammered out, and now we get to produce the art for Zax's demo. First, we need to answer some questions like, "What software do I use? What's an exporter?" And my personal favorite, "Why do I have to follow rules?"

In the art content section we look at all those questions along with a step-by-step process on setting up the software, exporter specifications, modeling,

texturing, and animating. Let's not forget about level design, playtesting, and lighting. Creating art for a game is a lot of work, but if you stick to some standard techniques and rules you will be able to cut out the work part and just have fun!

First things first. In order for any of our amazing artwork to get created and completed in a timely fashion we need to make sure the software, plug-ins, tools, and examples are all set up and working the way they should be.

Chapter 4

Getting Set Up

"Organization is the key to success." Is that not one of the greatest quotes around? What an amazing word. Let me just say it again, "organization." Before anything can get accomplished we need things set up on our computers and we need to get them organized. In the following sections we will get the software installed onto your computer and the plug-ins properly placed. In addition, we'll set up a directory structure for your art content.

Now, you may be thinking along the lines of "let's jump to the good stuff." I know I want to get there too, but how about we all start on the same page before we begin working.

Software

In the game industry we use a multitude of applications. There is literally a limitless amount of software available for use. After working with nearly all of them, I've narrowed it down to a few packages that work very well for game production. First on our list are the 2D software applications: Adobe Photoshop, GIMP, Corel Painter, Paint Shop Pro, and Microsoft Paint.

Adobe Photoshop — www.adobe.com
    Price — $649

Game artists, graphic designers, webmasters, and photographers can create original artwork, correct color, retouch and composite scanned images, and prepare professional-quality separations and electronic output with this tool. Photoshop CS is the new, full-upgrade version of Photoshop from Adobe.

GIMP — http://gimp.org/
    Price — Free

GIMP (GNU Image Manipulation Program) is a freely distributed piece of software suitable for such tasks as photo retouching, image composition, and image authoring. It is a powerful piece of software with capabilities not found in any other free software product. It can be used as a simple paint program, an expert-quality photo-retouching program, an online batch-processing system, a mass production image renderer, or an image-format converter. GIMP is modular, expandable, and extensible. It is designed to be augmented with plug-ins and extensions to do just about anything. The advanced scripting interface allows everything from the simplest task to the most complex image-manipulation procedures to be easily scripted. If you cannot afford Photoshop, this is an excellent free package to go with.

Corel Painter — www.corel.com
    Price — $429

Corel Painter IX — the world's most powerful Natural-Media painting and illustration software — features unique digital brushes, art materials, and textures that mirror the look and feel of their traditional counterparts. Corel Painter enables some of the

world's most accomplished creative professionals — including commercial designers,
artists, and photographers — to extend
their natural talents and techniques to create original works of breathtaking digital
art.

Paint Shop Pro — www.corel.com
Price — $129

Whether it's a photo, graphic, or digital art,
Paint Shop Pro is going to help you get that
vision out of your head and onto the screen.
Your pocketbook doesn't have to suffer for
your art and you don't have to settle on the
pricey standard for quality.

Microsoft Paint —

Comes standard with Windows and is found
under Start | Applications | Paint.

Next on the list are the most commonly
used 3D applications: 3D Studio MAX,
Maya, XSI, LightWave 3D, and MilkShape.

3D Studio MAX — www.discreet.com
Price — $3,495

3ds max 5, 6, and 7 were engineered to
accelerate both application and facility pipeline workflows, increasing studio productivity while providing intuitive artist-friendly
tools to a user base of 280,000 customers.
The releases include significant features
that offer animators and modelers the most
inclusive and sophisticated 3D toolsets in
the world.

Maya — www.alias.com
Price — $1,999

Maya integrates the world's foremost modeling, animation, visual effects, and
advanced rendering technologies into one
complete workflow solution. It's the most
comprehensive 3D software for producing
professional-quality graphics on desktop
PCs or graphics workstations.

XSI — www.softimage.com
Price — $495

Through the power of integration,
SOFTIMAGE|XSI gives you the most effi-
cient workflow in the industry. XSI takes
the guesswork out of creating 3D content
with in-context viewing and non-destruc-
tive non-linear control. The profound
integration of all functions and toolsets in
XSI means your clients can experience an
unmatched level of iterative control without
losing valuable production cycles.

LightWave 3D — www.newtek.com
Price — $1,595

LightWave's tools are designed for fast productivity and easy, intuitive use. They are
set in an interface that you can customize to
your needs, so the tools you use most are
right where you want them. Buttons are
plainly labeled with the names of the tools
so you know what they do instantly, not
with cryptic icons that take months to deci-
pher and memorize. Nothing in the industry
is faster to learn, easier to use, or more
productive.

MilkShape 3D — www.swissquake.ch/chumbalum-soft/index.html
Price — $25

MilkShape 3D is a low-polygon modeler
initially designed for Half-Life. During
development, many file formats were
added. MilkShape 3D has all the basic operations such as select, move, rotate, scale,
extrude, turn edge, and subdivide.
MilkShape 3D also allows low-level editing
with the vertex and face tool. Primitives
such as spheres, boxes, and cylinders are
also available. In addition, MilkShape 3D
has skeletal animation capabilities, which
allow you to export to morph target animation such as the ones in the Quake model
formats or to export to skeletal animation

such as Half-Life or Genesis3d. MilkShape 3D currently supports 37 different file formats from 27 different games, engines, and programs.

I believe each of these have free trial downloads if you are interested in learning or studying different applications.

The last and most certainly not least of programs on our list are what I would call an addition to the family. These programs work well with the ones above and help to create a more seamless flow between applications and game content creation.

Visual SourceSafe —
http://msdn.microsoft.com/vstudio/previous/ssafe
Price — $549

Through project-oriented version control and rich integration with Visual Studio, Visual SourceSafe provides individual developers and small development teams with tools to make safe alterations to existing code and track changes across users, projects, and time.

Visual SourceSafe is a version control system product that delivers restore point and parallel collaboration capabilities, thus allowing application development organizations to work on several versions of software simultaneously. The version control system introduces a check-in and check-out model in which an individual developer checks out a file, makes changes, and then checks the file back in. Other developers typically are not able to make changes to a file while it is checked out. Source code control systems also allow developers to roll back or undo any changes that later create problems.

BodyPaint 3D — www.bodypaint3d.com
Price — $495

BodyPaint 3D Release 2 will revolutionize the way you texture your 3D models. Regardless of how you've textured before, 3D texturing has never been easier. BodyPaint 3D makes painting by vectors as easy as painting by numbers.

Deep Paint 3D —
www.righthemisphere.com
Price — $595

Deep Paint 3D provides 3D artists with an intuitive, easy-to-use tool to paint and texture 3D models interactively in 3D. It uses textures or natural media that can be brushed directly or projected onto 3D models and scenes. This creative environment supports an integrated workflow with 3ds max, Maya, Softimage, and LightWave 3D. Deep Paint 3D comes complete with a bidirectional interface to Photoshop and special support for the Wacom Intuos pressure sensitive tablet. Deep Paint 3D can be used standalone or with Deep UV.

Pixologic ZBrush 2 —
http://pixologic.com/home/home.shtml
Price — $489

ZBrush 2 is a huge leap forward in speed, performance, and technology. Modeling, texturing, and painting features have all benefited from unprecedented code enhancements. New tools and options provide even more versatility in all areas, boosting the artist's productivity and streamlining workflow in surprising ways.

Z2 is fast. It boasts handsomely optimized code innovations combined with unique features, providing more power to create models with unparalleled detailing capabilities. Even medium- to high-resolution models respond instantly to sculpting actions, constantly rendered and shaded in real time.

Bryce 3D — http://bryce.daz3d.com
Price — $79.95

Featuring perhaps the most innovative and distinct user interface of any 3D application, DAZ|Bryce 5 combines exceptional power with incredible ease of use. Bryce 5 is a fun, feature-packed 3D environmental modeling and animation package. The entire program is designed to allow new users to quickly draw and render stunning landscapes, skyboxes, and 3D artwork. You can literally create a world of your own with this unique 3D program.

PolyTrans 3D Translation System — http://www.okino.com/default.htm
Price — $395

PolyTrans is a high fidelity and accurate 3D data translation, viewing, and model manipulation program that provides complete implementations of the most popular 3D file formats. PolyTrans is used for any task requiring manipulation, viewing, or conversion of 3D models and scenes. Supported export formats include 3ds max (via native plug-ins), .3ds, ACIS SAT, Apple 3DMF, Biovision, DirectX, DXF, Electric Image FACT, FilmBox, GameExchange, IGES, Lightscape, LightWave, Maya (via native plug-ins), OpenGL C code, OpenFlight, Parasolids, POV, Pro/Engineer (native), Protein Database PDB, Renderman RIB, Renderware/ActiveWorlds, Rhino-3D, SoftImage-3D and XSI, Solid Edge, SolidWorks, StereoLithography .stl, STEP,

trueSpace, USGS DEM, Vistapro, Viewpoint VET, VRML 1.0+2.0, Wavefront, and XGL. Some of these formats are import or export only. Used worldwide by thousands of 3D industry professionals, movie studios, institutions, etc., PolyTrans includes polygon reduction, batch conversion, and all 2D bitmap formats.

DirectX 9.0c — This will most certainly be mentioned in other places, but I just want to remind you that in order to get everything working you need the latest version of DirectX installed on your machine.

Note that many of these programs are found at www.sourceforge.net. The community there continues work on countless freeware and shareware applications that could save you and your development team some major bucks. Several applications on the companion CD are from the site.

So, which of these are we going to use for this book? Excellent question! We will use max 5.1/6 and Adobe Photoshop. That should set us up with everything needed to create the game demo.

> **Note:**
> Included on the companion CD are demos of many of the programs mentioned. If you don't own these applications, then go ahead and install the demos provided on the CD, which can be found in the Software directory.

Plug-ins/Utilities

On the root directory of the companion CD you will find a Tools folder. The folder contains plug-ins, scripts, utilities, and a viewer for the engine. Be sure max is closed before doing the following steps.

3DSMax_HgrExport

Inside the Tools\3DSMax_HgrExport folder are two 3dsmax .dle files. HgrExport is the exporter you will use to get art from max into the viewer and engine. Depending on which version of max you use, copy the appropriate .dle file to your hard disk.

Max 5.1 — Copy hgrexport-max5.dle from the CD to your …\3dsmax5\plugins folder.

Max 6 — Copy hgrexport-max6.dle from the CD to your …\3dsmax6\plugins folder.

Copy DevIL.dll (image loading library) to the C:\windows\system32 directory.

Max 7 — Copy hgrexport-max7.dle from the CD to your …\3dsmax7\plugins folder.

Script Files

Script files are generally created by artists to solve specific problems or to cut down on redundancy issues. Included on the companion CD are a handful of scripts that will help in your art creation. Check out the list below to see the scripts that have been included.

- **Advanced Painter** — A modular object distribution tool with a brush-based interface. Great tool for brushing on grass, rocks, trees, etc.

- **Asteroid Generator** — Creates asteroids, pebbles, and stones of varying sizes and polygons. It is an excellent tool for creating random rocks.

- **Edit Poly Tool** — Removes edges on loops and rings without distorting or messing up the UV coordinates.

- **GLB2** — Game Level Builder toolset. This has an awesome Handy Cam, which acts like a first person-style camera inside of max, and other great tools for creating walls and levels BSP style.

- **Layers** — A script from Blur Studio that allows more options for layering.

- **Mouse Planter** — Lets you distribute copies of objects across the surface of other objects in an interactive manner using the mouse.

- **Physique Mirror Weights** — Allows for mirroring of vertices in Physique mode.

- **Polygon Counter Poly Edit Mode** — Gives accurate polygon count in Edit Poly mode

- **Texporter** — Generates a map of the UV coordinates from 3ds max.

- **Tree Maker** — Creates low-polygon trees for games.

These, along with many other scripts, are available online at www.scriptspot.com.

HGR Viewer 1.x

Inside the Tools\HGR_Viewer folder is hgrviewer.exe. For the artist it's our keyhole into the engine. If we can export objects and view them here, then our world is a better place. It's a rather small application, so I stick it on my desktop for quick and easy access.

To place the file on your desktop simply left-click and drag hgrviewer.exe to your desktop, or press Ctrl+C to copy the file and press Ctrl+V on your desktop to paste it.

Environment Settings

Shaders

Place the Ka3D folder on your root directory, for example, C:\Ka3D, then set the Environment variable ka3d to point to the specified directory. This way you don't need multiple copies of shader files and particle files on your hard drive when you use the scene viewer or other applications using the engine.

1. Click on **Start | Control Panel | System | Advanced | Environment Variables**.

2. In the Environment Variables window under the System variables, click on the **New** button, then type **KA3D** for Variable name, and the path where your folder is located (e.g., C:\ka3d\) for Variable value.

3. Click **OK**, then click **OK** in the Environment Variables window. Finally, click **OK** in the System Properties window.

You're all set.

System DLLs

In order for the viewer and the engine to run properly, we need to copy some files to Windows.

Copy ...\Tools\SystemDLLs > mfc71.dll, mfc71enu.dll, msvcp71.dll, and msvcrt.dll to the C:\windows\system directory, unless they are there already.

.dds File Format and Normal Map Filter

Max Setup — .dds

In ...\Tools\Normal_Map_Tools you will see a set of folders that contain your plug-ins for the .dds format and normal mapping filters and exporters.

Open the 3dsMax_DDS_Plugins folder and choose your version of max. Copy and paste the dds.bmi file into the ...\3dsmax5\ stdplugs folder (or the folder for your version of max).

Max Setup — Normal Mapper UI

The Normal Mapper UI is a graphical front end to ATI's NormalMapper.exe, which is a utility to create Normal maps from source 3D objects. In order to get it working with max, simply follow the directions below:

1. Start 3ds max.

2. From the MAXScript menu, select **Run Script**.

3. Using the file open requestor, find the **NormalMapperUI.mzp** file and select **OK**.

4. From the Customize | Customize User Interface menu option you can now assign NormalMapperUI to a hotkey toolbar, menu, or quad menu. The command is located in the Lodestone Tools category. Once you've set it in place, select **Save**.

When you run the ATI Normal Mapper for the first time you will be asked to locate NormalMapper.exe. It is found in ...\Tools\ Normal_Map_Tools\3dsMax_NormalMapper_UI.

Once you have it set up, you are ready to go. Note that if you are using max 7, it now comes with a normal mapper so you won't need any outside applications.

Adobe Photoshop .dds and Normal Map Filter

In …\Tools\Normal_Map_Tools\Adobe_Photoshop_DDS_Plugins you will see two files.

1. Copy **dds.8bi** to …\Adobe\Photoshop x.0\Plug-Ins\File Formats.

2. Copy **NormalMapFilter.8bf** to …\Adobe\Photoshop x.0\Plug-Ins\Filters.

.dds Thumbnail Viewer

The Thumbnail viewer is simply an executable file that you run to allow Windows IE the ability to view .dds files in Thumbnail mode. It can be found in …\Tools\Normal_Map_Tools\DDS_ThumbNailViewer.

Normal Map Viewer

The Normal Map viewer contains the NMFView.exe. This ATI application is used to view your Normal map models. Be sure to have it somewhere handy, like on your desktop, for quick access.

Documentation

Inside …Tools\Normal_Map_Tools\ATI_Normal_Mapper\Documentation you will see a set of HTML documents that provide further explanation of the Normal map and .dds plug-ins.

Configuring and Customizing Software (max 5.1, 6, and/or 7)

The hgrexport.dle is an export class plug-in for 3dsmax 5.1, 6, and 7. Open the 3dsMax_DDS_Plugins folder and choose your version of max. Copy and paste the dds.bmi file into the …\3dsmax5\stdplugs folder (or the folder for your version of max).

Before we can start using max, let's be sure that it's working for us and not against us. Follow the steps below to ensure you are getting the "max"imum effectiveness.

Units and Grid

1. Double-click on **3dsMax.exe**. With max open, we need to define the units that we work with. The exporter allows us to use any form of unit and convert it to the engine specifics afterward.

2. On the menu bar click the **Configuration** button and then select **Units Setup**.

3. Click on **System Unit Setup**, then change the system Unit Scale to 1 Unit = **1.0 Feet** and click **OK**.

4. Next, under the Display Unit Scale, select **US Standard** and **Feet w/Decimal Inches**. Why feet? I know, I know, everyone uses the metric system, but I have used feet and find it the easiest to work with. If you want to use meters, just be aware that the lessons provided here are in U.S. standard measurements.

The Units Setup is used to measure geometry in the scene, but not the viewport display grid.

5. In order for us to have the grid set up the same, go to **Customize | Grid and Snap Settings | Home Grid**. Under the Grid Dimensions, you want to change the Grid Spacing to **1'0.0"**. This will allow you to have your grid set up every one foot in the viewport. Remember, the grid spacing is totally up to you. If you like grid spacing every six inches, then you can set it for that; just be mindful of the setting before you begin modeling.

Driver Setup

6. Next, we need to adjust the driver setup. Go to **Customize | Preference | Viewport | Choose Driver**.

7. Under Direct3D Version, select **DirectX 9.0** and click **OK**. A prompt will come up telling you that you need to restart max before it will take effect; don't worry about that just yet, we still have some more things to change.

Note:

In max 6, if you are running in DirectX mode, you will be able to view Normal maps real time in the viewport. In the Material Editor, select the DirectX 9.0 shader from the material type Standard button.

If you decide to go with OpenGL drivers, then be sure to get the most out of them.

8. Click on **Preference | Viewport | Configure Driver** and then change the Background Texture Size to **1024** and the Download Texture Size to **512**.

9. Change the Texel Lookup and the MipMap Lookup to **Linear**. That should do it.

I have consistently found that the OpenGL drivers assist in pushing more polygons and textures on screen in the viewport. So, if you plan on creating large levels in the future, you can always switch to the OpenGL drivers.

Now that everything is prepared, let's save this scene with the correct unit setup.

10. Go to **File | Save As** and call it **Scene_Setup.max**. By having a scene with everything set, you'll be able to give it to all your artists and level designers so that everyone is working with the same configurations. This may seem unimportant, but once you start creating hundreds of art assets, the last thing you want is to go back and rescale all the files until they are accurate.

Creating the Directory Structure

A directory structure is simply a set of folders giving you places to store your files, work in progress (wip), and the exported art. This is easily one of the world's evils for some artists and teams. I can't count how many times I've asked to see artwork or specific models from an artist and found myself waiting for hours (well, maybe just a few minutes) as he or she tirelessly clicks through one folder after another until the file is found. Setting up a solid directory structure and sticking to it is key to making sure things stay organized. Included on the CD under ...CD\Templates is a premade directory system for you to begin with.

Be sure to drop the whole directory onto your computer. Simply rename "Template" to your project name so that it's a little more personal. There are text files included with each subfolder to help you understand what should be in there.

The Exporter

The exporter is considered the crown jewel when it comes to artists and level designers. There is a distinct separation between artists and programmers. Some might say a language barrier. The exporter is our translator or interpreter, which means the better the exporter performs the greater our chances of communicating between each group.

With HGR Exporter, artists are able to work in complete unison with the programmers and engine. Being able to export art into the engine immediately determines whether the artist will love or passionately dislike the exporter and engine. Let's take a look at what makes this tool so great and why you'll be sold on the simplicity of how it works.

Exporter Definitions

The hgrexport.dle is an export class plug-in for 3ds max 5.1 and 6. It writes scene hierarchy, geometry, and key-framed animations to a single scene file .hgr as shown in Figure 4-1.

The Options dialog allows you to choose the following properties:

- **Scale world units to meters** — Temporarily scales all objects to the metric system
- **Copy textures to output path** — Copies

textures used in the scene to the same directory where the scene file is exported

- **Animation sample rate (Hz)** — Defines initial sampling rate for keyframe transformation animation data. After this initial sampling, the data is optimized.

- **Animation only** — Exports animations for characters

The position, rotation, and scale animations are extracted by resampling, so any controller can be used to animate objects.

- **Default shader** — Selects a default shader in case an object doesn't have any shader set to it

- **Fog parameters** — Fog is used in the scene if the Fog enabled check box is checked before exporting the level. Note that you only need to enable the fog for the main level scene. For example, separately exported characters don't need fog to be set, since only the level file scene fog settings are used.

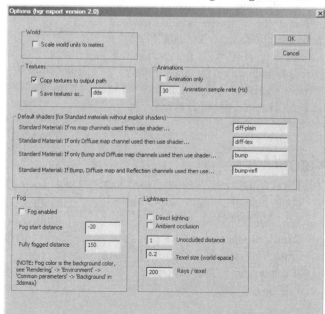

Figure 4-1: HGR Exporter

Fog uses 3ds max Rendering | Environment | Background Color as the fog color (there is also a comment about it in the exporter dialog box), and fog range is defined in the exporter dialog. Fog is always linear, since it's easier to control. Fog range, on the other hand, is not limited; in other words you can set fog start behind the camera to create a more subtle effect.

Note that all export dialog options are saved next to the target exported file; for example, an exported scene.hgr would have its export config saved as scene.hgr.cfg, so you need to set them only once, and you can also check the plain text .cfg file afterward to see the settings that were used.

Fog is independent of material. The only exception is the unlit-tex-nofog shader, which ignores fog totally (it was done for a skydome). Other nofog shaders can be easily added as well if needed.

Support for Skinned Characters

Character skinning information is extracted both from the Character Studio Physique modifier and 3ds max Skin modifier. I just want to repeat that part: You can use the Physique and/or Skin modifier! I don't know of another engine that allows both to be used. For an artist, that is really speaking my language!

Light Maps

- **Direct Lighting** — Bakes direct lighting to light maps. It can be combined with Ambient Occlusion.
- **Ambient Occlusion** — Bakes the ambient occlusion factor to light maps. It can be combined with Direct Lighting.

- **Unoccluded distance** — The distance that is considered unoccluded by the ambient occlusion factor ray-tracing
- **Texel size** — The size of a single light map texel in world space coordinates (Smaller texels in world space equals more light map data.)
- **Rays/texel** — Number of rays used to determine the ambient occlusion factor

Lightmapping, when enabled, is used by default on all objects. Lightmapping can be disabled on a per-object basis by setting the **Receive shadows** check box as disabled from Edit | Object Properties.

If the object is not supposed to cast shadows, then disable the **Cast shadows** check box from Edit | Object Properties.

> **Reminder:**
>
> Examples of everything are included on the companion CD, so don't worry if things feel overwhelming at first. You'll have it down in no time.

Materials, Shaders, and Lights

The preferred way to set materials to objects is to use the DirectX 9 Shader material type in 3ds max 6 or 7.

The Standard material is also supported for 3ds max 5.1.

The Multi-Sub Object Material is also supported when multiple DX materials/Standard materials need to be used in one object. So each exported object must use either DX material, Standard material, or Multi-Sub Object material, which has DX/Standard materials as sub-materials.

Specifications, Usage, and Limitations

Here we go with some more rules. Or put another way, the "Dos and Don'ts" of the HGR Exporter.

As discussed previously, the exporter writes scene hierarchy, geometry, and keyframed animations to a single .hgr scene file. With the exporter we can export our levels, characters, weapons, physics, animations, and particle setups through a simple click. There are a few things you should factor into your geometry creation:

- If your models come in flipped, with normals facing the wrong direction or scaled improperly, simply reset the Xform and export again.

- Be sure the naming conventions for the object name, shaders, and collision are set up properly. We will get to this soon enough, so don't worry right now.

Polygon and texture suggestions:

- **Hero character** — 3,500 to 8,000 polygons (could be more depending on the game), 512x512 or 1024x1024 texture size.

- **Enemy characters** — 2,500 to 5,500 polygons (depends on how many you plan to have on screen at once), 512x512 or 1024x1024 texture size.

- **Static mesh objects** — 200 to 2,500 polygons per object (once again, it just depends on how many you have in the scene), 256x256 or 512x512 texture size.

- **Weapons** — 500 to 2,500+ polygons (dependent on whether it's a FPS or third-person), 512x512 or 1024x1024 texture size.

- **Scene** — Polygon limit is totally dependent on game style and layout, 32x32 to 1024x1024 texture size. (There's a lot of play here because of the variation of objects, visibility, etc., that can occur in a level.)

■ ■ ■

The best way to check what your limitations are is to push the engine and max out the geometry and textures. Then you will be in a much better position to judge your game's limitations.

That's about it. I think it's time we jump over to Chapter 5 and start working on art.

Chapter 5

2D Art for the Game

thing up and going from the start. We need art in the game pretty quick so that the team (programmers, level guys, and manager types) can get a first-hand impression of the look in game.

Typically, as artists we want to jump straight to characters and animations, but first let's use our talents to come up with a couple of illustrations for interface screens, special power effects, particle effects, and more.

Let's begin with UI screens, then move to the HUD and other elements.

The 2D stage in game development includes sprites, particles, interface screens, blood splatters, bullet holes, and anything else that's flat! When beginning to develop a game, it's important to get every-

What Are UIs and HUDs?

Have you ever played a game where there were no instructions or no buttons to click on for start or exit? What about a game that didn't have any information about what the character was holding or how many more bullets you had left in your gun? Games require some sort of cohesiveness with instructions and prompts in order for the user to know what's going on. Fortunately, as artists of the gaming world we have the pleasurable task of creating UIs and HUDs.

The Innovative and Intuitive UI

A *UI* (user interface) is an image prompt that allows the player/user to input information into a game or read information about a choice or an action. For instance, if you were playing a game and clicked the pause button, a screen would appear giving you a list of options to choose from. The list could be "Objectives, Controls, Save, Exit" or something of that nature. The user/player would have the option of selecting from the choices. If the player chooses to "Exit," then the game would end and he/she would have to go back to reality. Maybe not the best of choices, but one we must make every so often.

Let's start by creating some interface screens for Zax's demo and work our way through the design.

The start screen is first on the list. What type of options do we have when creating the screen? We can render a cool 3D scene from max or work over a highly detailed 2D illustration inside of Photoshop. Also, we could take advantage of using the engine for an in-game background and environment with some typical 2D selection options, so that there's lots of movement and immediate immersion into the game.

Let's take the best of both worlds and put them together.

Start Screen

The Start screen is a bit of a tricky item to work with. The opening screen needs to portray the entire game in one scene or set the standard for all user interface screens while keeping with the theme of the game.

The opening screen for the Zax demo looks like Figure 5-1. We decided to go with the straight through approach. What's that, you ask? Notice the layout of the page doesn't strongly suggest a back and forth pattern. It's centralized and very straightforward, which is a great technique for demos. Also, notice how the flow runs straight down from the title through the words while the silhouetted buildings make sure that your eyes move back up the screen and not directly off. When you run the demo you should see the sky in the background moving along with spaceships flying around, which helps to add a bit of life and movement to the start screen. All the textures and the max file are included on

the companion CD at …\Tutorials\ Art_Tutorials\Tutorial_UI_Start_Screen.

> **Note:**
>
> The start screen is probably one of the most important interface screens to get "right." If it confuses the player, he will likely start the game off with reservations or hit the Exit button once it appears. So, we have kept it simple by having the Start button at the top of the list, Options second, Load/Save Game, Credits, Website, and lastly the Exit button. That's all we need to get going. The player will be happy not to have any more choices than that and should be able to jump into the game quickly.

Once you establish the "look" of your start screen, it should become your user interface template. By this I mean it's important to keep the "look and feel" of the game consistent. The rest of the screens should contain the same fonts, layout style, texture, and color sets as the start screen. If things change for every UI, the players may assume they are playing different games or characters instead of the one they intended to play.

Note:

By sticking with the same look and feel, you will also increase your speed for creating the rest of the interface screens in the game.

Figure 5-1: Screen shot of start screen

Creating the User Interface Using Photoshop

Creating the title for the Zax demo is an excellent place to introduce some techniques and steps for Photoshop.

The sketch shown in Figure 5-2 should give you a good idea of what we are trying to accomplish.

1. Open Photoshop. Go to **File | New** (**Ctrl+N**) and make a new image with the following settings:

   Name: **Zax_Demo_Title**
   Width: **500** pixels
   Height: **215** pixels
   Resolution: **72** pixels/inch
   Mode: **RGB Color**

Figure 5-2: Sketch work from the art style guide

2. Double-click in the viewport inside Photoshop or click on **File | Open** (**Ctrl+O**). Browse to ...\Tutorials\Art_Tutorials\Zax_Demo_Title and open the two files in the folder.

3. Navigate to **Layer | New | Layer...** (**Shift+Ctrl+N**). Call this new layer **Blue Background 1** and then click **OK**. Be sure that the Layers window is open. If you don't see it, click on **Window | Layers** (**F7**) to bring the window up.

4. Using the sketch we drew, click on the Polygonal Lasso tool (**L**) and make the outlining shape as shown in Figure 5-3.

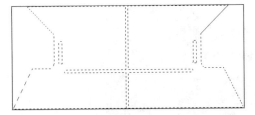

Figure 5-3: Outlining shape

5. Next we want to fill the area that we have outlined with blue. Click on the first color selection button and change the color to **0, 0, 255** for blue (see Figure 5-4).

6. Using the Paint Bucket tool (**G**), fill the outlined shape with the blue color.

7. Press **Ctrl+D** to drop the marquee selection.

We need to add some depth to the blue shape. Photoshop has many tools for doing just that. I would highly suggest going to Adobe's web site as well as the links on the CD for some great plug-ins, filters, and brushes that will make the creating process all the more fun.

Paint Bucket Tool (G)

Blue

Figure 5-4

8. Click on **Layer | Layer Style | Bevel and Emboss**. We'll use the default settings, so click **OK**. (See Figure 5-5.)

9. Make sure metal_01.bmp is open. (Metal_01 is simply a photo reference of a scratched metal surface.) We want to add this texture to our set of Title textures. Select the Move tool (**V**) and left-click and drag the metal texture into our Title window. Photoshop automatically creates a new layer for it called **Layer 1**. Let's change the name by double-clicking on the layer name inside the Layers window. Rename this layer **Metal Background 1** and hit Enter. Move the metal texture so that it fits directly inside the window. If the Snap tool is on, you will have a much easier time lining up the texture to the edge. It's found under View | Snap (**Shift+Ctrl+;**).

Figure 5-5: Bevel and Emboss selection

Note:

Another option for moving textures from one window to the next is to simply press Ctrl+A for Select All in the metal_01 window and then press Ctrl+C for copy. Select the current project and press Ctrl+V. Photoshop will automatically paste a new layer of metal_01 inside.

Currently, the metal texture doesn't allow us to see the blue color underneath. We need to change the blending mode so that the layers work with each other. Figure 5-6 illustrates where the Blending mode is on the Layers window.

10. Change the Blending mode to Pin Light. This will allow some details from the layer to carry over on to the blue texture.

11. Let's get rid of the run-off texture on the sides of the title. Select the Magic Wand tool (**W**). Select the Blue Background layer. Hold **Shift** (allows multiple selections) and click on the area next to the blue color with the Magic Wand tool as shown in Figure 5-7.

12. Select the Metal Background 1 layer and then press the **Backspace** key to delete the selected area. Next press **Ctrl+D** to drop the marquee selection.

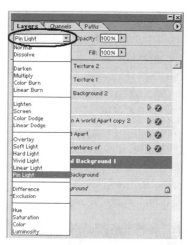

Figure 5-6: Blending mode drop-down selection

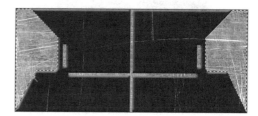

Figure 5-7: Magic Wand tool selection

Choosing Fonts

While creating the artwork for the art style guide, we had to come up with the fonts that would be just perfect for use in this demo. In Figure 5-8 you can see the font style we chose to go with. It's playful like a cartoon, but has an undertone of seriousness. A great technique for choosing your font is to use either Microsoft Word or Photoshop, type in the name of your game, and then simply browse through the list of fonts until you get a top 10 workable fonts list. Then pick the top three from that list and finally choose the lucky winner. Oftentimes you can choose two or three styles to go with your main font if they complement each other. The two other fonts shown in Figure 5-8 are our complementary fonts.

Figure 5-8: Fonts

It's time to add text to Title.psd.

1. Select the Text tool (**T**). Click inside the Title window to start the text. Next go to the top on the info bar and change the font type to **Morse Kode**, the text size to **35.5** pt, and the color to **white**. Type **The Adventures of**, then click the **check mark** button (Commit any current edits) at the top right of the

info bar. Click inside the Title window again to create another text layer and, using the same setup, type **In**.

2. Create another text layer and type **Zax** using the Morse Kode font, but change the text size to **150** pt.

3. Finally, create the last text layer using font type **Motor**, text size **71** pt, white color, and type **A World Apart**.

4. Position the text with the Move tool (**V**) until it looks like Figure 5-9.

Figure 5-9: Text placed on image

5. Select the Zax text layer. Click on the **Layer Style** button on the bottom of the Layers window and select **Inner Shadow**. In the Structure area be sure that Distance and Size are set to **5**.

6. Next, click on **Bevel** and **Emboss**. In the Structure area make sure your setup is as follows:

   Style: **Inner Bevel**
   Technique: **Smooth**
   Direction: **Down**
   Size: **2**
   Soften: **0**

7. In the Layers window, left-click and drag the Effects bar into the other three text layers.

Now, we need to rough the text up some so that it blends in better with the background textures.

1. Right-click on the **Metal Background 1** layer and select **Duplicate Layer**. Change the name to **Metal Background 2**, then click **OK**.

2. Drag the new Metal Background 2 layer up to the top of the stack. (Make sure it's above the text layers.)

3. It's time to change the background color. Click on the Gradient Bucket tool (**G**) and make sure you have **black** chosen for the Foreground Color. Then click on the Background layer and fill it with black.

4. Select the Zax text layer. Using the Magic Wand tool (**W**), select the letters.

5. With the letters selected, click on the **Metal Background 2** layer. Navigate to Layer | New | Layer via **Cut** (**Shift+Ctrl+J**). With the new layer selected, take the opacity down to **36%**.

6. Click on the **A World Apart** text layer. Let's look at another way we can select the letters all at once. Choose the Magic Wand tool (**W**) and click outside the letters. Then hold down the **Shift** key and click on the insides of the letters where there are spaces. Once you get that completed, choose **Select | Inverse** (**Shift+Ctrl+I**). You should have all the letters highlighted.

7. Select the **Metal Background 2** layer from the Layers window and make a copy of that selection by going to Layer | New | Layer via **Copy** (**Ctrl+J**).

8. With the new layer selected, navigate to **Image | Adjustments | Color Balance.** Change the Color Levels to **+86, –11, –38,** then click **OK** (see Figure 5-10).

That's it! We just made the title and logo for Zax's demo game! Be sure to save it.

Figure 5-10: Title image complete

The second user interface screen (Figure 5-11) will accomplish the rest of the tasks needed for the demo. The interface screens will consist of Options, Pause, Menu, Yes/No, Play Again, etc. So what I did was create a generic style box to put all the text into. For demo purposes this helps keep the art load down, but the quality is still very high, meaning I am able to concentrate on making the one interface screen look just right for the demo. I included the .psd file on the CD at: ...\Tutorials\Art_Tutorials\Tutorial_UI_Screen. This should help you see what type of layer styles I used and how I put things together. Make sure that you decompose it before moving on to the next section.

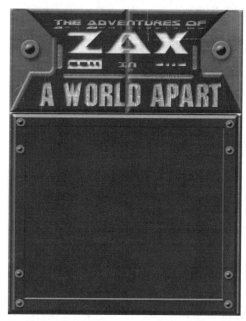

Figure 5-11: Interface screen

Creating the Heads-Up Display

The next item on our list is the HUD (heads-up display). Think of this as what you want the player to see on screen during gameplay. So, what should a player see during gameplay? That's an excellent question. Let's list some of the variables seen on HUDs for console and PC-style games.

- Life
- Health
- Weapons
- Ammunition
- Special powers

- Communications
- Control variables
- Player information
- Enemy information
- Status information
- Timer or counter
- Selection menus
- Onscreen help
- Objectives
- Inventory
- Arrows
- Maps

As you can see, these are just a few of the options that designers enjoy sticking on screen while the user is playing. It can be a bit tricky at first trying to make everything work without filling up the entire screen with options. Typically an artist will take those words and do drawings or illustrations to capture that word with a picture, which is commonly referred to as an *icon*. An icon takes away the language barrier and gives users from all backgrounds the ability to play games without difficulty.

Our job is to create a smooth flowing layout that gives the player exactly what he needs when he needs it.

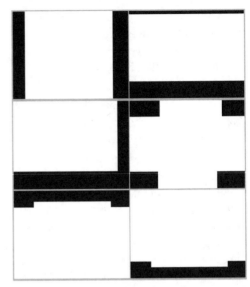

Figure 5-12: Examples of good HUD layouts

> **Note:**
>
> Remember, you may not always need HUD pieces on screen all the time. Some may only come up when particular events happen.

A good rule of thumb for laying out HUD elements on screen is to go from left to right and top to bottom. Therefore, when you work on layouts for the HUD keep in mind that your audience has been trained to look and read that direction. I've blocked in a few examples of solid HUD layouts in Figure 5-12. Notice how the images keep you concentrated on the screen while maintaining a balance between what is important and what is secondary.

Bad examples of HUD layouts are just as useful, especially if your current idea fits into one of these categories. See Figure 5-13.

These four examples definitely show what not to do. As you can see from the top-left example, the HUD is placed in the center of the screen. A user interface would be optional for that position but a HUD element — well, let's just say it's not the best idea. The ones below and to the right are cut up so much that you can't tell whether

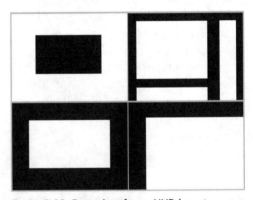

Figure 5-13: Examples of poor HUD layouts

the gameplay is more important or the HUD pieces. Personally, I want as much real estate as I can get from the gameplay. The last example shows how things placed on the left side of the screen make the player feel boxed in, simply because we read things from left to right. Those types of layouts force me to either fall off the screen on the right or bump my head every time I look to the left.

For the Zax demo, we need to know what Zax will be using during gameplay and whether the character will need options on screen such as help menus, control variables, ammo amount, etc. Let's create a list and find out.

- **Health** — The health icon has got to be fun looking and cool. The game itself requires a lot of screen real estate, so we do not want to burden the player with huge images, but it needs to be large enough so you don't have to squint to see if you're almost dead. The health will be a fixed icon on the screen (meaning it won't disappear during gameplay).

- **Weapon** — Zax's arsenal will consist of a mounted laser, lights on his shoulder pads, and a gun. We want the ammunition and the weapon to be one icon. Basically, whatever weapon you have selected will show up in the display box while the corresponding ammunition will be next to it. The idea is to keep it simple and slick.

- **Weapon Selection** — When the player has multiple guns you simply press the defined scroll weapon button and the character will switch to whichever gun he has on him. If you are developing strictly for a PC title, then you could go for the standard number of key selection sets, too.

- **Inventory Selection** — The player will have the option to pick up a few extra items along the way. We don't want the player to have to learn some new inventory action, so what you will do is press a defined button, cycle through to your item, and hit the button again. That will work out well for our purposes.

- **Usable Item** — The usable item will appear on screen and will have a count of how many of that item is left. This

item should be a simple one-button click to operate. If there are complexities to it, you may want to add more specifics on screen to help guide the player.

- **Ammunition** — For the Zax demo we use a bar system set in with the weapon icon. It defines the weapon and colored bars show the amount used and left.

- **Map/Objectives** — The map and objectives will be a separate screen. Many games place screens up in the top corners with a set opacity, but for this demo we are going for a very open HUD screen. Here we have a defined button to press that will stop the gameplay and allow you to view a map and player objectives at the same time.

- **Communications** — A communications window will be defined when the player is receiving incoming calls on Zax's telecom device. We should try to keep it out of the way like at the bottom of the screen, but visible enough that the player will notice it when text appears.

Now that we have the icon list, it's time to create a screenshot mockup of the game. For me, the best way to do this is to render out scenes in max after I've sketched out the icons.

In Figure 5-14 you notice that we have a mockup of the gameplay, which helps us better position the HUD elements. It's important to a project to get the look and feel of your game before moving on much further. Typically this would be a sketch colored in using Photoshop, but I wanted to bring the full look of it to life a bit early.

Note:

Take your time with this portion of the game. If it takes you two months to come up with the proper look, then that was time well spent.

Notice that the major elements on the screen have not been placed one on top of the other. This is ideally what you want. Be sure to use the earlier example about creating a solid layout to help you produce the placement needed for the game.

Once you have the items positioned on screen, we need to find the x and y coordinates for the programmers. So how does one go about finding such a thing? In Photoshop, go to Windows | Info. With the Info Window open, choose Palette Options. In the Info Options under Mouse Coordinates, change the Ruler Units to Pixels from the drop-down list and click OK.

This will give you the exact location for where the HUD elements x and y coordinates are on the screen. We will jot them down and give them as a text file to a programmer or scripter. Simply move your mouse to the top-left corner of the image and write down the x and y coordinates for the programmer.

Figure 5-14: HUD mockup

Decals and Particles

The next step is to create special effects and particles for the game demo. We will create the decals with Photoshop and use similar techniques for making the particle effect images.

Decals

A decal is anything that requires 2D art such as blood splatters, burn marks, bullet holes, and even rain or snowflakes. The decals involved in this game are listed below.

- Muzzle flash
- Explosion sequence
- Pickup effects
- Water textures
- Splash texture
- Smoke textures
- Wood and spark textures
- Bullet holes
- Burn marks
- Steam

Particles

Particle effects can be either 3D objects or 2D images that typically face the camera (billboards), giving the appearance of a particular shape. You can have animated textures like fire being displayed or a single image like a raindrop. What we need to figure out is how to use the particle effects and what to use them for.

The particle effects system that is used with the engine creates particles directly from Lua scripts and text files. In order to get a better handle on the particle effects, let's look at some definitions and an example to find out what makes it work.

The Insides of the Particle System

The particle system is heavily based on the concept of "domains." It is a bit abstract, but understanding it is essential for effective usage of the particle effects. Once you understand it, using particle systems becomes very intuitive and orthogonal, as nearly all properties of particle systems are simply defined by setting appropriate value domains for each property.

"Domains" are source ranges for various random values needed by particle systems. Domains can be sources for scalar values, 2D and 3D vectors used in the simulation. You're probably thinking, "I need an example right about now." So, for example, saying that some particle effect has particle initial position domain set as "Sphere with radius 4," means that the initial positions of new particles are randomized inside a sphere that has a radius of 4.

Here's another example:

If the particle initial velocity domain is set as point {–50,0,0}, then all particles get initial velocity of –50 along the negative X-axis.

With various domains it is easy to make pretty much any kind of particle effect. For example, rain could be done by setting a position box above the sky, and then changing velocity Point (0,–1,0) and Gravity=–9.8. In addition, ParticleSpriteElasticity could be set above 0 (say, 0.1) to stretch the particle bitmap along the movement speed. (Note that the system is very flexible.)

Even with all this power you are probably still wondering how particles are created. Let's look at an example.

Fire Particle Effects Example

As an artist you will want to familiarize yourself with the following information on the particle system. It's not too difficult; it only took me 15 minutes to read through the programmer comments to find out what was important to the artists. We'll step through the code so that you'll understand what's going on and what major things you need to understand.

1. Open the max file **Tutorial_1_Particle_Effects** found in the \Tutorials\Art_Tutorials\ folder.

We have a simple scene with barrels and an alleyway. Take a look inside the barrel. You will notice that there is a dummy box that is labeled "dummy box fire." This is our "tag" for the particle system.

The following properties are the ones you use for the particle effects: Particle Effect, Supports User Property tags, and Time.

Note:

User Property is found by right-clicking on the selected dummy box, choosing Properties from the quad menu, then selecting the User Defined tab.

The Time property allows you to write a user-defined sequence like the following:

Time=3
Particle=fire
Time=6
Particle=snow

This will launch fire particles at time=3 seconds and snow particles at time=6 seconds. Both tags are case-sensitive. With timing it is also possible to make cut scenes (which use particles) in 3ds max.

2. In the same location you should see a **Particle_Effects.hgr** file. Double-click on it to start the viewer and take a look at the current scene.

```
-----------------------
-- System properties --
-----------------------


-- Maximum number of simultaneous emissions
SystemMaxEmissions = 1


-- How emission limit is maintained: kill NONE, OLDEST, RANDOM
SystemLimitKill = "NONE"


-- Number of new emissions/second
SystemRate = Constant(100) -- to light it up fast


-- Time after no more new emissions are launched
SystemStopTime = Infinity()


-- Lifetime of the whole system
SystemLifeTime = Infinity()


-----------------------------------
-- Particle emission properties --
-----------------------------------

-- Maximum number of particles simultaneously
EmissionMaxParticles = 150


-- How max particle limit is maintained: kill NONE, OLDEST, RANDOM
```

```
EmissionLimitKill = "NONE"

-- Emission rate, particles/second
EmissionRate = Range (250,300)

-- Time after no more new particles are emitted
EmissionStopTime = Infinity()

-- Lifetime of particle emitter
EmissionLifeTime = Infinity()

-- Pivot point for the emissions
EmissionPosition = Point(0,0,0)


-------------------------
-- Particle properties --
-------------------------
-- Particle lifetime in seconds
ParticleLifeTime = Range(0.2,5)

-- If true, then particles are updated even though they are not visible.
-- Note: Normally this should be set to false
ParticleUpdateAlways = false

-- Volume in which the particles are born
ParticleStartPosition = Sphere(0,-0.2,0.1,0.2,0.12)

-- Domain for velocity vector values. This works the same way as position, but instead of randomizing
-- initial positions for the particles, this time velocity vectors are randomized so that the length and
-- direction of the velocity is randomized from the specified domain when the velocity vector is con-
-- sidered to start at origin.

ParticleStartVelocity = Sphere(0,1.4,0,0,0)

-- Start size of particle
ParticleStartSize = Range(0.3,0.4)

-- Lifetime end size of particle
ParticleEndSize = Range (0.4,0.7)

-- Start color (R,G,B in range 0-1) of particle
ParticleStartColor = Box(1,1,1,1,1,1)

-- End color (R,G,B in range 0-1) of particle
ParticleEndColor = Box(1,1,1,1,1,1)

-- Start opacity of particle
ParticleStartAlpha = Constant(1)

-- End opacity of particle
ParticleEndAlpha = Constant(0)

-- Particle sprite elasticity with particle velocity, set Constant(0) to disable
-- (note that elasticity and rotation are mutually exclusive)
ParticleSpriteElasticity = Constant(0)
```

```
-- Particle sprite initial rotation (degrees)
-- (note that elasticity and rotation are mutually exclusive)
ParticleSpriteRotation = Range(20,360)

-- Particle sprite initial rotation speed (degrees/sec)
ParticleSpriteStartRotationSpeed = Constant(0)

-- Particle sprite end rotation speed (degrees/sec)
ParticleSpriteEndRotationSpeed = Constant(0)


-------------------------------
-- Particle bitmap animation --
-------------------------------
--
-- View mode: CAMERAUP, WORLDUP
--
-- View mode defines are particles rotated when camera rotates along Z-axis.
-- If view mode is WORLDUP, then particle "up" direction is the same as world Y-axis.
-- If view mode is CAMERAUP, then particle "up" direction is the same as camera Y-axis.
--
-- Note: View mode does not affect if ParticleSpriteElasticity is set. Particle sprite elasticity
defines the "up" direction based on particle velocity
--
TextureView = "WORLDUP"

-- Texture bitmap
Texture = "textures/fire1.bmp"

-- Number of frames embedded to texture (nxn grid)
TextureFrames = 16

-- Method of selecting which frame to display:
-- LOOP plays back animation in constant frame rate (TextureFramerate)
-- LIFE starts from first frame and gradually animates until end-of-life
-- RANDOM selects random frame in interval defined by TextureFramerate
TextureAnimation = "LIFE"

-- Playback rate if TextureAnimation is LOOP
TextureFramerate = 10

-- Shader
Shader = "sprite-add"


-------------------------------------
-- World forces affecting particles --
-------------------------------------
-- Gravity affecting particles. Positive number particles go up; negative number particles go down.
Gravity = -1.7

-- Wind affecting particles. You can pick and choose between the x, y, and z coordinates.
Wind = {0.3,1.8,0}
```

There you go. We stepped through the code of the particle system. (I'm guessing we're not experts at it just yet, but with some work we'll get there.) The best way to become comfortable with it is to just create two or three more effects. Try creating a laser beam with particles that glow red. When you get that completed, make chimney smoke that you can add to give movement to an outdoor environment. And if you've created those, then your third one should be up to you.

On a side note, it took me about 2½ hours of just playing around with it — changing numbers, function calls, and textures — until I got to a point where I was creating things easily and on my own. So, if you're reading this and you are the "particle person" for the team, just spend an afternoon or lunch break reading through the code and changing variables until you remember what each thing does. The particle system may not be Windows (coming soon), but it is extremely friendly and easy to use. Good luck!

On the companion CD in \Tutorials\ Art_Tutorials\Particle_ Example_1_Fire I have set up a scene in max that shows how to use the particle effect system. Let's take a quick look at it to be sure you've got everything straight.

1. Open the max scene **Particle_Example_1_Fire.max** found in the \Tutorials\Art_Tutorials\Particle_ Example_1_Fire folder.

2. This scene when exported looks like Particle_Example_1_Fire.hgr in the HGR viewer. If you haven't run any scenes in the viewer, go ahead and open the HGR viewer. Click on **File | Open** and then select the file **Particle_Example_1_Fire.hgr**. You should see something similar to Figure 5-15.

3. Select the dummy box creatively labeled Dummy01. Right-click on the viewport and choose **Properties** from the quad menu. Click on the User Defined tab. The Particle properties should read Tutorial_1_Particle_ Effects_Fire.

That's all it takes to get a particle inside the engine. Whatever you label the particle here, just be sure to label the .prt file (the particle effects text file) the same. When you export the scene it will automatically

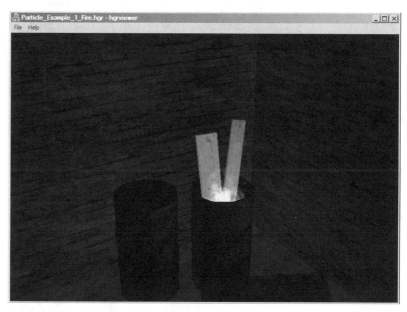

Figure 5-15: Particle effects in the viewer

look up the labeled .prt file in the particle folder and load its settings in the exported scene. Let's assume we want to change up the scene a bit.

1. With Dummy01 still selected, go to the Top viewport, press **Shift**, left-click, and drag Dummy01 to the other barrel. When the Clone Options dialog comes up, press **OK**.

2. Click on **File | Export**. Under Save as type, select **hgr export (*.HGR)**. Save the file as **Particle_Example_2_Fire.hgr** and click **OK**.

3. When the Options (.hgr export) dialog comes up, be sure to check **Scale world units to meters** and **Export vertex colors**, then click **OK**.

4. Open the new file in the HGR viewer. You should be looking at a fire burning in both barrels.

Important:

One of the key benefits of using the particle system is that you can create and manipulate multiple effects at one time, which means you will be able to view an entire sequence at once and tweak it as necessary.

Fog

"I can't see! It's too foggy and dark in here." Fog can be an excellent effect for games, certainly if you are attempting to create a mood or limit the player's view to only a particular distance. So how exactly does it work?

Fog is used in the scene if the Fog enabled check box in the exporter dialog is checked while exporting the level. Since only the level file scene fog settings are used, you will only have to set fog once for a level.

Fog uses 3ds max's Rendering | Environment | Background Color setting as the fog color (there is also a comment about it in the exporter dialog box) and fog range is defined in the exporter dialog. Fog is always linear, since it's easier to control. Fog range,

on the other hand, is not limited. In other words, you can set fog to start behind the camera to create more subtle effects.

Note:

All the export dialog options are saved next to the target exported file. For example, an exported scene.hgr would have an export config saved as scene.hgr.cfg, so you need to set them only once and you can also check which settings were used afterward from the plain text .cfg file.

Also, fog is independent of material. The only exception is the unlit-tex-nofog shader, which ignores fog totally. Other nofog shaders can be easily added as well if needed.

Shaders

Shaders are predefined and changeable material/texture files. If you want the character to have a glow map applied to it in certain areas, that can be created with a texture map and defined with a shader. The shader system is set up for the artist. Shaders use the Material Editor and specific naming conventions. We'll be going over the shaders in the tutorials coming up, so don't worry if you are not getting it or haven't ever used them. Let's take a look at how they work and some of the predefined shaders already supported.

Shader Usage in 3ds max

Shaders are used in 3ds max by assigning the FX=<shader> tag to the end of the material name. For example, to change the "Default-1" material to use the bump.fx shader you could change the name of the material to "Default-1 FX=bump."

The following conventions are used in naming shaders:

XXX.fx = shader XXX
s-XXX.fx = shader XXX for skinned objects
XXX-alpha.fx = transparent (alpha) shader XXX
s-XXX-alpha.fx = transparent (alpha) shader XXX for skinned objects

Please refer to the individual shader files (.fx) to see the details about each shader. Following is an overview of the included shaders.

Shaders for Skinned Characters

(in character/directory)

- **s-bump** — Skinned bump shader
- **s-bump-glow** — Skinned bump shader with glow support

- **s-bump-refl-glow** — Skinned bump and specular shader with glow and reflective support
- **s-bump-selfillum** — Skinned bump shader with conventional self-illumination
- **s-bump-alpha** — Skinned bump shader with transparency
- **s-hair-alpha** — Skinned bump shader with transparency and special hair sorting

Shaders for Static Geometry

(in level/directory)

- **bump** — Bump (normal map) shader
- **bump-alpha** — Bump shader with transparency
- **bump-glow** — Bump shader with glow support
- **bump-glow-refl** — Bump and specular shader with glow and reflective support
- **bump-selfillum** — Bump shader with conventional self-illumination support
- **bump-selfillum-refl** — Bump and specular shader with self-illuminated and reflective support
- **diff-plain** — Simple gouraud diffuse shader with no texture
- **diff-tex** — Simple diffuse shader
- **diff-tex-alpha** — Simple diffuse shader with transparency
- **unlit-plain** — Simple shader with plain, non-shaded texture with additive blending. It can be used as a basic "self-illuminating" material.
- **unlit-tex** — Simple plain texture (no shading)

- **unlit-tex-add** — Simple plain texture (no shading) with additive blending

- **unlit-tex-add-nofog** — Simple plain texture (no shading) with additive blending, without fog

- **unlit-tex-alpha** — Simple plain texture (no shading) with transparency

- **unlit-tex-alpha-nofog** — Simple plain texture (no shading) with transparency, without fog

- **unlit-tex-nofog** — Simple plain texture (no shading), without fog

- **vcolor-glow** — Static vertex color shader with transparency support

- **vcolor-tex** — Static vertex color

- **vcolor-tex-alpha** — Static vertex color with texture transparency

Post-Process Effect Shaders

(in post-process/directory) These shaders cannot be used directly by the artists.

Debug Shaders

(in debug/directory) These shaders cannot be used directly by the artists.

■ ■ ■

The shaders listed above were enough to create everything in the demo games and more. If you make it through all the tutorials you will really start realizing the full potential and ease in creating and using shaders directly through max.

Also, remember if you are a max 6 or 7 user, you will be able to apply and view all the shaders directly in the viewport, which is very cool! (We'll discuss this in the tutorials to come.)

Creating 3D Content for Games

The creation of art assets and content for PC and console game development is one of the larger tasks involved in developing a project that fully encompasses one's ideas. In this chapter we cover the technical issues and software usage. Also included are tutorials that demonstrate everything from creating your first character, weapon, and animation cycles to exporting and testing them in a game.

There's a lot of work ahead of us, so the sooner we get going on all this, the closer you will be in creating your first "world exclusive" game demo. You will have the publishers eating out of your hands.

> **Note:**
>
> Publishers eating out of your hands might be an exaggeration of terminology.

Modeling 101

Wow, we are finally to the modeling section of the book. All the documents have been created, the designer (me) has approved everything, all the software is properly installed and configured, and we have the art task list sitting next to us dictating what to create. It's time to begin modeling. We are going to warm up with world objects and then move to characters, animations, and level creation. Remember, the tutorials start easy and advance. Each tutorial will have relevant topics and techniques about creating artwork in 3ds max for the engine, so I would suggest reading and/or studying the max files closely.

The Max Window

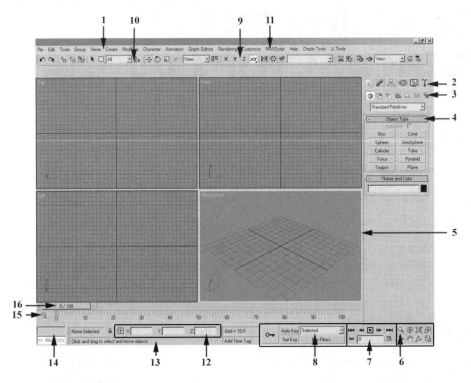

Figure 6-1: Max interface

Important:

Figure 6-1 depicts the user interface and provides a short description of what you will need to know about navigating in max. If you are unfamiliar with modeling inside of 3ds max, be sure to look over this carefully, as well as the Beginners Guide included with your copy of max, before beginning. The tutorials in this book are set up to help you gain an understanding of 3ds max and the engine but in no way replace all the information contained inside the official max tutorials.

1 — Menu bar
2 — Command panels
3 — Object categories
4 — Rollout

5 — Active viewport
6 — Viewport navigation controls
7 — Animation playback controls
8 — Animation keying controls
9 — Selection and transform tools
10 — Window/Crossing selection toggle
11 — Keyboard shortcut override toggle
12 — Absolute/Relative coordinate toggle and coordinate display
13 — Prompt line and status bar
14 — MAXScript mini-listener
15 — Track bar
16 — Time slider

The Main Sections of max

I like to think of max as being divided into four main sections: the menu bar, viewports, tabs, and animation tools. If we keep things to a minimum, then learning about and navigating in 3ds max will be a breeze.

Menu Bar

The menu bar is at the top of screen and is used for quick access to the tools, buttons, and options available to the artist. Manipulating, modeling, and even rendering your scene can all be done in this section.

Viewports

The viewports are the large boxes in the center of your screen. Each box has a name located in the top-left corner that lets you know which view you are currently in. A yellow highlight is displayed for the active viewport. The viewports can also be moved and resized however you like. Presets of viewport layouts can be found at Customize | Viewport Configuration | Layout.

Command Panels

The command panels are located on the right side of the screen. The command panel is comprised of six tabs that give you access to most of the modeling features of 3ds max, as well as some animation features, display choices, and miscellaneous utilities.

The Create tab 🖉 is used to create everything from boxes to lights, cameras, helpers, and more.

The Modify tab 🖉 is used to modify and change the current state of your geometry. You can also apply modifiers to adjust the geometry of an object or a set of objects.

The Hierarchy tab 🖧 provides access to tools to adjust the hierarchical linkage between objects. The Hierarchy tab adjusts and creates linkage through the Pivot, IK, and Link Information options.

The Motions tab 🞊 is made available when you start working with animations and Character Studio. It provides all the necessary tools you'll need to work with CS.

The Display tab 🖳 gives you all the options for hiding, freezing, or displaying anything in the max scene.

The Utilities tab 🕈 gives you access to plug-ins and miscellaneous utility programs.

Animation Tools

The animation tools are located at the bottom of the screen. The time slider, keyframes, track bar, playback controls, and more are on the main interface. The Animation menu provides a set of commands related to animation, constraints, controllers, and inverse kinematics solvers as well.

As long as you keep things simple, you shouldn't have too much trouble working through the tutorials and learning the interface. For a fuller explanation of 3ds max, consult your reference books and help section that come with max.

Max Modeling and Guidelines

Save Often

Saving should be your number one priority. Be sure that when you are working on any model that you save the file even before you start working on it. Max does a good job of saving the backup copy, but you cannot always count on it to save your work. A good way to save your files is to open 3ds max and load Setup_scene.max. Then go to File | Save As "Your next model name".max. If you start the process off by saving, you are likely to hit Ctrl+S more often during the work.

Naming Conventions

To stay organized, you need to maintain proper naming conventions. Let's assume we have created a baseball bat and need to properly label everything.

Model Name — baseball_bat.max
Base Texture — baseball_bat.dds
Specular Color — baseball_bat_spec.dds
Normal Map — baseball_bat_bump.dds or
 baseball_bat_nrm.dds

Okay, let's examine what we have. When you create a file, be sure to name related files similarly so that finding textures for models and vice versa will be a breeze. I can't stress this enough. If you begin naming things differently it creates a world of problems for you and others on your team. For instance, just imagine if you create a model named handgun09.max and use textures named metal05.jpeg and image22j.png. I've seen it done time and time again; after months of work like this, everything becomes a huge mess. The cleaner we make the naming conventions,

the better our chances of organization and reusability.

> **Tip:**
>
> During the modeling process you need to ask yourself whether the model will be used more than once in a scene. If so, make sure that the model name has _01 attached to the end. You should have something similar to barrel_01, barrel_02, etc.

When developing games — whether with a large team or a small group — you need to organize your files so that they are intuitive and easily readable by anyone.

STL Check

The STL Check modifier checks an object to see if it's correctly built, similar to a real building. It runs a check for double faces, open edges, spikes, and multiple edges, then highlights the parts of the model that need correcting. Using STL Check to test the geometry before you export it can save time and work.

Select an object, then choose Modify panel | Modifier List | STL Check.

Reset Xform

One key rule in modeling is to reset the Xform. Use the Reset Transform utility to push an object's rotation and scale values onto the Modifier Stack display and align the object's pivot points and bounding boxes with the world coordinate system. Reset Transform removes all rotation and scale values from the selected objects and places those transforms in an Xform modifier. After you reset the Xform, make it an editable mesh or editable poly again.

Photo Reference

Photo references are key to creating solid, detailed texture maps. You will need a digital camera (2 gigapixels is plenty) to take reference photos. Below are some helpful hints on starting a reference library.

- Photos for textures are best taken during the morning hours of the day before the sun begins casting heavy shadows on the world around you, and on cloudy days where the sun isn't casting too many shadows. Be careful taking photos during the afternoon or nighttime hours as you might have shades of yellow and blue in the photos.

- If you don't have any photos or reference resources, then begin by taking at least 10 pictures a day of objects and environments near your home or work. Just think — by the end of the month you could have up to 300 textures at your disposal. Pretty cool! Keep it up for a year and you are looking at over 3,600 photos.

- When you take the pictures, be sure to take a photo of the entire object so that you can get the full scale. You also want the front, back, left, right, and, if applicable, top and bottom views of the object. The more views you get of the object or scene, the easier it will be to

duplicate it in a 3D software application. Once you have the entire image photographed, you can then move in and take some closeup shots of the detail pieces.

- Think of the textures as covering an 8x8 square foot section. If the object goes outside those parameters, the texture quality may go down a notch or two. Take multiple photos for larger areas in order to keep the quality high.

Remember:

We artists need boundaries and rules to make things work extra well together. And usually we need lots of extra documentation so that we don't waste weeks trying to figure out how to export an object or animation into an engine.

The following tutorials will take you step by step through creating, managing, and exporting your first models into the Ka3D engine. Each tutorial is designed to take you from the conceptual stage through viewing it inside the Ka3D viewer. By the time you work through each tutorial you should have a strong working knowledge of max, the HGR Exporter, and the HGR Viewer.

Tutorial 1: Building a Crate

This is it, time to build our first crate! When working with any engine for the first time, I typically build a simple crate to test the boundaries of the exporter and check quickly to see whether or not I can get things working right off the bat. In this first tutorial we will look at working with 3ds max, creating a high-polygon object for normal mapping, texturing techniques, and much more.

Reference

The first thing we need is reference photos. In order to create anything of real value we should always have reference on hand. In each tutorial we will create the models in a different fashion so that you will be introduced to multiple methods. The crate model will be created by using only two photo reference pictures.

Let's go ahead and open Adobe Photoshop or whichever 2D software application you have. Click on File | Save As. You will find the crate_reference.bmp in ...\Tutorials\Art_Tutorials\Tutorial_1_Crate. Open it and examine the different styles of crates.

Modeling

After we have the reference, the next step is to model. The first technique we will use is simply called sighting the object. What does this mean exactly? Well, oftentimes when you first begin modeling you go through a phase of modeling with little or no reference in the viewport of 3ds max. This technique forces the artist to come up with the shapes and details on his own. It's a great help for learning how to make models by sight and helps the artist begin visually working inside of max. I don't disregard this method, but I would strongly

suggest that you always have some sort of reference nearby. Let's take a look at how this is done.

1. Open max. Then go to **File | Open**. Select the **Scene_Setup.max** file so that we are all working with the same settings.

2. Click on the **Create** tab and choose **Extended Primitives** from the drop-down list as seen in Figure 6-2. Select **ChamferBox**.

3. Expand the keyboard entry bar and type in the parameters shown in Figure 6-3.

4. Make sure the Top viewport is selected (you should have a yellow box around the viewport). Press **Create**.

Figure 6-2: ChamferBox selected

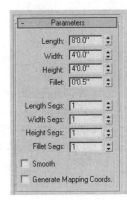

Figure 6-3: ChamferBox parameters

Note:

So, why did we put an edge around the crate? In the real world, not many things have a perfect 90 degree edge, and they typically catch light down the edge or side. How do we create that highlight? Simple. We add an extra set of polygons around the crate.

5. Go to the object name and rename ChamferBox01 to **crate**.

6. Click on the object color. Change the object color to **black**, then click **OK**.

Hint:

The object color box is right next to the object name.

7. Click Material Editor (**M**). With the crate selected, click on Assign Material to Selection . Then close the Material Editor window.

8. Right-click in the Perspective viewport to activate it. With the crate selected, right-click in the viewport to bring up the quad menu. Select **Convert To | Convert to Editable Poly**.

9. Under the Selection Parameters choose **Polygon mode** (4).

Max Tool Tip:

Press **F4** to see Edge Facing on the model. **F4** is the on/off toggle between Edge Facing modes. You can also view it by right-clicking on the viewport name and selecting it from the drop-down.

10. Select **Inset** from the Edit Polygons parameters. Select the Uniform Scale button   and left-click and drag the side polygon inward as shown in Figure 6-5.

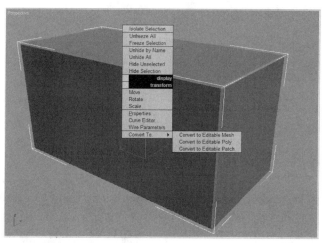

Figure 6-4: Editable poly crate

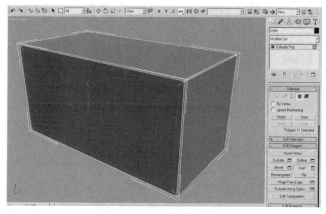

Figure 6-5: Polygon selected and scaled in with the Inset tool

99

11. Now click on the **Extrude** button. Left-click and drag the selected polygon inward, like in Figure 6-6.

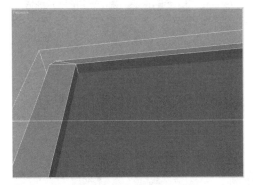

Figure 6-6: Polygon extruded inward

12. Repeat the inset and extruding procedures for the other five sides of the crate.

13. Let's chamfer the edges on the inside of our crate. Select **Edge mode** (**2**) and left-click on the top inside edge as shown in Figure 6-7.

Figure 6-7: Edge selected on crate

Max Tool Tip:

One of the great things about Edit Poly is that you can select one edge and then choose **Loop** from the Selection menu and it will (usually) go around the object, selecting all adjacent edges.

14. Click on **Loop**. You should have all the inside top edges selected. Press the **Spacebar** to lock selection.

15. Select the Chamfer folder to the right of the name. In the Chamfer Edges window, set the Chamfer Amount to 0'0.4". Click **OK**.

16. Repeat these two steps for the other five sides.

We are right under 200 polygons with the crate. So, let's bump it up to about 250 by adding some boards through the middle of the crate.

17. Go to the Left viewport. While you are still in Edge mode, under Edit Geometry select the **Cut** tool.

18. Follow along with Figure 6-8 and cut two slots out from the sides of the crate.

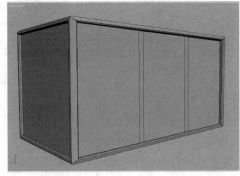

Figure 6-8: Cut tool used to cut into the crate

19. Change to **Face mode** (**4**) and select both faces. Then click on the **Extrude** button and extrude the polygons outward as shown in Figure 6-9.

Be sure that they don't go past or line up with the initial boards. It should be set in just a bit to give some depth variation.

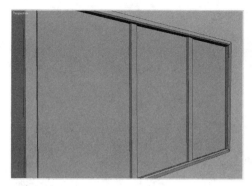

Figure 6-9: Extruded boards on crate

20. Do the same for the opposite side of the crate to finish it.

That's it! We have our first model for the game — all we need now is to unwrap the crate and work up some awesome textures.

UVW Map

We will use the Unwrap UVW modifier, which is used to assign planar maps to sub-object selections and to edit the UVW coordinates of those selections. It is very much like putting a big puzzle together, only you're making the pieces and the puzzle board.

Max Tool Tip:

If you use Unwrap UVW, there's a little something you should know. If Edit Mesh (or Poly) is highlighted (in vertex, edge, poly, face, or element mode), you will not have the **Select Face** option in the drop-down + under Unwrap UVW. So, be sure that if you want to select faces in the viewports while editing the UV coordinates that Edit Mesh/ Poly is deselected before applying the Unwrap UVW modifier.

1. In the Modify tab, click on **Modifier List | Unwrap UVW**.

2. With the modifier selected, click on **Unwrap UVW** to highlight it. Under Parameters, click on **Edit**. This will

bring up the Edit UVWs window. See Figure 6-10.

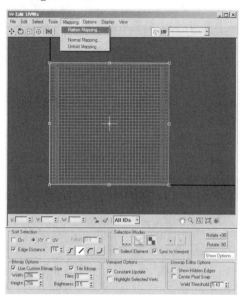

Figure 6-10: Edit UVWs window

3. Under Selection mode parameters, click the **Face Sub-Object** mode. Select all of the faces in the viewport and then click **Mapping** from the menu bar and choose **Flatten Mapping**.

4. Change the Face Angle Threshold to **65.0** and then click **OK**.

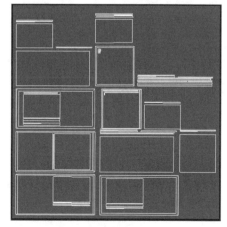

Figure 6-11: Crate UVs flattened

Figure 6-11 shows the flattened UV coordinates.

When using Flatten Mapping, there are times when it flattens everything just the way you want. And then there are times where you need to do a few extra steps. This would be one of those times. We are going to do a little unfolding and a little more flattening.

5. Select the top and side of a wood slat in the modeling viewport. Then click on **Mapping | Unfold Mapping**. Click **OK**.

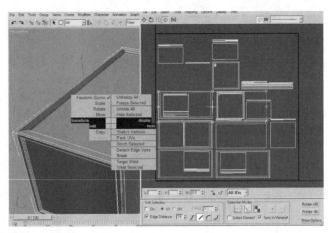

Figure 6-12: Copy UV coordinates

Flatten Mapping works great on simple to slightly complex shapes. As you can tell, Flatten Mapping kept all the pieces together and laid them out flat. With this one complete, let's do a little something to make the adjacent ones even easier.

6. While the slat is still selected, right-click in the Edit UVWs viewport. In the quad menu click on **Copy**. See Figure 6-12.

7. In the viewport, select the next wood slat pieces.

8. Right-click and select **Paste** from the quad menu.

Notice how Paste moves all the UVs directly onto the first set. This is really a great tool from 3ds max; just remember that sometimes it won't work as well with an overly complex shape. If you run into problems copying the UV coordinates, try doing smaller sections at a time.

9. Next, select a set of vertical wood slats and apply **Unfold Mapping** to it. Then right-click and select **Copy** from the quad menu.

10. Go around to each vertical slat and paste the coordinates to them. Check out Figure 6-13.

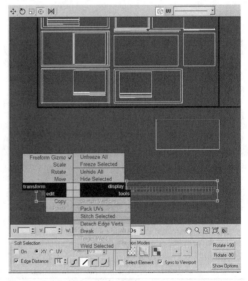

Figure 6-13: UV coordinates

The coordinates mapping portion is complete. As you can tell, I have a lot of pieces still on my map. We need to lay UVs on top of each other to get the most bang for the pixel. Check out the map in Figure 6-14 to see how I managed to compress the maps.

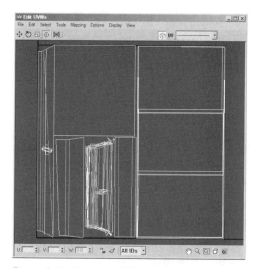

Figure 6-14: Rearranged UV coordinates

Can you tell what was done? The large panels were placed on the right side of the image while the ends were placed separately so we could change out the texture on them. After moving everything around I found the best place for the slats was in the bottom corner. As you can tell, I decided to keep them separate so that each slat could have a different texture applied. If you wanted to compress things even more you

could lay out the map like Figure 6-15. This map really shows how compressed you could actually make it.

Texporter

Texporter converts mapping coordinates of a mesh object to a bitmap. What Texporter generates is a bitmap on which you can see topology of the mesh in UV space (not 3D space). It can be thought of as the unfolded mesh that is saved out and used inside of Photoshop to paint the texture onto.

1. To find Texporter, navigate to **Utilities tab | More... | Texporter**, then click **OK**.

2. Under the Parameters bar change the Width and Height to **512**. Then go to the Display section and be sure that Polygon Fill is unchecked and then check **Edges**.

3. Click on the **Pick Object** button and then choose the crate. Texporter should generate the mapping coordinates for you similar to Figure 6-16.

4. Save the file as **crate_map.bmp**.

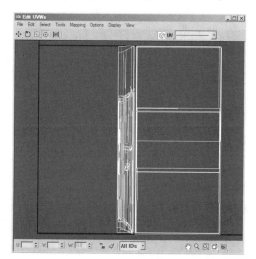

Figure 6-15: Different arrangement for the UV coordinates

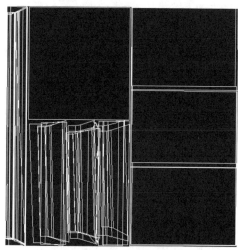

Figure 6-16: Texporter map

103

Texture

We are going to use Photoshop to create the crate texture. It's a pretty simple process, so work along with me as we texture the crate.

1. Open Photoshop. Double-click inside the viewport area or click on **File | Open (Ctrl+O)**.

2. Select and open **crate_textures.psd** and **crate_map.bmp** from …\Tutorials\Art_Tutorials\Tutorial_1_Crate.

There are several different wood textures on the crate_textures file, so you have the option of creating multiple crates with the different textures.

3. Let's place the old wood texture across the bottom-left side for the trim boards. Then drop and drag the new wood textures onto the other two sections. See Figure 6-17.

Figure 6-17: Crate texture being worked on

4. The last thing we want to add is the picture and some letters. Drag and drop the symbol onto the wooden panel. Then with the Text tool (**T**) write a couple of letters and numbers across the bottom. I went with **Arabic Transparent**, **Bold**, and **Font** size **50**.

Hint:

Open crate.dds. This is what we are working toward. Sometimes it helps to see the end result if it is your first time texturing an object.

5. Click on **File | Save As (Ctrl+Shift+S)** and save the file as **crate.dds**. When the .dds window opens, click **Save**.

Textures Inside of max

There are two ways you can go about applying the maps to max models.

Max 5.x

1. Open max. Click the Material Editor (**M**).

2. Click on the **Maps** rollout tab. Then in the Diffuse slot, click on **None**. When the Material/Map browser opens, select **Bitmap** from the options and click **OK**.

3. Navigate to the **crate.dds** file and select it.

4. Click on the **Go to Parent** button (Up arrow). Change the name of the material from 1 - Default to **crate FX=bump**. The Material Editor window should look like Figure 6-18.

Max 6 and 7

1. With the Crate model loaded, click the Material Editor (**M**).

2. Click on the **Standard** button (Material type) and select **DirectX 9 Shader** from the Material/Map browser.

Important:

Make sure you are using the DirectX rendering mode. If you have OpenGL selected for the rendering, the DirectX 9 Shader option will be grayed out.

3. In the DirectX 9 Shader tab, click on the **Shader** button, navigate to the shaders included with the Ka3D engine, and select **bump.fx**.

4. Right below that you should have a tab called bump.fx Parameters. Place the crate.dds, crate_bump.dds, and phong-20.png files in the proper slots as shown in Figure 6-18.

5. In order to see the Normal map and the light affecting it, select the **Omni01** light that is currently in the scene with the Light position drop-down.

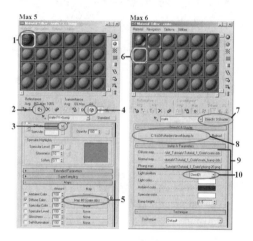

Figure 6-18: Material Editor in max 5 and 6

1 — Max 5.x material slot

2 — Assign material to selection (You can also click on the material and drag it to the image.)

3 — Quick button to access the Diffuse map options

4 — Show Map in viewport (Click on this if you want to see your map in the viewport.)

5 — Map's diffuse color

6 — Max 6 material slot

7 — DirectX 9 Shader is the material type

8 — Shader button. Click to display a file dialog that lets you select a DX9 FX effect (.fx) file. Instead of labeling it in the Material name section, you can choose it here.

9 — FX Parameters provides the maps available for each FX file. The FX file is selected from the KA3D shader folder.

10 — Light position. Choose the light in the scene so that you can view the objects with the proper light setup.

Specular Map

1. Let's jump back into Photoshop. The Specular map is stored inside the diffuse channel. Press **Ctrl+A**, then **Ctrl+C**.

2. In the Channel window click on **Create a new channel**. Then press **Ctrl+V**. This will paste your texture into the Alpha 1 layer (it should be grayscale).

3. The specular amount on wood does not need to be bright white. Let's darken it just a bit. Click on **Image | Adjust-ments | Brightness/Contrast**. Change Brightness to **–25** and Contrast to **+15**.

4. Save crate.dds. Be sure to change the Save Format to **8:8:8:8 ARGB (32 bit)**. This will ensure that your alpha map is saved without optimizations. See Figure 6-19.

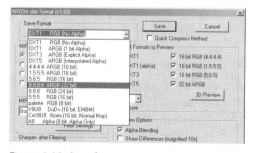

Figure 6-19: Save format

105

Specular Level

1. In max, go to **Material Editor | Maps | Specular Level | None.** Select **phong-20.png** and click **OK.**

Bump/Normal Map

The Bump/Normal map is our last map for the crate. We are going to create a high-polygon crate inside of max and generate a Normal map from it. The steps below show the technique I use in creating Normal maps. Try it out and see if you like it.

1. Make sure that you have the crate.max file open. Click on **File | Save As.** Save the file as **crate_normal_ map.max.**

2. Go to the Left viewport, right-click on the crate, and from the quad menu select **Convert To | Convert to Editable Poly.**

3. Select **Edge Mode** (2).

4. Under the Edit Geometry tab, click on **QuickSlice.**

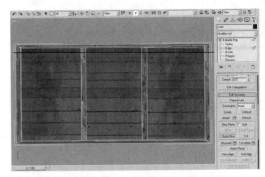

Figure 6-20: QuickSlice cut

Figure 6-21: Crate sliced all the way down

> ### Max Tool Tip:
>
> QuickSlice cuts an edge plane directly across the model. The cool thing about it is that you have control of where and how you want it cut. Since we are not worried about the polygon count of the model, it's time to make a bunch of cuts.

5. In the Left viewport, left-click once to start the QuickSlice tool. Then moving the mouse around, rotate it until it runs along the wood panel as shown in Figure 6-20. Then left-click again to have it cut across.

6. Continue doing this all the way down the image in sets of three as shown in Figure 6-21. Why three? Well, what I'm creating is a set of vertices that I can push and pull with. By having three vertices, we'll be able to move the

middle one inward and create more shape between the wood. If you have wood pieces that are not perfectly straight, use the Cut tool and cut around that shape.

7. Select **Edge Mode.** Click on the top row middle edge of the wood panel and move it inward, creating a divot in the model. See Figure 6-22.

Figure 6-22: Edges pulled inward

8. Now grab the two outside set of edges. Click on the **Chamfer Folder** and change Chamfer Amount to **0'0.15"**. Click **Apply**. Then change Chamfer Amount to **0'0.07"** and click **OK**.

There are many rows left to work on. A good time-saving technique is to select all the middle row edges and pull them back. Then select all the outer edges and chamfer them as we just did. That should save you a good 10 minutes or more.

With all the horizontal boards worked over, we still need to smooth out the vertical boards through the middle.

9. Select one of the edges as shown in Figure 6-23.

Figure 6-23: Edge selected

10. In the Selection tab, click on **Ring** and then click on **Loop**. This will select all your edges for both sides.

11. Click on the Chamfer folder. Change Chamfer Amount to **0'0.2"**. Click **OK**.

12. Do this for the other three boards. The last thing to do is grab the selected vertices around the crate and pull them in or out. Check out crate_9_Normal_

Map3.max in ...\Tutorials\Art_Tutorials\Tutorial_1_Crate.

Time to normal map the crate!

1. Select the high-poly crate and then go to **File | Export Selected**. Choose the .nmf file type and export the crate as **crate_high.nmf**.

2. Select the low-poly crate and choose **Export Selected**. Save this file as **crate_low.nmf**.

3. Open the **ATI NormalMapper**. In the Input Files section load the low- and high-polygon crates into their respective places.

4. Down at the bottom be sure to check **512 x 512**, then click on **Browse** and save the file in the same directory as the model.

5. Click on **Create Normal Map**.

6. Once the Normal map is created, we need to open the crate_normal-map.bmp file in Photoshop and then resave the file as **crate_bump.dds**.

7. Open the Material Editor (**M**). In the Maps drop-down, click the **None** button next to bump. Select your Normal map file and click **OK**.

Collision

Collision geometry is essentially what the object created is tested by to see whether or not it's been hit or collided with. The collision has been set up to benefit the artist and allow more control of the design and implementation. Creating the collision detection on an object with as few polygons as possible is ideal for game development. The more times collision is checked the more processing it has to do, so you should always try to cut corners. There are three ways collision works in the Ka3D engine.

- The **Collision=only** user-defined object property can be used to add static level collision objects that are not visible in the level.

- The **Collision=none** user-defined object property can be used to add level objects that are not collided against. All objects that can never be collided against should be tagged this way.

- The last way is to leave the object with no collision properties. The exporter automatically assumes the actual mesh is to be used for the collision object as well. (This is the default.)

1. In the Top viewport, create a box (Create | Geometry | Box) equivalent to the crate. Name it **crate_collision**. Open the Material Editor (**M**) and assign the second Material slot to the collision box. Then rename the material to **collision** and in the Shader Basic Parameters click the **Wire** box so that the crate_collision mesh is simply an outline in the viewports. Right-click and select **Properties** from the quad menu. In the User Defined tab type the following in the User Defined properties: **Collision=only**.

2. Remember that the default collision is having an object with no user-defined property stating collision. So, select the crate object, right-click, and choose **Properties** from the quad menu. Then in the User Defined tab, type **Collision=none**.

3. Click **OK**. By doing that, we have made the six-sided collision box the only thing the computer will check on collision. The crate object has no collision and will not be checked, meaning its 230 faces are not checked for collision, saving us 218 polygons. That's a pretty good save right there.

Physics

Physics has become so popular in games that everyone wants objects that move, get pushed around, or topple over. So, what if we wanted physics on the crate instead of static collision? Fortunately for the artist it's changeable inside of 3ds max. Let's look at the properties first, then we'll change the crate's properties.

- **Physics=<x>**, where <x> is box or sphere, enables rigid body physics for the object. Body size is computed automatically from the object's bounding box.

- **Mass=<x>** sets total mass for the object when Physics=<x> is used. Note that Mass and Density are mutually exclusive.

- **Density=<x>** sets size-relative mass for the object when Physics=<x> is used. Note that Mass and Density are mutually exclusive.

1. Select the crate object.

2. Right-click and choose **Properties** from the quad menu. Then under the User Defined tab in the User Defined properties section, type **Physics=box** and **Mass=500**.

3. Click **OK**.

> **Note:**
>
> If you have collision applied to an object, you can't have physics applied. It needs to be one or the other. Also, if you decide to apply physics, be sure to add a plane (the ground) for the box to fall onto.

The geometry is complete, the maps are loaded, and the collision or physics is set — we are ready to export the model.

Export

Let's make sure the crate is exporter friendly. Currently, the exporter will basically export anything and it will show up in the viewer. It's extremely friendly and has been set up in such a way that you don't have to export with proper naming conventions, lights, or even cameras. Simple enough, right?

The exporter automatically places a light and camera in the world if the exported model doesn't come with one. If you have a particular light scheme and camera angle to view the model, I would suggest including the light and camera.

1. Select the crate model. Navigate to **Utilities | Reset Xform.** Under the Reset Transform tab, click on **Reset Selected.**

2. Navigate to **Hierarchy | Affect Pivot Only | Center to Object.** Then move the transform gizmo to the bottom of the object as shown in Figure 6-24. Click on **Affect Pivot Only** again to deactivate it.

3. Right-click on the **Select and Move** tool to bring up the Move Transform Type-In. Under Absolute: World, type **X: 0, Y: 0, Z: 0.** Close the window.

4. Select **Create | Lights | Omni.**

5. Go to the Top viewport and left-click to drop a light into the scene in the bottom-right corner. In the Front viewport raise the light up about 12 feet.

6. Position the Perspective viewport to the angle at which you want to see the crate in Ka3D.

7. Select **Create | Camera | Free.**

8. In the Perspective viewport, left-click to create a camera. Then press **Ctrl+C** to automatically position the camera at the same angle as the Perspective viewport. Press **C** to view the camera in the viewport.

9. Click on **File | Export.** Choose the file location you are saving the crate in. Save the File Name as **crate.hgr** and the Save as type as **hgr export** (*.HGR).

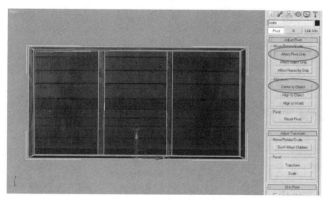

Figure 6-24: Transform gizmo moved down to the bottom of the model

10. The HGR export Options dialog is displayed as shown in Figure 6-25. Be sure that the check boxes for Scale world units to meters and Copy textures to output path are checked. Then click **OK**.

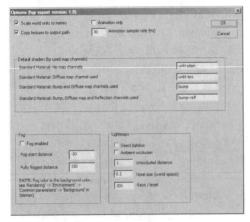

Figure 6-25: HGR exporter options

That's it!

HGR Viewer

The HGR Viewer is set up so that you can view the models in Ka3D instantly. This makes it much easier to preview things, add corrections, and make changes before they are handed off.

There are three ways to view a scene:

● Choose File | Open from the menu bar.

● Drag and drop the file to the scene viewer window.

● Double-click the .hgr file to start the scene viewer.

> **Note:**
>
> When you view the crate_physics.hgr file you can press **F5** to watch the crate fall again and again.

The following keys are used in the HGR Viewer.

Key	Action
WASD	Move forward, left, backward, right
Left/Right arrow keys	Rotate left/right
Up/Down arrow keys	Rotate up/down
Shift+Left/Right arrow keys	Move left/right
Shift+Up/Down arrow keys	Move up/down
1-9	Select movement speed 1-9; default is 5
Pause/Break	Pause animation playback
F12	Toggle fog rendering pass on/off
F11+Shift	Toggle sprite rendering pass on/off
F12+Shift	Toggle glow rendering pass on/off
F5	Refresh/reload scene file

Tutorial 2: Building a Light Post

In Tutorial 2 we are going to build a light post, make a glow shader, and create a Normal map through Photoshop. The reference, texture, model, and exported file are in \Tutorials\Art_Tutorials\Tutorial_2_ Light_Post if you need any help. Sounds simple enough, right?

Let's start with the photo reference.

Photo Reference

I usually divide art styles and textures into three categories. You have photorealistic, painted stylized, and cartoon shading. Each one still requires either photo reference of some sort or reference from that style. Since we are working on improving our modeling skills we are going to create a very real (photorealistic) light post.

1. Open Photoshop and double-click anywhere inside the workspace or go to File | Open. That will bring up your Open window.

2. Navigate to \Tutorials\Art_Tutorials\ Tutorial_2_Light_Post\light_post_ref-erence.bmp. I've taken four photos of a light post, cropped them down, and placed them on the Reference.bmp.

Before we start working on the texture map, we need to model the light post from the reference. Since the shape is the same all the way around, we will use the full light post image called light_post_front.jpg. If you want to take a look at it you will notice the red line up the side of the image. Typically, when you first start modeling it's best to draw out the division lines and even place red dots on your picture where you think the vertex points will go. By doing this you will cut down the thinking time in max and ensure exact placement of vertices while outlining.

Modeling

The technique for modeling the light post is a bit different from the crate we did before. Since max is so full of different options for modeling we are going to look at another way to go about it.

Note:

We will demonstrate at least three different ways to model so that you can have multiple options to choose from — no one wants just one.

1. Open max and then go to **File | Open**. Select your **Scene_Setup.max** file so that we are all working with the same settings.

2. Right-click in the Front viewport to activate it. You should see a yellow border around the viewport window.

3. From the menu bar go to **Views | Viewport Background** (**Alt+B**).

4. Right below the Background Source you should see Files... Click on **Files...** and then navigate to **\Art_Tutorials\Tutorial_2_ Light_ Post\light_post_front.jpg**. Click **OK**.

5. The aspect ratio at the bottom left of the viewport background needs to be changed to **Match Bitmap**. Click **OK**. Using the viewport background can be a bit confusing at first, but once you get the hang of it, creating objects is a breeze. If the image comes in too large in the viewport, just zoom out until you can see the whole thing. If you want to move your viewport separate from the background image, just click the check box off of **Lock Zoom/Pan**.

6. Go to **Create | Shapes | Line tool**.

111

7. Click on the Rendering tab; you will see a set of parameters. Change Thickness to **2'0.0"** and Sides to **8**.

8. Click the check boxes for **Renderable**, **Generate Mapping Coords**, and **Display Render Mesh**. You should now see a cylindrical shape in the viewport. You might be asking yourself, "Why didn't I just use the cylinder and make segments?" Well, the best answer is because when you create segments max automatically divides it evenly for you. By using the Line tool you are able to specify instantly where you want your segments.

9. With the Line tool, click a vertex point everywhere you see the red dashed line on the left of the image. This should help you to understand where vertex points should be placed. Create a line up to the base of the light. Then right-click to finish the base line. Create one more light that is from the base of the light to the top of the light.

Max Tool Tip:

If you are using the Line Tool and you make it to a corner of your viewport, press the letter **l** and the screen will automatically move over toward the direction of your mouse cursor.

10. Right-click in the viewport. You should have the quad menu on screen. From the bottom-right menu (Transform) choose **Convert To | Convert to Editable Mesh**.

11. Under the Modify tab you should see the Edit Mesh modifier at the top of your stack. Click on the plus sign

to drop down the options. Select the **Vertex mode**. It should now be highlighted. Max gives you a variety of ways to choose between Vertex, Edge, Face, Polygon, and Element modes. Under the Selection tab there are five buttons representing each mode. If you select them, you will switch between the modes. The way I use most often is the quick keys: **1**, **2**, **3**, **4**, and **5**. Each key represents each mode in left to right order. Give it a try to get the feel for it.

12. We want to scale the vertex points inward to line up with the outlining shape of the light post. Left-click and drag over the second row of vertices on the bottom. All the vertex points should be lit up.

13. Select the **Uniform Scale** tool from the menu bar. Then click the **Selection Lock** toggle (**Spacebar**) to lock the vertex points. This allows you to scale from anywhere in the viewport. Scale the vertices inward until they line up with the edge of the light post picture. See Figure 6-26.

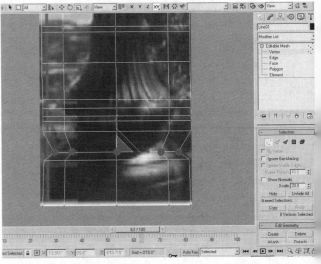

Figure 6-26: Vertices lined up with the light post photo

14. Unlock the Selection Lock toggle (**Spacebar**).

15. Repeat Steps 12 through 14 until all the vertices are aligned with the photo. The image should look like Figure 6-27 when you get all the vertices adjusted.

Figure 6-27: The vertices should line up with the outline of the light post as shown here.

16. Select the small line that represents the light bulb. Under the Line tool parameters change Thickness to **1'0.0"** and Sides to **5**.

This will allow us to place a bit more detail into the light geometry and still maintain a decent polygon count. Work up the outlining shape the same way the base of the light post was created.

17. With the light post and the base created we need to attach them together. Select the base of the light post.

18. In the Modify tab under the Edit Geometry drop-down, click on **Attach**. Once it's highlighted, left-click to select the bulb in the viewport. Both objects should now be highlighted.

19. Let's optimize the light post. Select the faces directly under the light bulb and on the bottom side of the base as shown in Figure 6-28.

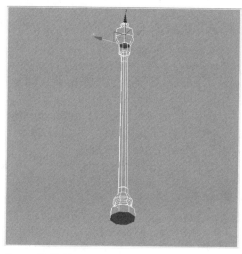

Figure 6-28: Unnecessary polygons selected

20. Hit the **Delete** key to delete these unwanted polygons.

Now that it is optimized, let's give it an appropriate name and apply a gray-toned texture to the light post.

1. Select the light post. Right under the Modify tab you should see a text box with a name like Line01 in it. Replace the name with **light_post**.

2. Open the Material Editor. With the first material box highlighted, click on **Assign Material to Selection**. The light post should now be gray.

3. With the Material Editor still open, rename your material **light_post FX=bump-glow**. The FX=bump-glow is our shader effect for the material.

4. Deselect the light post by left-clicking in the viewport away from the light post. Now switch to wireframe view by pressing **F3** or by right-clicking the Viewport name and selecting Wireframe from the options list.

UV Mapping

The model is ready to be UV mapped! If you notice, the basic shape of the light post is a cylinder. Right? Okay, then we will apply a new modifier to our stack called the UVW Map. The UVW Map is the first step in applying mapping coordinates to an object. The UVW Map modifier controls how mapped and procedural materials appear on the surface of an object. Mapping coordinates specify how bitmaps are projected onto an object. The UVW coordinate system is similar to the XYZ coordinate system. The U- and V-axes of a bitmap correspond to the X- and Y-axes. The W-axis, which corresponds to the Z-axis, is generally only used for procedural maps.

1. Select the light post.

2. Click on the Modify tab and left-click on the drop-down Modifier list.

3. Choose **UVW Map** from the list.

4. In the Parameters | Mapping option, select **Cylindrical** and then click the check box for **Cap.**

5. Choose **Alignment: Fit** from the bottom of the list. Also note that the X, Y, Z radio buttons are used to rotate the gizmo around your object.

6. In the Modifier list, select the **Unwrap UVW** modifier.

7. Click on the Unwrap UVW modifier so that it is lit (should be yellow now).

8. Under Parameters, click on **Edit.** The Edit UVWs window should open and look something like Figure 6-29.

As you can see, the cylindrical map did a decent job, but it's not perfect. After looking at the model, there are three major areas that stick out — the base of the light post, the pole area, and the light itself. We'll separate these three areas and stick them on our mapping space.

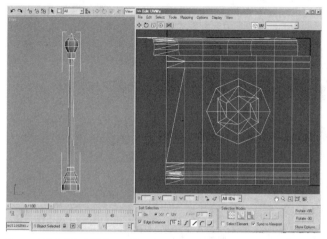

Figure 6-29: Edit UVWs window

9. Inside the viewport, select the pole area of the light post model. You should notice the vertex points become lit in Edit UVWs.

Max Tool Tip:

What if you wanted to convert the vertices to faces or edges without having to reselect them? Great question! To convert from one mode to the next, go to Select | Convert Vertex to Edge and click on it. All the vertex points you had lit should now be converted into edges.

10. On the Edit UVWs menu bar, choose **Select | Convert Vertex to Face.**

11. Click on **Tools | Break (Ctrl+B).** This will make sure that no extra vertices or edges are attached to the selected areas.

12. With the Move tool selected, move the pole area to the side as shown in Figure 6-30.

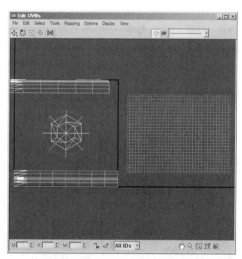

Figure 6-30: Pole area UVs are moved to the side to start working with them.

13. Click on the Vertex Sub-Object mode ⋰ . Select the first four columns on the pole area as shown in Figure 6-31.

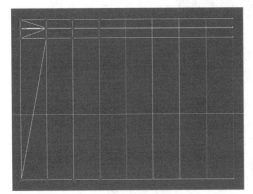

Figure 6-31: Four columns selected

14. Select **Move Horizontal** ↔ from the Move tool drop-down list. Then click **Mirror Horizontal** ⋈ . The vertices should be flipped horizontally.

15. With the Move Horizontal tool selected, move the vertices over the unselected set as shown in Figure 6-32.

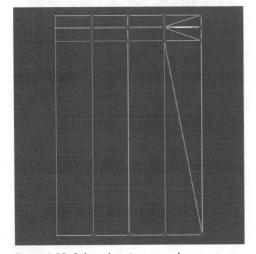

Figure 6-32: Selected vertices moved

16. Repeat the process again. Select the left two rows and mirror them horizontally. Move them in until they line up like the ones before.

17. Finally, select the one row of vertices on the left and move them over to the right side. This should leave you with a simple, compact shape like Figure 6-33.

Figure 6-33: Vertex points optimized

The last thing we want to do is weld the edges together so that it appears "pretty" on the screen.

18. Select the top-right set of vertices as shown in Figure 6-34. Click on **Tools | Weld Selected** (**Ctrl+W**) to weld your vertices together. Repeat that step for all the vertices where there is more than one set.

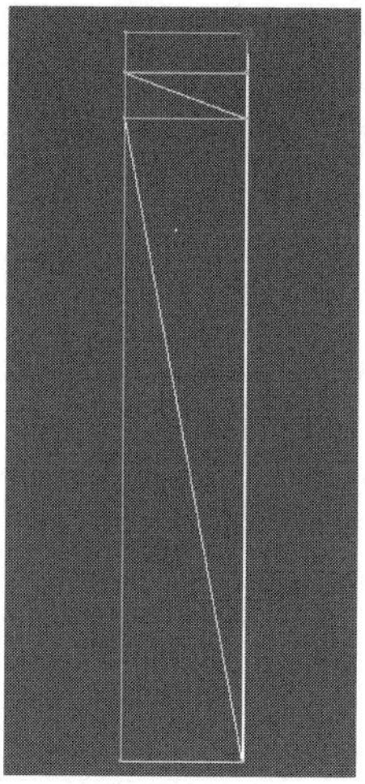

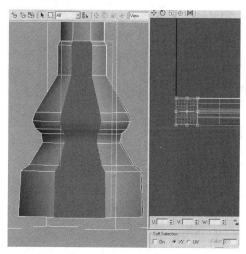

Figure 6-34: Vertices welded together

19. Use the same procedure for the light portion.

Note:

There may be a bit of streaking but don't worry about it. The player won't be able to make out much of the light bulb texture because it will be given a glow shader.

20. Select one row of the base as shown in Figure 6-35.

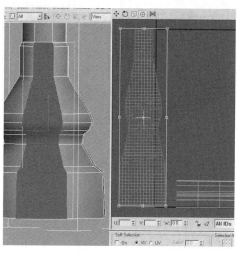

Figure 6-35: Base row selected

21. Click on **Mapping | Unfold Mapping**, then click **OK**. It should look like Figure 6-36.

Figure 6-36: Unfold Mapping applied to selected UVs

Max Technique:

When you really begin creating complex shapes, sometimes it's easier to take one strip of the whole and unfold it all together. By doing this I have the exact shape of the UVs as well as a perfect piece to copy onto the rest of my base UVs. Let's take a look at how that's done.

22. With the faces still selected, right-click in the Edit UVWs viewport. On the quad menu selection click on **Copy**. See Figure 6-37.

117

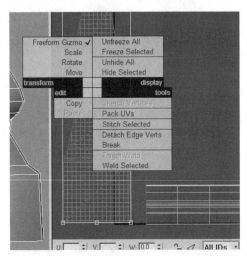

Figure 6-37: Copy UV coordinates

23. Select the next row of UVs, right-click in the Edit UVWs viewport, and click **Paste**.

Your copied UV coordinates are automatically pasted onto the selected UVs. Pretty cool, huh?

24. Select the next row of UVs, right-click, and select **Paste**. Follow these steps until you have pasted the remaining UVs.

Finally, let's move all the pieces together inside the blue map area. Figure 6-38 illustrates one way of arranging it. When scaling the UVs, try to scale them proportionately to keep from stretching the texture coordinates.

25. The last thing we want to do is copy and paste the map into Photoshop. Make sure your Edit UVWs window is open and the map is completely visible. Press the **Print Screen** button.

Texturing

The next stage in our process is texturing. Typically, texturing goes hand in hand with UV mapping since you need to check how things look on the model.

1. Open Photoshop (or another paint program). Click on **File | New (Ctrl+N)**. Click **OK**.

2. Press **Ctrl+V** to paste the copied image from max inside of the window. Select the Crop tool (**C**) and crop the picture similar to Figure 6-39.

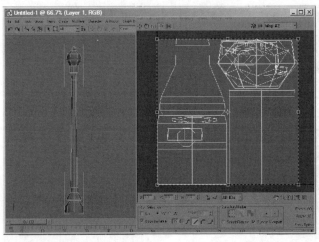

Figure 6-38: UV map complete

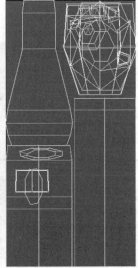

Figure 6-39: The copied image pasted in the Photoshop window

3. Click on **Image | Image Size** (Alt/i/i). Resize the picture to 256 pixels by 512 pixels. Be sure that Constrain Proportions is unchecked.

4. Click **OK**. Click on **File | Save As**. Save your file as **light_post.psd**.

Your texture map is ready to be worked up.

5. Open **light_post_reference.bmp**.

Let's take a moment to look at the photos we have taken. They show a cylindrical post, so as you can tell there is only one side that can actually be used for tiling purposes. In Figure 6-40, I have outlined the areas in black that would be most beneficial to you.

Figure 6-41: Photos placed into light post file

Figure 6-40: Outlined shapes depict the most useful portions of the photos.

6. Select the Rectangular Marquee tool (**M**) or the Polygonal Lasso tool (**L**) and select the areas indicated. Then choose the Move tool (**V**). Drag and drop the selections into the light_post.psd file as shown in Figure 6-41.

Adobe Note:

Depending on how you work, it could be beneficial to have the UV map layer at the top of the stack. Left-click on the UV map layer and drag it to the top of the stack. The Blending mode for the layer should be set to Multiply or Screen as shown in Figure 6-42.

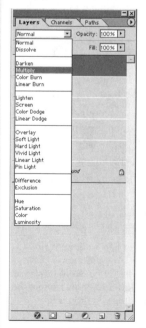

Figure 6-42: Multiply layer selected

7. Scale each layer down so that they fit the proper section on the map. Then go ahead and trim the edges so that everything fits tightly onto the texture. See Figure 6-43.

Figure 6-43: Scaled down textures

Look at the bottom-right portion of the map. We have only one piece of the pole and it's pretty small. Let's make this into a larger map. We could just stretch it, but that would lose a lot of the major detail. Let's try it another way.

8. Select the Move tool (**V**). With the post layer selected, **left-click+Shift+Alt and drag** the selection directly above the original. Another way to create a new layer with the shape is to go to **Layer | Duplicate Layer** and click **OK**.

Adobe Tool Tip:

Creating a new layer can be done by left-clicking, holding Alt, and dragging it somewhere. But if you want to have the new layer move exactly in a 45 or 90 degree angle, be sure to hold Shift while you drag it around.

9. With the new layer selected, click on **Edit | Transform | Scale (Ctrl+T)**.

10. Right-click and choose **Flip Vertical** from the drop-down list. The image will now be flipped around. As long as you don't see any major mirroring issues, you should be good to go.

11. Press **Ctrl+E** to flatten the two post layers together. Then **left-click+Shift+Alt and drag** the selection directly above the original. That should take you to the top of the UV section. See Figure 6-44.

Figure 6-44: Pole texture repeated and flattened

12. Navigate to **Filter | Sharpen** and click on the **Sharpen** option to crisp up the image a bit more. If the image needs to be sharpened again, press **Ctrl+F** to redo the last filter effect.

13. Select the light bulb layer. Let's brighten the darker portions of the texture next. Select the **Dodge** tool (see Figure 6-45). Be sure the Exposure setting is around **50%**.

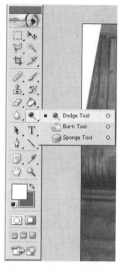

Figure 6-45: Dodge tool selected

Figure 6-47: Rectangle marquee selection

14. Click and hold the left mouse button. Then go back and forth over the darker portions of the texture until it resembles the whiter section of the bulb texture as shown in Figure 6-46.

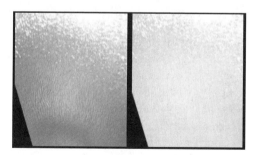

Figure 6-46: Light bulb before and after

Time to clean up those rounded edges. The base of the light post texture is curved, but the UV coordinates are straight. Let's get everything on the straight and narrow.

15. Select the Rectangular Marquee tool (**M**) and drag a rectangle out over the line as shown in Figure 6-47.

16. Select the Clone Stamp tool (**S**). Hold down the **Alt** key and left-click on the middle area of the selection. That will be the starting point for the cloning. Next, go to the left side of the texture map and left-click to start the cloning process.

Adobe Tool Tip:

Be sure that when you clone a particular area, you start the cloning directly horizontal from that location. This will ensure a straight line and less cleanup to follow.

17. Repeat the process for the other side as well. It should look similar to Figure 6-48.

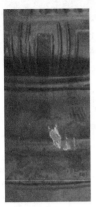

Figure 6-48: Areas filled in with the Clone Stamp tool

Figure 6-50: Light post texture

With the inside selection fixed we need to work on the outside area next.

18. Choose **Select | Inverse** (**Shift+Ctrl+I**) to flip the selection. Use the Clone Stamp tool (**S**) and repeat the process from before except on the outside areas. Check out Figure 6-49 for the results.

Figure 6-49: Inverse selected and cloned

There you go! You are only a few more lines away from completely flattening the texture. Use the same techniques for the top portion of the map as well. When you get done with that, check out the final texture in Figure 6-50 to see what other changes and improvements you can make.

The final steps are to crisp the colors up and sharpen the straight lines. A quick way to make your colors stand out better is to change the Brightness/Contrast (Image | Adjustments | Brightness/Contrast). Change the Brightness setting to –8 and the Contrast setting to +20. In order to get sharper straight lines I used the Rectangular Marquee tool (M), selected one of the groove sections, and with the Burn tool, I darkened the colors just a bit. This allows the lines to pop off a bit more as well. One final note: The base texture at the top has been given an extra angle line. This helps keep everything straight on the model. After playing with it a bit, I found this to be the best solution.

Time to save! Save now if you haven't saved in a while.

One texture map down, only three more to go!

As we learned before, the Diffuse map (the one we just created) will contain the specular level in the alpha channel. The Bump map (Normal map) contains the glow information, which is a simple grayscale image. Let's take a look at how to create them.

Specular Level Map

Make sure the light post texture is still open.

1. Press **Ctrl+A** to select the entire image.

2. Press **Ctrl+C** to copy the image.

3. In the Channels window click on the **Create a New Layer** button 🔲.

4. Press **Ctrl+V** to paste the Diffuse map into the Alpha Channel map. It should have come in as a grayscale image.

5. Select the metal portions of the texture with the Polygonal Lasso tool (**L**).

6. Navigate to **Image | Adjustments | Brightness/Contrast**. Change the Brightness setting to **–14**. That should darken the metal enough that it has a shine to it but doesn't appear brand new.

It should look like Figure 6-51.

Figure 6-51: Specular Level map

7. Click **File | Save As**. Save the file as **light_post.dds**. Just like we did before, be sure that the Save Format is set to **8:8:8:8 ARGB (32 bit)**. Then click **Save**.

Bump Map (Normal Map)

The Normal map is going to be created differently than our previous crate Normal map. We will use a plug-in filter from Photoshop.

1. Make a duplicate image of the light post texture by clicking on **Image | Duplicate**. Change the name to **light_post_bump**, then click **OK**.

2. Select **Filter | nvTools | Normal-MapFilter**. You will have an Info window come up saying, "Only three channels selected, alpha height will not be available." Click **OK**. The window that appears will look like Figure 6-52.

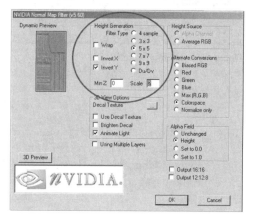

Figure 6-52: Normal Map Filter window

For a detailed explanation of the Normal Map Filter, please consult the Read me file that came with it. Right now, we are concentrating on the circled area of information. The Height Generation section provides us with the shadow direction, height scale, and sharpness value.

3. Change Filter Type to **3 x 3** and Scale to **4**. Then click **OK**. Figure 6-53 shows the Normal map filter before and after I cleaned it up a bit.

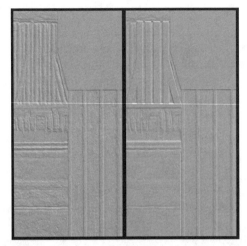

Figure 6-53: Normal maps

Glow Map

The Glow map shader is simply a grayscale image indicating sources to self illuminate or glow. Black indicates no glow, while values of gray/white become lit. Be sure you place the Glow map in the Normal Maps alpha channel.

1. Select the Channel window. Click on the **Create a new channel** button at the bottom right of the Channels window.

2. Select the RGB channel and press **Ctrl+A**. Then copy (**Ctrl+C**) and paste (**Ctrl+V**) the image into the Alpha 1 channel. This will let you see where and what to outline. See Figure 6-54.

3. Outline the metal with the **Polygonal Lasso tool** (**L**). With Black selected as the background color, press the **Backspace** key.

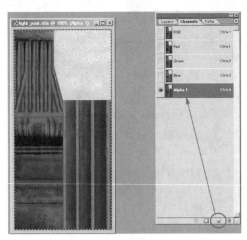

Figure 6-54: Alpha channel

4. Choose **Select | Inverse** (**Shift+Ctrl+I**) to flip the selection.

5. Click on **Set Background Color** and in the Color Picker window, change the R, G, B values all to **87**. Click **OK**.

6. Press the **Backspace** key to have the area turn gray. The Glow map should look like Figure 6-55.

Figure 6-55: Glow map

7. Choose **File | Save As**. Save the file as **light_post_bump.dds**. Just like we did before, be sure that the Save Format is set to **8:8:8:8 ARGB (32 bit)**. Then click **Save**.

Assigning the Texture Maps to the Model

1. Open max and go to **File | Open**. Choose **light_post.max**.

2. Select the Material Editor (**M**). Set up your materials just like the ones in Figure 6-56.

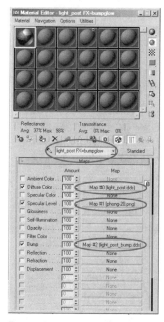

Figure 6-56: Material for light post

Material Name

3. Be sure that your material name is light_post. When you begin merging this file with others, you want a texture file name that is associated with the model.

Shader Name

4. We are going to use the bump-glow shader for objects on this study. If you want to find out specifically what makes the bump-glow.fx shader work, check out the file in the Shader directory. To have the shader working

properly, type the following next to the material's name: **FX=bumpglow**.

Maps

5. Click on the Maps rollout tab to expand it.

Diffuse Map

6. Next to Diffuse Color, you should see the word **None**. Click on it. This will open the Material/Map browser. Double-click on **Bitmap**. Now choose the **light_post.dds** file and click **OK**. Then click on the up arrow, which is Go to Parent.

Specular Level

7. Follow the same process as above, but select **phong-20.png**.

Bump

8. Follow the same process as above, but load **light_post_bump.dds**.

Once the maps are loaded in correctly and the material and shader are named appropriately, let's be sure it's assigned to the model and showing in the viewport.

9. Select the light post model. In the Material Editor be sure you have **Assign Material to Selection** selected.

10. Then click on **Show Map in Viewport**, which is the blue and white checked box.

Important:

Save before moving on. (Just a friendly reminder.)

Exporting

Just to be sure that we haven't skipped anything, it's time to prepare the model for export. What's the scale currently? The light post stands roughly 15'6".

1. Click on **Create | Geometry | Box**. In the Front viewport left-click and drag a box approximately **15'6"**. (This is just a simple way to judge the height of the model. Once you have the light post the same height, delete the box from the scene.)

2. Select the light post.

3. Use the **Select and Uniform Scale** tool to resize your light post to the correct height.

Remember:

Once the model is selected, press the Spacebar to turn the Selection Lock toggle on.

4. Select **Utilities | Reset Xform**. Under Reset Transform, click on **Reset Selected**. Then right-click in the viewport to bring up the quad menu. Select **Convert To | Convert to Editable Mesh**.

Reset the Pivot

The pivot should be set to 0, 0, 0 and at the bottom of the model. What's the quickest way to do that? Follow these steps:

1. Click on **Hierarchy | Affect Pivot Only | Center to Object**. That should center your object. Now with the **Move** tool selected, move the pivot point down to the bottom of the light post.

2. Click back on **Affect Pivot Only** to deselect the mode.

3. Right-click on the **Select and Move** tool to bring up the Move Transform Type-In window. In the Absolute: World properties area, make X, Y, Z all equal to **0**. This will center the light post in the world at the origin.

When viewing models in the editor you can set up a camera and light source (just like we did before).

4. Navigate to **Create | Cameras | Free**. Place a Free Camera in the Perspective viewport.

5. Go to the Perspective viewport in max and line the light post up in the viewport. You can quickly make the Perspective viewport the Camera viewport by pressing **Ctrl+C**. Pretty cool! (Be sure the camera is selected before pressing Ctrl+C.) The camera will automatically move to match the perspective settings.

6. Let's place a light in the scene. Go to **Create | Lights | Omni**.

7. In the Top viewport drop a light in the front part of the scene. Then go to the Front viewport and use the Move tool to move the light upward in the scene as shown in Figure 6-57.

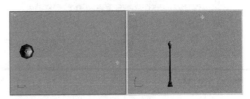

Figure 6-57: Light setup

Let's save the light post scene one last time.

8. Select **File | Export**. For File Name, type **light_post**. Then click on the drop-down list for Save as type: and choose **hgr export (*.HGR)**. Make sure you save it in the Tutorials directory.

9. Click **Save**. The HGR export Options window appears. Click on the check box for **Scale world units to meters**. Be sure the check box for **Copy textures to output path** is also checked as shown in Figure 6-58. Then click **OK**.

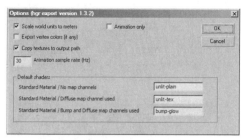

Figure 6-58: HGR export Options window

Viewing

We've exported the light post; now we need to view it! You can view it two different ways:

- Double-click on the exported light_post.hgr file. It will automatically pull up the viewer and allow you to view the scene.

- Open the HGR Viewer and click on Open | File. Navigate to your exported light_post.hgr file and select it.

That's it. We are on to the next model.

Tutorial 3: Building a Weapon and Ammunition

Up to this point we have created some pretty basic shapes. It is time to move on to a more complex object like a handgun. We will look at yet another way of modeling and learn how to set up weapons for exporting. If you managed to get the first two objects modeled and exported, then you are two steps closer to jumping on your own game demo!

Modeling

A handgun, like many types of weapons, is best modeled with splines. If it is your first time modeling this way, then you are in for a great experience. This will be an introduction to splines so we will touch on the basic

principles now and the more in-depth stuff later. It may seem a bit awkward at first, but once you do it two or three times, I think you'll enjoy this form of modeling more than most modeling techniques.

We will work up a new background for placing images on. So, rather than working with the "background" inside the viewport, let's build multiple rectangle meshes and place the texture references on them.

1. Open max. Load **File | Open | Scene_Setup.max**.

2. Use **File | Save As** and save the file as **weapon_handgun.max**.

127

3. Click on **Create | Shapes | Rectangle**. In the Right viewport, left-click and drag a rectangle as shown in Figure 6-59. Make its length **0'8.0"** and width **1'0.0"**.

Figure 6-59: Rectangle created

4. Right-click in the viewport and from the quad menu select **Convert To | Convert to Editable Mesh**. Change the name to **ref_handgun_right**.

5. Click on the Modify tab, then select the Modifier list and choose **UVW Map**. Under the Parameters tab, make sure **Planar** is selected. You should see an orange square appear around ref_handgun_right.

6. Open the Material Editor (**M**). We're going to use a shortcut button to apply a Diffuse map to the object. Click on the Map button as shown in Figure 6-60. Then double-click on **Bitmap**. Browse to ...\Tutorials\Art_Tutorials\Tutorial_3_Weapon and select **side1.jpg**.

Figure 6-60: Map button for the Diffuse slot

7. Assign this material to the rectangle by clicking on the **Assign Material to Selection** button. Be sure that the object you want assigned is selected. You should see brackets around the texture slot, showing that it is assigned. See Figure 6-61.

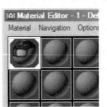

Figure 6-61: Material assigned

8. Click on the **Go to Parent** button to take you back up to the top of the material stack. See Figure 6-62. Then click on the checked box right next to it called **Show Map in Viewport**. This will allow you to see your texture inside the viewports.

Figure 6-62: Go to Parent button

9. Check **2-Sided** under the Shader Basic Parameters tab. Also, we want to be able to see through it, so in the Blinn Basic Parameters tab there is an Opacity setting on the right-hand side. Take the percentage down to **50**. In order to see it properly in the viewports, right-click on the Viewport name. In the drop-down list, go to **Transparency | Best**. That should do it.

Next we need to make sure the bitmap isn't squashed or stretched onto the rectangle.

10. Click the **UVW Mapping** button so that it becomes highlighted. Scroll

down to the Alignment section and click on **Bitmap Fit**. This will bring up a window to select an image. Double-click on the **side1.jpeg** image. The texture map is now stretched across the rectangle.

11. To make sure that the whole texture map is visible, click on the **Selection Lock** toggle button, then choose the **Select and Uniform Scale** tool. Left-click and drag in the viewport until the handgun becomes completely visible. Once you have it correct, turn off the Selection Lock toggle button.

12. Follow the same procedure for the top view and front view of the handgun. Check out weapon_handgun_01_reference_setup.max.

13. Select all the rectangles and right-click to bring up the quad menu. Then click on **Properties**. In the General tab, go to the Display Properties and check the **Freeze** box and uncheck the Show Frozen in Gray, then click **OK**.

Time to start tracing!

1. With the Line tool selected (**Create | Shapes | Line**), go to the Right viewport and trace the outlined shape as shown in Figure 6-63.

Figure 6-63: Handgun outlined

Max Tool Tip:

Don't forget, if you are outlining and get to the edge of the screen, press **I** and it will reset the screen from that point so you can continue to outline the shape.

2. Outline the trigger, barrel, sight, and cock separately. See Figure 6-64.

Figure 6-64: Handgun outline complete

3. Now we need to give the handgun some depth. Extrude the shapes as follows:

Handgun body — **0'1.0"**

Trigger — **0'0.3"**

Trigger hole — **0'1.5"**

Sight — **0'0.2"**

Cock — **0'1.9"**

Barrel-Top — Click on the Rendering tab. Check the **Renderable, Generate Mapping Coords**, and **Display Render Mesh** boxes. Then change Thickness to **0'1.175"** and Sides to **10**.

Cylinder-Bottom — Click on the Rendering tab. Check the **Renderable, Generate Mapping Coords** and **Display Render Mesh** boxes. Then change Thickness to **0'0.47"** and Sides to **6**.

The next step in the process is to begin detailing each shape. We have only half the handgun body because we are going to mirror the shape. Also, notice that the cock is the full length. We are going to carry it all the way through the handgun.

4. Select all the objects, right-click in the viewport and click on **Convert To | Convert to Editable Mesh**. Now all the objects are editable meshes and ready to be refined and detailed.

5. Let's go ahead and get the trigger hole defined. Select the handgun body.

6. Navigate to **Create | Geometry | Compound Objects** (drop-down list) and choose **Boolean**. Make sure Operation is set to **Subtraction (A-B)**.

7. Under the Pick Boolean tab, click on **Pick Operand B**, then choose the trigger hole geometry. When you click on the trigger hole, the geometry should disappear. It should look like Figure 6-65.

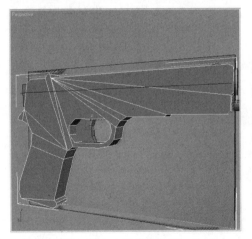

Figure 6-65: Trigger hole defined with a Boolean operation

8. Convert the gun back to an editable mesh.

9. Activate **Edge mode (2)**. Left-click and drag over the handgun to show all the edges on the gun. In Edit Geometry, choose the **Turn** button and begin

turning the edges until it looks similar to Figure 6-66. By cleaning up the geometry we will have an easier time working over the body details.

Figure 6-66: Edges turned

If we rotate the handgun toward the front view, we can see that the front.jpeg image shows a curve at the top edge and a smaller rounded edge on the bottom side.

10. Activate **Edge mode (2)** and select the top-front edges of the handgun body. Under the Edit Geometry tab, click on **Chamfer** and take it out **0'0.3"**. See Figure 6-67.

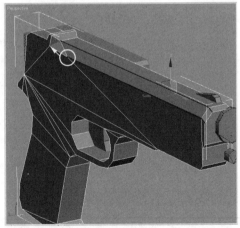

Figure 6-67: Chamfered edges

11. Notice the extra edge created in Figure 6-67. In **Vertex mode (1)**, select the circled vertex. Move it down the gun body and weld it to the nearest vertex point (indicated by the arrow).

12. Select the back edges of the handgun and chamfer them out **0'0.2"**. Then in Vertex mode, move the circled vertices down and in as shown in Figure 6-68.

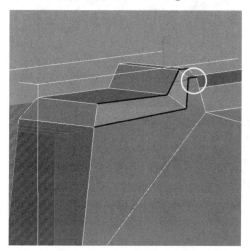

Figure 6-68: Edges chamfered and vertices moved inward

13. In Edge mode, select the body edge once more and chamfer it out **0'0.1"**. This should give us just enough curves to have the gun appear smooth on the top and not boxy. See Figure 6-69.

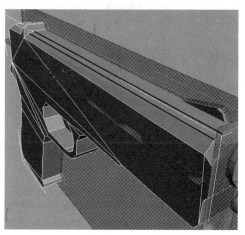

Figure 6-69: Edges

14. Right-click in the viewport and from the quad menu select **Convert To | Convert to Editable Poly**. Activate the **Edge mode (2)**, then select the **Cut** tool under Edit Geometry. Cut the bottom edge out so that we can have a rounded and smaller casing in the front. Check out Figure 6-70 for where to cut it. Then remove (hide) the "extra" edges. Select the edges that are not part of the outlining shape we cut out. Then under the Edit Edges tab, click **Remove**.

Figure 6-70: New cut and edges removed

15. Select the new edges and chamfer them out **0'0.002"**. With the new edge created, move it inward until the front view works. Then chamfer the side edge once more to smooth it out. See Figure 6-71.

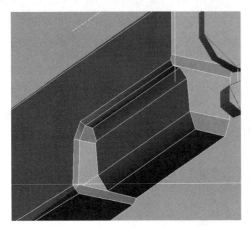

Figure 6-71: Underside refined

16. Select the trigger hole edges and chamfer them out as shown in Figure 6-72. Then clean up and weld the extra vertices it created. Use the Cut tool to cut an edge from the trigger hole to the handle.

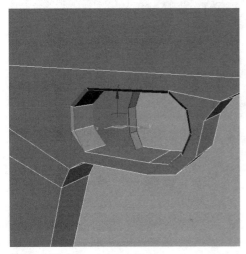

Figure 6-72: Trigger area refined

We are nearly finished with the body of the gun. After all this, the rest will seem really simple. Let's tackle the trigger area and the handle.

17. Use the Cut tool to cut around the trigger area. See Figure 6-73. After you

finish cutting, take some time to clean up the extra edges and vertices so that it looks like this figure.

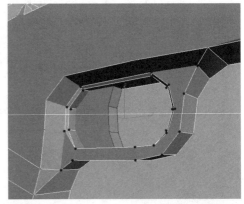

Figure 6-73: Trigger area defined and pulled inward

In Figure 6-74 all the edges around the trigger and handle have been chamfered to smooth out the hard edges.

Figure 6-74: Trigger and handle refined more

That does it for the main body of the handgun. Great job!

18. The cock just needs the edges chamfered on the sides. In the top view move the back vertices out to line up with top1.jpeg of the handgun. See Figure 6-75.

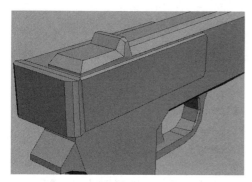

Figure 6-75: Refined geometry

19. Let's optimize the gun before we move on. Select the body and click on **Polygon mode** (**4**). Click on all the side faces that we didn't work on and delete them. Then do the same for the back of the barrel pieces and the back side of the trigger. Got it? Great! Let's move on.

20. Select the body of the handgun in the top view. Hold **Shift**, left-click, and drag to make a new copy of the handgun body. For the Mirror: Screen Coordinates be sure that Mirror Axis is set to **X**, then click **OK**.

21. Line up the copy right next to the original and attach the two together. Select the vertices down the center and weld them together.

22. In Figure 6-76 you can see we need to optimize a bit more. Select the center vertices and move them over, then weld it shut.

Figure 6-76: Optimizing

23. Once you have it optimized, attach the rest of the pieces and rename it **weapon_handgun**.

The handgun is rounding off to about 600 polygons, which is just about right for third-person and even first-person games. Take your time refining the weapon before moving on to texturing.

Texturing

I know what you're thinking. I've made a mistake. What is texturing doing before the unwrap section? Oftentimes you can actually create the texture first and then work the UVs into it. All right, are you ready to try something different?

1. Start Photoshop. Open the handgun texture files.

2. Let's start off by pulling in all the major pieces of the photos to a single file and then saving it as **weapon_handgun.psd**. See Figure 6-77.

Figure 6-77: Handgun texture pieces

By building the texture map up first we are going to have to think slightly differently. If we were unwrapping the handgun first,

133

chances are each UV piece would encompass an equal portion of the map since nothing on the weapon is overly important. The initial idea is to unwrap the body pieces all the way around.

3. Take the side view of the handgun and blend it with the top and underside of the gun. Be sure that you scale the pieces down so that they are equal to one another. If you do it right, everything should line up from the top to the side and underneath. In Figure 6-78 there is a before and after of the top and side blending together. All I did was erase the highlights and clone the area in between.

Figure 6-78: Texture cleanup

4. Take the remaining pieces and place them below the gun body. In Figure 6-79 notice how not much has changed. I've just placed the trigger, barrels, and side pieces on and darkened the background to keep things from standing out too much.

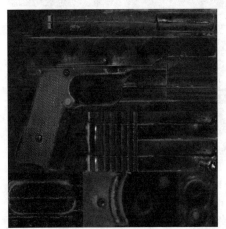

Figure 6-79: Finished texture

Okay, it's time to find out if the handgun texture is going to work or not. So, let's jump back to unwrapping the object and find out.

UVW Mapping

We have looked at unwrapping objects in the previous two tutorials. This time around, I'm going to assume that you have a greater understanding of how the Unwrap Editor works. Be sure you have weapon_handgun.max opened in max.

1. With the handgun selected, open the Material Editor (**M**) and assign the **weapon_handgun.dds** file to it.

2. Click on the Modifier list and choose the **Unwrap UVW** modifier.

3. Click on the Unwrap UVW modifier to activate it. Next, press the **Edit** button under the Parameters rollout to open the Edit UVWs window.

4. Under Selection mode, change to **Face Sub-Object** mode. Then select the entire gun.

5. Click on **Mapping | Flatten Mapping**. Make sure Face Angle Threshold is **70** and uncheck Rotate Clusters and Fill Holes. Click **OK**. See Figure 6-80.

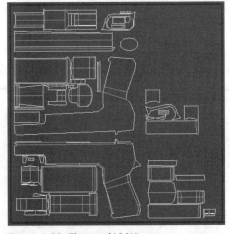

Figure 6-80: Flattened UVW map

Let's work the UVWs the same way we did the texture by unwrapping the top, side, and bottom together.

6. Select the side views of the handgun and move them off the center area. Next, select the rest of the UVWs and move them off the center area to the other side. With the puzzle board all clean, we can begin putting the pieces together.

7. Take one side panel of the handgun and properly scale it to the texture as shown in Figure 6-81.

That's all there is to it. Take the top piece of the handgun and connect it to the side piece and start building everything around it. When you are finished, you should have something similar to Figure 6-82.

Awesome! The texture map was a perfect fit. My suggestion to you is that if you really dislike unwrapping objects, then texture first so that the chore of unwrapping doesn't seem so unpleasant.

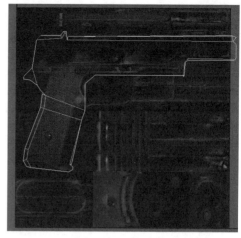

Figure 6-81: Side panel of gun scaled onto texture

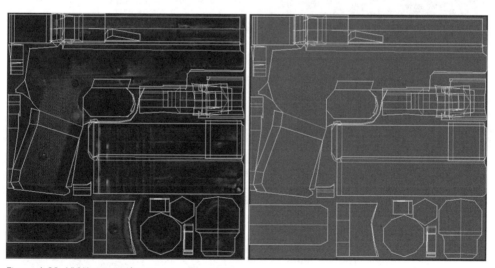

Figure 6-82: UVW map and texture

Exporting

For the artist, setting up the weapon can be dependent upon the programmer/scripter. Currently, the setup for a weapon in the Ka3D engine is as follows.

1. Be sure the weapon_handgun model is open. With the handgun selected, go to the Hierarchy tab and click on **Affect Pivot Only** and then below it press the **Center to Object** button. Using the Move tool, move the pivot point slightly behind the handle as shown in Figure 6-83.

Figure 6-83: Pivot point moved back

2. Navigate to **Create | Helpers | Dummy**. Make three dummy boxes.

   a) Dummy_flame — Make a dummy box and place it directly in front of the weapon.

   b) Dummy_shell_exit — Place the dummy box wherever the shells or used ammo will exit the weapon.

   c) Dummy_slug — Place the dummy box at the front of the weapon. Slugs can start from the same dummy as muzzle flash.

> **Note:**
>
> Slugs, shells, and muzzle flash need to be triggered from the scripts, so basically it's enough that the artist provides the meshes to the programmer and tells him from which dummies each should be initiated, and in which frames of the shooting animation sequence.

3. Link the dummy boxes to the weapon. On the toolbar at the top click on the **Select and Link** button. Select the **Dummy_flame** box. Click and drag it to the handgun, then let go. The handgun should highlight for a second, letting you know that it is now linked. Do the same for Dummy_shell_exit and Dummy_slug.

> **Tip:**
>
> You can also link up dummy box particle effects to the weapon for the bullets, muzzle flashes, or whatever else you feel it could be used for. The system is very flexible.

4. Next we can attach the muzzle flash to the weapon. Merge the muzzle flash object into the handgun scene and place it at the front of the weapon as shown in Figure 6-84. Be sure to link it up to Dummy_flame.

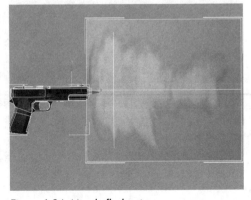

Figure 6-84: Muzzle flash setup

5. The last thing we need to add is the type of bullet the handgun shoots. Be sure the "shell" and "slug" model are included in the scene. The max file weapon_handgun_7_export shows an example of the weapon setup with all the art included. Be sure to look it over.

That's all the artist needs to do. The rest is on the shoulders of our fearless scripters and programmers.

Viewing

You can view the handgun scene in two different ways.

- Double-click on the exported weapon_handgun.hgr file. It will automatically pull up the viewer and allow you to look at the scene.

- Open the HGR Viewer and click on Open | File. Navigate to your exported weapon_handgun.hgr file and double-click on it.

Okay, if you've managed to get through these models, then you are probably ready to destroy something. That's right, in the next tutorial there are two examples of breakables. Put your thinking cap on and meet me in the next tutorial!

Tutorial 4: Breakable Models

The ability to break models and blow stuff to pieces in games has always been a fascination with game players and designers. Luckily for us, the Ka3d engine takes one file with both the breakable pieces and the original model, making the job very easy. Sounds simple enough, right? Let's take a look at breaking the light post that we made earlier in the book and destroying a wooden crate.

Broken Light Post

Let's look at what is going to happen before we jump in. When building a breakable model we need some structure and naming conventions.

- **Intact** — The original model.
- **Damage** — Model that is dented and/or bent but remains one piece.

- **Broken** — The base piece left after the pieces break off. This is optional for use with pieces.

- **Pieces** — Chunks and pieces from the original model that go flying off.

1. Open the light_post file found at …\Tutorials\Art_Tutorials\Tutorial_4 _Breakable_Models\light_post.

2. Select the light_post model. Hold **Shift** and click to duplicate the model. In the Clone Options window, change Name to **light_post_damage1**, then press **OK**.

Tip:

Hide the original model so that it doesn't get in your way while modeling.

3. In Editable Mesh mode, choose **Vertex selection**. Then dent the pole up a bit and start bending the top of the light downward. Check out Figure 6-85.

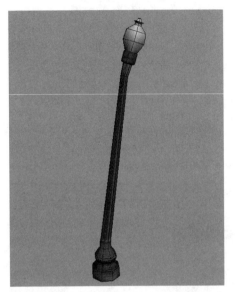

Figure 6-85: Pole bent

4. Do the same steps again except this time push the pose even more for **light_post_damage2**.

When you are done working the damage states over, unhide all the models so that it looks like Figure 6-86.

Figure 6-86: Light post damage states

Now that the models are created we need to work up the system that the scripters use to hook everything together.

5. Create a dummy object to which you parent (link) all the parts (breakables) and then add in the **Trigger=breakable** user property to this dummy.

6. Add the following User Property tags to each child object (all the different forms of the light post): **Breakable=intact**, **Breakable=damage1**, and **Breakable=damage2**.

7. In each sub-part, you can add Sound= and Particle= tags to trigger sounds and particles when specific parts become active. For instance, if we wanted the first damage state to have some sparks from the light we could add a particle to it that the scripters would call up at the necessary time.

The light post is complete! We have all the textures and models created and the multiple breakable states are set in place. The light_post_breakable.max file contains everything we have done to this point if you need to take a look at it. Now, what if we wanted to have it actually break into pieces? Let's check out the broken crate example to get an idea of using another method.

Broken Crate

In the previous example, we were looking at damaged models. This example looks at creating an object that does more than dent; it's actually going to be broken into lots of pieces!

1. Open **crate.max** found in ...\Art_Tutorials\Tutorial_4_Breakable_Models\ crate.

2. Select the crate. Hold Shift and click on the model to duplicate it. In the Clone

Options window change Name to **crate_1_Piece-01**, then press **OK**.

3. Hide the original crate.

4. Select the new crate and go into Edit Poly mode, then turn on Edge selection.

5. Scroll down to Edit Geometry and choose the **Cut** tool. This tool will allow you to cut directly on the box whichever way you would like. In Figure 6-87 you can see that I've cut into the side, keeping with the basic wooden slats and adding a few breaks here and there to help give it that broken appearance.

Figure 6-87: Cutting into the crate

6. Choose **Face** selection. Select each cut piece individually and detach it from the model. Be sure it goes under the crate_1_Piece-xx name.

7. Now take each piece one at a time and extrude the face out, then build the inside face as shown in Figure 6-88.

Continue with these steps until all the pieces have been blocked out. In crate_pieces.max you can see the end result, which has about 23 pieces including the "Broken" piece, which is the base of the model (Figure 6-89).

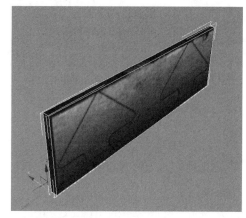

Figure 6-88: Extruded piece

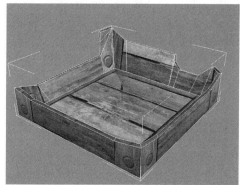

Figure 6-89: Broken piece

We have broken pieces galore! Remember that when designing breakables, you can go as far as having everything in the game breakable — there's no limit to what you could break!

8. Now it's time to add a dummy box and set up the pieces like we did on the light post. In Create | Helpers, select **Dummy** and place it inside the crate.

9. Link all the parts of the crate to the dummy and then add in the **Trigger=breakable** user property to this dummy.

10. Add the following User Property tags to each child object (all the different forms of the crate): **Breakable=**

139

intact, **Breakable=broken, Break-able=pieces, Breakable=pieces**, and **Breakable=pieces**.

Note:

Notice the same Breakable=pieces property is applied to all the pieces that fly off.

Just like the light post, on each sub-part, you can add Sound= and Particle= tags to trigger sounds and particles when specific parts become active. Check out crate_ breakable.max for the completed version.

Okay, it's time we take on the next task of modeling — vehicles!

Tutorial 5: Vehicle Modeling

In Tutorial 5, we will be modeling, UV unwrapping, and texturing a delivery truck. Before modeling, I try to get as many pictures as I can of that type of vehicle for reference and textures. The best way to do this is to have your own digital camera and easy access to the object that you are trying to model.

Tip:

Don't try taking photos at a stop light; there's not enough time.

Setting Up

There are generally three types of pictures that I take when preparing for a vehicle model. The first are orthographic shots from the front, side (left/right), top, and back. I begin making the model by using these reference shots to "trace" the outline of the object from the different orthographic windows. Because of the simplicity of a delivery truck, this method takes care of most of the shape. I then load these pictures into max as textures and put them onto planes. It's not too difficult punching in the dimensions of the plane to match up

with the dimensions of the picture; just make sure you get the perfect proportions.

The second type of pictures I take are used for the texture itself. In the case of the truck, these include details such as the lights, handles, front grille, rearview mirror, windows, tires, and any other details that would be faster to do as photo manipulation rather than straight painting. Like the first type of pictures, these work best from a head-on angle and with a good front light source.

The third type of pictures, which are also for modeling reference (and often for texture reference as well), consist of three-quarter view angled shots, closeups of three-dimensional detail, and any other shots that would help with an understanding of the structure and surface texture. It's always best to go overboard with these pictures. At first glance it may be obvious what sort of details you will want to capture for reference, but there are always plenty of details that you may not think of until you have to model them. Oftentimes, the pictures I think will help the most end up being used the least, and the more obscure shots I take end up capturing some detail that I wasn't aware of at the time.

Modeling the Vehicle

For many models that I make, including this one, I work with the geometry as an editable poly. Keep in mind that some functions and options that we use throughout Tutorial 5 may not work if the model is an editable mesh.

Before modeling, I set up any reference that will be in the scene. In this case, the back and side pictures of the truck are put onto reference planes as shown in Figure 6-90. I used a front reference picture also, but mostly for small details like where the window molding and headlights line up and not so much to help with the overall shape of the model.

Figure 6-90: Vehicle reference planes

1. Start off by identifying a basic shape that the model resembles the closest. In this case, the truck is quite boxy. Make a box and, because the model will look the same on one side as it looks on the other, only model half and then mirror the other half. This saves a lot of time in the long run, as well as making sure that the model is perfectly aligned on both sides.

2. Convert the box to an editable poly. Using the front orthographic view and reference plane, align the box's left edge along the midline of the world. Go into the Perspective viewport and

delete the face that aligns with the midline. Go into Top-level mode (hotkey **6** with the model selected). See Figure 6-91.

Figure 6-91: Refining the box

3. Under the Hierarchy tab, select the **Affect Pivot Only** button. Now you will use the **Snap Toggle** to snap the pivot of the box to the world's midline. Hit **S** to toggle snapping. The button is also on the top icon bar. It is a magnet with a number above it. If the button is yellow, that means snapping is on. For now, make sure that the number on the button is **3**. If it's not, you can right-click the button and select **3**.

4. Next, left-click the same button to bring up the Grid and Snap Settings window. From here, you can select which things in the scene will be "snapable." Since we are only snapping the pivot to the midline, just have **Grid Lines** turned on. Now you can grab the transform gizmo and snap it to the midline.

> **Tip:**
>
> Keep in mind that snapping doesn't work in this instance when grabbing just one direction of the gizmo. Try selecting the whole gizmo by selecting it where the three arrows meet in the middle. This should let you free-form move around, making it easier to snap with.

5. With the pivot at the midline of the world, select the model and click the

Mirror Selected Objects button from the top icon bar. With the Options window open, be sure you do a **Reference** mirror and not a copy. Also, make sure that **X** is the mirror axis. Hit **OK**.

6. Once you have a reference mirror of the box, you can begin modeling the original half, and any adjustment will automatically update on the other side. One thing to keep in mind is that the reference update does not work if you are moving the original half in Top-Level mode. If you need to move the entire model, simply select all the vertices and move it that way. It will allow the reference mirror to move as well.

7. Now you can begin adding some real detail to the vehicle. The first step is to get a basic outline shape of the truck. Using the Front and Side orthographic viewports, use the reference planes to block out the shape as shown in Figure 6-92.

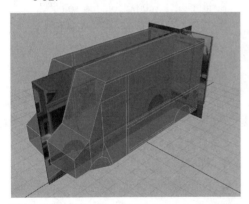

Figure 6-92: Reference planes

From this point, I generally use only a small number of tools to complete the rest of the model. Use the Cut tool to add any extra edges where you may need them. Weld vertices to merge more than one vertex together. Target Weld is also a helpful welding tool. It allows you to select a vertex and drag it to another vertex, and then it welds the vertices there. Extrude any faces to pull them out or push them in. If you want to take an edge away, use the Remove button. Simply hitting Delete will get rid of the edge, but it will also make a hole in the geometry. Snapping can come in handy many times when modeling. If you want to get more mathematical accuracy with edge cutting, you can use snap options like Midpoint, which will cut the edge at the exact midpoint of any other edge you are cutting to. Play around with the different settings for snapping to figure out a system that works for you.

Figure 6-93 shows the cut edges that define the door, windshield, wheel area, and the strips on the side. Select the faces of those side strips and extrude them out a small amount. The door is extruded in too.

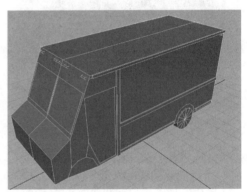

Figure 6-93: Cut edges

Starting from cylinders, I made the wheels. I also extruded the wheel area in, and added some other details like headlights, bumpers, and other small lights. I made these separate, and as of right now, they are separate objects from the main truck body. See Figure 6-94.

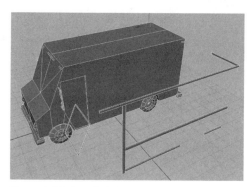

Figure 6-94: Detail objects

8. Once the details on the truck are complete, select their faces, and holding down **Shift**, move in the **X** direction. On the window that pops up, select **Clone to Object** (see Figure 6-95).

Note:

Holding down the Shift button and moving an object is the shortcut for making a copy of that object. It also works all the way down to the vertex level. You can duplicate any selected faces, edges, or vertices using this shortcut.

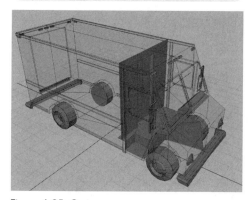

Figure 6-95: Copy

9. With these details separate from the truck, you can delete them from the main truck body. The reason for making them separate is to keep the poly count down. Fewer polys are needed if

the details are separate from the face that makes up the side of the truck. It also makes UV unwrapping a little easier.

After adding a few more small details, like the back door, rearview mirrors, and several more window seals, it is time to start on the interior.

Figure 6-96 shows progress shots of the interior. All the modeling was done using the same set of tools that I mentioned earlier.

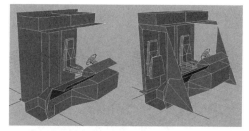

Figure 6-96: Interior work up

10. Once the interior is finished, convert the reference mirror half of the truck exterior to an editable poly and attach it to the original half. Then remove the midline edge to reduce the polycount as shown in Figure 6-97.

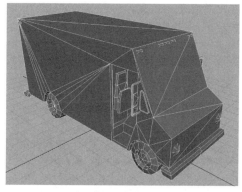

Figure 6-97: Vehicle mirrored and cleaned up

Check out the finished geometry in Figures 6-98 and 6-99.

143

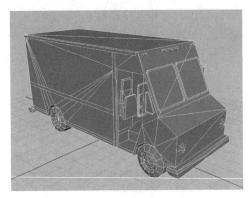

Figure 6-98: Truck geometry complete

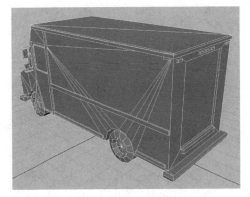

Figure 6-99: Truck geometry complete

UV Unwrapping

Now that the modeling is finished, it is time to start unwrapping UVs. The unwrapping process gets more complicated the more detailed and organic the model is. However, with a simple boxy truck, it's hard to ask for a more UV friendly model. With minor exceptions, all of the faces are generally directly facing an axis.

Before unwrapping I split the model into two textures, one texture for the exterior and the other for the interior and wheels.

1. Giving the model an **Unwrap UVW** modifier, I begin laying out the UVs. On the Modifier list, next to Unwrap UVW there is a small + sign. Click this to

open up the **Select Face** option. With it highlighted you can select a number of faces on the model, select an axis under the Sub Object Params below, and hit **Planar Map**. This lays out the UVs of those selected faces according to what axis was selected.

2. Click the **Edit...** button under Parameters to open the Edit UVWs window. In this window there are many options that are similar to the viewport options, such as Move, Rotate, Scale, Mirror, etc. This is the window where you will tweak your UVs to their desired location. Under the Tools menu of the window, there are weld options that work similarly to the vertex weld options.

Similar to modeling, there are typically just a few options that we use when UV unwrapping. Typically, use the Planer Map button to get the initial UV layout and then tweak the UVs in the Edit UVWs window using the Transform, Rotate, Scale, and Weld options.

> **Note:**
> You can right-click to get to the quad menu and choose the Move and Scale buttons within the Edit UVWs window to change the tool. If you only want to move in one linear direction or scale along one axis, select them from the drop-down on the menu bar.

Another way to think of the texture is as wrapping paper for the model. The model is the present itself, and your UVs are the shapes of wrapping paper that you cut out to wrap the present with. It is best to keep the number of pieces of wrapping paper to a minimum. This means that you will want to try to connect the UVs to each other as much as possible. Whenever you have two connecting faces of a model whose UVs aren't attached, this creates a texture seam.

Imagine you are wrapping a box for someone's birthday. You could cut out a piece of wrapping paper for each side of the box, but it would be very time consuming to perfectly match up the paper pattern where the different edges meet. Even if you could get the pattern reasonably close to matching up, it would still be fairly obvious that each side has its own separate piece of paper. Now, imagine that you have the same box but one large piece of wrapping paper that you fold over the edges. Not only would the pattern be completely seamless on the edges, but you have saved yourself the time of having to tediously match up the separate pieces. UVs work very much the same way. The smaller the number of UV pieces that you have, the easier the texturing will be in the long run.

It is also important to keep the proportions of the UVs as close to the proportions of the faces on the model as possible. If you get it perfect, then the resolution of the texture will be consistent all the way through the model. If you are sloppy with the proportions of your UVs, then you will have parts of the model that have a high-resolution texture, and other parts that look more blocky and low quality.

Try to use up as much of the texture space as possible by really packing the UV shapes close together as shown in Figures 6-100 and 6-101. The more empty space that you have in your texture, the more the computer processing is being spent on useless information. It also means that the model has a smaller resolution texture than it could have without adding to the processing time of the machine running it.

Once you have the UVs laid out, put a checked pattern texture on the model. This lets you see how well the UVs are set up. If any of the squares are zigzagging at all, you know you have some tweaking to do. If

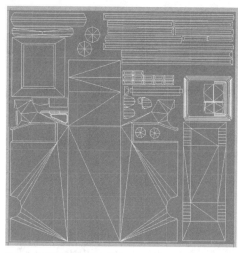

Figure 6-100: Exterior UV map

Figure 6-101: Interior UV map

there are parts of the model where the checked boxes are smaller or larger than on other parts, you know you have some proportion issues. Once you have the boxes perfectly square and the same size throughout, then you know the setup is good and you can move on to the actual texturing. See Figure 6-102.

Figure 6-102: Checked pattern on the truck

When the UVs are complete, use Texporter to save out a picture of them and take it into Photoshop and begin texturing.

Texturing

The first thing to do on the texture is to block out the basic colors. This allows you to get at least some color on all parts of the model right at the beginning and gives you a full understanding of the UV setup, at least as far as coloring goes. See Figure 6-103.

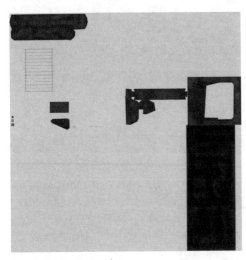

Figure 6-103: Base color

Figure 6-104 is where we need to add some of the minor photo details. Most of these came directly from the pictures I took at the very beginning. After bringing in the photo details, go in and tweak the color, brightness, saturation, and other parts to get it to blend in with the painted areas as much as possible. It's important to focus on these details to get an overall sense of unity on the model.

Do the shadows on the photo details match the shadows on the painted areas of the texture? Are the highlights similarly matched?

These are the kinds of things we should always think about when tweaking the details.

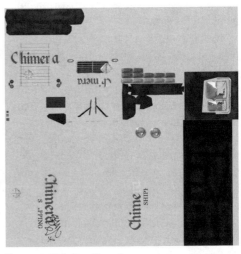

Figure 6-104: Detail work

A trick that I use often is shadow baking. For this model I didn't use it to get the actual shadows for the texture, but instead to use as a reference image. At one point in the modeling process, the extruded strips along the side of the truck were actually connected to the side face but were taken away to save on the poly count. If they were still connected, it would be easy to see where exactly they lie along the side because the UV lines would show them. Since the strips are not connected I have used a texture bake to show the shadow of these strips. This also tells me where the window molding lies along the doors and front windshield. Also, the small red and orange lights that run along the top of the vehicle are shown. Bring this reference image into Photoshop and use it to see where you need to paint in shadows for the details. See Figure 6-105.

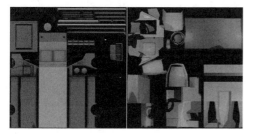

Figure 6-105: Texture bake

1. To bake lighting into the texture have the model selected and press zero (**0**). This will open the Render to Texture option box.

2. First, uncheck **Automatic Unwrap Mapping** at the top. Scroll down and click the **Add** button under Output. Select **Diffuse Map** from the list that pops up. After you choose it, a list of options will become usable in the window.

3. In the same Output rollout, select the resolution of the baked texture, as well as the file name, type, and destination. Also, be sure to have **Lighting** and **Shadows** checked. Figure 6-106 shows the finished exterior texture.

While the overall texture is very white, I tried to dirty it up a bit. I cannot think of too many trucks I have seen that don't have that thin layer of dirt on them. One of the most important things to do while making

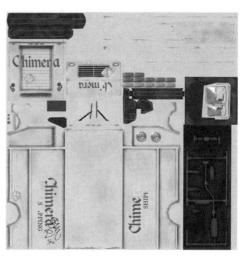

Figure 6-106: Texture completed

the texture is to think of it not as a model but as an actual object. For this model I pictured the truck driving down the road. What kind of wear does a truck like this take? Where along its surface does it collect the most dirt? You will want to add details that give the impression that not only is the model believable, but it has its own personal history. For the truck, lettering has worn off to show the less sun damaged surface underneath. Some juvenile has tagged the side while it was making a delivery in a sketchy part of town. The driver no doubt isn't too concerned with the cleanliness of the exterior. These are details I added to give the model more character. It's always best to go overboard with dirt and details than to not have enough. Something that is really dirty comes off as more believable than the same object that has a perfectly clean surface.

Also, it is important to constantly think about how close the model is going to be to the camera in the game, so that you have a sense of what kind of detail is too small. Spending an hour on a minor detail that will ultimately make up only a couple of pixels in the final game may be a waste of time.

147

I am always breaking down real objects I see in life and studying their surface qualities, trying to figure out how I would recreate them in 3D. Over time, this sort of analytical view of your surroundings becomes second nature. Even if you were to take one day and really study the surfaces you come in contact with, you might be surprised at how many imperfections there are in everything. You would also come to a better understanding of how these small details speak visually to you about an object. They tell of its age, how often it's used, what kind of condition its owner keeps it in, what sort of elements it has been exposed to, etc. Each aspect blends together to give that object a story, and objects that can communicate a story are infinitely more interesting than ones that cannot.

In Figure 6-107 we can see the finished interior texture. Not as much time went into the interior texture as on the exterior because this part of the model is smaller, and more importantly it won't be seen by the player as much.

Figure 6-107: Interior texture complete

Figure 6-108 is another example of how to use a texture bake to see where shadows need to be and where window molding is.

Figure 6-108: Texture bake

The shadow of the window molding is also very helpful in showing where to make the transparency alpha map so that you can see through the windows. Since the interior of the truck does not have the windshield molding that the exterior does, simply duplicate the exterior molding and move it inside the truck so that it creates a shadow on the texture bake. Do the same trick for the side window moldings as well.

Figure 6-109 shows the transparency alpha channels for the exterior and interior texture maps.

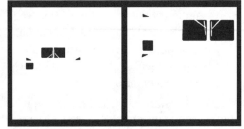

Figure 6-109: Transparency alpha map

The finished model with the final texture is shown in Figures 6-110 and 6-111.

Figure 6-111: Completed model with texture

Figure 6-110: Completed model with texture

Tutorial 6: Character Modeling

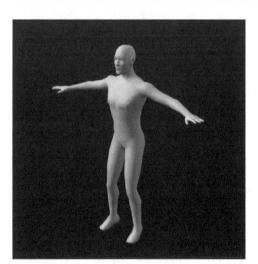

Figure 6-112: Getting started

In this tutorial you learn to create a complete human model while developing your skills with various tools and techniques. All of the techniques used throughout this tutorial can easily be applied to other models and projects of varying complexity.

Tutorial Files

All the files needed for this model can be found on the companion CD in …\Tutorials\Art_Tutorials\Tutorial_6_Character_Modeling. Before starting this section, copy the files to your hard drive.

Preparing the Workspace

In this first section we set up your workspace to create an efficient and consistent layout for the best workflow throughout the project. You then create the reference material needed and bring it into max for modeling purposes.

Note:

If you're still using the original setup, then you can skip this section, but if you still haven't even touched the Unit setup or any button under Customize, I would suggest following these steps before proceeding.

149

UI Setup

1. Let's get 3ds max up and going. If it's already started, go ahead and hit Reset Function under the File menu just to be sure we are starting fresh.

2. Next, choose the **Unit Setup** button under the Customize menu.

3. Choose **US Standard** and **Feet w/ Decimal Inches**. This will be our unit of measurement for the models we deal with. If you are more comfortable with another setting, please choose that one now. Be aware though that the models will be addressed using the U.S. standard feet dimensions. See Figure 6-113.

Figure 6-114: Inch setting

Grid and Snap Settings

1. Locate the Grid and Snap settings under the Customize menu or right-click on one of the Grid tools in the toolbar.

2. The Grid and Snap window gives you a number of options to customize this part of your working environment. For now we want to change the Grid Spacing. Set this value to **1'0"**. Change the Perspective View Grid Extent to **10**.

3. Close this window and return to your viewport.

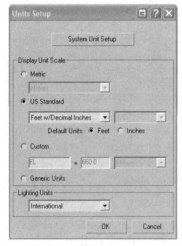

Figure 6-113: Units Setup window

4. Next choose the **System Unit Setup** button at the top of this window and set the default to **Inch**. Press **OK** and accept the settings. See Figure 6-114.

Reference Image Layout

Now that the workspace is set we will create the planes and load our reference material.

When creating a 3D plane to place an image on, it is helpful to keep in mind the dimensions of your image so that there is no stretching when it is mapped to the reference plane in max.

For instance, if your image was created in a 512x512 pixel area, it is best to work with those same ratios in max. You could create a 5x5 or 2x2 plane, or if it were 512x256 you could use a 6x3 plane.

For our project we will use a plane that is 7'x7'. Note our image is 512x512.

1. Click on the Create tab and select the **Geometry** button.

2. From the list of Object Types, choose the **Plane** button.

3. In the Front viewport, click and drag a plane in the viewport. Do not worry about the size of the plane just yet. See Figure 6-115.

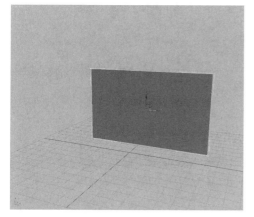

Figure 6-115: Plane created

4. Once you have drawn the plane, the values for this object will be displayed to the right under the Parameters rollout. Set the length to **7'** and the width to **7'**. The rest of the options you may leave as the default.

5. Let's center our reference plane in the world. Select the plane and then right-click on the **Select and Move** icon on the top bar. This will bring up the Transform window for you to center the object with. Set x and y to **0** and leave z as it is. We will manually set this one in the viewport. Notice in Figure 6-116 we have resized the plane and centered it on the X and Y axes.

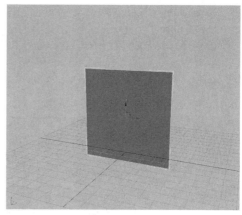

Figure 6-116: Plane resized

Note:

You can also use the transform options on the bottom bar of the interface.

6. Next, select the Z-axis and move it up until the bottom of your plane is even with the surface grid as seen in Figure 6-117. This will place our character on the ground plane of the world. If we choose to recenter the character later we could do so, but for now it is best modeled from this position.

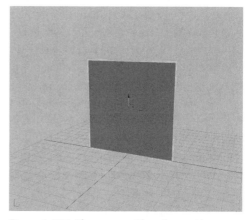

Figure 6-117: Plane even with surface grid

7. Next we need to create a second plane to put our side view image on. It will be the same size as our front view plane, so let's make a copy of the front view plane and rotate it 90 degrees as seen in Figure 6-118.

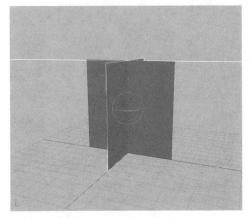

Figure 6-118: Plane rotated 90 degrees

Note:

Using the Angle Snap option will help with rotating an object around to a 90 degree position (shortcut key **A**).

8. Open the Material Editor (**M**). The reference material is already loaded into the slots for you. You should notice in Figure 6-119 the three materials representing the front, side, and top view of our character.

9. Select the front view reference material and apply it to the first plane. Select the side view reference material and apply it to the second plane.

These images do have an alpha channel in case you want to remove the excess image surrounding the character.

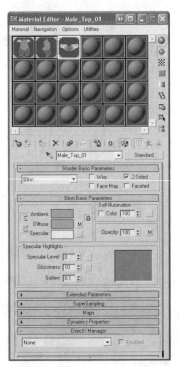

Figure 6-119: Materials for character

Note:

To make the alpha visible in max right-click on the Viewport label name, select **Transparency**, then set the option to either **Simple** or **Best**.

10. Lastly, we should freeze the reference to make it easier to work with. Select the reference planes, then right-click on them, and choose **Properties** from the drop-down menu.

11. On the middle left of the Object Properties window, check the **Freeze** box and then below it in the Display Properties make sure to uncheck Show Frozen in Gray. This will allow us to keep the image visible and unselectable as we work within the scene.

Initial Shapes

We now have everything ready to begin modeling the character. The reference images are set to display the most defining of views for the character, those being the front and side views. Notice in Figure 6-120 a top view has been added to give further assistance in modeling this character. The top plane is the same size as the other planes and was copied using the same process as the side plane.

The next step will be to trace the outline of our reference with the Line tool. By tracing the outline of the reference images we will capture our character's look and feel and have the basic building blocks for taking this concept and turning it into a game-ready 3D model.

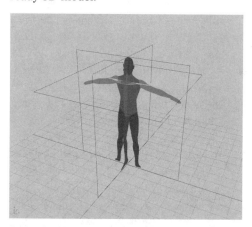

Figure 6-120: Top view

1. First select the **Line** tool from the Create menu under the Shapes icon.

2. Start with your side view and outline the torso of the reference image plane. In Figure 6-121 notice the placement of the vertex points and how they are aligned with the most prominent points of the outline. These are the points we want to work with, so be sure to have these areas marked. Everything has

been broken down into colored regions to identify the division points useful when creating your model. These areas provide you with transitional joint sections that help in connecting the arms, legs, and head with the torso.

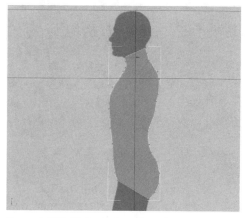

Figure 6-121: Vertex points aligned

Note:

The more points you place in the outline of the character, the higher the poly count will end up becoming. For this model we are going for a medium poly count, so we can be somewhat generous with our vertex point placement.

3. Next outline the side view of the head as seen in Figure 6-122.

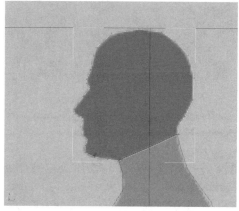

Figure 6-122: Side view of Head

153

4. Next we outline the side view of the foot as shown in Figure 6-123.

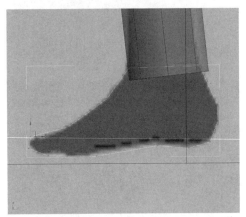

Figure 6-123: Side view of Foot

5. Our hand is outlined from the Top viewport. This is the most defining of views for the hand and provides us with the detail we need to model it. The model needs to have a vertex placed at each bendable joint on the hand. In Figure 6-124, there is a vertex at each of the finger joints.

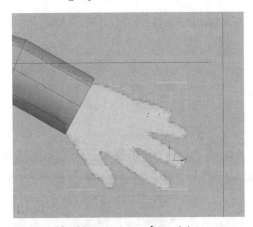

Figure 6-124: Vertex points at finger joints

The last two shapes to be dealt with are the leg and arm. For these we are going to take a different approach. We could continue to model them like we did the previous

shapes, but for the leg and arm it is easier to use the Line tool in a different fashion.

6. Select the Line tool from **Create Tab | Shapes Button | Line**.

7. Under the roll-out options choose **Rendering**. There are five settings we want to change:

    a) Set Thickness to **5'.0"**.

    b) Set Sides to **8**.

    c) Check the **Renderable Setting** option.

    d) Check the **Generate Mapping Coords** option.

    e) Check the **Display Render Mesh** option.

8. You are now ready to draw a line through the center of the leg. We are not going to outline this shape, because with the new settings we automatically have a three-dimensional shape to work with instead of just a line. As you draw this line take note of the thickness of the leg; at times it is wider and then thinner. At each of these points place a vertex so that when we move into defining the shape you will have what's needed to work with. See Figure 6-125.

Figure 6-125: Line defined

9. Next select the Top viewport and do the same with the arm. Be sure to set the arm line to **4'.0"**. The closer in size to the actual reference image, the easier it will be to work with later. In Figure 6-126, notice that the arm line has been moved up to the highest point of the arm (the deltoid). Move your line up as well to get it ready for when we match it with the front view.

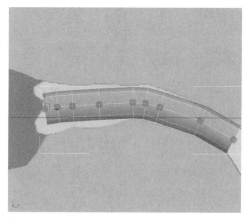

Figure 6-126: Arm line adjusted

Note:

You can copy and paste the arm and leg to the other side as a reference copy to watch both sides come together at the same time. This can be helpful at times but is purely a preference of the artist.

Defining the Initial Shapes

The initial character outline is complete and we have a good starting point to get the character going. Before we start please keep one thing in mind: The human figure is a complex set of shapes and can be intimidating when you first approach it, but if you take it in sections and break it down into approachable pieces, as we are going to do, then I think you will fly through this model with ease and be on your way to creating whatever you can imagine.

You can start anywhere you want on the character like the head, big toe, teeth, etc., but for this example we are going to start on the leg. It will provide us with some quick and easy results and let you see how the right approach can make the difference in a task being difficult or easy.

As you recall, we have a line going down the center of the side view leg that has the Display Render Mesh option checked so it appears as a three-dimensional shape. We get a lot of detail out of working this over, so let's get started with it!

The Leg and Foot

Our next focus brings us to the wonderful world of the all-important leg. Our leg's initial position has already been well defined in the side view as far as the overall flow. But as you can see from the front view we are still a little stiff to say the least. Let's get to work on this.

1. Start by selecting the **leg line**. Using the Front viewport, set the vertices of the leg line to the center of the front view reference. This can be seen in Figure 6-127. The first section of the line has been modified correctly with only a handful left.

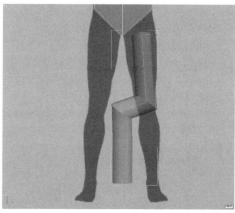

Figure 6-127: Leg line moved to center

155

In Figure 6-128 the line is properly adjusted within the reference image. Even at this point you can begin to see the shape of the leg in 3D take on more of the appearance of a real leg.

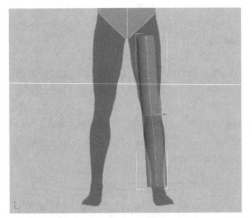

Figure 6-128: Line adjusted to match reference image

Now that we have the leg line prepared and a good solid flow in both the front and side views, we want to start defining a more accurate geometry that best represents the leg. In order to do this we will add a new modifier to the stack.

2. With the leg selected make your way to the Modify tab and select the **Editable Mesh** option from the Modify drop-down list. Select the Vertex mode, grab your Scale tool, and let's get to work. Select the bottom row of vertices and, with the Scale tool constrained to only the X-axis, pull the vertices in until they line up with the edges of the reference image. Continue this process all the way up the leg, as shown in Figure 6-129.

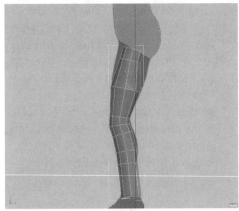

Figure 6-129: Scale vertices in and out to match the reference image.

3. Once you have gotten all the way up the leg (see Figure 6-130) move to the front view and work it over the same way. Be sure that as you do this you are scaling the selection in only one direction. As long as we tackle one view at a time, everything will go down just fine. See Figure 6-131.

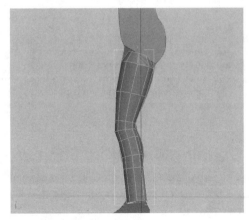

Figure 6-130: Side view adjusted

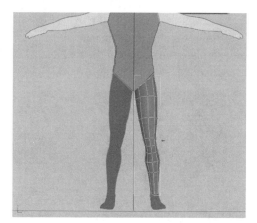

Figure 6-131: Scaling selections

4. At times you may need to use the Move tool to adjust the placement of a vertex so that it better aligns with the outlining shape. After you have scaled the object as closely to the reference image as you can, go back through and adjust the outer edges of the model by only selecting the outerlying vertices and moving them into position.

Note:

You should be able to leave the inside vertices alone, as they will not affect the reference lines all that much. In Figure 6-132, we have made a reference copy of the leg and mirrored it and lined it up with the other side of the body. We are basically done with the modeling of the leg with respect to the attachment process with the torso and foot.

Take a moment to look at the leg and make sure it all looks correct. Rotate it around a bit and get a good view from a number of angles. As you can see it has a great deal of shape and definition and looks amazingly like a human leg. It may be hard to believe, but it really is as simple as drawing a line, scaling the vertices to the reference material, and adjusting a few points here and there. This technique works great for limbs

of all types, whether you're working on an animal, monster, or even the unthinkable. See Figure 6-132.

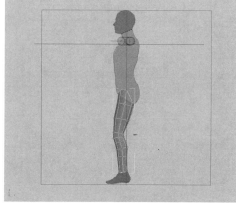

Figure 6-132: Leg copied and mirrored

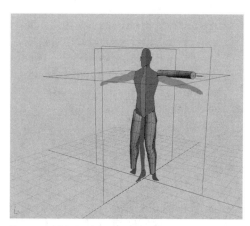

Figure 6-133: Limbs complete

The next section of the model is the foot. The foot has been well represented with the side view outline, and because of the blocky nature of the foot we are going to use a different method here as well.

5. Select the foot in the viewport and move it until it lines up with the left leg, as seen in Figure 6-134. Get it roughly placed near the inside edge of the ankle, go into the modify list, and add an Extrude modifier to the stack.

157

There are several options in the rollout that we need to change.

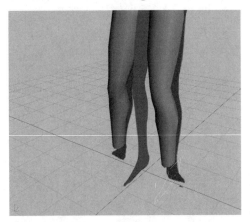

Figure 6-134: Foot moved

6. The amount of extrusion should be set to **0'3.0"** and the Segments should be set to **2**. You may also want to check **Generate mapping coords** if it is not selected. The extruded ankle should have moved out until it reached the outer ankle. See Figure 6-135.

Figure 6-135: Foot extruded

7. Next we address the rather blocky shape of the foot. Select the outside vertices and move them slightly down to create a more curved surface for the top of the foot. As seen in Figure 6-136,

you will want to scale the top and bottom rows of vertices in and out to emulate the outline of the foot image provided, shown in Figure 6-137.

Figure 6-136: Vertices adjusted

Figure 6-137: Vertices scaled in and out

8. Next select the **Edge** tool and divide both the inside and outside ankle areas. We need a little more to work with here to soften up the shape and flesh it out better, as seen in Figures 6-138, 6-139, and 6-140. The edges have been divided and made visible to make it easier to work with than in Vertex mode.

Figure 6-138: Edges divided

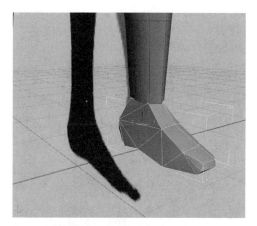

Figure 6-139: Edges worked up

Figure 6-140: Edges worked up

9. With the edges divided, switch to **Ver-tex** mode. Select the new vertices and move them outward a little to soften up this plane of the foot. Adjust the foot as necessary and when you are ready we will prepare to attach the foot to the leg model. After reviewing the foot model in Figure 6-141, we can safely say we now have a good looking foot and are ready to attach it to the leg.

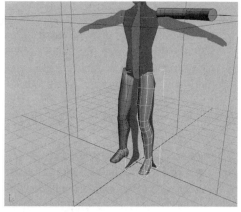

Figure 6-141: Foot model

10. Select the leg model and click on the **Attach** button under the Edit Geometry rollout. Click on the foot model and it is now attached to the leg. We are now ready to move in closer to

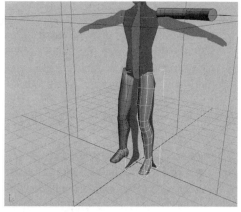

Figure 6-142: Leg and foot attached

attaching the geometry at our joint. See Figure 6-142.

11. The next order of business is to clean up the geometry a little before we start welding vertices. Select **Poly** mode in the Edit Mesh modifier and move your view to the joint of the ankle and lower leg. As you can see there is a surface on the top of the foot and the bottom of the leg. This geometry will not be seen, so we can get rid of it now while it is easy to get to and before we move on to something else and forget about it. With Poly mode on, go in and select the top faces of the foot and the bottom faces of the leg as seen in Figure 6-143.

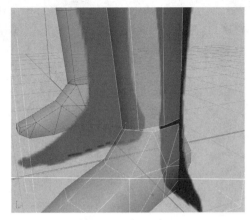

Figure 6-144: Geometry cleaned

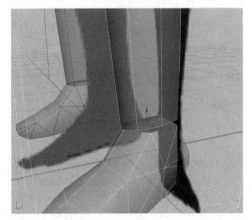

Figure 6-143: Selected faces

12. Once you have them selected, press the Delete key and delete the polys. In Figure 6-144, you can see that we now have an open area, but more importantly it is cleaned up and ready to be welded together.

13. In Figure 6-145, the front two vertices have been selected and welded together. You can use two different methods to achieve this. One way is to select both vertices and then under the Edit Geometry rollout, under the Weld section change the Selected value to

0'5.0". This will allow the tolerance more leeway and allow you to weld vertices that are farther apart. At the same time it will find a fairly good median between the two points. Click the **Selected** button and the vertices are now good to go.

The other approach is to use the Target weld option. By pressing the Target Weld button you are able to select a vertex and then move it on top of another vertex to weld the two together. It all depends on what you need to do to get the job done. The options are there, so just keep them in mind and it will make things go a little more smoothly down the road.

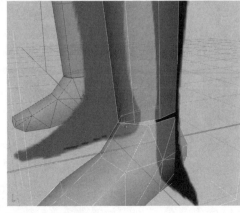

Figure 6-145: Vertices welded

14. Take a moment to look at the leg model and think through the connection before you start welding vertices. Notice there are eight vertices on the leg model and only six on the foot model. You need to divide your foot geometry once on each side and then you can weld everything together as shown in Figure 6-146.

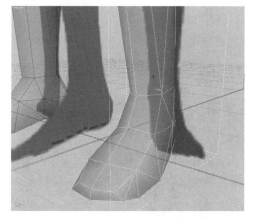

Figure 6-146: Foot geometry divided and welded

Once you have everything welded together, reset your view and take a look at the foot and leg as a whole. Make sure that everything looks correct and that the foot and leg look like they belong together. This is a good opportunity to reevaluate the leg model as a whole and make any adjustments that you may feel are necessary. A few edges turned and some vertices tweaked and we end up with Figure 6-147.

Note:

When you start working over all the edges, rotate around the model looking at the outlining shape (the edges) to tell if there's a good connection or if some of the edges sink into the mesh or away from it.

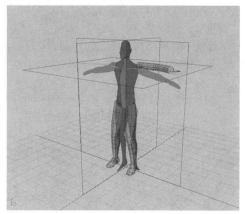

Figure 6-147: Edges turned and vertices adjusted

The Arm and Hand

The arm is our next subject of attention. Because of the similarities between the leg and the arm and the process used to model them, we will tackle it next. This will allow you a good chance to see what you remember from the last section and hopefully solidify the modeling technique that we used.

The arm model is ready to go and already prepped in the Top view, as shown in Figure 6-148, so let's move to the Front view and get started.

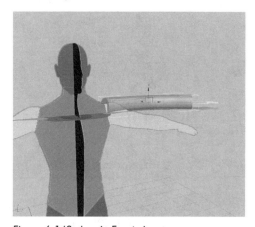

Figure 6-148: Arm in Front view

1. Select the **Vertex** mode and begin moving the lines/vertices to the center of the front view reference plane. Because the Top view is set correctly, you may want to drag the vertices locked along the Z- or Y-axis to keep from changing the overall shape by accident. Refer to Figure 6-149.

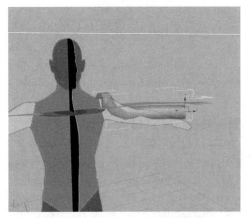

Figure 6-149: Vertices moved on locked axis

2. In Figure 6-150 we have adjusted the center line and have the arm looking more or less like an arm.

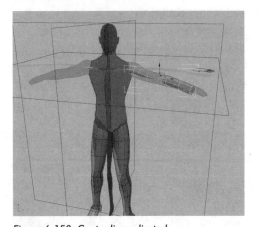

Figure 6-150: Center line adjusted

3. After looking back over the arm we should add another set of edges to the shoulder area. Select the arm model

and add an Edit Mesh modifier to the stack. Select the **Edge** mode and then go through and select the edges highlighted in Figure 6-151. We are adding these extra edges so that when we bone and animate the character we will have a better mesh to work with on the bends and folds when the arm is in action punching through a giant boulder or waving to the fans at a press conference.

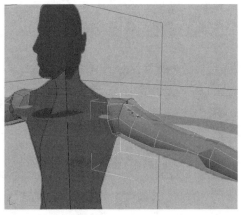

Figure 6-151: Edges highlighted

4. Once you have all of the edges selected, click on the **Chamfer** button under the Edit Geometry rollout and set it to **0'0.5"** or somewhere close to that. We just need a little distance between the vertices to work with them better. In Figure 6-152, we have the edges all chamfered out and ready to modify them a little to soften it up and blend it in better with the shoulder.

5. With the new additions done we can move on to scaling the vertices in and out to match up with our reference planes. Staying in the Front viewport, change to Vertex mode and begin scaling the vertices along a single axis. Notice when it is the first pass with the Scaling tool you can choose to scale as

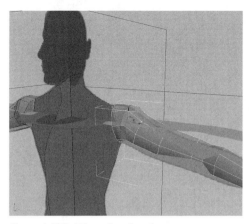

Figure 6-152: Edges chamfered

a whole instead of along one axis. Sometimes when the shape is much larger or smaller it is worth scaling the whole selection at once.

6. Starting at the shoulder, begin working your way across. Be sure to work over the new edges a little as you get to them; they may need to be tweaked up or down slightly to keep the smooth feel of the shoulder going, as seen in Figure 6-153.

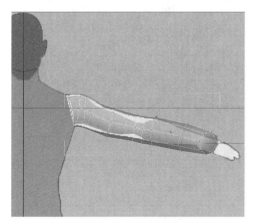

Figure 6-153: Edges worked over

7. Continue lining up the widths and work it all the way through until you get to the end. In Figure 6-154 it is almost

complete, with just one last section left to go. Scale the last section down as shown in Figure 6-155, and you can call this part done.

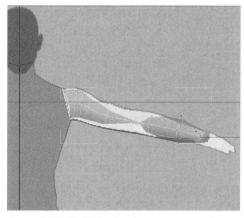

Figure 6-154: Refining the shape

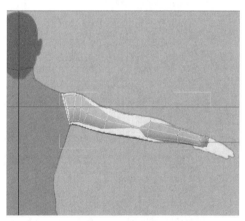

Figure 6-155: Front view complete

8. Next move to the Top viewport and make the necessary adjustments to have the arm lined up with your top view reference plane. It should look like Figure 6-156 when you have it completed.

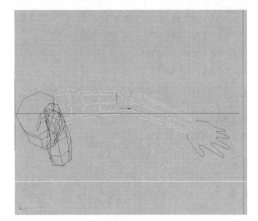

Figure 6-156: Top view complete

We have now completed the upper and lower arm and should take a few moments to look at it and make adjustments as needed. In Figure 6-157 we see the arm in all its glory. The shoulder has a nice rounded definition, while the rest of the arm maintains a very strong, solid flow. We have plenty of mesh for animating with and the overall look is very smooth with soft angles that you won't get with a lower poly character.

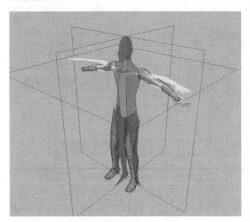

Figure 6-157: Arms displayed

9.   The hand line is next up. As seen in Figure 6-157 it has been moved down to the center of the wrist, ready to be

worked on. Select the hand line and apply an **Extrude** modifier to the stack. Very similar to the process of the foot, we extrude the hand and then soften the edges where needed. In Figures 6-158 and 6-159, you can see the hand extruded. From this view it is obvious that the hand appears very blocky and in need of some fine tuning.

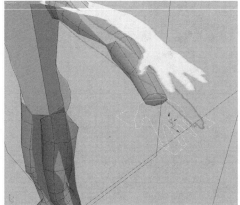

Figure 6-158: Selected

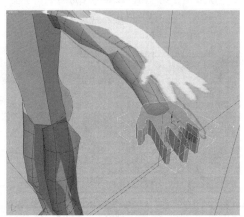

Figure 6-159: Extruded

10. To start with, change to Vertex mode and go to the Top view. Select the vertices shown in Figure 6-160 and switch to the Scale tool. We are going to scale all of this down at once and then detail each finger on its own next.

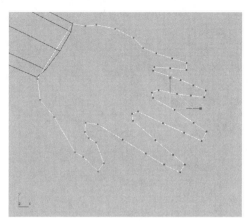

Figure 6-160: Vertices selected

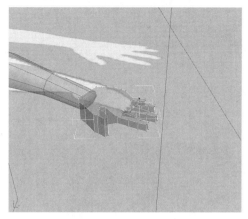

Figure 6-162: Correcting fingers

11. In Figures 6-161, 6-162, and 6-163 we can see the process of scaling the fingers down and scaling the fingertips down smaller as well after the overall scaling has been done. Notice the thumb has been included in this scaling.

Figure 6-163: Correcting fingers

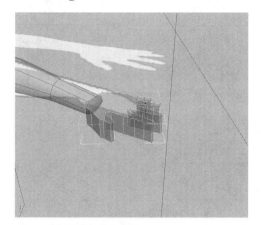

Figure 6-161: Correcting fingers

12. The fingers are scaled roughly to a good size to work with but before we start on them, let's go ahead and get the wrist prepared. As shown in Figure 6-164, change to Edge mode and select the wrist portion of the hand. We want to add some edges to this area in order to attach the arm to the hand. The arm is set to eight sides and our hand is at four. We will need to add another four edges to this end of the hand. In Figure 6-165 we have four edges added, one on each side of the wrist.

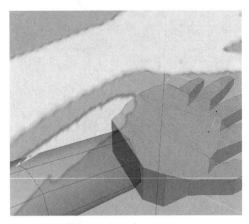

Figure 6-164: Wrist selected

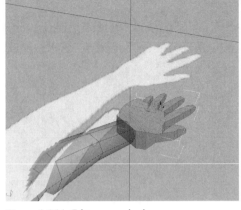

Figure 6-166: Edges reworked

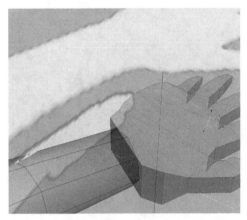

Figure 6-165: Four edges added

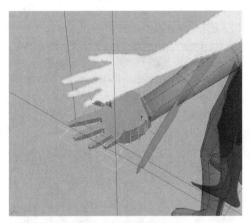

Figure 6-167: Vertices selected

13. In Figure 6-166, we've reworked a few of the edges to make the geometry work better for when we connect the arm and hand together.

14. Before we attach the hand let's make a few minor adjustments to the outer palm region. Select the vertices shown in Figure 6-167 and then scale them down until they look similar to Figure 6-168.

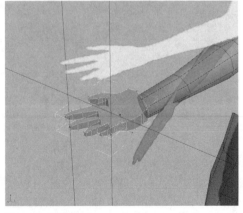

Figure 6-168: Vertices scaled down

The hand is now close enough that we can attach it to the arm. It still requires a good deal of tweaking to finish it, but a large part of the tweaking takes place directly with the connection of the arm and hand.

15. It's time to switch back to the arm and attach the hand to the arm, as shown in Figures 6-169 and 6-170.

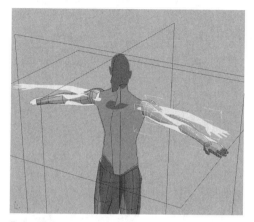

Figure 6-169: Arm selected

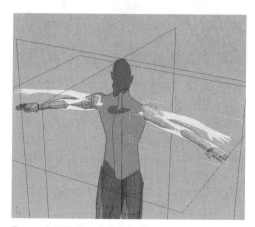

Figure 6-170: Hand attached to arm

16. As with the foot, we need to get rid of the interior polys at the end of the hand and the lower arm. Change to Poly mode, select these polys, and delete them from the model as shown in Figure 6-171.

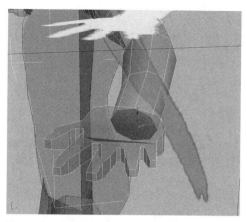

Figure 6-171: Polys selected and deleted

17. The next step is to attach the vertices from the hand to the lower arm. Most of the vertices line up fine, but the ones selected in Figure 6-172 need to be welded using the Target Weld method. Select each one individually and drag it to the corresponding vertex located on the lower arm.

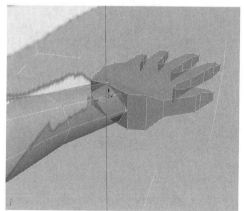

Figure 6-172: Vertices welded

18. In Figure 6-173 the vertices have been welded and we move on to cleaning up the edges on the top and bottom of the hand. Right now they are not helping the flow or appearance of the hand, so we want to turn a number of the edges

and get them to a point that is more manageable for us to work with. Begin turning the edges so that they run from the wrist to the knuckles, as shown in Figure 6-174.

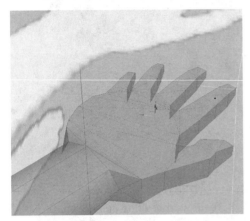

Figure 6-173: Vertices welded

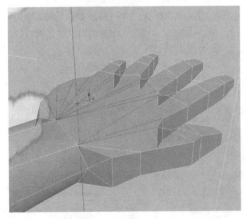

Figure 6-174: Edges turned

19. Next, rotate the thumb box around a little and move it down just a little as well. Select the vertices shown in Figure 6-175 and change to the Rotation tool. Rotate the thumb around until yours looks close to Figure 6-176. You can make adjustments as needed. It would be best to rotate the model around a little, pulling and pushing polys where needed.

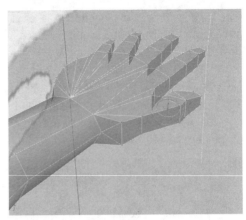

Figure 6-175: Vertices selected

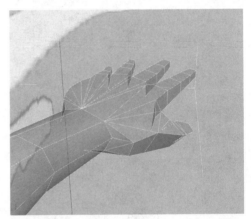

Figure 6-176: Thumb rotated

20. The next step involves the outer palm of the hand. In Figure 6-177, the edges are selected and you need to divide the outer edge down the middle so we can soften this part of the hand more than it is currently.

21. In Figure 6-178, the edges have been divided and made visible. Make sure yours is looking the same and then select the Vertex mode and move to the Top viewport to quickly select the outer vertices. From another view be sure to deselect the center vertices. Once you have them deselected, move

the vertices inward toward the palm as shown in Figures 6-179 and 6-180.

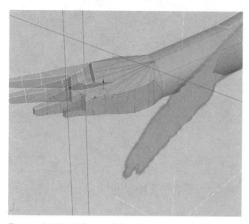

Figure 6-177: Edges selected

Figure 6-180: Vertices adjusted

22. We need to do the same to the pointer finger and the inner thumb. Using the Edge tool, divide these two areas and move the vertices inward to create a softer edge for the hand as shown in Figure 6-181.

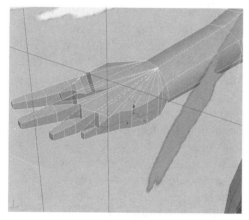

Figure 6-178: Edges divided

Figure 6-181: Hand softened

23. Lastly, Figure 6-182 shows the palm of the hand and how it has been reworked to add more detail. A set of edges were added to the center of the palm and between the fingers and the palm wedge. This is a good chance for you to play around with the model and see

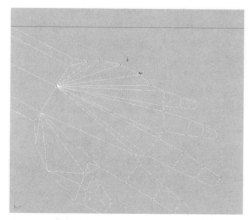

Figure 6-179: Vertices adjusted

what kind of detail you can add with the polys that are there.

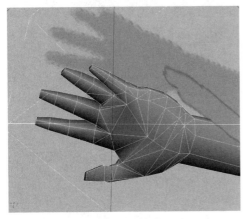

Figure 6-182: Hand detail added

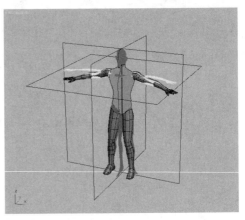

Figure 6-183: Limbs completed

When you are done with the hand you can zoom back out and check the progress that has been made. Figure 6-183 shows off an excellent looking model that has been started. We really can see what this character is going to look like and we've only made it halfway through. Now that we have modeled using the Extrude and Line Render Mesh mode, we will try out a couple of different techniques on the torso and head pieces. Overall the arm was not too difficult a model to create and at the same time we have one great looking piece of the overall body completed.

The Torso and Pelvis

We now move to the torso and the pelvis region of the human body. These are two very powerful regions of the body and will be the major connecting blocks for all of the limbs we have been creating. The arms, legs, and the eventual head will tie in directly to this section, so there are a number of things to keep in mind while we model it.

By keeping the joint sections relatively similar to one another we make it much easier on ourselves down the road when we do attach this all together. Also the poly count is something to be mindful of, as we want this model to look like it belongs together. If it were too high or too low it would not mesh well and would feel like it was not part of the rest of the model. The torso and the pelvis are both attached as one section in this model and will be addressed at the same time while creating the model.

Okay, the sooner we get started with this model, the sooner we'll have it completed, so let's get things rolling!

1. We already have the outline of the torso and pelvis created from earlier. Let's select the front torso and then under the rollout in the Modify tab, select the **Attach** button. Then click on the side line of the torso to make this all one selection. See Figure 6-184.

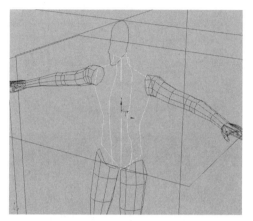

Figure 6-184: Attaching lines

2. Now that we have the line segments connected we can get rid of the interior segments. Switch the line mode to **Segment** and then select the interior segments that are no longer needed. Delete them once you have them selected. When that's done it should look like what you see in Figure 6-185.

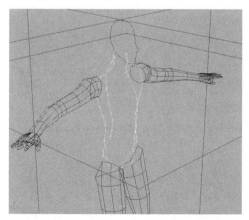

Figure 6-185: Segments cleaned up

3. For the next step, I want you to switch to **Vertex** mode and then under the Geometry rollout, check the **Connect** box next to the Refine button and then click on the **Refine** button. This allows us to connect our vertices together with a segment. With the Refine button selected go to the neck section of the model and click on one of the vertices at the top of the neck. Usually, a pop-up window will come up the first time around and ask you about connecting or refining. Choose **connect only** and check the **Do not show again** box as well, then click **OK**.

4. Now work your way around the top portion of the neck and when you get back to the first vertex you started with, right-click to end the line.

Your model should now look similar to what we see in Figure 6-186. Connecting the splines together is a fairly simple process, and the action you just did represents the gist of the entire operation that we are going to undertake to make the rest of the torso.

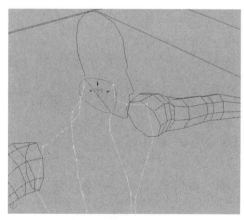

Figure 6-186: Connecting splines

Before we get into connecting any more vertices we need to add a few more lines to help us define the shape of the character

171

better. In Figure 6-187 we have changed out our texture image for the front view with the Male_Front_01-Lines texture file. On this image you will notice a chest line and a collarbone line has been drawn in for you to follow along with.

5. Select **Create Line** under the Geometry rollout. Then using the Front viewport, trace the chest line and the collarbone line as seen in Figure 6-187.

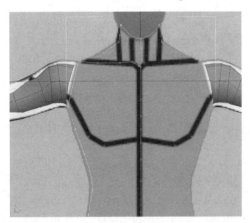

Figure 6-187: Chest and collarbone lines created

6. The next line we want to create is the abdominal section. This has not been drawn but you can reference it from Figure 6-188.

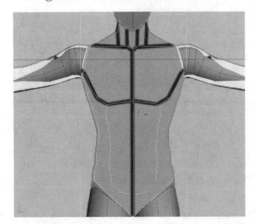

Figure 6-188: Abdominal line

7. In Figure 6-189 you see that the line is in the center of the body and will need to be adjusted in order for us to begin connecting the vertices together. Select the vertices for these two pieces and move the line forward until it resembles the image in Figure 6-190. This gets us far enough out that we can begin working on the overall shape of these segments.

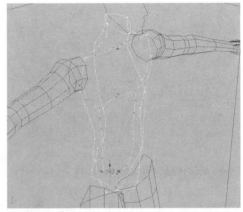

Figure 6-189: Center line point

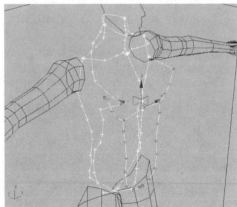

Figure 6-190: Vertices selected and moved

8. We now want to weld several of the vertices together. Starting at the clavicles, select and weld the three vertices together, as seen in Figures 6-191 and 6-192. To weld them together, select

the vertices you want welded and then press the **Fuse** button in the Geometry rollout.

> **Note:**
>
> The Fuse button will simply connect the two vertices together by moving all vertices selected equally toward each other.

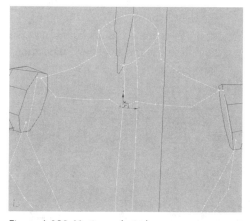

Figure 6-191: Vertices selected

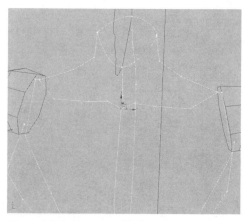

Figure 6-192: Vertices welded

9. The next pair of vertices are on the end of the clavicles. You can see the selection highlighted in Figure 6-193. Select one pair at a time and fuse them together. In Figure 6-194 we are fusing together the abdominal segments with the lower chest region as well as the

inside section of the chest with the center line.

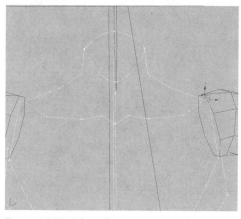

Figure 6-193: Selected vertices

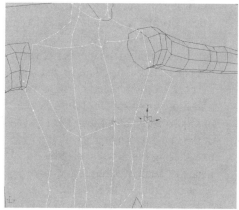

Figure 6-194: Fused vertices

10. Next up, we start moving the chest and abdominal segments around. The top section of the chest line can be moved back toward the deltoids where they will eventually be connected. The abdominal lines can be moved back as well. These lines should not be placed farther out than the center line of the body. Refer to Figure 6-195 for the changes.

173

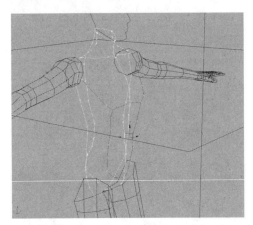

Figure 6-195: Revised vertex positions of the chest and abdominal segments

11. We now want to add another chest line to work with. In the Front viewport, select **Create New Line** and add a second line above the first chest line. You should mimic the number of vertices placed in the first line so that when we connect them together there will be a well-prepared spot for them. Notice in Figure 6-196 how the left-hand side of the line ends right at the deltoid vertex. Placing the newly created vertex near that section of the arm is a good habit to get into when modeling separate pieces that will eventually get welded together.

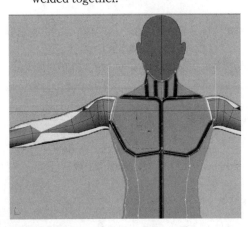

Figure 6-196: New chest line is created

12. In Figures 6-197 and 6-198 we move the new chest line out to the front of the model and then manipulate the vertices by shifting them in toward the body to mimic the same flow of the first chest lines. This set of lines is going to be offset from the body more than the first set of chest lines. Also notice how the top vertices are pulled in line with the deltoid mesh. As with the other chest lines and abdominal lines, it is helpful to use the side view to position the vertices.

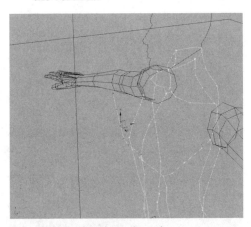

Figure 6-197: Chest line adjusted

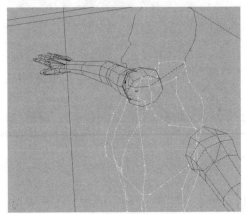

Figure 6-198: Chest line adjusted

13. With the front of the character outlined, we now move to the back of the model.

Select the center line down the back as seen in Figure 6-199. Make three copies of this segment to be used for the back. We could make a new set of back lines separately but this tends to offer us the same results without the extra overhead. A few minor tweaks and these copies will work just fine. In Figure 6-200 we have made a single copy of the segment to the right of the model. In Figure 6-201 we have made a copy of this segment to the left of the model and placed each copy near the outer neck line region.

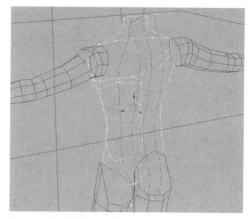

Figure 6-201: Segment copy

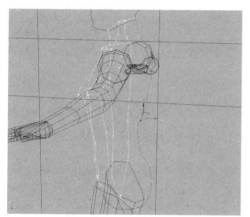

Figure 6-199: Back center line selected

14. Starting at the top of the model we get the neck ready to have the new back lines attached in. Place two new vertices on the back of the neck line as seen in Figure 6-202 by selecting the **Refine** button under the Geometry rollout. To add another vertex to work with, make sure that the Connect check box is not checked.

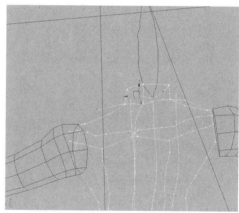

Figure 6-202: New vertices on the neck

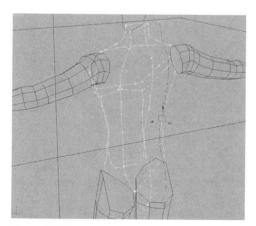

Figure 6-200: Segment copy

15. With the two new neck vertices created we can now weld our back lines to them as shown in Figure 6-203. The neck lines have been repositioned slightly away from the body to round

out the neck a little better and the back lines have been adjusted to tie in with the neck. Go ahead at this point and weld these together.

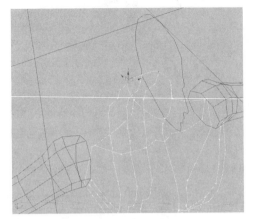

Figure 6-203: Vertices welded

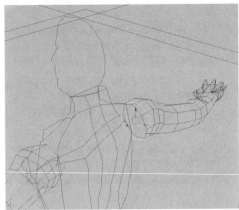

Figure 6-204: Circle created and moved to deltoid

16. In order to tie the arm into the body and give the body the necessary shape to fit with the arm we add a circle line to the scene. The Circle tool is found under Create tab | Shapes. Draw the circle in using the Right viewport near the shoulder so that you can get the size of the shape close without too much adjusting later. Once you have the circle drawn, move it over and position it between the deltoids and the torso as seen in Figure 6-204. We want this to be positioned fairly close, so using the Rotate tool, rotate the circle around until the line is reasonably close to that of the deltoid's outer edge. See Figure 6-205.

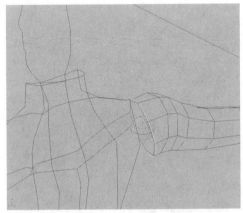

Figure 6-205: Rotated to match deltoid angle

17. Next select the torso and attach the two circles to the torso object as seen in Figure 6-206. You'll notice in Figure 6-206 that two segments have been selected that lie within the open area of the deltoids. These two segments can be selected and deleted now.

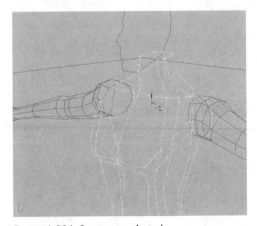

Figure 6-206: Segments selected

18. In Figure 6-207 all of the vertices have been selected to show you what needs to be welded together. At this time go through your model and weld the vertices together that line up with the four major positions of the circle line. The chest line needs to be connected as well, but we must first add a new vertex to both circles before we can do this. Place the vertices similar to those shown in Figure 6-208 and then weld the chest and circle lines together.

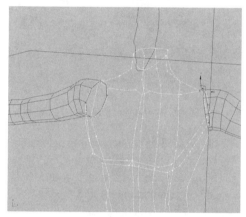

Figure 6-207: Vertices highlighted

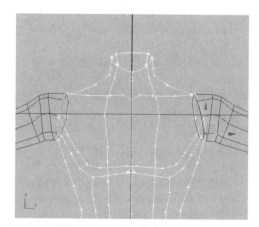

Figure 6-208: Chest area refined

The model is now ready to begin connecting a set of segments around the body lines. These segment lines will help round out

the shape and allow us to create a 3D workable mesh. You can start anywhere you want; we have chosen to start at the waist and work our way up.

19. Check the **Connect** check box, select the **Refine** button, and left-click on the back vertex. Follow the vertices that tend to be at the same height as the one you selected and work your way around. When you get all the way back to the first one you selected, right-click on it and that will place the new segment in. Refer to Figure 6-209. Continue to do this, working over the pelvis region and then working your way around and up. Remember to maintain the same height level in your line as you work around the model. If you get off and need to start again, just use the trusty ol' Ctrl+Z and try again.

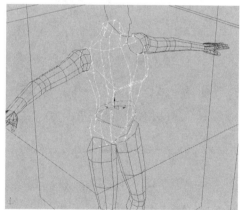

Figure 6-209: New segment created

20. Work the new segments all the way up to the bottom of the chest, covering as much of the back and buttocks area as you can.

21. At this point it would be helpful to have more visual feedback with what you are doing. To do this we can add a Surface modifier to the stack. Under the

177

Parameters rollout for the Surface modifier, you need to check the **Flip normals** check box and possibly increase the threshold a few inches. Patch Topology is another option that we can play with. Steps allow us to increase or decrease the number of polygons used in the model we are working on. Try setting it to 5 or 6 and take a look at the model. It will have a much smoother look and feel to it as it has a much higher poly count. Go ahead and change the Topology setting to **0**. This gives us an exact look at what we are doing and what we are going to end up with. See Figure 6-210.

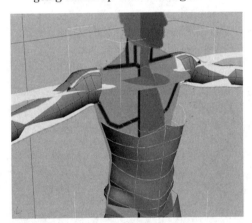

Figure 6-210: Surface modifier applied

22. Let's clean up the workspace before we continue with the rest of this model. At the moment the arms, legs, and our reference material make it difficult to work on this model from every view, so select the torso model and go to the Tools menu. On the top bar select the **Isolate Selection** option. The model is now centered and everything that was not selected has been hidden, as shown in Figure 6-211.

We now have a much better working environment for completing the torso model.

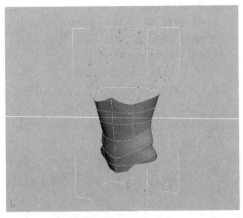

Figure 6-211: Cleanup time

23. Move to the neck region of the model and continue connecting the vertices like we did on the waist area before. You may want to add new vertices in while you connect things together; these are adjustments that are best done while winding around the character. Sometimes as you make your way around the character you may find that there are no vertices in place to keep the flow of the line going smoothly. In such cases, just click on the line and add a new vertex. In Figure 6-212, we have roughed in the neck faces, but don't stop there; continue to work it on around.

24. While we work with it, we can finish up the rest of the back. Check out Figure 6-213. The back is now mostly complete — just two more polys to create and then it's back to the front.

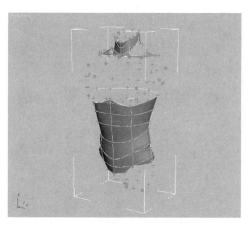

Figure 6-212: Neck detail

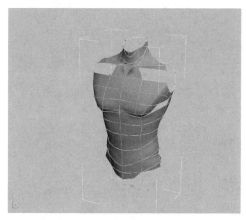

Figure 6-214: New segments created

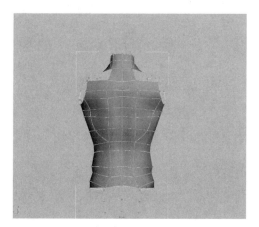

Figure 6-213: Back refined

26. In Figure 6-215 we complete the connections and have an amazing looking chest model that is ready for a head! You may now press the **Exit Isolation mode** button at this time and return to the scene with all of our other models. So far, so good. Figure 6-216 gives us a solid look at the model thus far and everything appears to be in order. The limbs are lining up nicely with the torso, everything seems to be scaled well with one another, and the poly count for each section is matching up just right. We are definitely on course

25. On the front of the model, add several new segments to the pectoral region. Start by adding a horizontal line across the chest from the outer edge in to the center line. Add two lines here and then add the vertical lines down the chest. The vertical lines need adjusting, so move the vertices out a little to round out the chest nicely. Continue connecting the vertices together and adding extra ones where needed. Refer to Figure 6-214 for some of the new segment additions.

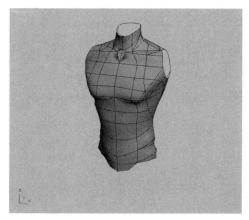

Figure 6-215: Connections completed

179

and it would appear that we only lack one final piece to cap this off with.

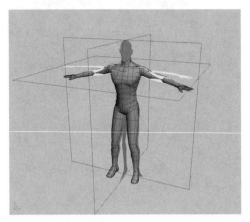

Figure 6-216: Model

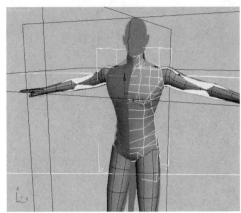

Figure 6-217: Right side selected

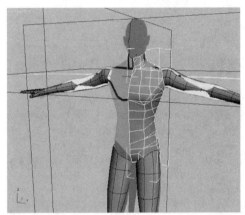

Figure 6-218: Polys deleted

27. Before we begin modeling the head, we should connect the arm and leg models to the torso. Since the torso was created as a whole model, we only need half of this model to attach the limbs to. So, select the torso and add an Edit Mesh modifier to the stack. Select Polygon mode and select the right side of the model as seen in Figure 6-217. Once you have these polys selected, delete them from the mesh as shown in Figure 6-218. You should also delete the leg and arm reference copies as they will not be used from here on out. They served their purpose well as we modeled and gave us a good peek into what it was going to look like.

28. With only half of the chest remaining, select it and attach the arm and leg models to it. See Figure 6-219. With the body now attached we can make a reference copy and mirror it next to the original as seen in Figure 6-220.

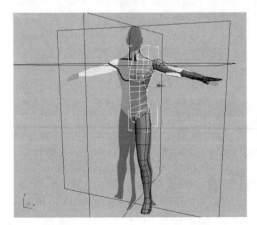

Figure 6-219: Arm and leg attached

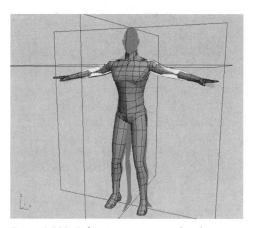

Figure 6-220: Reference copy created and mirrored

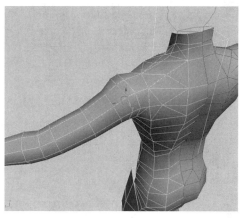

Figure 6-222: Vertices welded

29. Next, go to Vertex mode and zoom in on the shoulder joint. Most of the vertices have been placed very close to the adjoining vertex, making discerning the pairs of vertices that are to be connected very simple. Start by selecting one pair at a time and weld them together, as seen in Figure 6-221, until you have made it all the way around. See Figures 6-222 and 6-223.

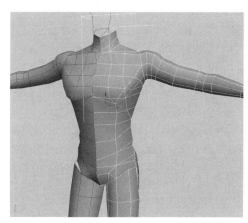

Figure 6-223: Vertices welded

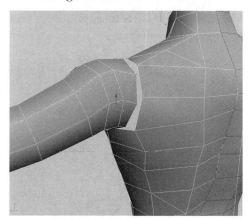

Figure 6-221: Weld vertices

30. Next we want to weld the leg to the pelvis. We will have to move a few of these vertices in or out to better align with the overall shape. Start selecting and welding vertices, working your way from the front to the back. See Figure 6-224.

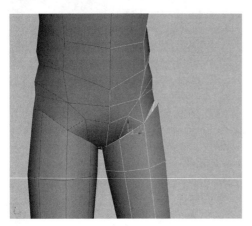

Figure 6-224: Vertices welded

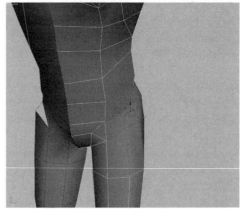

Figure 6-226: Bottom edge divided

31. Like we saw with the foot and the hand models, there are times when we need to divide a polygon to get an extra vertex to work with. In Figure 6-225 we do just that. Change to Edge mode and select the side of the pelvis. Next, divide the bottom edge in half. See Figure 6-226. Switch back to Vertex mode and select the vertices in Figure 6-227. Weld them together and adjust each slightly to smooth out the connection. See Figure 6-228.

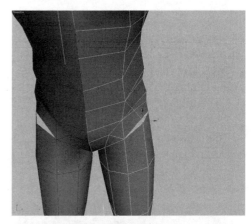

Figure 6-227: Vertices selected

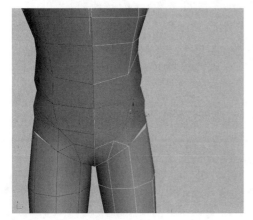

Figure 6-225: Edges selected

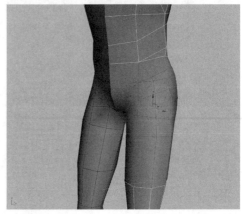

Figure 6-228: Vertices welded and adjusted

The Head

The last step in the modeling process takes us to the very top, the head itself. So far the model is looking really good, so let's top it off with an awesome looking head that will be the crowning achievement of the model!

We already have a side view and a front view of the head outlined. We may only use the side lines in the model, but the front will be useful for reference.

1. Let's check the right view of the profile. We need an extra set of lines in there as well as an ear, so get the Line tool and add a line in the face to represent the side plane of the face, the jaw line, and the ear as seen in Figure 6-229.

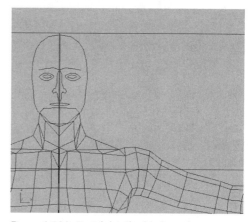

Figure 6-230: Facial detail added

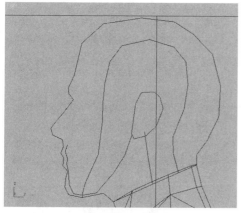

Figure 6-229: Jaw and ear lines

2. Next we switch to the Front viewport and draw in the eye, the eyebrow, the nose, and a reference line for the mouth. See Figure 6-230.

3. Move both the front and side lines into place. For this, please refer to the 3ds max files on the companion CD. There are several small changes and tweaks that are best reviewed with the actual file worked on at the time the model was adjusted. See Figure 6-231.

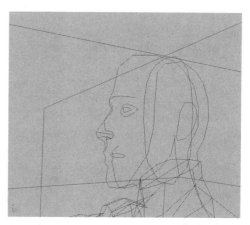

Figure 6-231: Lines moved forward and adjusted to face

4. The next step is to attach all the lines together and then start connecting the vertices. In Figure 6-232 we have attached the lines together and have begun adding segments to the top and front of the face.

183

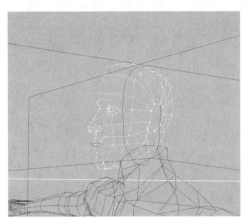

Figure 6-232: Lines attached

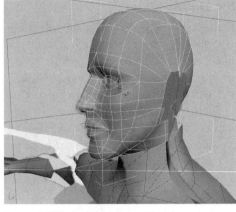

Figure 6-233: Open areas connected

5. We continue working over the face, adding more detail in the cheekbone areas and connecting the nose, eye, and brow together. Be sure to add a Surface modifier to the stack so we can watch the progress as we work.

> **Note:**
>
> To view the surface property while you work in the Line mode, be sure to set the **Show end result** button on.

6. In Figure 6-233 we see a good deal of progress has been made in connecting the open areas together. Another set of lines has been added to the top of the head and helped round out that part of the model. The cheekbone region has also had several line segments added horizontally and vertically to give us more mesh to work with and a better sculpted cheekbone.

7. We have only a few open polys left to wrap up. Go ahead and build these polys and then take a moment to look it over. Some adjustments around the nose and mouth may be needed. In Figure 6-234 we see the end result after the model has all of the open polygons

filled and a few minor tweaks to the facial features. You can see the front view finished off as well in Figure 6-235. The face has a solid overall appearance and will work great for animating and texturing. Modifications to the head will also be easy to do; by simply playing around with the brow lines, nose lines, and other features you can quickly adjust the mesh to look more individual and less generic.

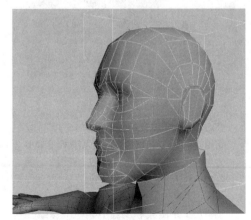

Figure 6-234: Face geometry filled

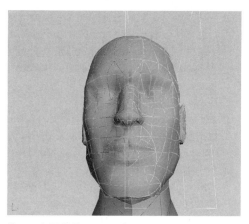

Figure 6-235: Face complete

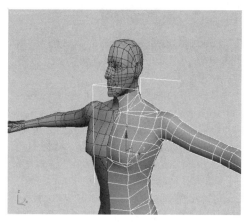

Figure 6-236: Body selected

8. We are now ready to attach the head to the rest of the body. Select the body mesh, as shown in Figure 6-236, and then attach the face model to it. See Figure 6-237. The reference model helps us to quickly see the overall effect. Take a moment to zoom out and look at the model from different angles.

9. Only a few tweaks are needed here and there, but for now those can wait as we concentrate on welding the neck joint together. Zoom in on the neck and select Vertex mode. Most of these vertices line up well enough that you can see which ones are going to go with each other. Select these vertices and weld them together like we have been doing with the other joints. Start at the front of the model and work your way around to the back. If there are any "extra" vertices, simply add one by dividing an edge near the extra vertex. See Figure 6-238.

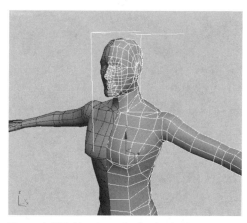

Figure 6-237: Head attached to body

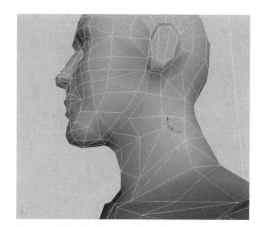

Figure 6-238: Vertices welded together

185

Tweak and Review

The body is now complete and ready to be inspected for minor changes and/or additions.

1. After looking over the model we see that the face would benefit from a more well-defined ear. Select the character mesh and choose Poly Edit mode. Select the inner polygons of the ear, as shown in Figure 6-239, and using the Bevel tool, extrude them toward the head and then slightly bevel them in as seen in Figure 6-240.

2. In Figures 6-241 and 6-242 we have a chance to study the creation and make sure that everything is in place the way we want it to be. It is best to make any changes to the model now before we begin breaking down the UV maps. Several small changes have been made to the model such as softening the chest and decreasing the outward size. Several edges have been turned to allow for both better lighting and better folds during animations. Take a moment to look over the finished model and see if you can locate the

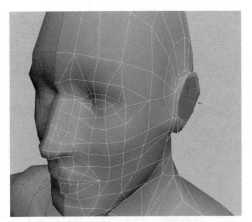

Figure 6-239: Inner ear polygons selected

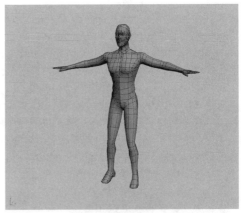

Figure 6-241: Character model

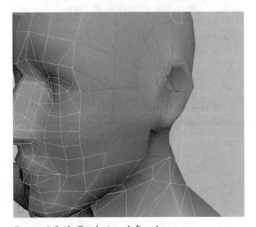

Figure 6-240: Ear being defined

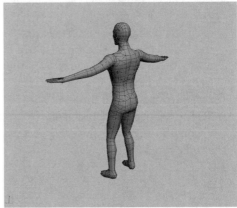

Figure 6-242: Character model

changes. By looking at the model in its finished and unfinished states you will have a better understanding of the subtle changes and begin developing an eye for seeing the minor imperfections in the model. A few simple tweaks and we are ready to run this character through the UV process!

UV Mapping

UV mapping has been covered in detail previously, so here we will only touch on the aspects that affect this model. There are countless variations for UV mapping a human character, and a number of gameplay concerns will determine what to apply the most detail to, whether or not there will be separate maps for different uses, etc.

We are going to make this simple, straightforward, and easy to manipulate at any point in time by any other artist. For our purposes it will provide the amount of detail we need and lay out the body in a manner that is simple to work on. Everything will be placed on a single map and the UV coordinates will be overlapped to save on space and allow for more texture detail.

1. Select the character mesh and, in the Modifier drop-down list, add an Unwrap UVW modifier to the stack. Under the Parameters rollout, click on the **Edit** button. The UV coordinates are all stacked on each other and twisted around in an unusable manner as seen in Figure 6-243.

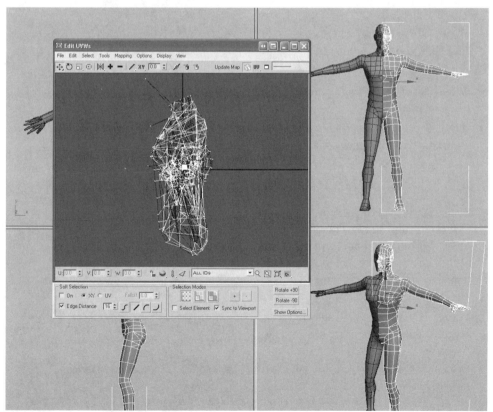

Figure 6-243: UVW coordinates

2. Let's clean up the UVs a little so we can see what we're working with. Click on the **Unwrap UVW** modifier in the stack so that it is highlighted. Once it is highlighted you can then work with the model in the viewport. Select all the faces of the model either in the viewport or in the Edit UVWs window. With everything selected, check the Y axis under Sub Object Parms and then click on the **Planar Map** button. The results should look like Figure 6-244.

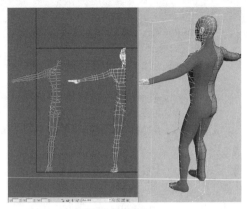

Figure 6-245: Back half selected

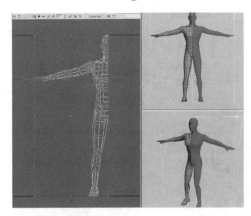

Figure 6-244: Planar map

3. Working with the viewport and the Edit UVWs window, select the back side of the mesh. Move your cursor into the Edit UVWs window and right-click on one of the selected vertices. Choose **Detach Edge Verts**. The edges are now separated and can be moved to the left. Lock the Move tool to **Horizontal** and move it over. See Figure 6-245.

4. Next select the hand polys and apply a planar map to the whole selected mesh. Scale it down to a smaller size and then separate it in half, similar to the way you did with the body, as seen in Figure 6-246.

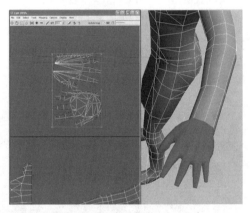

Figure 6-246: Hand polys planar mapped

5. Select the head poly as seen in Figure 6-247. Apply another planar map to this one and scale it down like in Figure 6-247.

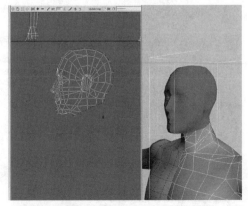

Figure 6-247: Head side planar mapped

6. Now select the front plane of the head from the Perspective window and apply a planar map. Scale it down and align it with the side view, as seen in Figure 6-248. We now have everything in place; let's weld these two edges together. Select one side of vertices, right-click on a selected vertex, and choose the **Stitch** function. You may need to weld some of the vertices independently from the whole selection. If you get a strange result where the edges pull across each other, undo the operation and go at it one vertex pair at a time. The result will look like Figure 6-249.

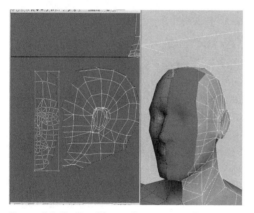

Figure 6-248: Head front planar mapped

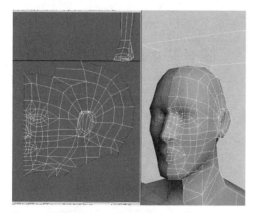

Figure 6-249: Front and side connected

7. The foot is next up. Select the bottom of the foot and apply a planar map to it. We are going to do the same for each side of the foot, the top of the foot, and the back of the foot. With these pieces mapped out we can now align them next to one another and then weld the edges of the top and sides. Leave the bottom of the foot as a separate piece. See Figure 6-250.

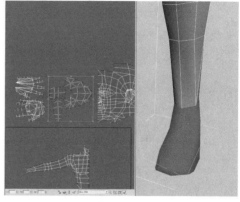

Figure 6-250: Foot mapped

8. The pieces of the map are flattened out but still need a few tweaks to the outer edges. The major points of interest here are the top of the head and the outer portions of the arms, legs, and torso. Select the vertices in these areas and expand them out close to the width of the other faces on the body. See Figure 6-251.

189

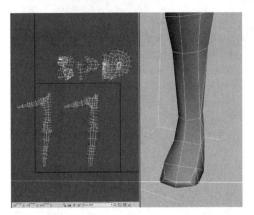

Figure 6-251: UVs adjusted

9. We can now reposition the UV map within the blue box. Use Figure 6-252 as an example for where to place the UV map. As we mentioned earlier, there is a wide range of possible place-ments for the UV map, so take this as one example. For other projects you may need to adjust the UV map in a completely different pattern.

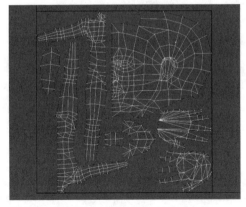

Figure 6-252: UV map example

10. Included with the model is a burned UVW map. See Figure 6-253.

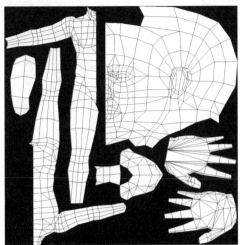

Figure 6-253: Burned UVW map

Texturing

It's time to move on to a rather simple but effective texture map that will be used in conjunction with the Normal map. Because we will be applying a normal to the model, we have no need of making a texture with shadows or overly detailing the base map. Our texture will be used mostly for color and texture detail purposes.

1. Open up your 2D paint program, pref-erably Photoshop, and then find the Burned UVW map shown in Figure 6-253. This map has all the information we need in order to work over the tex-ture. It provides us with a detailed outline and boundary of the character's UV map.

2. The first step is to create a color layer for each of the separate UV sections. Create a new layer in Photoshop and, using the Draw Selection tool, outline the head UV and then place a fleshtone color inside this selection. Use this same process to create the rest of the colored layers for the texture map. The

results should look similar to Figure
6-254.

Figure 6-254: Color layers

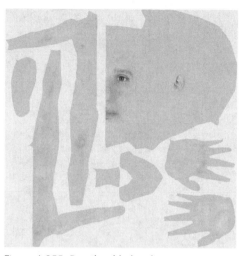

Figure 6-255: Details added to the texture

3. We can continue to add some detail to
    this texture that will enhance the skin
    tone and flesh-like look of the model.
    For this example, let's go very light on
    these areas, but if you want to add
    more detail and push it to its limits feel
    free to do so. For our purposes we are
    simply setting up a very solid generic
    model and texture that can be quickly
    and easily manipulated for varying
    results.

4. In Figure 6-255 we add eye details, fin-
    gernails, skin wrinkles, ear details, and
    an overall skin texture to give the
    model more realism. Notice along the
    edges of the model we have kept the
    color the same so that the seams will
    not become an issue. Sometimes when
    working over seams you can copy and
    paste the textured edge to the non-tex-
    tured edge and then blend the
    overlaying areas with the Erase tool to
    match the edges.

5. Save the file with whatever extension
    you want and then switch back to 3D
    Studio MAX to see the results of the
    new texture maps. You may need to
    apply a material to the model and then
    load in the texture file you just saved.
    Once you have it up and running, take a
    few moments to look it over and see
    what you think. This is where we can
    spend countless hours going back and
    forth between tweaking in Photoshop
    and viewing the results in max.

For your first go at this type of model I suggest that you stick with a simple map that
has some very straightforward edges for
blending and then work your way up to a
more photorealistic texture.

The final results of the model look quite solid and can be seen in Figure 6-256.

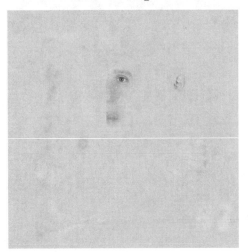

Figure 6-256: The end results of the texturing process

Rigging

The last phase of this project takes us to the rigging portion of the character. We've reached the point of doing some serious surgery to the character. We are going to implant an entire skeleton system and then affix it to the skin. So let's begin by creating a biped that will fit our model.

1. Go to **Create | Systems** and then click on the **Biped** button.

2. Inside the Perspective viewport, click and drag upward to create the biped. The biped will grow in height as you drag up, so go ahead and get it close to the height of your model. When you get it close, let go of the left mouse button to stop the sizing of the biped.

The biped has a very robust skeletal structure with a number of options for adjusting it to fit with your creations. For our character we are going to break it down like Figure 6-257. Let's review this image and

set up the skeleton with the same parameters.

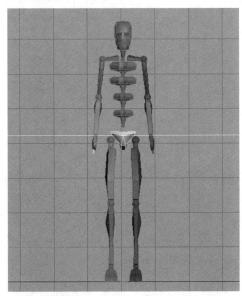

Figure 6-257: Biped that has not been adjusted to fit the model

3. We need to bring up the parameters for the biped, which can be found under the Motions tab. Be sure you have the biped selected so you can see the options available. Under the Biped rollout there is a stickman icon (aka Figure mode). Click this icon and then go to the Structure rollout. Under this rollout we find several options for the biped model.

4. First, set the Biped Spine links to **3**. Set the Fingers to **5** and the Finger Links to **3**. Set the Toes to **1** and the Toe Links to **1** as well. Continue down the list and check the **Forearm Twist** box and set the Forearm Links to **2**. This allows for a better twist for the forearm and wrist.

Now that we have all of the bones needed, we can scale the biped to fit our character. In Figure 6-258 we see the unscaled biped.

You can tell that things do not line up and that the arms and legs are not even close to being set in the right place. We'll work over the spine first.

5. While still in Figure mode select the **Scale** tool and then select a spine link on your biped. We are going to scale each of these down to fit into our character and line up with the cross sections of the mesh where we want it to bend. We want an area where edges cut all the way around the midsection, not in the middle of a polygon, because the edges act as hinges and make the bends and folds much more manageable.

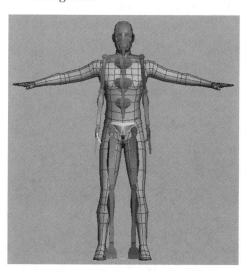

Figure 6-258: Unscaled biped

6. In Figure 6-259 we have scaled the spine down and placed the joints in three specific places. Please take note of the placement: the middle of the abdomen, directly below the chest, and the top of the chest. These are three very good places to work with. You will also notice the arms and the legs are rotated. Go ahead and rotate the arms and legs into position and move the

clavicles down to line up with Figure 6-259.

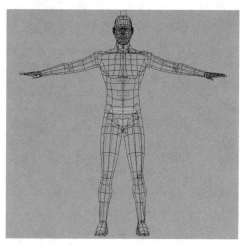

Figure 6-259: Refined biped in front view

Note:

The biped has been aligned and fitted from the front view only to work with our mesh.

7. The biped works in the front view, but as you can tell from any other view it's not exactly good to go. From the Top viewport, select the clavicle bone and get ready to rotate it back a little as seen in Figure 6-260. Continue to work the arm on down, aligning it with the mesh. In Figure 6-261 notice where the elbow joint is placed and configure yours appropriately. We have three sets of edges on the elbow joint; we want to place our hinge in the midsection of these three as seen in Figure 6-261. The hand is the last in line and can be worked over the same as everything else has been.

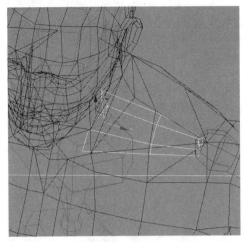

Figure 6-260: Arm bone selected

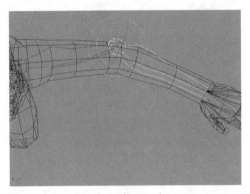

Figure 6-261: Biped nearly complete

8. Copy and paste this section of the biped to the other side; since we have perfect symmetry it makes things much quicker. Select the arm (double-click on the clavicle and it will automatically select the lower extremities) as seen in Figure 6-262.

Note:

The hand has been scaled and rotated to fit the hand properly.

9. Under the Copy/Paste rollout click on the **Posture** button, then press the

Copy Posture button below it to copy the current selection.

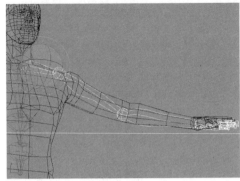

Figure 6-262: Biped arm is selected and ready to be copied.

10. Next, press the **Paste Posture opposite** button. In Figure 6-263 the right arm now has the properties of the left arm. This makes our job that much easier and keeps things more even in the long run. Rotate around just to make sure everything is in place and get ready to work on the legs.

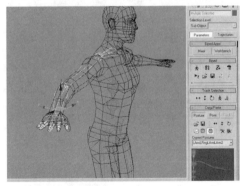

Figure 6-263: Biped's left arm has been copied and pasted to the right arm.

11. The legs need to be scaled and rotated as well as moved over a little to fit correctly as seen in Figure 6-264. Starting with the upper thigh, scale and rotate it to fit. Similar to the arm, the knee joint is broken down into three sections. We

set the joint to the center section which should do fine, as seen in Figure 6-265. Next, set the rest of the leg placement to mimic Figure 6-265. Once you have that ready, select the biped's leg bones and copy them.

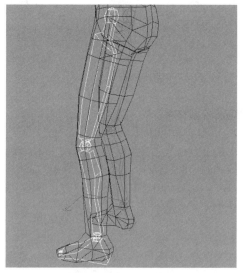

Figure 6-264: Legs ready to be scaled

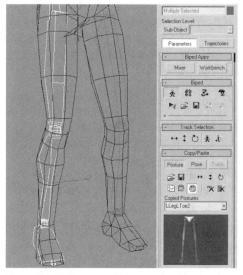

Figure 6-265: Leg is scaled, copied, and pasted to the other side.

12. Lastly, make sure the head and neck are in place. With that completed, zoom out and take a look at the biped figure you created. Take another look at the joints and the placement of the bones to make sure that everything will bend and twist in the right place. See Figure 6-266.

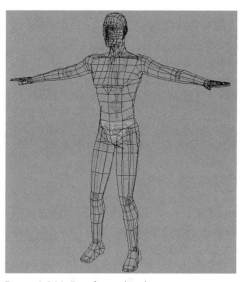

Figure 6-266: Biped completed

The next phase is to create the advanced rig setup, which is simply an addition to the biped skeleton.

Advanced Rig Setup

Have you have ever rigged a character or created a skeleton? If you have, you might be the first to say that it's not the greatest job in the world. Well, it's probably because the process wasn't easy and it was cumbersome due to limitations with the skeleton and weighting systems.

Let's just say we found a great way to use what's already there and simply make it better. The basic biped character put on adrenaline. Typically, the areas around the shoulder and the front and side of the legs always take a beating when it comes to extreme movement with the animations.

Not anymore! An excellent system, which I learned from Juan Martinez and Blur Studios, helps out in big ways for creating near unbreakable shoulders and legs.

Let's briefly talk about what we are going to do and then we'll walk through each step involved.

When a character rotates its arm upward and twists or places it in front with a weapon, the shoulder tends to take a beating. Oftentimes if it's not a proper physique, you will get shoulder polys that pop into the chest area or dip down and distort the actual character. The leg tends to have the same problems since it cannot tuck into the body without going directly into and through the body.

To put it simply, the devised system adds an extra bone to each shoulder area and two extra bones to each leg area. That, in essence, is all we are doing. By adding these bones we eliminate the problems.

Advanced_Rig_Biped.max is found at \Tutorials\Art_Tutorials\Advanced_Rig_ Setup.

Let's use the biped character that we have been working on.

1. In the Front view create two dummy boxes by the shoulder and clavicle joint. You can find dummy boxes by going to the **Create tab | Helpers | Dummy**.

2. Call the larger dummy box **bone_ Slerp_left** and the smaller box **Shoulder_left_nub**.

Now we need to link them to their respective bones.

3. With the Link tool selected, link Shoulder_left_nub to **bone_Slerp_left**. Then link bone_Slerp_left to **Bip01 Spine2**.

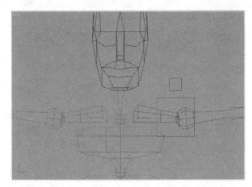

Figure 6-267: Dummy boxes

Why link it there? Here's where a little understanding will go a long way. The bone_Slerp_left is linked to Bip01 Spine2 because of the need to have it affect the clavicle and upper arm bones. If we were to link the Slerp bone to either of the two bones, we would be unable to properly weight this as a separate bone. Remember, we need a bone that will be independent of the clavicle and the upper arm.

Now that the bones are linked we need to apply one more thing to the bones. If you rotate or move the arm or clavicle right now, the boxes would stay in the same place (give it a try). That presents a problem since it's linked to the spine and we want it to follow the movement and rotation of the clavicle and upper arm.

4. Click on **bone_Slerp_left**. Go to the Motions tab and under the Assign Controller rollout, click (highlight) the **Position: Position XYZ** controller. When you click on this it makes the Assign Controller button above it active. Click on the **Assign Controller** button to bring up the Assign Position Controller window. See Figure 6-268.

5. Select **Position Constraint** and click **OK**. You should see a new set of rollout options below. Under the Position

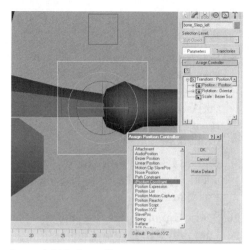

Figure 6-268: Controller options

If Shoulder_left_nub should move down into the bone_Slerp_left box, simply move it back up to its original position.

That's it. Test the new bone to see it in action. As you rotate the upper arm, you should see that the Slerp bone stays with the movement but just slightly behind it.

Do the same procedure for the right shoulder.

Let's move on to the legs. The setup for the legs is the same, yet different. As you can see, we don't have the advantage of using the spine for the "extra bone" to link the dummy boxes to. That means we need to create a new bone and use it as our extra bone.

Constraint rollout tab, click on **Add Position Target**.

6. Select **Bip01 L Clavicle** and **Bip01 L UpperArm**. Inside the Position Constraint rollout, the two bones you clicked on should appear in the Target Weight window. Select the **Clavicle** and change the weight to **15**. Then select the **upper arm** and change its weight to **70**.

Note:

Watch the Slerp box as you change the weight of the bones. The box moves from left to right, adjusting to the amount you type in.

7. Now select **Rotation: Euler XYZ** from the Assign Controller rollout. Click on the **Assign Controller** tab and select **Orientation Constraint**.

8. Under the Orientation Constraint rollout, select **Add Orientation Target**. Click on **Bip01 L Clavicle** and **Bip01 L UpperArm** to add them to the list. Change the Bip01 L Clavicle weight to **70** and Bip01 L UpperArm to **50**.

9. In the Front view create four dummy boxes on the side of the biped approximately the same size as shown in Figure 6-269. Notice that the center box is positioned just above the rotation point of the leg.

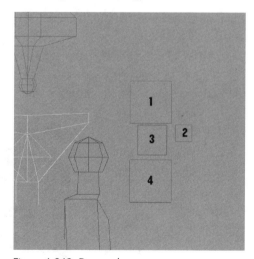

Figure 6-269: Dummy boxes

10. Name them as follows:

1 — Hipjoint_left_Top_nub
2 — Hipjoint_left_nub
3 — bone_Hipjoint_left
4 — Hipjoint_left_Bottom_nub

> **Note:**
>
> Remember when you set up the bones that they need to be placed just slightly away from the actual model geometry. In order for the bones to have a good effect, it's important that they reside next to the model. This applies to the shoulder and leg setups. If the bone is too far away, the rotation effect will be too much. If the bone is too close, the effect will be too small.

The top and bottom hip joints will become the constraint controllers since we don't have the extra bone to work with like we did with the shoulder setup.

11. Link Hipjoint_left_Top_nub and bone_Hipjoint_left to **Bip01 Pelvis**.

12. Link Hipjoint_left_nub to **bone_Hipjoint_left**.

13. Link Hipjoint_left_Bottom_nub to **Bip01 L Thigh**.

That will do it for the linking information.

14. In the Front view, create the same set of boxes and place them in front of the leg as shown in Figure 6-270.

1 — Thigh_left_Top_nub
2 — Thigh_left_nub
3 — bone_Thigh_left
4 — Thigh_left_Bottom_nub

15. Link Thigh_left_Top_nub and bone_Thigh_left to **Bip01 Pelvis**.

16. Link Thigh_left_nub to **bone_Thigh_left**.

17. Link Thigh_left_Bottom_nub to **Bip01 R Thigh**.

18. Let's go back to the Front view and select **bone_Hipjoint_left**. Do just like we did with the shoulder. Under the Assign Controller rollout, select **Position** and then click the **Assign Controller** button.

19. Choose **Position Constraint**. Then under Position Constraint click on **Add Position Target**.

20. Select **Hipjoint_left_Top_nub** and **Hipjoint_left_Bottom_nub**.

21. Change the weight for Hipjoint_left_Top_nub to **75** and Hipjoint_left_Bottom_nub to **50**.

22. Next, assign the **Orientation Constraint** to the Rotation controller.

23. Under the Orientation Constraint rollout, click on **Add Orientation Target** and select **Hipjoint_left_top_nub** and **Hipjoint_left_Bottom_nub**.

24. Change the weight for Hipjoint_left_Top_nub to **75** and Hipjoint_left_Bottom_nub to **50**.

25. Apply the same steps to the front boxes as well. Then repeat the procedure for the right leg setup.

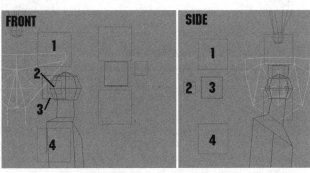

Figure 6-270: Dummy boxes

26. Once you have completed the new rig setup, be sure to save it separately as **Advanced_Rig_Biped.max**. The file can be reused for any and all characters you wish to create.

> **Note:**
>
> This type of setup can be used for any joint on the biped. The reason we chose these sections is because they tend to be the most problematic areas when weighting characters for advanced movement and animations.

Now that we have all these cool new bones added, we should skin the character and get it ready for animations.

1. Select the character and apply a Physique modifier to it. Under the Physique rollout, click on the **Attach to Node** button. Then select the hip

box of the biped as seen in Figure 6-271. This brings up the Physique Initialization window in which we need only change one setting. There are a number of options in here and I encourage you to play around with them, but for our immediate project we only need to deal with Vertex — Link Assignment. Change the selection from Deformable to **Rigid** and then click **Initialize**.

Your mesh should look like Figure 6-272 with the orange link lines going through the whole body. If it only appears on one section of the body, then you may have selected the wrong biped bone. You will need to **Ctrl+Z** your way back and then make sure you select the hip bone of the biped and do the previous steps again.

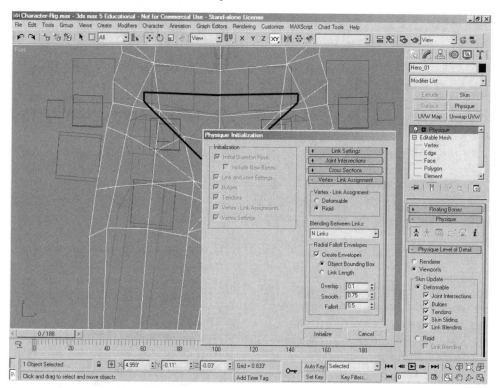

Figure 6-271: Physique Initialization window

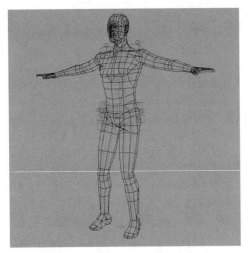

Figure 6-272: Physiqued mesh

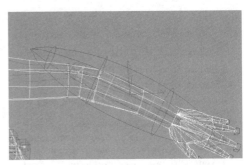

Figure 6-274: Arm links selected and envelopes adjusted

We are going to look at two ways to adjust our weights to the character. The first one is with envelopes.

2. Next select an arm link and, using the envelope parameters, adjust the envelope to fit around the mesh as seen in Figures 6-273 and 6-274.

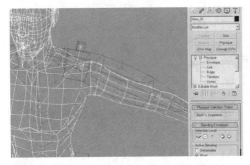

Figure 6-273: Arm links selected and envelopes adjusted

3. Continue to do this with the rest of the links until you have all the envelopes encompassing each part of the mesh just right. You can also use the Copy Paste function under the Edit Commands section of the command panel as shown in Figure 6-275.

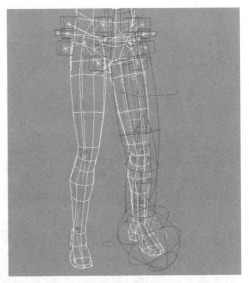

Figure 6-275: Leg links copied and pasted from the left leg to the right leg

The second way to adjust the vertex assignment and weights of our character is to use the Vertex mode.

4. Under the Physique modifier select **Vertex** mode. In this mode, assign vertices to the links that affect how things bend and what moves with what.

5. In Vertex mode, click on the **Select by Link** button. Select the head link and then notice the vertices that are currently assigned to it. Not all of them are vertices we want assigned to it as seen in Figure 6-276.

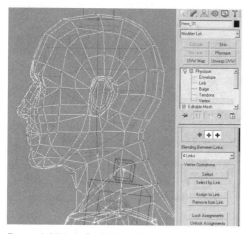

Figure 6-276: Default linked head vertices

now see the head vertices highlighted in bright green as seen in Figure 6-278.

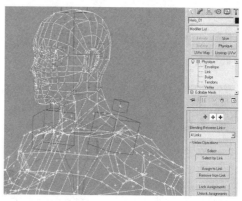

Figure 6-278: Head link selected and the vertices highlighted

6.   The next step may seem a little backward but what we want to do is deselect all the vertices that we want assigned to this link. Select them and under the Vertex operations click on the **Remove from Link** button. Before you remove these vertices make sure that the Vertex Type has the **green** vertex checked. Then click on the head link to deselect those selected vertices from this link. See Figure 6-277.

Let's move on to the forearm now.

8.   Select the vertices that you don't want in this link. With **Remove from Link** selected, click on the forearm links. This is the basic process you will use for the entire character. At times you may need to add vertices to a link that they may not currently be linked to. To do this, simply select the vertex you want added and then use the **Assign to Link** button to assign it to whatever link you select with it. See Figures 6-279 and 6-280.

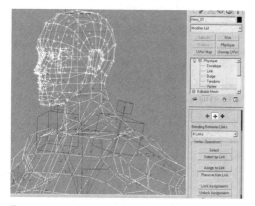

Figure 6-277: Unwanted vertices selected

7.   Change back to the **Select by Link** mode and select the head link. You'll

> **Tip:**
>
> In order to make unattached vertices selectable, be sure to have the blue "+" box (root vertices) checked under the Vertex Link Assignment rollout.

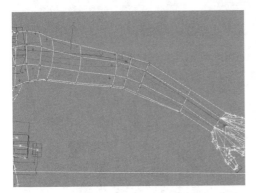

Figure 6-279: Forearm vertices need to be adjusted.

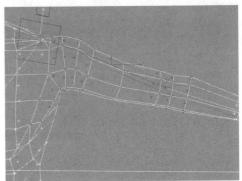

Figure 6-281: Upper arm vertices selected

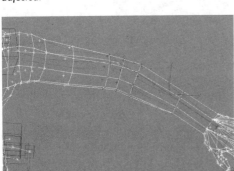

Figure 6-280: Forearm adjusted

Note:

The knee has a darker green color that represents the overlap of the upper thigh and lower leg.

9. Next we work over the upper arm. Take a look at Figure 6-281. Make sure that you overlap the elbow vertices from the forearm to the upper arm. This allows us to have multiple influences over a single vertex, so that when the arm bends it does not completely fold in on itself. See Figure 6-281.

10. The next order of business has to do with the legs. In Figure 6-282 the vertices in the leg have been selected and then removed from the links around the legs and hip section to remove some confusion. This is just one option. In Figure 6-283 the left leg vertices have been applied/added to the leg links.

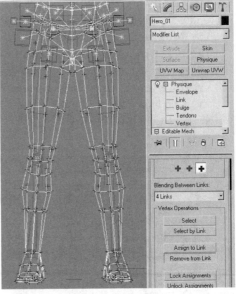

Figure 6-282: Vertices removed from the leg and hip links

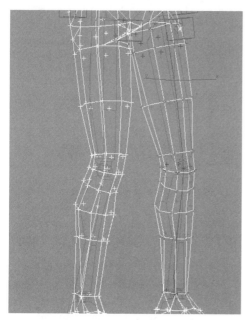

Figure 6-283: Leg links are now applied to the left leg.

11. Continue this same process though the rest of the model. Work the torso over as seen in Figure 6-284, and notice the extra bones added as seen in Figure 6-285.

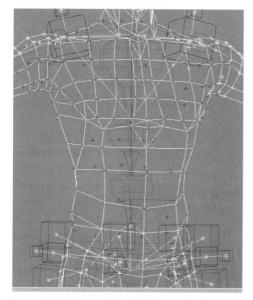

Figure 6-284: Torso of mesh being worked over

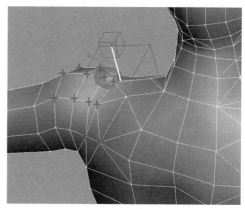

Figure 6-285: Shoulder sections applied to the new bones highlighted

After you have applied the vertices to the body links, you can then select the biped and test the joints by bending the biped into several different positions. Keep an eye on the joints and bends and make sure they do what you want. You may find that some vertices need to be adjusted. If so, go ahead and jump back into it and make those adjustments!

Overall, this can be a fairly simple process. The more complex the geometry and/or the character, the longer it may take, but the basic principle is still the same.

Exporting the Character

Exporting the character is as simple as clicking the Export button. When the character is complete and the physique is properly set up, simply export the model.

1. Click on **File | Export**. Choose the file location you are saving the character in. Then type **character.hgr** for the File Name and **hgr export (*.HGR)** for Save as type.

2. Click **Save**.

3. The HGR export Options dialog is displayed. Be sure that the check box for

Copy textures to output path is checked. Then click **OK**.

Note:

To see the character in action you will need to apply some animations. You can, however, change out the current figure in the game. Navigate to ...\Art_Tutorials\Animation_Export_Test\data\mesh. Inside that folder you will find the Zax_mesh.hgr file. Simply save your character over that file (rename character.hgr to Zax_mesh.hgr) and copy your textures to that directory.

Important:

If your character is not similar in size to the Zax_mesh character, then you will notice some distortion in the animation. That's why we are about to learn how to animate!

■ ■ ■

You've done it! All the modeling tutorials have been accomplished. You have gone from modeling a simple crate to a complex human character. Give yourself a pat on the back!

Now that we have the models completed, it's time to find out how animation works. But first take a slight break; get some rest so that you will be refreshed and raring to go. I'll meet you back here in Chapter 7 with my special guest David March.

Chapter 7

Animation

This chapter contains a fairly complete overview of animation, with some directed tutorials created to give you a start on animating game characters, exporting them into the Ka3D engine, and leading you on your way to an incredible new and exciting skill.

Introduction to Animation

With the creation of moving pictures in the late 1800s and with many new inventions and improvements to the motion picture camera, a new art form arose. The art form known as animation has since made its stain on history and it keeps adapting and growing as it moves into the digital age.

The first 2D animated characters that evoked emotion were created in the early 1900s. With that beginning, a famous studio arose, led by Walt Disney. Since then great strides in technique and artistry have been mastered and passed on.

So what is animation? It's simply a way of bringing things to life. You can also bring storytelling and video gaming to the table in any genre you want to. Furthermore, animation can also give you complete control over your story in the way things move and the way things look.

The following is a timeline of animation in history.

1824 — Peter Mark Roget, who did research in physiology at the University of London, publishs *Persistence of Vision with Regard to Moving Objects*. This book presented the idea that a succession of still images could create the appearance of motion.

1832 — Joseph Plateau develops the phenakistiscope.

1889 — Emile Reynaud patents the praxinoscope, a device that used mirrors to project a sequence of images (along with a fixed background) onto a screen. It was sufficiently complex that only he could run it. The infinite length tape changed the medium from a curiosity into entertainment.

1895 — The age of movie camera and projector begins. Experimentors discover they can stop the crank and restart it to obtain special effects. Example: James Stuart Blackton creates *The Enchanted Drawing* in 1900; a caricature is drawn with no evidence of an artist.

1914 — Windsor McCay produces perhaps the first popular animation, *Gertie the Dinosaur,* which becomes part of his vaudeville act.

1915 — John Bray patents the use of clear cels over a background.

1917 —John Bray patents rotoscoping (developed by Max Fleischer).

1919 — Koko the clown (Max Fleischer) appears.

1920s — Otto Mesmer creates Felix the Cat.

1928 — Walt Disney releases *Steamboat Willie*, an early cartoon with sound; cartoons are now seen as entertainment. Disney innovations over the next 10 to 20 years include the storyboard, pencil tests, and the multi-plane camera stand (3D effects). Disney also promoted the analysis of real-life motion.

1937 — *Snow White* is released at a cost of $1.5 million.

1930s — Fleischer Studios creates Betty Boop and Popeye. Warner Bros. creates Porky Pig, Daffy Duck, and Bugs Bunny.

1940s — Walter Lantz and Woody Woodpecker, Paul Terry and Mighty Mouse, MGM with Tom & Jerry (animators William Hanna and Joseph Barbera)

1963 — Ivan Sutherland and SKETCHPAD at MIT/Lincoln Labs

1972 — At the University of Utah, Ed Catmull develops an animation scripting language and creates an animation of a smooth shaded hand, and Fred Parke creates first computer-generated facial animation.

1974 — National Research Council of Canada releases *Hunger/La Faim* directed by Peter Foldes and featuring Burtnyk and Wein interactive keyframing techniques.

1982 — MAGI releases *Tron*, a movie with a CG premise.

1983 — Bill Reeves at Lucasfilm publishes techniques for modeling particle systems. Demo is *Star Trek II: The Wrath of Khan*. The paper also promotes motion blur.

1984 — In *The Last Starfighter*, CG is used in place of models. Porter and Duff at Lucasfilm publish paper on digital compositing using an alpha channel.

1985 — Girard and Maciejewski at OSU publish a paper describing the use of inverse kinematics and dynamics for animation. Their techniques are used in the animation *Eurythmy*. Ken Perlin at NYU publishes a paper on noise functions for textures. He later applied this technique to add realism to character animations.

1987 — John Lasseter at Pixar publishes a paper describing traditional animation principles. Demos are *Andre and Wally B* and *Luxo Jr.* Craig Reynolds at Symbolics (now at Dreamworks SKG) publishes a paper on self-organizing behavior for groups. Demos are *Stanley and Stella* and *Batman Returns*.

1988 — *Willow* uses morphing in live-action film.

1992 — Beier and Neely, at SGI and PDI respectively, publish an algorithm where line correspondences guide morphing between 2D images. Demo is Michael Jackson video *Black and White*.

1993 — Chen and Williams at Apple publish a paper on view interpolation for 3D walkthroughs. *Jurassic Park* uses CG for realistic living creatures.

1995 — *Toy Story* is the first full-length 3D CG feature film.

Principles of Animation

Animation is all about timing and spacing. The simplest example, and we'll get to animating it soon enough, is the bouncing ball. Of course, there are many more principles that can make a world of difference. The masters in the past have laid all this out for us. It's now just about taking their knowledge and learning and practicing it.

The Illusion of Life by Frank Thomas and Ollie Johnston is an awesome source of animation material and I highly recommend it.

Listed below are the "12 principles of animation" developed by the two Disney animators.

- **Solid Drawing** — Appropriate weight, depth, and balance in drawing

- **Squash and Stretch** — Non-rigid deformation

- **Timing** — Precise movement at which a given character motion occurs

- **Anticipation** — The technique by which the audience's eyes are drawn to where action will occur on screen

- **Staging** — Refers to the way in which character motion and camera movements are set up to convey the mood and intent of a scene

- **Follow-through and Overlapping** — Follow-through refers to the reactive animation that occurs after an action is completed, telling the audience how the character feels about that action.

- **Straight Ahead vs. Pose to Pose** — Characters' actions are either drawn from beginning to end, creating an unpredictable look and feel, or they are broken down into a more predictable set of key poses.

- **Slow In and Slow Out** — Characters' motions tend to be quicker in the middle of an action than at the beginning and end.

- **Arcs** — Organic characters almost always move in motion arcs rather than straight lines.

- **Exaggeration** — Action is enhanced by exaggerated motion.

- **Secondary Action** — Small, complementary motions occurring in a scene.

- **Appeal** — Developed character with interesting and distinct personality.

The two main mediums for animation are 2D and 3D. Both mediums are used for gaming and films. To understand these mediums you must understand the attributes each possesses. An easy way to understand something's attributes is to compare it to something else to see what the differences actually are. In addition to comparing the differences, examples of these mediums also help the association.

Forms of 2D Animation

Cel Animation

The two-dimensional animations created in the early 1900s used a series of drawings placed on pieces of celluloid (cels) and flipped to create the illusion of movement. Walt Disney perfected this technique with his first full-feature film, *Snow White*.

Cut-out Animation

Cut-out animation is a two-dimensional technique that uses flat cutouts to create images. Each shot changes to create a sense of movement. *Monty Python* is well remembered for this method. *South Park* is a newer example of this type of animation.

Forms of 3D Animation

Computer-Generated Animation

Computer-generated, or CG, animation has three-dimensional models, or "wire meshes," that are animated with the use of computers through X, Y, and Z space. Powerful 3D packages can interpolate keys through a series of frames. This form gained its popularity in the 1990s with the introduction of Pixar's *Toy Story*. *Toy Story* was also the first animated feature created entirely on computers. Since then there has been a huge competitive move toward 3D animation. Films like *Finding Nemo* have recently crushed box office sales records.

Claymation

Claymation is three-dimensional animation that involves any number of clay models that are remolded between each shot or frame to create movement. *Celebrity Death Match* on MTV and *Chicken Run* are great examples of this technique.

Model/Puppet Animation

This type of three-dimensional animation is similar to claymation. It uses moveable figures that are posed in each shot to produce motion. Tim Burton's film *The Nightmare Before Christmas* is a great example of this type of work.

Combined Techniques

Many studios today are using different types of animation with their films. *Titan AE* is an example of a 2D animated film that also contains composite CG animation. Compositing allows movies to have CG animation interact with live actors and cameras. Movies like *Jurassic Park* and *Spider-Man* are chock full of CG animation mixed in with real actors and scenes.

2D vs. 3D in Gaming

A great early example of a 2D animated style video game would be Don Bluth's *Dragon's Lair*. A recent favorite of mine is the prerendered real-time strategy game *StarCraft*, created by Blizzard Entertainment. Cap Com's *Marvel* and *Street Fighter* games also have a 2D animated style. Real-time 3D game engines are also making huge strides at the moment. Newer graphic cards can take advantage of powerful shaders and have added a whole new level to the amount of detail, effects, and polygon pushing power. 3D real-time games like *Far Cry* took advantage of new features such as normal mapping and real-time physics, which set it apart from the 2D animated styles. Ultimately, however, gameplay determines which technique to use.

Learning Your Basic Motion Curves and What They Can Do

These simple tutorials assume you have a basic knowledge of the 3ds max user interface.

1. Start by creating a simple sphere and placing it at **0, 0, 0**, then move it up so the bottom of the sphere is placed right above the grid line from the right or left. The base grid line is a great reference point for an imaginary floor.

2. Click on the Auto Key button near the bottom right. It will turn red once you have clicked on it. Now, right-click on the timeline at the bottom on frame **0**. A dialog box should pop up like the one in Figure 7-1.

Figure 7-1: Create Key dialog

Notice you have three check boxes: Position, Rotation, and Scale. They are checked by default.

These three options are important tools that can be used to copy any keyframe for P, R, and S to a new destination frame. We will play around more with this after we have covered motion curves.

3. You should now have a set of keys for P, R, and S at frame 0. Now move your time slider to frame **15**. Move the sphere on the X-axis roughly 100 units to the right and up on the Y-axis roughly 100 units (or any position up and away from the current one).

4. Hit the **Play** button on the lower left and voilà, you should have your first animation.

5. Now drag your time slider over to frame **30** and then move the ball 100 more units to the right and back down to the base of the grid. You should now have an animation that moves up and then back down.

Now that you have an example animation to use, we are going to cover some different types of motion curves and their uses. Understanding a few of the different types of motion curves will help you while you are animating and are quite honestly a must.

On reviewing the simple animation you just completed, notice the ball interpolates from one position to the next in a nonlinear fashion. This is because the ball probably has attributes for its position set to X, Y, Z. We need to check what type of curve is set on the ball first, so click on the Motion tool in 3ds max. It's the icon that looks like a wheel. First select Position, then click on the question mark icon (circled in Figure 7-2).

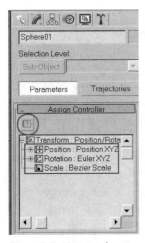

Figure 7-2: Motion tab

You should see a list pop up of different types of motion curves that you can use for position controllers. Also notice that you could have selected Rotation and Scale as well. I am only going to briefly cover Position and Rotation because I use them the most for production animation in games.

- **Position**

Linear Position – Bezier Position – TCB Position

- **Rotation**

Euler XYZ – Linear Rotation – Smooth Rotation – TCB Rotation

The best way to understand these curves is by testing them on the simple animation we just completed. First, let's change the

Animation Controller to **Linear.** Now notice the movement. It's as if it were on a straight line. It will also make a more linear turn as it changes directions. I usually use linear position for anything mechanical.

Let's change the curve to Bezier and play the animation. These curves have more control to them because they can interpolate between keys using an adjustable spline curve. Using the same animation, go to the middle frame and change the icons to match Figure 7-3. Use the PRS Parameters rollout located under the Assign Controller window.

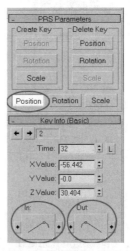

Figure 7-3: PRS Parameters rollout

Notice how the sphere moves as it did when it was set to Linear. Your default start key and end key should still be set like Figure 7-4.

Note again the small arrows at the top left. You

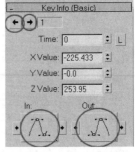

Figure 7-4: Key information

can click on the right one and it will immediately skip over to your middle key. This is quite handy if you want to skip around to change the In and Out curves.

To change the curves, you just hold down the left mouse button on top of the In or Out curve icons and a list of the different curve types will pop up. See Figure 7-5.

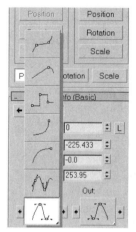

Figure 7-5: Curve types

Feel free to start changing the curve types on any keys now. The best way to understand these curves is by playing with them.

The last position curve we will cover is TCB (Tension, Continuity, and Bias) position. I use TCB position controllers for most of my animations. Tension can make an impact on the amount of curvature on the curve. Continuity is smooth by default and can cause fast changes in the curve upon manipulation. Bias controls where the key will occur with respect to the curve. And once again, you should play with these curves to understand them.

Let's make a new example animation this time. Create a sphere again from a new scene. Now, move the ball above the grid line. We basically copy the movements from the previous example except we are going from up to down to up again. When the ball hits the bottom, you want the base of the

sphere to hit the line. (This is the middle keyframe this time.)

Set Tension and Continuity for position at 50 on the middle keyframe. Your TCB controller should look like Figure 7-6.

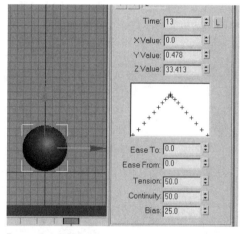

Figure 7-6: TCB curve

Notice the ball touches and pauses just a bit. Also notice if you crank Bias up to 50 and then to 0, you will get no change. Now go to the first frame and crank Bias to 50, then 0. Notice the curve will move left to right. As you will see later, for production purposes, I will usually just stick to Tension and Continuity for beginning and ending frames in a loop.

Now, let's add some rotation to the sphere. Change the default rotation to Smooth rotation for now. You will change the rotation controller the same as you did for Position. Go to the middle key and rotate the ball –185 degrees on the Y-axis. You will now see it rotating from keyframe 1 to the middle keyframe and then stopping.

Basically, use these settings for a smooth look when rotating. You will get less control, however, because you get no display properties or function curves as you would in TCB. Repeat the steps above for each of the curves. The characteristics are pretty much the same as discussed for the position controllers except for the Euler curve, which we will cover later in more detail. Switch the controller curve back to Euler XYZ. Euler XYZ gives us additional control in the Curve Editor for rotation on the XYZ axes, but first let's cover some basics in the Track View – Curve Editor (Figure 7-7).

If you hold the mouse curser over any of the above icons for a moment, a tool tip will pop up, letting you know what the icon is. The icon with four arrows is the **Move** icon. Click on the Move icon and then select any key in the graph; it will turn white. You could then move the key in any direction. The icon to the right of the Move icon is the Slide Key icon. The **Slide Key** icon allows you to slide the key along the dotted line axis.

The next icon to the right, **Scaling keys**, will scale your animation over time. You may also scale time down. The next icon will scale its value up and down. The next icon is the Add Keys function. This will plot new keys along your existing curve. The little pencil icon next to that one is for drawing curves in the Curve Editor.

The **Reduce** icon does exactly what it says. Use this tool when you have a key set on bones for every key set to create the same animation with fewer keys. It is easier to manipulate fewer keys in an animation.

If you have not tried them out yet, go back through the icons we have covered and test them on the simple animation.

Let's go back to your animation and to the center key.

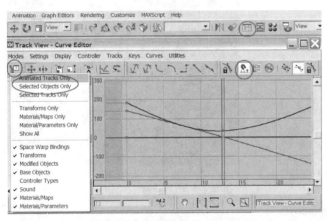

Figure 7-7: Track View – Curve Editor

Figure 7-8: Track View toolbar

A few quick points to cover first in the Track View are circled in Figure 7-7. On the top right side is the icon to open up the Track View. Right below this is the Snap to Frames icon, which looks like a magnet. This will keep the keys snapped to frames when moving keys in the editor. Right-click on the question mark icon to get the drop-down you see here. These first two selections make it easy to view which objects you want to select. They will show up underneath this window. Figure 7-8 shows the Move icon selected.

1. Select the sphere and rotate it 99 degrees on the X-axis.

2. Now open up the Curve Editor and highlight the X rotation as above. Your curve should also look similar to the above example.

3. Now right-click on the same key centered in red. The Sphere\X Rotation dialog should appear. Notice the Value area circled in red in Figure 7-8. Scroll the arrow slider up and down. The ball should rotate in the view accordingly. I usually use Euler Rotations for specific rotations and 360 degree turns or more.

4. Select two keys and click on each of the Curve icons, one at a time. You should notice the curves change according to which curve type is selected. You can use the Lock icon to lock your keys and then manipulate them as a group. I find this useful when scaling multiple keys.

The **Parameters** icon opens the dialog box shown in Figure 7-9.

5. The default is Constant so switch it to **Cycle** and click **OK**. Now notice the dotted lines in the Track View. Go to the animation and extend the frames to view the cycled animation. Feel free to try the others now. Select **Constant** once more when you are finished to go back to the original state.

6. Now rotate the ball on any frame you like and then try pasting it on another frame by holding down the right mouse button and scrolling the time slider to a new frame and pasting it. Try the dialog box again. Right-click the time slider

on frame 0 except this time hold down the mouse button and drag it over to frame 30. After you release the time slider button you see the dialog box pop up. Select **OK**. Notice the ball has now been copied back to frame 0. Quite easy!

7. Press **Ctrl+Z** to undo, and go to frame 0 and scale up the sphere quite a bit. Play the animation again. It slowly scales down back to its previous state at frame 15. Let's now go back to frame 0 and right-click the time slider again and drag it to frame 25. This time, only flag the **Scale** box. Notice that the scale key from frame 0 was copied to frame 25 only.

Note:

This is a powerful way to adjust your keys on the fly in 3ds max.

You can also make the changes in the control Curve Editor, which we will briefly touch upon in a moment. Rotate the ball on any frame you like and then try pasting it on another frame as explained above. After you have succeeded here keep playing around with whatever you like and practice dropping and pasting keys with T, R, and S. Practicing will make it easier as we move to animating a bouncing ball.

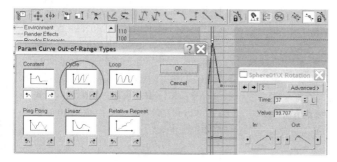

Figure 7-9: Curves in the Track View – Curve Editor

Tutorial 7: Basic Bouncing Ball

Animating a ball bouncing is a great way to learn some basic principles in animation. We'll be using a paper drawing as a guideline, which will help coach us through the process. I think this exercise is kind of like using tracing paper and is helpful for anyone who has never animated before. Furthermore, this exercise helps us understand the basic principles of timing, spacing, squashing, stretching, and arcs. I have to give credit to the creators of the Idleworm web site. I adapted their simple 2D exercise for this 3D animation training lesson.

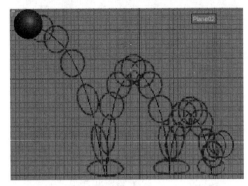

Figure 7-11: Sphere created

1. Let's start by taking the reference from Figure 7-10 and adding it to an image plane in 3ds max.

Note:

Be sure to use Bitmap Fit.

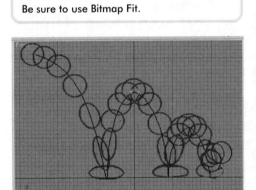

Figure 7-10: Reference image

2. Next, create a 3D sphere exactly the same size as the one in the top-left corner of Figure 7-11.

3. Right-click on the time slider at frame 0 to set a key for T, R, and S.

4. Set keys on all the major transitions. Follow the example from Figure 7-12 and right-click a key on each frame as noted in the figure.

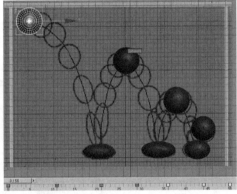

Figure 7-12: Keyframes

5. In Figure 7-13 I have placed multiple copies of the ball for your reference. Remember, yours will not look like this, as yours should animate across time. The main keys I have added are at 0, 12, 22, 29, 36, 44, and 50. (Just eyeball it for now and make more key changes later.)

6. After scaling the ball at frame 12, go back and select the ball again at frame 0, hold down the right mouse button, and drag the time slider to frame 22. When you release the mouse button, uncheck the Position and Rotation check boxes and select **OK** as shown in Figure 7-13. This is the best way to keep the same volume of the ball. You will be repeating this step many times during this exercise. While scaling try using the Squash and Scale icon.

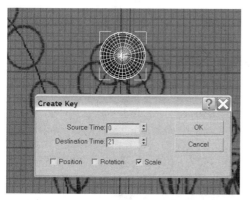

Figure 7-13: Key info

7. Next, move (translate) the ball to the areas between our main poses. Notice if you played the above animation it interpolates right to each key. We want to move the ball and pose it for all the keys shown in Figure 7-14. On frame 9, we begin to stretch the ball before it hits. You will also want to "trace" the stretching after the squash again as the ball moves away on frame 13.

Note:

I did not add a ball object on frame 13 as I did not want to clutter all the reference poses. Frames 14 and 15 marked in Figure 7-14 also have no keys on the time line. That is because frame 16 has a key on it. Pretend it is in between 15 and 19. Use common sense with Figure 7-14. You can see my keys on the timeline. Therefore use the reference as a guide to see many of the positions that have no keys and just interpolate between the set keys.

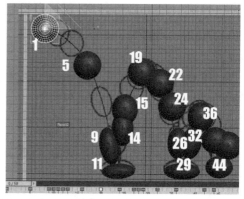

Figure 7-14: Ball movement

8. You will have to use Rotate on the stretching keys (9 and after 11) to make it adjust to the correct position(s). Notice the keys that have three colors. I set a key for P, R, and S often just to make sure everything is set and will not interpolate incorrectly. Be sure to use the right mouse button and drag several times to place your keys. This technique will increase your animation speed since you won't have to adjust volumes manually.

9. After you get your major keys set, feel free to play around with your Curve Editor. Practice what you learned with animation curves on the new animation. Also, try to drag (box select) the keys on your timeline and slide them around to change the timing. More

space between your keys means it will go slower.

Also, be careful of setting too many keys next to each other. Deleting keys in between to see how it interpolates is always a great way to see how things are moving. Not only will it smooth your animation at times, but you will be able to see if you really need the key there or not. Again, practice makes perfect, so after mastering this exercise try making a new animation without the reference help.

Challenge: Create a bouncing ball that rotates into a wall and bounces back. After completing this, make the wall fall down after the ball hits it. Don't forget to set a key for the wall's T, R, and S right before you make the wall fall down. Good luck!

10. Once the animation is complete, it's time to see it in action in the viewer. Click on **File | Export**, then be sure that Copy Textures to Output Path is checked.

In the viewer you should be able to see the ball bouncing.

Tutorial 8: Creating a Simple Idle Breath Animation

This is it — our first character animation!

1. Let's start off by creating a new biped in the middle of the grid. Make sure the red Auto Key button is turned on at the bottom before you start to set any keys.

2. We first want to set a pretty basic pose that you will want the character in for most of the loops. Typically, the loops will have a pretty basic start and stop pose, which is standard for game animations. See Figure 7-15.

3. Spread the legs outward, then move and bend the arms out as shown in Figure 7-16.

4. Next, click on the left foot and set a planted key by selecting the circled icon after selecting the foot. Now repeat it for the right foot. The feet should now be planted to the ground. Using Figure 7-17 as a guide, select the root bone called **bip01** and move the biped down a bit. Notice there is only a slight bend in the knees now. The

leftmost icon under Track Selection will move him left and right if needed.

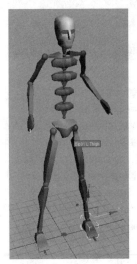

Figure 7-15: Basic pose

Note:

You must always have a part of the biped selected to access the rollouts for bipeds in 3ds max.

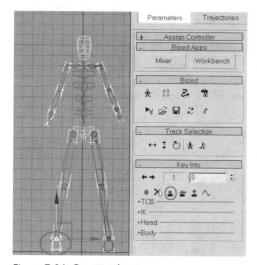

Figure 7-16: Creating the stance

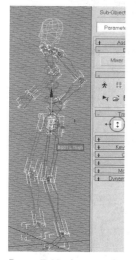

Figure 7-17: Continued adjustments

5. Give yourself about 31 frames to work with. (Note: Frames 1 to 31 is 30 frames.) We are going to copy some poses. Under Copy/Paste click on the first icon to copy the pose, then paste it at frame 1. This sets animation on the entire pose. Now, move to frame 31 and hit the Paste key only. You could hit Copy Pose again and paste it, but the pose has already been pasted to your

copied poses. The icons you need to press are circled in Figure 7-18.

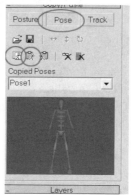

Figure 7-18: Copy and Paste

6. Be sure to note that if you grab bip01 again and move it, the biped's feet are no longer anchored to the floor. You could go back and use the set planted key again on frame 1 and 31, but we are going to get the same result another way.

7. On frame 1 select the right foot and press the green **Anchor Right Leg** icon (circled in Figure 7-19). This will anchor the foot down on your biped in 3ds max. Go ahead and move the bip01 bone around and see. (Press **Ctrl+Z** to go back after you have tested it.)

Figure 7-19: Anchoring right leg

There have been no keys set yet and if you unclicked the icon, the foot would move around again. To set a key, click the Set Key icon. You will now have a key set on the foot. Before releasing the foot anchor, be sure and set one at frames 1 and 31 again. Do the same for the right foot now. Click on bip01 again and you will see that the feet are now planted again. Go to frame 16 and move bip01 down slightly.

Note:

Always make sure your Auto Key icon is red before you ever set any keys

8. Play the animation. Your character should now move up and down slowly. Select the clavicle on frame 16 and click on the **Symmetrical** icon. Rotate the clavicles down a bit as shown in Figure 7-20.

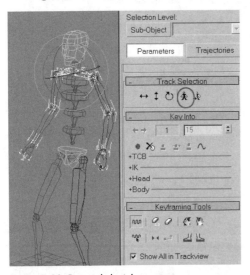

Figure 7-20: Rotated clavicles

9. Hit the **Play** button or press the / key to view the animation.

Note:

While animating you should always check to see what you have done after setting some keys. Also remember that using the < key and the > key are great for flipping frame by frame to view or even manipulate your work.

10. Next, rotate the head and torso ever so slightly on frame 16 (see Figure 7-21).

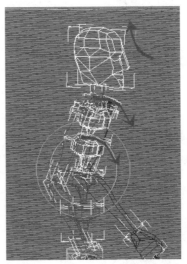

Figure 7-21: Head and torso rotated

11. Play the animation and make any adjustments you see fit. "Subtlety" is the key in making cool animations, but for games and learning purposes it's great to add more exaggeration. So try some extreme bends and then some subtle ones also.

12. Expand the TCB drop-down under the Key Info area. Crank up the Tension and Continuity to **50** on frames 1 and 31. Notice all the spine bones on the biped also change. Use Figure 7-22 as reference. After playing the animation, notice how it loops more smoothly. Repeat the above process for the clavicle, head, and bip01 bones.

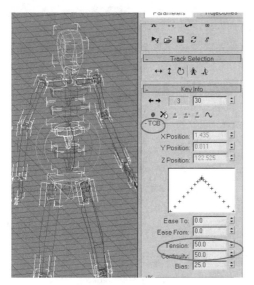

Figure 7-22: TCB Tension and Continuity settings

on frame 16 and rotating the right and left calves out a tad. You should now have your first basic idle breath loop! Again, this is very basic, so try experimenting with cool poses and shifting and rotating the root bone for slight weight changes.

Challenge: Practice makes perfect, so try a few new idles on your own. Attempt to make the character scratch his head, then try a new loop of the character turning left and right as if to look.

> **Hint:**
>
> Pay attention to the way you move in a mirror. If you are lucky you can get a friend to act out the motions for you while you animate. This is a great learning tool.

13. If you do not have a key on frame 31 for the root bone (bip01), add one by selecting the Set Key icon right above the TCB rollout and then crank up both Tension and Continuity again. Try translating the arms out very slightly

With every action there is a reaction. It is important to think about this while animating. Also, try adding a ponytail swish or some secondary movement to the animations. The more you practice, the better you will get. Next, we animate a walk cycle.

Tutorial 9: Creating a Walk Cycle

We are going to tackle the walk cycle by taking reference images and basically tracing over them like we did with the ball animation. First, let's import two sets of images onto two planes to animate over each frame. The images will update on each frame if imported correctly.

> **Note:**
>
> Use the provided bitmaps in the companion CD folder \Tutorials\Art_Tutorials\Tutorial_9_Walk_Cycle called walkfront0001.bmp and walkside0001.bmp. When applying the images to the planes, be sure to use Bitmap Fit under the UVWMap modifier.

The bitmaps will assure your proportions are correct.

1. Make sure the sequence is flagged again, and use the reference picture (Figure 7-23) to set up the scene. I have also offset the walk front and the walk right .bmp files a bit in my perspective view so you could see them better. Be sure to line both up in the middle of the X and Y on the graph at 0, 0, 0 with the feet right above the X line.

2. Now, create a biped in front of the reference picture. Additionally, change the biped from its default state to the

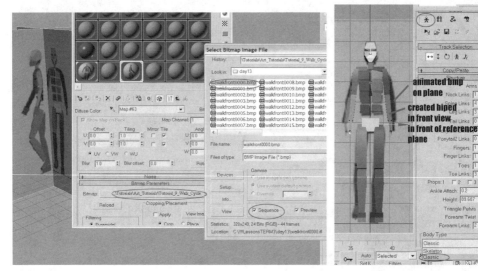

Figure 7-23: Walk images

Figure 7-24: Biped created

Classic state as highlighted and shown in Figure 7-24.

After scaling the biped to match the reference material, we start setting keys. Here's a quick summary of what we will do. First, set keys from the side on about every second frame. After you get a basic smooth motion, begin planting the feet down and work on a tricky part, the hips. Once the hips are working, release the feet and work on the upper torso movement.

Note:

Move the image reference plane behind the black grid lines so you can use the grid as a guide for the floor and for spacing.

3. On frame 0 pose the character from the side. I find just translating the limbs to be faster than making minor tweaks with rotations.

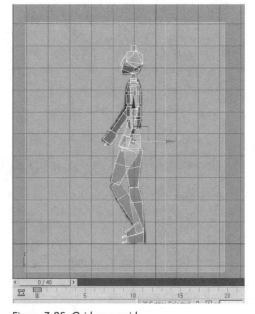

Figure 7-25: Grid as a guide

Note:

I have changed the colors on my biped by reversing the greens and reds. I also flipped the UVs on my reference image so I could animate if from the Right view. There are multiple ways you could get the same setup, or you can just leave it the way it is. You can also double-click the root bone (bip01), which selects all the bones, and then hit **Alt+X** to make it transparent.

4. Now animate the legs and arms every two frames. We use fewer keys on the arms to make the movement a bit smoother. Continue playing the animation to see where you have problems.

Max Tool Tip:

Use the < and > keys to scroll frame by frame in the viewport. I use these keys constantly while animating.

5. Don't worry about the arms; they should not match up perfectly, because you actually have not added the torso keys in yet. Once you have completed this for the entire character from frames 1 to 40, we will move on to the hips. Feel free to move the image plane to the left or right to visually check your work as well.

If you are having trouble with the feet in any areas, be sure the reference is matched up. Something to think about is that when the feet hit the ground they should be traveling about the same distance across each grid point. Also, they should be traveling at a constant pace, so if you have any hiccups use your < > keys to see if the foot is actually moving from a reference point on the grid. If it slows down or stays on the same frame for two in a row, then that is your problem. Try translating it on the key next to it on a few frames and then go back and delete the in-betweens.

6. Once you have all the keys set from the side view, you should have a pretty stiff loop with the arms and legs moving. You could have a few head keys and some side torso bend; if you do, no worries. What we must do now is set some sliding keys on the feet. Sliding keys are different from the set planted keys in that they will still translate forward but will give us the ability to

rotate the root (bip01) bone while keeping the feet planted down. If we set planted keys as we did earlier with the idle, then the feet would stop walking forward. See Figure 7-26.

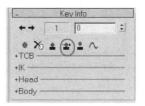

Figure 7-26: Sliding key

7. Use the > key and hold the mouse above the sliding key on every second key you have placed for both right (green) and left (blue) feet. See Figure 7-27. The > key will make the process go more quickly. You should now have a little red dot as shown in Figure 7-28 on every key for each foot.

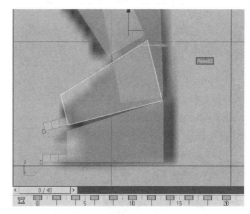

Figure 7-27: Keys set for animations

Figure 7-28: Red dot

When you're finished, go back through each foot with the < > keys and make sure the little red dot shows up. Next, we are ready to deal with the hips.

Note:

The feet should be a tiny bit jittery in some areas after placing the sliding keys. Don't worry about the way the biped has changed for now. We will eventually remove all the sliding keys.

1. Unless you adjusted the root bone earlier, make sure you add the up and down movement from the Side view port. Use the grid as a guideline, and remember that you choose the middle arrow to move the root bone (see Figure 7-29). You will also notice the red dot only shows when the feet are highlighted, as shown in Figure 7-30. As you move the root bone up and down, the feet stay in position. Make sure all

Figure 7-29: Middle arrow

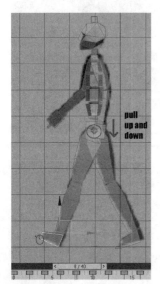

Figure 7-30: Up and down animation

of the adjustments are on keys. Keeping adjustments on previous keys instead of in random locations will make it easier to move or space keys out later and will look much more professional.

2. Let's rotate the hips from the Front viewport. Follow the reference on each key and mimic the rotation of the hips. Pay close attention to the way the shadow and block are moving in the reference. Also, pay extra attention to the side-to-side movement and the upward rotation. I have not adjusted the hands, feet, or torso yet because I'll do these steps after the hips are all set. Figure 7-31 is based on frame 8.

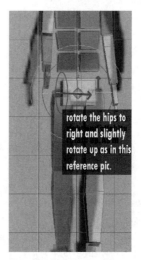

Figure 7-31: Hip rotation

3. After you have completed all the hip adjustments, remove the sliding keys. Repeat the steps you did when you added all the sliding keys, but this time as you > across the timeline on each frame click the **Set Free** key. This should release all your keys. You will no longer be able to move the hips while keeping the feet locked, so be sure the results are what you want.

Your feet should also lose that tiny jitter or popping after you add them.

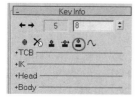

Figure 7-32: Removing sliding keys

It's time to begin adjusting the legs, arms, and feet from the Front view.

4. Go through all the other frames and begin to adjust the arms, torso, head, legs, and feet from the Front view as shown in Figure 7-33. It's all about the details. Look at the blocks and shadows once again to see how each part is moving.

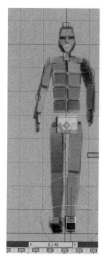

Figure 7-33: Adjusting and tweaking

Hopefully, as you have been working up to this point you have been studying the movement that we have been mimicking.

5. Adjust the torso from the Left and Right view and then make any remaining tweaks to the arms.

Practice and tweak this exercise many times. Once you understand the subtleties, try to animate a walk cycle with no reference material. The best way to accomplish this is by setting up the major keys at evenly spaced transitions, as shown in Figure 7-34.

Set these major keys and then try to fill in the gaps.

Figure 7-34: Walk example

You want to memorize four major transitions. The last frame will be the same as the first. Then look at the interpolations and begin to adjust the keys in between. Follow the steps for the hips and the rest of the body like above. Study the movement and practice it until you can animate a solid walk from memory. Once you understand this movement you can start using layers (described later) to plant feet with weight and exaggeration.

Challenge: After mastering this exercise, try to make a large character with a lot of weight and exaggeration.

Motion Capture Hardware

Animating with motion capture data is an excellent technology currently being used in today's game industry. With the proper tools and hardware you can turn a cool animated game into a stunning movie.

There are many different types of motion capture hardware on the market to choose from today. The two types I have used are a wireless magnetic system and an optical system. Magnetic systems have to have an environment that contains little or no metal. Metal in the environment requires more cleanup work later in the process. Programs like Filmbox/Motion Builder or iQ are almost a must when cleaning up poor data from capturing. Other than having to worry about the environment, magnetic systems can be quite useful if you have a proper setup. Two major

advantages of magnetic systems are that you can capture data with lots of non-metal props and the price is more affordable.

Even with these two advantages, however, a magnetic system is still no match for the Vicon optical motion capture system. These systems are used by medical research teams and the film industry but have since moved into the gaming industry. Games are becoming more lifelike and, with systems dropping in price to target games, a handful of companies are beginning to realize how powerful motion capture can be. From my experience, one person can do the work of several full-time animators with the use of a mocap system in production work.

Let's take a look at just what it means to use and work with motion capture data.

Tutorial 10: Manipulating Motion Capture Data

The best way to manipulate keys is by using a system that allows the use of layering animation or using control curves. There are many programs that can accomplish this task. The technique that is discussed here uses Character Studio. The first thing you will need is the vic-tory_dance.csm file provided on the companion CD at \Tutorials\Art_Tuto-rials\Tutorial_10_Motion_Capture_Data. We will be using the motion file to import onto the biped.

1. Begin by clicking anywhere on the biped to access the tools under the Motion panel of 3ds max. Scroll down to the + Motion Capture tab and click on the **Import Motion Capture File** icon (circled in Figure 7-35).

Figure 7-35: Import Motion Capture File icon

2. After clicking the icon, the dialog box shown in Figure 7-36 should appear.

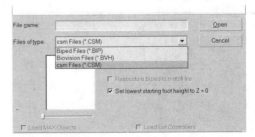

Figure 7-36: Choosing the .CSM file type

3. After choosing **csm Files** (*.csm), choose the **victory_dance.csm** file. The Motion Capture Conversion Parameters window appears next. This is where we choose some important settings (see Figure 7-37).

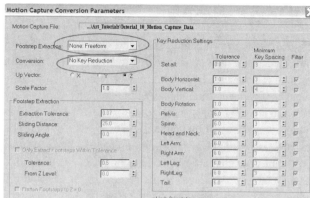

Notice the circled items. If you import an animation with No Key Reduction, you will get a key on every keyframe. This is fine for prerendered

Figure 7-37: Motion Capture Conversion Parameters window

animations, but not for games. Animation increases frame rate, and a key assigned to every bone on every frame is not encouraged for generating the best performance. Therefore, it is preferable to set Conversion to Use Key Reduction. Feel free to play with the scaling factor and any of the other tools in the window. You can usually get decent results with the default settings, however.

Figure 7-38: Footstep icon

The Footstep Extraction setting on this window is also important. Choosing None: Freeform will give you exactly that: There will be no Footstep icon on your biped model. If you set Footstep Extraction to ON, you will be able to use Character Studio's footstep manipulators. If you'd like to reorient the character in 3D space, for example, changing the biped character from facing right to facing the front, click on the Footstep icon as shown in Figure 7-38.

After clicking this icon you can select the feet in the window and rotate them in any direction you want. You can also change any of these icons to go up or down if you need to correct the feet. See Figure 7-39.

Figure 7-39: Footstep mode

Figure 7-40: Freeform mode

4. Now, convert them back to **Freeform** mode after making any corrections (Figure 7-40).

Once that's completed you have the data on the biped and you can begin tweaking.

225

Using Layers

The best way to tweak animation and motion capture data in Character Studio is by using the layers. Layers are powerful in that the biped will keep its current animation and let you translate and rotate biped bones over the existing animation. For example, if you have a walk animation and you want your character to be slouched down, you can add a layer to the spine bones and crouch the biped over on one frame with a layer and it will update the entire animation across all the frames. If this does not make sense, you will understand after the following exercise.

1. Using the existing animation we just imported, add a layer using the Layer icon (see Figure 7-41).

Figure 7-41: Layer icon

2. Notice a red stick figure inside the animation. Play the animation and note that nothing has changed. Select the biped's spine and rotate it a bit forward on frame 1. Also, go ahead and make an extreme adjustment to the head.

Important:

Make sure you have the **Auto Key** turned on in the corner or you will not be able to set keys.

3. Play the animation again, this time noticing the new position updates across all the frames. The red stick figure keeps its original position. You may add new layers on top of this by selecting the Layer icon again. You can make multiple changes on separate layers. I tend to work with one layer at a time, but it depends on what you are trying to accomplish or your working preference. Use the up and down arrow icons to go up or down a layer. Lastly, we need to collapse the layers for the end result.

Note:

If you would like to delete the layer, just click on the X'ed-out Layer icon. Check out Figure 7-42.

Figure 7-42: Layer options

Note:

Notice if you try to do this on frame 1 without layers it will only update the first frame and immediately pop to the original animation on the next keyed frame. This is a powerful tool to update your animations and motion capture data.

Now let's look at how to use layers with mocap animation in a way that is quite easy.

Using the Copy/Paste Tools in Character Studio

Before we start, let's talk briefly about how we would set up animations for games. First, think about the amount of time the animation takes. You want it just long enough to cover what you want to see; that way we keep the amount of keyframing down to a minimum. Second, depending on the animation required, it should have the same start and stop frames. This also depends on the game and how well the blending system works. For this example let's go ahead and use the same .csm file again.

Note:

Make sure you import it with Feet Conversion and Key Clean Up on. You will also want to use Footstep mode to face the front.

When we are close to finishing the tweaks we will import the idle animation like we did earlier. This pose is what you would want to use as your start and stop positions for the idles and other minor movements. Most of the action movements will be loops of themselves. For example, the runs and walks would not have the same pose but loop themselves.

1. Start by converting the feet back to Freeform mode. Next, cut out a good portion of the ending part of the animation to shorten it up. Box select all the biped bones and box select all the keys from 54 to the last key and hit **Delete**. Be sure the correct keys are selected as shown in Figure 7-43. If the biped disappears, that means you are still on the bones. You want to Ctrl+Z to get the biped back. Re-box select the biped again, this time clicking on the **timeslider** bar on a free area, then selecting the keys again to delete.

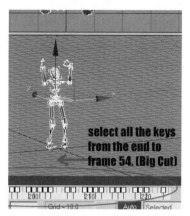

Figure 7-43: Delete keys

2. Change the range from 0 to about **80** so we can see the beginning keys easier. See Figure 7-44.

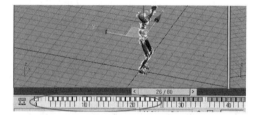

Figure 7-44: Key selection

3. Delete keys 0 to 24. You want frame 25. (See Figure 7-45.)

Figure 7-45: Delete keys

4. Slide all the keys you have back to 0.

Now we are ready to create a layer and use the Copy/Paste Pose tool.

Note:

One thing you do not want to do is grab multiple bones and drag the slider bar to copy keys. Be sure to use the Copy/Paste tool with the biped for any key copying.

227

5. After creating the layer, use the **Copy/Paste** tool (Figure 7-46) to set some random poses across the entire animation. When using motion capture, the two things to look for are important points in the movement and the spaces in those movements between keys.

Figure 7-46: Copy/Paste rollout

6. Use the left icon shown circled in Figure 7-46 to copy the pose and the right icon to paste the pose. Repeat the process across the entire animation.

Figure 7-47: Copy and paste victory pose

7. Place one at **0** and then decide on the ups and downs. The next step is to begin tweaking the body parts. Basically, tweak the feet, legs, and arms on each of the keyframes set below. After that, rotate the calves to match up better. You will see the hand get really bent out of shape, too. Correct the forearms first before working on the hands. Once they are cleaned

up, then straighten the hands out. Go ahead and try to fix the problems I have mentioned and any other small details you see.

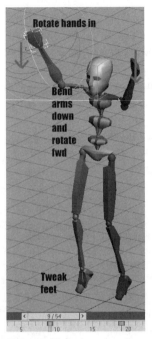

Figure 7-48: Body parts adjusted

The reason for setting intermittent keys is so you will not lose the main movements that make the animation look good. For example, you could have made fewer keys and fixed the errors in only a couple. It is best to set more and tweak more. The more experience you have, the easier and better you will get at locating problem areas.

8. After pasting the important keys it's time to start manipulating the animation, as if it were a new animation. First, correct all the keys of the biped on all the frames you have set. It is important to correct these frames first as it will help you when you are updating the in-betweens. Once they are all set you can start to reanimate the character to do what you want him to do.

I find this to be the most simple and effective way to animate the existing animation and/or motion capture data. The example provided is an easy one as the character is not moving very much. Use this same technique for any movement you do. Don't forget that you can use the Anchor Feet tools to plant the feet, but don't use them in the Layers mode. Do the layering first, then go back and delete frames for the feet and replant them.

9. After tweaking, move the arms down a bit on frame 0 and copy frame 0 to the last frame, frame **53**. Collapse the layers. You should now have a loop; however, we are not finished yet.

10. Go through each foot and set free keys to remove all the red dots, then play the animation. A few of the frames seem to be a bit sticky, so delete some keys for the right (green) foot on frames 6, 21, and 39. Replay and do the same for the keys that act identically on the left (blue) foot. Select all the bones and delete key 52, the key right before the last key. All of these deletions should make things smoother. Delete the jittery key, then set some layers up again and go back through and try to blend these keys more smoothly. Feel free to practice your layers again and set some more blending keys.

> **Note:**
>
> You can paste an opposite pose if need be. Try one to see the outcome, then **Ctrl+Z**. You may select one or multiple biped bones and use the **Posture** icon, which will paste only the position(s) of the bone(s) selected.

11. Save your work if you haven't already.

12. We are going to add the first pose of the idle animation that we did earlier. Open the idle and examine where the character is oriented compared to the grid and the direction. The idle should be facing forward in the Front viewport. If not, you need to add some planted keys back to the idle animation on each key for the foot and convert it back to Footstep mode. Set planted keys on the feet if they are not there already, click on the **Convert** icon to get back to Footstep mode, and then make any corrections needed. Now save a .cpy pose for the idle.

Figure 7-49: Footstep mode

13. The circled icons at the right in Figure 7-50 are for deleting single poses and all poses. To keep things clean we are going to delete all the poses and then copy/paste the poses again. This time name it **idle_stance** as shown in Figure 7-50.

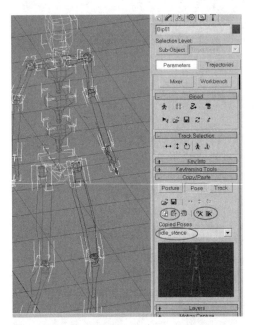

Figure 7-50: Copy and paste pose

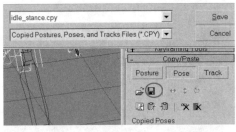

Figure 7-51: Save option

14. Copy the pose and name it **Idle Stance**. If you had multiple poses, we would save them as well. See Figure 7-51.

15. Reopen the victory animation. Create a new layer and paste a pose at frames **5** and **50**. See Figure 7-52.

16. Click on the biped and import the new **idle_stance.cpy** file by clicking on the **Open** icon (see Figure 7-53).

Figure 7-53: Import .cpy file

17. Make sure you are still in Layers mode. Go to frame 0 of the idle pose and paste the idle_stance pose. Copy the first pose of the idle into the new animation and let it interpolate from there to the next current frame on 5 or 6. See Figure 7-54. Again, copy a base pose from the idle animation into the first frame of the victory animation.

18. Once it's pasted you can paste idle_stance again to the last frame after frame 50. You should now have a loop that starts from the idle pose and transitions into the victory pose and back again. We have a simple game loop animation usable whenever needed for a cool victory dance.

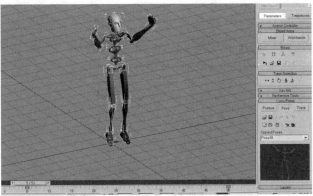

Figure 7-52: New layer with pasted frames

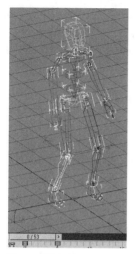

Figure 7-54: Motion

The Motion Flow Editor, another powerful tool provided by Character Studio, could have been used to accomplish this task; however, the transition was quite simple so there was no real need to use it. I will not cover the Motion Flow Editor here, but feel free to use Character Studio's Help menu to learn more about the tool. There is plenty of information on how to use it.

Animation for Games

Animation for games requires a different direction and focus than full-featured cinematic film work. Games require many techniques for optimizing, playtesting, and maintaining your release schedule.

As discussed previously, games require cleaned up keyframes because they have limited memory and animation can be quite memory intensive with a key set on every frame. Therefore, games must try to optimize the keys and still look as good as possible. Game playability is greatly affected by the length of time required to accomplish a character's task. For example, if you want a character to punch when you click on the keypad or action button, you usually want the character to punch immediately. The reaction speed is very important. Generally, you want a speedy reaction to cause damage as soon as the key is hit. For example, gameplay would feel interrupted if you pressed the hit key and the character slowly breathed and then punched. The same principle should be applied for most of the actions in a game.

Another important factor is the game's production cycle. You must playtest your running speeds, attacks, jumps, deaths, etc. Scaling times and tweaking moves add extra polish and are well worth the effort. There is quite a bit of back and forth testing in games that can indirectly affect your schedule as an animator.

Furthermore, characters and animations must "loop." *Looping*, as we demonstrated in some of the earlier lessons, is creating a short animation file that has the ending frame the same as the starting frame. For example, a walking loop for an animation must begin on a certain posed frame, make one complete cycle, and end on a frame that matches exactly with the beginning frame. You don't want a short, jerky motion or a long drawn-out walk with multiple loops within a set of frames.

In addition to being mindful of keys, the list of animations for the characters must be well thought out so the designers and animators can efficiently accomplish the many tasks required of them. The list should be discussed seriously and also looked at according to time and schedule.

Tip:

Scheduling is imperative in creating games. As stated in other chapters, preparing and maintaining a tight schedule for all the aspects of a game will help ensure your team's success.

With the Ka3D engine, your animation parameters are set very high, allowing you extensive use of animations and keyframe detail. We'll discuss exporting animations into the Ka3D engine soon, for right now we need to further our animation skills by looking into morph animations.

Morphing Facial Animations

Although there have been many technological advances in computer graphic facial animation, it is an area that still has quite a way to go. Humans are hard wired on what facial expressions and movements look like. Our minds are so trained on what movement looks like that any imperfections are strikingly noticeable. Even with the tools available, it is very difficult to create realism in the field of facial animation.

There are quite a few different software programs and ways of capturing facial animation, and fortunately they appear to be getting better and better. We may master it yet. In addition, many of the games we play today are also adding facial animations. This is an excellent animation feature that the Ka3D engine takes full advantage of.

The next lesson includes an introduction to creating facial morph targets in 3ds max and demonstrates how easy morph targets are to create. (The tedious part is adjusting all the phonemes and facial expressions.) Basically, you take a copy of a "base" mesh pose and remodel all the vertices in each face to create a new phoneme or expression on each additional copy. All of these separate copies are referenced back to the base mesh for creating the animations. You will

understand more after completing the next tutorial, so let's get to it!

Tip:

When modeling a face you want to make sure the areas around the eyes and mouth are built correctly. You want to build loops around these areas to enable nice deformations similar to Figure 7-55.

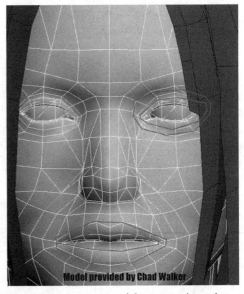

Model provided by Chad Walker

Figure 7-55: Loops around the eyes and mouth

Creating Facial Morphs

1. Once the base (original mesh) face pose is set up, bone the eyes, jaw, and tongue. Depending on the character you may modify any of the above parts. I use bones to rotate the eyes when creating my morphs as well as the jaw and the tongue, if I have them. For example, it's much easier to open the jaw all the way on the mesh and then move the vertices into an O position (Figure 7-56). Using this same technique with the eyes you would move them to the left, right, up, down, etc., and then create the target.

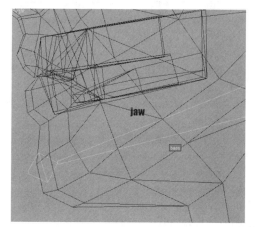

Figure 7-56: Jaw bone

2. Place the bone in the eye from the center and back. Only bone and weight one eye and test the rotation in the socket. Keep repositioning the pivot and pressing the Reinitialize key under biped to update the mesh.

3. Do the same for the jaw. Be sure to test the jaw

bone's rotation until you have the proper location.

4. After everything is boned properly to the character, select the morph target modifier in the stack.

Figure 7-57: Morph modifier

5. Add the Morpher icon under the configure modifier stack and use the reference in Figure 7-57 to create a morph target. First make a copy of the mesh. If you have boned it, then it is best to use the Snapshot tool. Do this after selecting the base mesh and then select **Tools | Snapshot** from the menu bar. This will create a copy of the mesh. Drag it over to the side. Make sure you do not have the original mesh.

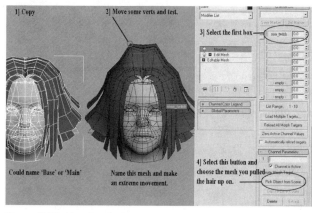

Figure 7-58: Morph setup

Note:

If you have any modifiers on the copied mesh, go ahead and delete them.

Note:

To delete a morph target, just highlight the button you want and hit **Delete**.

Hint:

I find morphs that I have already manipulated easier to use than the base one. For example, if I already created the "O" phoneme I could copy it again and change it into a "U" phoneme or even a surprise expression. This can be a smart way to save yourself some time.

6. Next, make some major adjustments to the new copy. For example, I made some extreme hair moves and turned the nose. Be sure to name the new mesh. (The name of the mesh should reflect the new action.)

7. Now go back to the original and reselect it. Notice all the empty slots in the window. Click on the first slot and then click **Pick Object** from the Scene icon. Select the modified mesh. You have now created your first morph target as shown in Figure 7-58.

8. Test it by dragging the spinner up to 100 on the nose twitch button. Notice as you drag the slider up that the base face begins to morph into the new manipulation. If you want to create an animation in 3ds max, first set a key at frame 0 with anything from 0 to 10. Then drag the slider up to 100. Play the animation! (Be sure you have Auto Key turned on before animating.)

9. Now that you understand how to create morph targets, let's use the reference material provided in Figure 7-59 to create more morph targets. Feel free to also turn the eyes with the bones and make snapshots as well.

For game animations you will want to make all the expressions separate from the phonemes. You can blend multiple sliders to get the desired result. For example, create one morph target for each eye direction. The "smile" would not have the "eyes to the left." If you created a smile expression with the eyes to the left, then every time the character smiled, the eyes would move to the left. The smile should also be separate from the phonemes.

To use it with the Ka3D engine, you will typically have the scripter create the setup for you to use as shown in Part 3 of this book, which simply calls up the morphs needed at any given time during the game. This is certainly a very efficient and

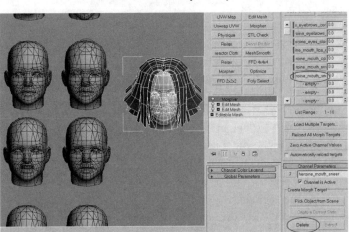

Figure 7-59: Motion

productive way to give expression and life to characters throughout the game.

> **Hint:**
>
> Sometimes the bind pose can conflict with the morphs if you have selected another modifier in the stack. That is why you always want to test your targets with some animation on the biped or character. For example, if the character bones animate but when you scroll the target, the character moves back to the bind pose instead of keeping his animation, you have made a mistake. If you are not checking the work you can waste hours of time.

Finally, be sure the character is green-lighted and ready to go. If there is a call back or the model is incorrect, you will typically have to redo all of the targets again, which can be quite time consuming.

The Morpher modifier in Figure 7-60 shows the Physique modifier applied, if the biped is used.

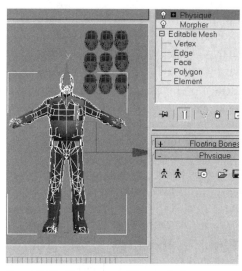

Figure 7-60: Physique modifier applied

As my brother Scott says, "reference is king." Study expressions online and in books, and use a mirror.

Exporting Animation

Now that we have a working knowledge of animation, it's time to test some animations in the engine. The Ka3D engine allows us to use a set of animations for single characters and/or multiple characters (as long as the rigs are similar). It has an extremely smooth interpolation system for animations and is set up for morph animations, which could be used for virtually anything from facial expressions to changing body forms.

So, what does it take to actually get animation working properly in a game? In the following exercise we'll go over that and more but first let's lay down the rules.

Rules for Exporting Animations

Rule 1: When exporting animations you should have Animation only checked in the Export window. With this option selected, the engine simply looks for the animations, not the geometry.

Rule 2: The movement speed of the character is extracted directly from animations, so "in-place" animation edit mode should be disabled while exporting; otherwise, the character won't be moving (translating) in the game either.

Rule 3: When exporting "new" characters that have entirely different bone heights, scales, and structures, it's best not to use the existing exported animation files because of the distortion that could occur.

Simply use the .bip files from the old character and place them on the new character in max. Then export the animations to ensure a proper fit with the new character.

Rule 4: Remember from Chapter 6 that the final rigged character needs to be exported. So when you create your own character, export the mesh as a normal scene to the data\mesh\ folder. If the mesh scene contains animation, it is ignored in the game since all we need is the character mesh and rig.

Time to Export!

1. In the Art Tutorial folder navigate to the Animation_Export_Test folder. Inside the folder you should find zaxdemo.exe. Double-click on it and walk the Zax character around using the arrow keys and jump by pressing the Spacebar. Once you have played with it for a bit, come back here for the rest of the exercise.

2. Let's say we want to change Zax's animation from a walk to a run. Open the Zax animation **walk_frwd.max** file found in the Animation_Export_Test folder. Once it loads, press the **Play**

button to view the run animation for Zax. Now go to **File | Export**. In the \data\anim folder you want to replace walk_frwd.hgr with this new one. When the HGR Options window comes up, be sure that only the **Animation only** check box is checked. Click **OK**.

3. Run the zaxdemo.exe once again to see the change. Pretty easy, right? What if you wanted to check out the walk animation you created previously? If that's the case, be sure you have saved the animation as a .bip file. Then open the walk_frwd.max file and apply your walk.bip to the Zax character. Once you have it looking smooth on Zax, export it once again, then run the .exe to see how it looks.

If you have a character of your own that you want to test out, simply export the mesh character over the Zax character in \data\mesh and export the character's animations like we just did.

It looks like we are almost ready to move on to Chapter 8, which is all about level design! Before you jump over there, be sure to take a break, get something to eat, and then meet me there for more max mayhem.

Level Design

Are you an interior designer? What type of engineering or architectural degree do you have? Have you helped create a city, the road systems, and the waterways? What about lighting, color theory, mood, and expressional context? Suppose I wanted a roof of a house to have a 6/12 pitch; would you know what I was asking for or the mathematical equation behind it?

Fortunately, the job of a level designer does not require all these things. It's very important, however, for a level designer to have an understanding of how the real world works and definitely how to read a blueprint and create one to scale. One of the more difficult positions in game creation is that of a level designer because of the multitude of tasks. Let's list a few things you have to know how to do:

- Create environment concepts including blueprints

- Design
- Create proper game flow
- Use 3D software applications (for example, max, Maya, engine editors, etc.)
- Follow gameplay aspects and design techniques
- Scripting
- Develop game logic and AI
- Research and development
- Talk with artists and programmers

You have probably noticed that a "good" level designer is familiar with the jobs of just about everyone. A great level designer should be skilled with and knowledgeable of everything above and more. With that in mind, let's go over a few things to help us on our journey into level design.

Editors vs. 3D Applications

The majority of level designers create levels and sets in programs such as Hammer or Radiant, or in engine editors such as Unreal, Doom, or Half-Life. The Ka3D engine takes a different approach to level design. Instead of forcing the level designer to use specific small toolsets and limiting the control of level creation and design, it is open to the world of 3D modeling applications such as max and Maya. Rather than forcing level designers to comprehend both a 3D app and multiple editors, and subtraction and addition modeling, it is all placed into one program. One of the major advantages to this type of level design is that the artists and level designers will be speaking the same language. If all the artists (art and level designers) are using one toolset, then they will easily be able to help one another out and focus more on the game creation and less on conflicts with the engine editor, exporters, and limitations.

One of the other advantages is that you have all the tools inside of max at your disposal. That means if you decide to create an entire opening cinematic for the game inside of max, you have all the levels and artwork readily available. The toolsets available include animation, reactor, rendering and lighting, video post, and more.

> **Note:**
> There's also no need to write an importer to bring the levels from Radiant or Unreal into max since everything is there to begin with.

Let's find out what the true advantages of using max are.

Basic Rules for Designers Working in 3ds max

First, let's go over some basic rules for creating levels inside of max.

Rule 1. Know what you want to create before starting.

This means you need to have blueprints, color mockups, and concepts created prior to sitting down and modeling the level. I know many people who just start working on a level and then about halfway through the process, start questioning things, changing major parts of the level, etc. If you take the time in the initial stage and develop a strong blueprint (top-down view) and color guides, then you won't have to change things drastically during the development cycle.

Rule 2. Be mindful of polygons and texture space.

The Ka3D engine does an excellent job of processing, but that isn't reason enough to be wasteful of polygon or texture space. When creating geometry and textures, be sure you stick with the familiar phrase, "If it's not seen or very distant, keep it low and simple." One other point to keep in mind is that you can create any type of geometrical shape you want inside of max. If you can imagine it, then most likely it can be created and used in the engine.

Rule 3. Everything except for scripting and programming is done inside of max.

What does that mean for the level guy? The player start point, the enemy locations, paths, lights, breakables, in-game cinematics, level design, animations, cut scenes, triggers, and more are created in 3ds max. That's pretty cool!

Rule 4. Know before you test.

Just like when you were in school, before you took a test you (I'm assuming here) spent the day or week before preparing. The same should be true when creating levels. Before you export/test levels, be sure that you know what you are testing for.

> **Note:**
> I've seen people spend/waste hours and hours of time simply looking at the level they created. If you find yourself running around the level aimlessly, chances are you stopped testing it long ago. There is a time to play the level and a time to make sure it's working properly.

Rule 5. Save and back up.

Save the levels often and when the final level is completed, be sure to save a backup copy just in case.

Sticking with these simple rules will help you create and maintain a solid workflow.

Guidelines and Naming Conventions

Guidelines and naming conventions. What are they and why should we use them? If you have ever created a game, you realized firsthand that there were guidelines that told you what, when, and how to create something. Using the Ka3D engine is similar but incredibly more open to variations and workflows.

When creating levels for the Ka3D engine, I follow a couple of steps that help keep me organized and on top of everything in the level.

1. Block in the level. By this I mean you need to place some basic blocks and layouts into the level. This helps you find out whether your scale is too small or too large. Also, by laying out the basic level you can begin running through the level and testing the timing and playability.

Note:

You will want to test the block level carefully. If you run through this portion of your level and find that the character is aimlessly running a mile and nothing happens along the way, it can become boring and stale for the player. Things should be relatively close together and scripted to maintain the player's interest.

2. With the level blocked in, it's time to work up the actual details of the scene. The environment can be anything from the terrain in a WW II recreation to an indoor apartment complex or restaurant.

3. Scene dressing and level assets need to be added. At this point we need to dress up the level. This means artistically placing crates, trees, rocks, bookcases, vehicles, and whatever else the level calls for. It's always a good idea to test the scenes to be sure the frame count stays balanced with the added objects.

4. Work up the particles, paths, spawn points, doors, pickups, sound boxes, breakables, etc. This is the time to get everything "technical" placed into the scene and prepared for exporting.

5. Finally, light the scene so that you can enhance the mood and capture the feeling of the level.

Tip:

These steps are a basic order to working through a level. Typically, you will want to make multiple passes on steps 2 through 5 until everything works together efficiently.

In terms of art guidelines for level designers, that's pretty much it. Later in the book you will learn all about the scripting side, which is also part of the job of a level designer. (Remember, you are a multitasking creator!)

The best way to get everyone working with the same guidelines and naming conventions is to create several small test levels that will encompass all the essential points in using the Ka3D engine.

Note:

It's important to point out that you don't have to use the naming convention provided. The script files will need to change what they call up. Remember this is max; it's not an editor that is name-centric. If the team you work with wants to do things differently, then you most certainly can.

Tutorial 11: Designing Levels

So what are we going to accomplish with this level? First off, we will learn several different ways to create rooms inside of max and the different ways to use textures and the UVW Editor. After creating the final "Test Level," we look at bringing art assets into the level as well as placing particles, physics, paths, start points, animations, and more into the scene. Finally, we are going to check out a few max scripts and plug-ins that will help us with level design.

1. Start max and open **My_First_Level.max**.

2. The max file should start up in the Top view with the level map in the viewport background.

3. On the Create tab, select **Geometry Box**. Create a box around the purple room at the top of Figure 8-1.

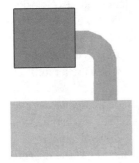

Figure 8-1: Box

4. With the box selected, right-click in the viewport and select **Convert To | Convert to Editable Poly** from the quad menu.

5. Change the outline color to black and then in the Material Editor (**M**), apply a gray diffuse color slot. Change the name Box01 to **Room_01**.

6. Select **Element** mode (**5**) and left-click on **Room_01**. The box should become highlighted. In the Edit Elements rollout, select **Flip**. In the viewport you should notice the normal direction is now pointing inward.

7. Select **Edge** mode (**2**). In the Perspective viewport, zoom in until you see where the hallway is supposed to be.

8. Under the Edit Geometry rollout, select **Cut**. In the Perspective viewport, cut the shape shown in Figure 8-2 out of the geometry.

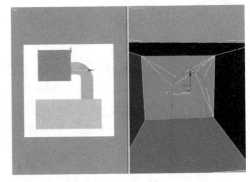

Figure 8-2: Perspective view of box

9. In the Left viewport, clean up and align the vertices so that everything is straight. Next, in Edge mode, select all the extra edges that were created, then

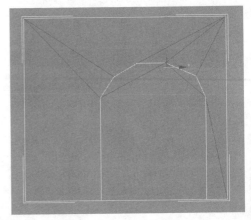

Figure 8-3: Edges cleaned up and removed

in the Edit Edges rollout, click on **Remove**.

10. Select the **Line** tool and draw the line for the hallway as shown in Figure 8-4.

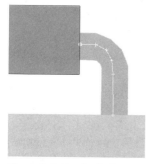

Figure 8-4: Line for hallway

11. Now select the **Room_01** box and, in Face mode, select the doorway that you cut out. In the Edit Polygons rollout, select the **Extrude Along Spline** folder as shown in Figure 8-5. Click on **Pick Spline** and **OK** in the Extrude Polygons Along Spline window, then choose the **Line01** you just created.

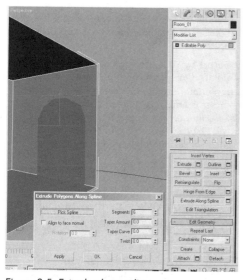

Figure 8-5: Extrude along spline

Note:

Play with options in this window. Segments indicates how many edges will be created. Taper Amount, Taper Curve, and Twist allow you the options of actually changing the shape of the geometry.

12. With the hallway created we need only to create the last room box. In the Top viewport draw the shape of the room box with the **Line** tool, then select the **Extrude** modifier and make the amount **25'0.0"**. See Figure 8-6.

Figure 8-6: Line tool creates room

13. Convert it to an editable poly, then with Element mode selected, highlight the faces and flip the faces.

14. In Edge mode, cut the doorway out as shown in Figure 8-7.

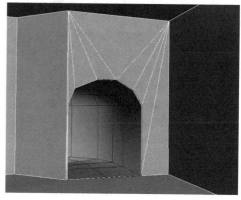

Figure 8-7: Doorway complete

Note:

Be sure to line up the existing doorway so that you can trace around it with the Cut tool.

15. Choose **Vertex** mode and weld all the vertices together.

16. Be sure to clean up the scene and delete the **Line01** that we created earlier.

Note:

Save if you haven't done so already.

17. Let's do one more thing to the room. The second box we created needs to be larger so that we'll have more room to move around. Select the outside wall (the one opposite the doorway) with the Face tool, then extrude it out an equal distance. You should have something like Figure 8-8.

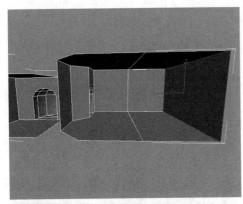

Figure 8-8: Wall extruded

18. Let's go ahead and assign textures to the level. Open the Material Editor (**M**).

19. Select the first Color slot. Click on the Map rollout tab and choose the **None** button in the Diffuse Color tab, then click on **Bitmap** and **OK**. Browse to

...\Tutorials\Art_Tutorials\Tutorial_ 11_My_First_Level and select **wall_01.bmp**.

20. Click on the **Go to Parent** button to take you back up. In the material name, change 1 – Default to **wall FX=unlit-tex**.

21. Change the Material Effects Channel to **3**.

22. Select all the polygons that make up the wall section and assign the wall material to them. Be sure to change the Material ID to **3** as well. It's found in **Editable Mesh | Surface Properties | Material ID**.

Max Tool Tip:

If you haven't used the ID properties here's some information that will help you out:

In Edit Mesh or Edit Poly, under the Surface Properties rollout, you will see ID and Select by ID options.

ID — Lets you assign a particular material ID number to selected faces (polygons, elements) for use with multi/sub-object materials and other applications. Use the spinner or enter the number from the keyboard. The total number of available IDs is 65,535.

Select by ID — Displays a Select by Material ID dialog that you use to enter a material ID number. Clicking OK selects the faces assigned that material ID. If Clear Selection is on, any previously selected faces are first deselected. If Clear Selection is off, the new selection is added to any previous selection set.

23. Repeat the same process for the ceiling and floor. Make sure the floor and ceiling have their own material ID numbers.

24. With the object selected, go to the Modify tab and choose **Unwrap UVW** from the Modifier drop-down list.

25. Click on the **Unwrap UVW** modifier to highlight it. By having this on, you will be able to select polygons in the viewport and have them show in the Edit UVWs window. Under the Parameters rollout, click **Edit**. This will bring up the Edit UVWs window.

26. Navigate to **Mapping | Flatten Mapping**. Make sure the Face Angle Threshold is set to **70**, then click **OK**. The map should look something like Figure 8-9.

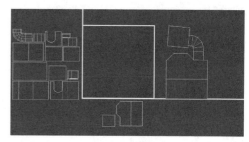

Figure 8-10: Map pieces

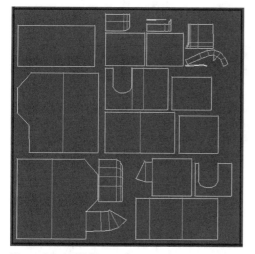

Figure 8-9: UVW flattened map

27. Select the floor maps and pull them off to the side. If you would like the floor to resemble the actual floor, select **Mapping**, choose **Flatten Mapping**, and click **OK**.

28. After the floor is moved out of the way, select the ceiling faces and separate them from the bunch. Finally, select the wall pieces and move them to the side as well. Figure 8-10 shows the map with the pieces arranged correctly.

29. Select the wall pieces and begin placing them inside the map area on top of each other. This is my easy mapping method. Easy. Be sure that when you place the wall pieces together they stay the same size (don't start scaling anything up or down just yet). Since each wall piece is currently equal in scale, we will scale the UVWs all up at one time. Figure 8-11 shows the pieces all laying on top of each other. After you have them as shown, scale them up with the Scale tool or choose the Freeform Mode tool, then Ctrl + left-click and drag a corner to scale proportionately as shown in the right side of the figure.

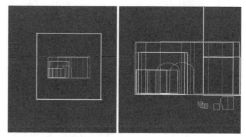

Figure 8-11: Wall scaled

30. The walls are not finished just yet. Using the Perspective view, check all the corners and connecting areas of the rooms and hallway. You will probably start noticing places where the bricks don't line up just right. Simply select

the face in the viewport, then move the UVWs until they line up properly with the adjoining texture. See Figure 8-12. Go around to any area that needs extra attention and make it look pretty.

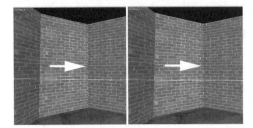

Figure 8-12: Texture corrected

31. Next select the hallway and the floor UVs for room 1. See Figure 8-13. Go to Tools and select **Break** (**Ctrl+B**). Then flip the UVs with the **Mirror Vertical** tool and move them down as shown in Figure 8-13.

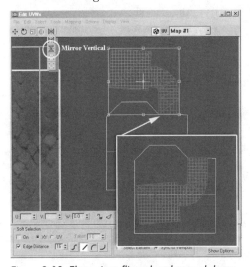

Figure 8-13: Floor piece flipped and moved down

32. Move the UV pieces to the yellow outlined box area and scale it up like Figure 8-14.

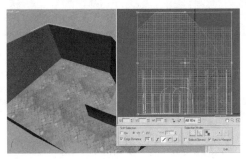

Figure 8-14: Floor scaled

33. Now, do the same thing for the ceiling UV coordinates. The textured room should look similar to Figure 8-15.

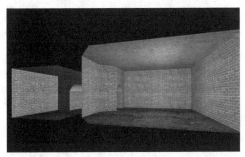

Figure 8-15: Level textured

Time to check out the level using a great tool from Game Level Builder (GLB). If you haven't installed the files, go ahead and do that now (refer back to Chapter 4). A text file inside the GLB2 folder will walk you through installing the plug-in.

Once you have GLB installed, open the Handy Cam. The Handy Cam works just like an FPS camera, which allows you to move around in your level more freely. Left-click on the Start Cam button to activate the camera. Simply left-click in the viewport to start the camera and right-click to stop the camera.

Take a moment to move around the two rooms with the Handy Cam. Pretty cool, huh?

Okay, let's do a quick breakdown of the good and the bad in creating levels this way.

Pros

- Quick level building (you can make it however you want…no thinking involved)
- "Easy" unwrapping of UVW coordinates
- Simple and effective texturing
- Tiling speeds up the process

Cons

- Can't reuse pieces or structures very easily (not modular)
- Hard to hand off to another level designer to work with
- Detailing specific texture areas is a bit more difficult
- UVW maps are very messy and hard to read

It's time to work up a different design with a brand new approach. We are going to reverse the roles and make things more modular. The completed level is Modular_Building.max found in the same folder.

1. Open max. In the Front viewport create a rectangle with length and width set to **8** feet.

2. In the Modifier list, select **UVW Mapping**. Be sure **Planar Mapping** is chosen. You should see an orange outline around the rectangle.

3. Open the Material Editor (**M**) and apply the **wall_02.dds** texture to the rectangle. See Figure 8-16.

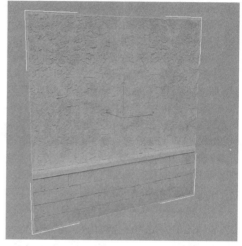

Figure 8-16: Texture applied to the rectangle

The applied texture has some trim about midway on the rectangle that we need to cut out and extrude.

4. Convert the rectangle to an editable poly. Then select **Edge mode** and click on the **Cut** tool. Cut into the rectangle as shown in Figure 8-17.

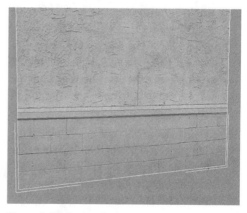

Figure 8-17: Rectangle cut

5. Select **Poly mode** and click on the newly created trim board. In Figure 8-18, I've pulled it out to give the impression of trim.

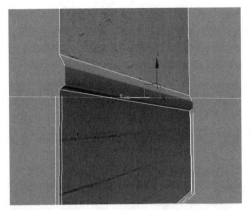

Figure 8-18: Trim pulled out

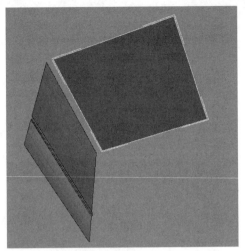

Figure 8-19: Ceiling texture

6. Excellent! You have created your first modular piece of art. Change the name to **wall_trim_01** and then be sure the pivot point is centered at the bottom of the wall.

Let's work on the ceiling next.

7. In the Top viewport, create a rectangle with a length and width of **8** feet. Go ahead and apply the **UVW Mapping** modifier to it and be sure it's using Planar mapping.

8. Assign the **ceiling_02.dds** texture to the rectangle and then rename both the material and the model to **ceiling_stucco_01**.

9. Convert the rectangle to an editable mesh. Now, select the faces and flip the normals so that you can see it from underneath. See Figure 8-19.

10. Finally, create one more rectangle with a length and width of **8** feet. Name this rectangle **floor_tile_01**. Do the same steps as before, just be sure to apply **floor_02.dds** to the rectangle.

That's it! The three pieces you created should look like Figure 8-20.

Figure 8-20: Modular pieces

Let's build a room with these pieces!

11. Start off by attaching and welding these pieces together. Then Shift+click and drag a copy of the piece next to it. In the Clone Options window, choose **5** for the Number of Copies. Figure 8-21 shows the five copies next to the original.

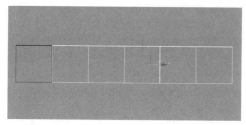

Figure 8-21: Wall copies

12. Attach all the wall pieces together. Now Shift+click and drag another three copies of the wall. Rotate them around to match Figure 8-22.

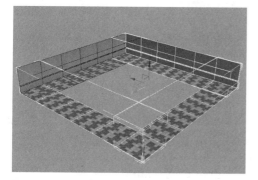

Figure 8-22: Wall copied and rotated

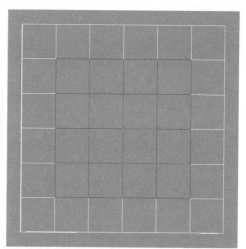

Figure 8-23: Wall and ceiling pieces copied

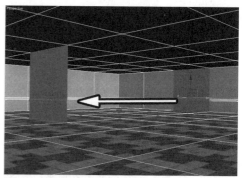

Figure 8-24: Copied wall to center

13. Attach all the walls together and then delete the overlapping faces. Once you have the faces deleted, weld all the vertices together.

14. In the Top viewport, select the three center rows of the wall. Be sure you only select the ceiling and floor pieces. Copy them throughout the center of the room as shown in Figure 8-23.

15. Select the back wall piece and drag a copy up toward the center. (See Figure 8-24.)

16. Once you have the first wall piece copied, simply copy it around, creating a smaller square inside the room. See Figure 8-25. Then delete any unused

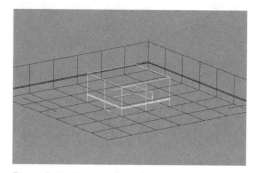

Figure 8-25: New inside walls

polygons after you weld the walls together.

Inside the room it should look like Figure 8-26.

Now that we have gone over a few different types of level creation, it's time to put our abilities to some practical use. I've created a test level for you. What we are going to do is apply the textures to the level as well as add dummy boxes and tags to it.

Figure 8-26: Inside the room

Tutorial 12: Test Level

1. Open max.
2. Navigate to ...\Art_Tutorials\Tutorial_12_Test_Level and open **Test_Level_01.max**.

It looks pretty boring right now. We are going to start off by applying the textures, and then add some art assets, lights, particles, and specific naming conventions. The finished level will look similar to Figure 8-27.

Figure 8-27: Test level

Before we jump into texturing the level, take a moment to look at the way the geometry was created. Everything is squared off,

right? Well, that's the idea. Creating the level with rectangles speeds up the mapping, texturing, and the overall process. We will work this way for the test level, then branch off into a few different ways for the "official" demo level.

3. Open the Material Editor (**M**) and select the first color slot. Rename it **floor1 FX=bump**.

4. In the Maps rollout, click on the **None** button and then select **Bitmap**. Double-click on **floor1.dds**.

5. Click on the **Go to Parent** button to take you back up to the Maps rollout. Click on the **Bump None** button and select **Bitmap**. Choose **floor1_bump.dds**. Click back on the **Go to Parent** button.

6. Once again, click on the **Go to Parent** button to take you back up to the Maps rollout. Click on the **Specular Level None** button and select **Bitmap**. Choose **phong-20.png**. Click back on the **Go to Parent** button.

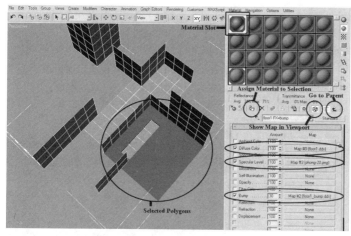

Figure 8-28: Floor selected and material applied

Tip:

If you work in max 5 or OpenGL mode, then you will most likely want to turn the Specular Level box off until you export. Try rendering with the specular level turned on and off; you'll see the difference immediately. If you are working in max 6 with the DirectX 9.0 Materials, then you don't have to worry about anything.

7. With the floor selected, click on **Assign Material to Selection**. You should now see brackets appear around the material slot identifying that the polygons selected have this texture applied to them. See Figure 8-28.

Max Tool Tip:

If you are using the shaded fill, you might only have red highlighted polygons. Press F2 to switch back and forth between the modes.

8. Press the **Show Map in Viewport** button so that you can see the texture in the viewport. If it's your first time to use the button, click it on and off a few times to get used to how it works.

Remember:

The diffuse, specular level, bump/normal, alpha, and glow maps are all stored in these two maps as we discussed in Chapter 6.

In the following steps I am going to assume you understand how to apply textures to materials, so there won't be tons of explaining. If you get lost or don't quite understand, simply refer to the earlier steps. Let's continue texturing the rest of the level.

9. In Polygon mode, select all the wall faces in the main room as shown in Figure 8-29.

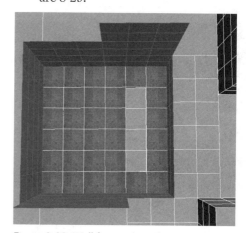

Figure 8-29: Wall faces selected

10. In the second material slot, rename it **wall_brick1 FX=bump**. Then load the **wall_brick1.dds** and **wall_brick1_bump.dds** files into the appropriate slots. Be sure to load the **phong-20.png** file into the Specular Level map as well.

11. Be sure you are at the parent level and then assign the material to the selection. Finally, click **Show Map in Viewport** to see it. (See Figure 8-30.)

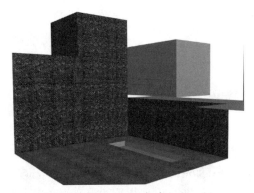

Figure 8-30: Wall texture applied

12. Now select the floor pieces in the hole area. In the third material slot, rename it to **floor2 FX=bump**. Then apply the **floor2.dds**, **floor2_bump.dds**, and **phong-20.png** files to the selected polygons. (See Figure 8-31.)

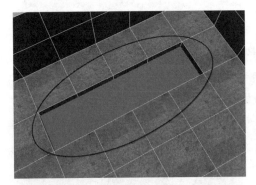

Figure 8-31: Floor area selected

13. Let's go ahead and finish off the area around the floor. Select the little wall pieces as shown in Figure 8-32.

14. In the fourth material slot, rename it **wall_brick3 FX=bump**. Apply the **wall_brick3.dds, wall_brick3_bump.dds,** and **phong-20.png** files to the selected polygons.

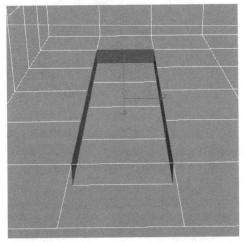

Figure 8-32: Small wall/edge polygons selected

The floor and walls on the main portion of the level are complete. That wasn't too difficult, was it? It should look something like Figure 8-33.

Figure 8-33: Main room textured

It's time to branch out and assign some textures to the walls around the testing area.

1. Select all the polygons on the back building as shown in Figure 8-34. In the Material Editor, select the fifth material slot and rename it **wall_building1 FX=bump**. Then apply the **wall_building1.dds**, **wall_building1_bump.dds**, and **phong-20.png** files to the selected polygons.

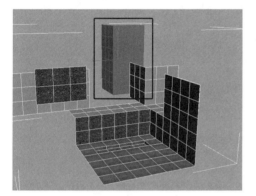

Figure 8-34: Building 1 selected

2. The next building on the list is the building on the far left as shown in Figure 8-35.

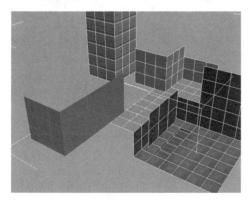

Figure 8-35: Building polygons selected

3. Name the next material slot **wall_building2 FX=bump**. Then apply the **wall_building2.dds**,

wall_building2_bump.dds, and **phong-20.png** files to the selected polygons.

4. In Figure 8-36, I've selected the next set of polygons. Select those and apply the **wall_building2** material.

Figure 8-36: Polygons selected

Two more things left to do.

5. Select the back building faces as shown in Figure 8-37.

6. In a new material slot, name it **wall_brick2 FX=bump**. Now apply the **wall_brick2.dds**, **wall_brick2_bump.dds**, and **phong-20.png** files to the selected polygons.

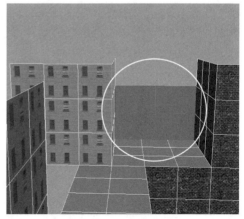

Figure 8-37: Back wall polygons selected

7. Now select the rooftop polygons shown outlined in Figure 8-38 and apply the **wall_brick1** material to them.

That's it! You have the entire level textured. See Figure 8-38. That was pretty easy, right?

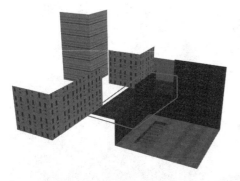

Figure 8-38: Test level textured

Let's take a second to load it into the viewer and see what it looks like.

1. Go to **File | Export** and name it **test_level.hgr**. Then check **Scale world units to meters** and **Copy textures to output path**, as shown in Figure 8-39, and click **OK**.

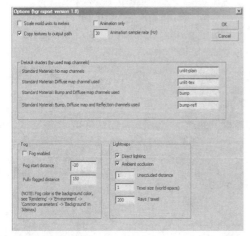

Figure 8-39: Exporter

2. Open the HGR Viewer and load **test_level.hgr**.

With the level textured it's time to work on the scene dressing; the objects we are going to use help in terms of bringing the level together, softening the corners, and making it look extra cool! Being level designers, we aren't required to create all the art. Fortunately for us, the art assets have already been created.

1. Be sure the level is open. Go to **File | Merge**. We will need to merge a few things into the scene to use in the level. In the Objects folder, select **barrel_set.max**. In the Merge window, select all the objects, then click **OK**.

2. Go ahead and load in all the max object files inside the Object folder. As you load the objects, be sure to move them to the side so you don't get a huge clutter of objects in the same spot. See Figure 8-40.

Figure 8-40: Items merged

Now that you have all the objects merged into the scene, it's time to start decorating. Let's go over a few pointers before we begin.

- **Corners and Edges** — Whenever you create any type of structure with sharp corners or edges, you begin losing the "flow" of the room. Remember, it's very important that a room's edges are softened a little. If a player enters a room and is immediately met with hard edges and walls that go to a point (corner), then it's likely the player will either head that way or leave the room. The objective is to place objects in the room that move the player around, guiding him through while keeping him from heading into a corner.

Natural — A natural look is important in a game. When you start placing objects in the level you want to keep in mind that it needs to look used, normal, just like an everyday scene. If things are all perfectly lined up in a row and the objects are all the same scale, then the scene becomes stale and predictable. You don't want to place a number of the same objects next to each other unless it's like a store shelf or an area that is expected to have similar objects. Try this: Don't clean your room for a month. If things fall on the floor, don't pick them up. Don't vacuum and lastly be sure to just "live" there. After a month, the room is undoubtedly going to look "natural." (**Hint**: If you actually attempt this experiment, be sure to clean it up after the month and stop living in a pig sty.)

Angles — Angles are needed in addition to softened corners and edges and a natural look. When you place objects into the scene, it's important to rotate them around to make the scene feel natural and flowing. Things that are placed on a ninety-degree angle will start to feel hard and fake. Also, use free-rotate in max so that objects don't just lie on a 45- or 30-degree angle. To keep things natural they need to lie at different angles.

Scale — The scale of objects is also important. Scaling an object larger or smaller in size immediately makes it feel like a new object. So, if you were to scale a cardboard box up in size and rotate it slightly from the original, there's an excellent chance it will appear like a new object.

Stacking — Stacking is definitely one of the best uses of objects in a scene. If you have all the objects lined up straight on the ground, your eye doesn't have to take in anything new vertically, just horizontally. But if you stack the objects on top of each other and lean boards around or on one another, then your eye will move in the vertical direction as well.

Sets — Creating a "set" or group of objects is an excellent tool. Let's say you had to fill an entire apartment complex with objects. You could take each room and personally design it, and three months later you might be done with the rooms. Another option is to create sets, which are groups of objects designed and laid out so that they can be reused. Then all you have to do is bring in a set to a room, change (rotate, scale, and add to) a few of the items around, and you instantly have an original-looking set of objects.

Snapshot — When playing a game you want to keep in mind that from any angle at any time during gameplay, you can take a snapshot of the game and it would be apparent which game it is and what level. By keeping this idea in mind when you design a level and/or populate the scene dressings you'll stick with items that go with the level. Another advantage of taking a "snapshot" of scenes is to be aware of whether or not the level and the objects go together. It's a chance to step back and look at the level objectively.

● **Quality vs. Quantity** — The quality of a scene will always win over quantity. If you cannot make two or three items look great in a scene, then it's only going to get worse by adding more to the level. Be sure that the quality is always first on the list before going for quantity.

Note:

These level creation pointers will keep your design team in check and will help you to create the best looking and most uniquely suited game around.

3. Go to the corner of the level as shown in Figure 8-41. Have the viewports configured similar to the image. I've chosen to have one viewport a "camera"-like setup, while keeping a Top view to move the objects around and a Front view to help in rotating and moving vertically.

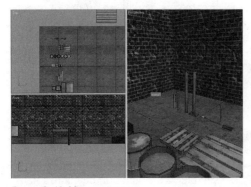

Figure 8-41: Viewport setup

We are going to start off with an easy set. Check out Figure 8-42 to see what I came up with.

4. Start off by placing three barrels in the corner. To throw off the monotony of barrels, place another one tipped over and rotated slightly. Place a couple of cardboard boxes around the barrels as well as one leaning up on top. Not too difficult. Finally, add the sign to the adjoining wall up top. I added in a couple of poles as well, to help divide the empty space between the sign and the ground.

Figure 8-42: Corner objects arranged

Ah, so you want more of a challenge? Let's work up the corner at the other end of the wall. See Figures 8-43 and 8-44.

Figure 8-43: Corner wall

5. Start with the largest objects and work down from there. As you can tell, I have placed stairs in the corner. After

Figure 8-44: Corner closeup

long and open the way it is. Divide up the hole with more wood posts about a third of the way down. Also, place the water and the crate to fill up the center areas. If you've done that, by now you have probably noticed that the back wall is just far enough from the hole to make it feel empty. An easy solution to that is to place five poles running down the back side. This will add just the right amount of vertical placement to keep things interesting on that side.

placing the stairs, you will immediately notice the large space under and next to them. It's time to fill that space with a large crate. Then place a few more crates and a couple of barrels around the large one. As you can tell I also leaned a pallet against the stairs. The steps leading to the top have not been broken up (in terms of design and flow), so I placed the pallet there to help add detail as well as flow to the stairs. Then at the top of the steps we've placed a pallet and a barrel in the corner so that when you get up there, you'll automatically want to go to the left and not toward the corner. Lastly, fill in the smaller empty areas with wood pieces scattered around and leaning up on the crates.

6. The pool area was certainly the most improved portion of the level. The first thing you should pay attention to are hard edges. The hole was cut clean out and extruded down. As you can tell, it needs to appear soft in order to flow with the rest of the scene. Let's take the large wood posts and line the hole with them as shown in Figure 8-45. The next thing we need to do is divide the hole up into separate sections. It's pretty apparent that the space is too

Figure 8-45: Hole area worked up

7. In the back corner I simply took the set from the first corner and copied it over, moved a few things around, and added some boards in front as shown in Figure 8-46.

Figure 8-46: Corner copied and adjusted

255

8. Now we need to add some light fix-
tures to the level so that we'll have a
reason to add actual light. If you look at
the poles that were just added to the
level, it certainly feels like the poles
point upward to nothing. We need some
objects to stop our eye movement
before we leave the wall. Place four or
five lights similar to the ones shown in
Figure 8-47.

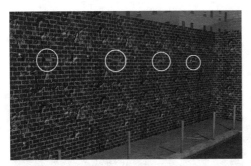

Figure 8-47: Lights

9. Then place the hanging light underneath the stairs as shown in Figure
8-48.

Figure 8-48: Hanging light fixture

I've included a couple of final images from
the level so you can see where I placed all
the other objects. See Figures 8-49 and
8-50.

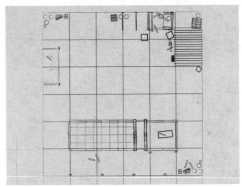

Figure 8-49: Top view wireframe

Figure 8-50: Top view textured

Let's place the lights into the level. Check
out Figure 8-51 to see where I've placed
them. I chose to use two lights against the
wall, the hanging light, and one light up in
the air to simulate moonlight.

1. Go to **Create | Lights | Omni**. Place
   three or four lights in the scene similar
   to Figure 8-51. Be sure to change the
   light color for the wall lights to R:**210**,
   G:**252**, B:**254** and the Multiplier to **0.3**.
   Set the "moon" light to R:**243**, G:**231**,
   B:**218** and the Multiplier to **0.5**. See
   Figure 8-52.

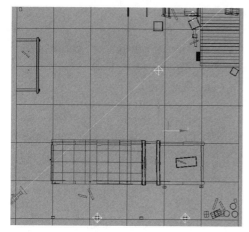

Figure 8-51: Light positions

quick but effective "radiosity"-style light.

Figure 8-52: Light parameters

2. For rendering inside of max, check **On** in the Shadows area and change the lighting style to **Area Shadows** for each light. This will provide you with a

Exporting the Level

The level is ready for exporting. Export the level and test it out in the HGR Viewer. Be sure to choose Scale world units to meters and Copy textures to output path. Also, make sure you check the Direct Lighting and Ambient Occlusion check boxes. This will generate the light map for the scene.

> **Tip:**
>
> If you'd like to see the scene really quick, be sure to leave Direct Lighting and Ambient Occlusion unchecked.

When you run the level, one of the first things you'll probably notice is the glow shaders applied to the sign and lights.

Pretty cool effect! Check out all the scene dressings and objects we've added. See if you like them and then look to see if it can be improved.

By now, you should have a clear understanding of the basics of level creation and design. This topic by itself could be an entire book, which means I've had to limit it and only touch on the essential issues. We will get into more of the details and tutorials on the web site (www.KA3D.com), so be sure to visit often. The last thing on the list for level design is the breakdown of the Zax demo level.

Tutorial 13: Zax Demo Level

The Zax demo level is a combination of modular building pieces and raw "artistic" geometry. Since I was using max for the level creation, I found that I would be able to use various modeling techniques inside the environment. Let's take a look at the steps involved.

1. Open **Level_1_Looney_Lava_1.max** found in the Tutorial_13 folder. You should see a wireframe view of the entire level.

We are going to pick apart the level from start to finish.

2. The initial design is very similar to the ones done earlier in the book. The following steps detail how I created the level. Start in the Top view with a box. Bump up the length and width of the segments until the squares are about **8** to **10** feet, to give you enough geometry to create a soft terrain and keep the textures crisp and clean.

3. Next, convert the box into an editable polygon, and use the **Cut** tool to cut out the outline shape of the mountain with the help of the concept design.

4. After the cuts are completed, delete the extra faces along the outside, then in Edge mode select the outline shape and began extruding it downward. Remember, when you work levels this way it's not exact, so you will have to clean up some of the UVs while texturing the shape later.

5. For the larger mountain, simply extrude the edges downward about 10 to 12 times, creating a somewhat smooth, modular feel to the geometry. Fortunately, the polygons are close enough to squares that it's possible to

apply one face map to the entire object and have it work for nearly everything.

6. The next option to decide on is the shape. Grab the vertices on each row and scale them out, growing the base enough each time to give it the look of a forceful mountain.

7. The design called for a floating, stationary mountain, so bring its base in as shown in Figure 8-53 to help define its softer, more refined side.

Use this same technique for each mountain.

8. Then with the Cut tool, cut into the top of the mountain and create a "lava pool" for the main bad guy.

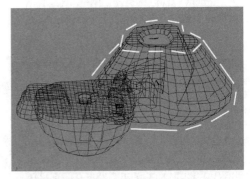

Figure 8-53: Mountains

9. The next step is to lay out the basic shapes for the mining shaft. The shaft followed a simple pattern and maintained a slope, giving the impression it was going down into the heart of the mountain. Using the Handy Cam, fly around the level and check out what type of geometry was created for it.

10. With the main level geometry created, begin loading in the art assets and place them in the world. This step typically takes the longest because it should be the time you have to start

really thinking. Make sure each section is totally refined and corners are treated properly as well as make sense. This is a floating mountain, so there is only a limited amount of area to successfully dress it up. In level_1_Looney_Lava_2.max, you can see all the objects that were placed around the level (see Figure 8-54).

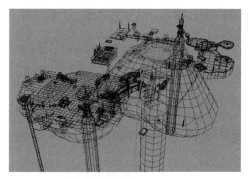

Figure 8-54: Scene dressings

11. At this point, I am still using the concept design for placement. Once the mountain was filled, it was time to add the skydome and some sort of brick divider between this level and the rest of the world. See Figure 8-55.

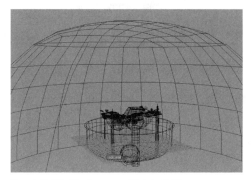

Figure 8-55: Skydome and brick divider

12. The skydome is not your average sphere. I've divided it up into five sections: four wall pieces and one top piece, which allows the skydome to have a solid place to stick the textures. The brick wall divider is a great idea to help keep the players within a boundary and create the feeling of needing/wanting to get out.

13. Once the geometry was created, I began working over the entire particle world. This consisted of placing dummy boxes and linking them to objects I knew would move, as well as defining their properties in the User Defined section. I also exported the level and began playing around with the actual particles through the HGR Viewer.

Note:

There's so much going on in this level that I created a square, boxy room in Tutorial Room Naming Convention, called naming_convention.max, and placed all the basic names and examples in it.

14. With the particles in place it was time to place the health, coins, weapons, and special items. The level design map does an excellent job of illustrating where they are. With the image in the Background viewport, I simply used the Top view and placed dummy boxes where I saw the need.

15. Finally, I placed the triggers, sound boxes, and lights where needed. Each one has user-defined properties, so be sure to take some time to pick apart the level to understand how each thing works with the others.

Final Tips on Environment Creation

Typically when you complete your first level, it's good to go back over your textures and geometry. With the level exported, you can begin testing everything for optimal performance. Let's look at some points of interest in both categories.

Optimizing the Final Level

Texture Size

It's very important to remember when you are creating level textures to start large and end small. I've seen companies create entire levels with 128x128 and 256x256 textures only to have to go back and recreate a large texture from the small texture or start over from scratch, so that they can have more detail for a splash screen, magazine cover, or because technology improves and allows them added texture memory. With that said, be sure that you create the original texture at either 512 or 1024 size and then once you have things looking great go back in and optimize where it's needed. Also, remember that if objects are at a distance, there may not be a need for a Normal map or Specular map. Test it out as you go to get a better feel of what's needed and what's not.

> ### Photoshop Tip:
>
> The most useful way I have found in replacing the larger textures with smaller ones is to simply go into Photoshop and run a batch file process that simply reduces the size and saves over the original file. Be sure that you save the original files elsewhere before replacing them.

Geometry Optimization

Once you have time to run through the levels and test the look and feel of the demo, there's a good chance you will notice things that could be reduced. "What exactly am I looking for?" you might be asking. There are many things you can look for. Check out these three ideas for some help in optimizing the geometry:

- Visibility — Can you really see the object in the game? Oftentimes designers will make geometry that is high in detail but is never close enough to the player to make it worth the expense. Run/walk through your levels and check to see if the objects you can actually get up next to are detailed enough, while the objects that are at a distance have shape but are not overly high poly.

- LOD — Level of detail is another great option to use for creating the most optimal geometry. For instance, if you have a rock in the scene that is 400 polygons, you should reduce it for the distance to something in the range of 40 polygons.

- Unseen polygons — If you have never created optimal geometry before, then be sure to remember and practice the following: "Always delete unseen, unused, back-faced polygons. If the player cannot see it, then there's no reason for the extra polygons to be in the scene."

Managing Large Worlds and Environments

We have been discussing ways to keep the design of large levels in check, but I want to be sure that you hear things one more time. In max, things can quickly become unorganized, messy, and "unprofessional." Using layers and selection sets allows you to maintain consistency, allows quick access to all parts of the level, and even helps force you to maintain an organized workflow. As you have seen in the demo level, I took the time to add each group of objects, paths, and even particles to its own selection name. Can you imagine needing to select all the paths in a level if there were literally hundreds of paths? I would prefer to click one button and have all the paths selected. Layers are excellent for control when it comes to outdoor and indoor portions of a level. Say you were working on an alleyway window and needed to jump into the building to work on the window from the inside. With layers you could have each part on a separate layer, as well as the collisions for each object on separate layers, so that it doesn't get in the way while you are

working on the scene. Another advantage of working with layers and selection sets is that it's easier to hide or unhide objects in the scene. Working with levels that are 100,000 to 500,000 polygons in size can make things go really slow if you have everything unhidden or you have to select objects continuously to hide and unhide them.

As long as you begin a project with organization in mind, control and accessibility will be much better. (And others who study the levels will be highly impressed with your professionalism!)

That wraps up the level design chapter. As I stated before, there are countless aspects to designing levels and those mentioned here are merely a few ideas and variations to the norm. If you are still in need of more explanations and ideas, just visit our web site at www.KA3D.com where we are working daily to provide you the best support, innovation, and ideas to help you with your understanding of game creation.

Time to move on to Part 3, "Game Programming." Good luck and keep smiling.

Part 3

Game Programming

Programming games is not an easy task. It involves many different areas of computer science, including computer graphics, computational geometry, finite automata, and artificial intelligence, so you need a wide variety of skills. But it is a very rewarding activity. It is exceptionally exciting to see your own hero character — something of your own creation — move on screen for the first time. It is even more rewarding when you implement the weapons and you can start shooting at the stuff you have created.

It is true that the best lessons teach by doing, but learning new techniques from a book can save you time if you end up avoiding even one painful mistake. Reading gives perspective, and more perspective is always good. At the end of each chapter in this part, I list a few books that can be helpful if you need more information.

Game programming starts by reviewing good development practices. It is always good to stop every once in a while and explicitly consider your own development practices. So even if you are an experienced programmer, I hope Chapter 9, "Good Development Practices," will at least give you something to think about.

We get into the actual code in Chapter 10, "Writing Robust Code." Here, we take a look at the issues of what makes a good piece of code, and what kind of conventions we're using and the reasons for them.

Graphics are the first thing you see in the game, and graphics have been the driving force behind game development. Chapter 11, "Graphics Programming," is also one of the longest chapters for a very good reason. Although there is more to learn about graphics programming than you can fit in a single chapter, or even a single book, this chapter gives you concrete examples of getting stuff to screen using the 3D engine provided with the book, Ka3D. The chapter starts with drawing a single polygon to screen, but by the end you'll also learn the basics of character animation and animating by physics simulation.

Chapter 12, "Collision Checking," gives you an overview of techniques available for making you stay above the ground, literally. Even if you're using some external library for collision checking, it's still useful to know the details to get the most out of the library you're using, and to solve the problems you might encounter while using it. The chapter also gives you a roadmap for implementing a moving sphere collision check against a triangle, probably the most used collision check in game development.

After graphics and collisions have been sorted out, we move to scripting in Chapter 13. Game content creation is as important as the game programming itself, so supporting it by scripting is pretty much a requirement for modern game

development. In this chapter we look at the basics of the Lua scripting language and the methods in C++ for providing easy-to-use support for scripting with it. At the end we give you an example of how to use the scripting support provided with the Ka3D engine, so you can start scripting your game without needing to implement a single line of scripting support yourself.

After scripting we're ready to look at typical interaction in games in Chapter 14. Here we focus on finite state machines and triggers, both fundamental building blocks in most games, especially in the action/adventure/platformer genres. As implementing both triggers and state machines is quite straightforward, this chapter focuses more on the concepts than actual code.

In Chapter 15, "Game Framework Design," we take a look at how we put all the pieces together. We use the game demo specification as the requirements for our design. Seeing the big picture helps you understand individual components better too, and their place in the whole. We also consider some generalizations — many seemingly different types of games are surprisingly similar in architecture if you look closer. Or further, in this case.

Chapter 16 gives you an annotated example of a technical document of a game demo. You might give this document to a potential publisher in your game pitch. They might not read it word for word, but at least it shows that you've thought about the stuff you're going to implement. The technical document also serves as an overview for new programmers involved in the project. Any high-level document helps, as it's quite a big effort just starting to look at the source without any big picture of the massive amount of source code.

Let's get started. Good luck with your game programming efforts!

Chapter 9

Good Development Practices

Software development is in some ways similar to many types of sports; when you have mastered the basics you can get quite close to the top. And game development is one branch of software development. Of course using good development practices won't guarantee your success as a game developer; successful software development is still mostly about people, the team building the software. But still, this doesn't mean you should underestimate the effect of these development fundamentals. It can be a great help in the effort of building better games, and everyone should use all the help they can find.

Countless projects done by even the biggest and the most stable companies have failed catastrophically — not just in the game development business but in all other software fields as well. The best-known example in the game industry might be Daikatana, but it certainly isn't the first or last failed project. Examples are easy to find — just ask anyone who has worked on a couple of moderate-sized software projects. Game development is a unique field, but it still shares many of the same issues with any software development, so if you spend some time reading software engineering

books, chances are you won't be wasting your time.

Problems in software development are often causes of catastrophic failures, both schedule- and product-wise. But in addition to severity, what makes software development problems worse is that they might surface only long after the actual mistake or mistakes have been made. The problems also surface bit by bit, so to speak, so it might take a long time before the project management team realizes they are in trouble. And then it might already be too late to react. Combined with the issue that often the problems are in fundamental development practices, this means that software development problems end up being very hideous and hard to fix. In some cases, the only fix may be a complete redo, and indeed, sometimes it might even make more sense than trying to fix the crippled project. You can always try to dump the whole thing and call it a prototype! But if you suspect you might end up in a situation where that is not a feasible approach, continue reading as we discuss the development fundamentals.

Define Clear Goals

Defining goals is a simple principle, but one that is surprisingly hard to follow. Lack of clear goals can appear in any level of abstraction in the project, from lack of overall project goals to design and implementation of individual functions in some specific programming language.

What's dangerous also is that even though some people might share common goals in the project, it might not be realized that all the people involved are not sharing them. For example, a client who will be using the software might not be an expert in software development, so he might not be able to ask the right questions or specify his needs accurately or even correctly. So it is not enough for a software developer to create the software right; he also must make sure that he is creating the right software. It is especially important that the management team shares the vision so the risk of compromising the product at later stages is minimized. Nothing is worse than having different producers each wanting his or her own kind of game from the poor developer.

The most common symptom of unclear goals is feature creep. Another is an overly general-purpose design, i.e., a "We want to make it ready for anything" attitude. If you want to be prepared for *everything*, then you are not *aiming* at anything.

Here is an example of a misguided low-level goal in a real-world game project. The team was making a realistic action game. The game world was managed using cells and portal technology, which means that the world consists of "rooms," or cells, which in turn are connected to each other by "doors," or portals. So whenever a character, bullet, or camera goes from one room to another, it passes through a portal. The team wanted the system to be very general-purpose, so it was decided that each room would have its own private coordinate space, including free rotation, and only the portals connecting the rooms knew how to transform a coordinate from one room to the next. This might sound like a good generalization, but the programmers ended up in a lot of trouble because of that decision, since it was unintuitive to need to transform every direction and position vector from one space to another when the possibility existed that the computations passed a portal. This had inconvenient consequences; for example, it was not possible to compute a distance between two points by simple subtraction of the position vectors. The team, in fact, ended up with this solution because *it didn't seem to do any harm*, not because it was needed in the game. So in fact they added a feature that was not needed and ended up in trouble.

Here's another example, this time from a higher abstraction level and a different game genre, a car racing game. The team was too busy to consider the overall target feeling of the game. Was the game supposed to be more like a stunt car simulation or arcade style racing? The racing tracks ended up looking like wild arcade tracks, but the car behavior was based on Newtonion mechanics; you can imagine what it feels like to try to do an upside-down loop with near realistic car physics. In the end, the team needed to hack the physics so that the game was even moderately playable, since it was out of the question to remodel the tracks due to time constraints.

Closely related to goals is the issue of coding priorities. If the project does not have clear goals, then each programmer will have his own priorities and the result is not consistent. What's worse, it might be completely unsuitable for the product and risk the whole development process. For example, if you need a product that is highly robust and the team is focused on making highly optimized, and risky, code, the project will end up in trouble sooner or later as misplaced priorities thwart the goal.

Despite the importance of coding priorities, project leads rarely inform the team about them. There are several priorities to consider:

- Clarity
- Simplicity
- Maintainability
- Testability
- Consistency
- Portability
- Code size
- Memory usage
- Reusability
- Robustness
- Execution speed

In addition to the order of priorities, you should also consider acceptable levels of quality for different priorities. Different components might also have different levels of quality standard. For example, should the function accept garbage as input? As a general principle, the lower the abstraction level you work on, the more robust the system should be with relation to these kinds of decisions. The operating system must not crash if some function gets called with invalid input, but the application level function might as well check the input with debug-build-only asserts and then continue assuming that the input was correct. In general, the code should not *hide* problems, even though it survives the problems

without crashing, so the problems should always be reported in one way or another.

Lack of goals can also surface in completely different circumstances; for example project management and corporate policies. The guiding principle to achieving efficient development should be that any work that does not result in an improved product is potentially wasted effort. The principle seems so self evident that you don't even think about it, but still in many companies the team spends too much time preparing for meetings, going to meetings, summarizing meetings, writing status reports, and answering e-mail. In context, this is a symptom of a lack of clear goals on a project management level: The team's focus and goal should be to make a better product, not waste time on corporate policies. Be sure that every report that is routinely written is really worth writing.

Some important properties of good goals in game development are:

- The goals are based on *player experience*. The goals should not be set by the merits of some technical solution or other reason; it's only the resulting experience that matters at the end.

- The goals are *concrete*. The more concrete the goals are, the better chance you'll have of achieving them. Good concrete goals directly imply actions.

- The goals are *realistic*. It is highly unmotivating to try to achieve something if you know you'll have no chance to succeed.

So how do you define good goals? There is really no magic in it; you just have to sit down and take some time to think of what you are really trying to achieve. The goals are there to help you build a better picture of what it is that you are trying to do.

Fix Problems Early

Fixing problems early is a general development fundamental that can be applied to a wide variety of problems. Usually software engineering books refer to the issue of fixing bugs early, but the same principle can be applied to any problem in any corner of the software triangle, whether it is product, people, or process that is in question.

Fixing problems early pays off. Software development is a kind of cyclic waterfall-like process by nature; even iterative development processes only make the cycle shorter. This has a direct implication that good decisions pay back early during the project, but wrong decisions end up costing more and more.

Maybe the most important benefit of fixing problems early is that it gives a much-needed negative feedback loop to the development process. When you develop software, for example, problems in the schedule tend to be apparent only later when the actual miss happened. It is a common saying that the last 10% of a software project takes 90% of the development time. The saying is referring partly to the fact that it is very hard to estimate how long it will take to fix some specific bug from the long list of all bugs. Also, new bugs might surface because of dependencies between different components. Fixing problems early addresses the issue by showing the delay in the development progress and schedule right away, when the problem occurs.

Getting immediate feedback in fixing problems early is also very good for an individual programmer in the project. Making mistakes and fixing them early gives the programmer a chance to learn from the mistakes. This is also the reason why every programmer should fix his own bugs: to get

a chance to learn from them and avoid making the same mistakes in the future.

Each programmer should try to learn from mistakes systematically, for example by following the steps shown below after finding or fixing each bug. A mini-postmortem or checklist for each bug could consist of the following steps:

1. How could I have prevented this bug?

2. How could I have detected this bug earlier?

3. How I will avoid this kind of bug in the future?

4. Could similar bugs be detected automatically by using some programming convention?

5. Did I step through the code when I tested it? If I did, then why didn't I notice the problem then?

It is much easier to fix problems at the time they occur. If we look at the issue from the pure implementation point of view, the conclusion follows directly from the fact that at the time you write the source code you also remember the internals of the source code much better than you will later.

Adding new code on top of incorrect code also makes the risk higher that the new code might hide the old bug, but the problem is still there waiting to surface. In addition to the possibility that circumstances might be worse, there will at least be more code to debug and so the problem will be even harder to find.

One must be careful that the *correct problem* is fixed. Programmers are usually optimistic by nature and generally hate bugs, so it is tempting to guess the reason for some new problem. By guessing what the problem is — and the fix as a consequence — the programmer can accidentally hide the actual problem, whether the problem is simpler or more complex than first thought. So be sure to find out what the real problem is before you try to fix it.

The attitude needs to be that bugs are serious and must not be ignored. If anything else is prevailing, then it follows that the bugs get collected, at best case, to some list that starts to grow and grow. Long bug lists are also bad for team morale, since there seems to be an endless number of issues to fix. By keeping a hard line on bug counts, you'll also have a much better chance to estimate when the project will be complete.

In the field of people management, the reasons for fixing problems early are basically the same as in coding: If you fix problems early, then the issues between people don't have time to escalate into larger problems, which might even destroy the whole development team in the worst case. If the chemistry doesn't work

between some people, find a permanent solution early on.

In the case of problems in the process, fixing early is also a good thing because the more an invalid process is used, the more consequences there will be, and the harder it is to replace the convention because of people getting used to using it. For example, one company used coding guidelines that required a pragma(pack) C preprocessor directive to be used around class declarations. There was almost never any reason for pragma(pack), but if the directives were missing even from one header, the usage of directives could cause serious and obscure bugs at run time because many other headers used them. Even though the problem was realized, the company continued to use the directives because of the large amount of legacy code that had the directives in place.

Keep It Simple

It isn't surprising that the most efficient way to speed up a development project is to narrow the scope of the project. The easiest requirement is the one that you don't need to fill. It is lucky from the developer's point of view that simple things tend to work better than more complex ones. I don't even remember how many times I've had to advise some less technical friend of mine how to get rid of that legendary Office Assistant.

The way the feature is specified can also make a huge difference. The same feature can take easily 10 times more work to implement, depending on the specifications. Consider, for example, the debug output. If you just dump the output to stdout, it takes practically no time to implement. But if you

specify to view the debug output in the same window in which the application is running, scroll through the output history, need proper, language-specific word iteration and line wrapping, need for the user to be able to insert comments between the output text, and so on, you can easily end up doing nothing but the debug output in the project. An extreme example maybe, but the issue should nevertheless be considered for every single feature: Is it really needed and is there a way to specify it more simply? This is especially important if the requirements originate from a nonprogrammer, because the wording could be poorly chosen, which programmers may not notice to question, even though the customer would be completely satisfied with a much simpler feature. As always, communication is vital.

Features are often added to the project because the goal is not clear. As an example, a game player who enjoys first-person action games (yep, me) probably won't be too excited about a platformer-style special level in the middle of the game. The feature might still be worth adding to the game if it doesn't require much work, but there are rarely any free lunches in that sense. Even if the addition takes very little code, there are always the issues of dependencies, resource usage, testing, documentation, and learning to use the added feature in gameplay and level design. In general, everything is usually more work than it initially seems.

In many game development projects you have to dump features at the end of the project because of the lack of time. In addition, most teams perform versioned development of some sort, which is to say that the developers keep a separate "to be added if we have time" list. But it's never too early to dump features — dumping should be started early, right after making the initial specification of the product. Or if you don't like "dumping," you can call it "feature-set control."

A key issue in controlling the feature set is to make sure that you know all the features. If the specification lacks features, then not only will you likely miss milestones, but your feature set looks better than it is because it looks *smaller* than it is in reality. So cutting down features shouldn't mean cutting down time spent on specifying the requirements.

Knowing all the features is not the same as overspecifying them. When the specifications aren't overly specified and thus restricted, the programmers are free to design and implement the software as efficiently as possible. Shorter specification documents also have a better chance of actually being read by someone every once in a while. Also, a less restrictive specification gives more ownership of the feature to the programmers, so that the product becomes *their* product. Ownership, in turn, increases motivation, and motivation is the most important factor for good productivity, as most studies have shown.

Keeping the feature set simple also has direct benefits right down to the implementation level. Writing bug-free code is difficult, but it's much easier to do if the design is simple to implement. Making a clear and consistent architecture design is in turn easier if the requirements are simple. Besides, if something feels complex to implement, the chances are good that you won't get it right.

Additional Reading

Steve Maguire, *Debugging the Development Process*, MS Press, 1994. (A very good read, and the style of Maguire's writing also makes it very easy to read.)

Frederick P. Brooks, *The Mythical Man-Month: Essays on Software Engineering*, Addison-Wesley, 1995. (A classic and also very easy to read.)

Steve McConnell, *Rapid Development: Taming Wild Software Schedules*, MS Press, 1996. (A bit heavy for my taste — I needed three tries to read it through — but the content is very good.)

Roger S. Pressman, *Software Engineering: A Practitioner's Approach, 5th Ed.*, McGraw-Hill, 2000. (A very good book for reference, but I doubt anyone has ever read this monster from cover to cover.)

Chapter 10

Writing Robust Code

In this chapter, we look at the properties of good source code. The properties are quite universal, but their priorities are not. What is the most important priority in one project might not be the best for yours. After properties we take a look at a set of source code writing conventions, which hopefully will help you on your path to creating quality code.

What Makes Good Code

Clarity

Clarity should usually be your number one concern. It is not rare to see programmers looking at their own source code and mumbling "WTH." What is even worse, later you might introduce new bugs into the code because you didn't understand the point you originally had with the solution you ended up with.

Simplicity

"Simple is beautiful." "Make it as simple as possible, but not simpler." — A.Einstein. "Keep it simple, stupid." "If you can't explain something in simple terms, you haven't understood it yourself either." — A.Einstein.

There are many sayings that underline this important goal. Simple solutions usually just end up working better, and if you can't understand something very thoroughly, there is a good chance that you won't be able to pull it off in practice. What's even worse, programmers who have less experience may end up with solutions that are way too complicated when they think too hard about what they are doing. And of course the end result is that they never get it working.

Maintainability

At first thought, maintainability doesn't seem to be an issue in game development projects. However, big projects last for years and have, for example, many different programmers, multiple DirectX versions, and multiple display adapter generations, so that you end up maintaining existing source code, whether you planned to or not. Scrapping everything and starting a total rewrite is usually a difficult choice to make after the project is finished as there are always useful components that can be reused. Or at least they could if you had written them with reuse in mind. Closely related to maintainability is the issue of dependencies — the fewer dependencies, the easier the code is to maintain.

Minimal Dependencies

Precompiled headers are a very useful feature in modern compilers, but this feature may be the number one reason why so many projects have ended up with unmaintainable dependencies. That's a pretty bold statement, but in my experience many people seem to take precompiled headers as the reason why they don't need to give a damn about dependencies and they can just put everything into one single header. One project I worked on used to compile for an hour when doing a full rebuild. And it happened a lot, because many of the low-level classes, for example 3-vector (float3), were included indirectly in every source file.

Avoiding cyclic dependencies is especially important because in addition to slowing down compilation, they are bad for maintenance, clarity, and testing. Use levelization techniques like refactoring, manager classes, escalation, and demotion for getting rid of cyclic dependencies. *Refactoring* is the process of changing the program structure without changing its functionality. Basically you just redesign the architecture a bit so that you avoid cyclic dependencies. Using *manager classes* means that instead of using low-level objects directly, you use the manager and avoid the internal cyclic dependencies that might otherwise occur. *Escalation* is moving mutually dependent functionality to a higher level in the dependency hierarchy. For example, instead of having two components dependent on each other, you can have one "super-component" that uses both lower-level ones. *Demotion* is doing the same thing the other way round; in other words, moving the functionality down to a shared component that is used by both.

Testability

Plan your code for testing. Even better, plan your code so that it can be automatically tested. For example, you can compare the results of unit tests against some known good results. This is harder to apply in very high-level code, but more often than not you can define very good unit tests and use a regression test suite for the components.

For example, when you have an image filter component that negates the image, you could negate some known test image and check it (by code) against some image manipulation software negated image to see if they match. You can easily do the test so that it can be run again later if needed. This way you can have a test suite that you *always* run when you modify an existing component, and you can be sure that your code works. Among other benefits, you avoid the anxiety that surrounds changing existing code, and the practice gives you a good night's sleep.

You should even consider using the practice of writing the test cases before writing the actual implementation of the component. This has an additional benefit that you actually prototype the user interface before doing the implementation, so that you have a chance to fix possible awkwardness in the interface before you write the implementation!

Consistency

Whatever you do, be consistent. First of all, it helps you to spot things when something is abnormal. It also helps you to understand stuff created by other people in the project, as everyone follows the same conventions. You should be consistent in all aspects, from function implementation level to high-level application design. Use the same order to pass parameters to a function and use the same logic as to how the buttons work in the game. The next section gives you an idea of the coding guidelines you might use when writing code, but consistency goes beyond that, so don't limit the practice just to coding.

Portability

With minimal dependencies and maintainable code, you're pretty well off already. But don't count on it if you have just developed the stuff for a single platform, since no matter how "portable" you planned the code, if you don't develop it on multiple platforms, then the code won't be portable in practice. This is especially true for porting source code to a PlayStation 2. As one major publisher put it: "We have had so many failed PlayStation 2 projects that started with a PC demo that we won't be even looking at anything that doesn't run on PlayStation 2."

Code Size

Code size is never an issue on desktop platforms, but it is definitely worth considering, especially if you're developing on mobile platforms. For example, compiling std::sort can add more than 23 kilobytes of executable code. Not exactly a good thing if you are aiming for a less than 100-kilobyte total application size.

Memory Usage

On the PC you have tons of memory and you can more or less transparently continue memory usage to the hard drive if you run out; but on consoles the situation isn't that relaxed and on mobile platforms the situation is even worse. You need to be *very* tight on memory consumption, since when you run out of memory, you just run out of memory and you have no swap disk or any

other magic operating system trick to save your game. But it doesn't hurt either to be aware of your memory consumption on the PC, since many customers might not have the latest PC with a gigabyte of memory. Besides, due to cache issues, lower memory consumption quite often means better performance, too.

Reusability

You need to plan for reusability before you can achieve it, but first you should consider its worth. Many times it is just cheaper to modify some old component instead of trying to generalize the component to apply to multiple situations. On the other hand, having robust code that works in both cases is excellent if you manage to pull it off. Many times programmers try to write reusable code and end up with obscure, non-reusable components that pretty much need a total rewrite in the next project anyway. As a rule of thumb, at least you should do something once before you try to generalize it.

Robustness

Don Knuth once promised a cash reward to anyone who found a bug in his TeX implementation. Respectable guy, respectable promise, and you should aim for the same. But make sure you're not hiding bugs — you're not writing a nuclear power-plant operating system that needs to run in every possible error scenario without interruptions. Instead, you should aim at making every bug visible and unavoidable in every step. For example, make sure that after a sorting routine, the elements are in the proper order and show a big flashing message box to the user of the application if this is not the case. Dumping warnings to some log file is not enough. This is the only way to verify that your code actually works.

275

Execution Speed

Many programmers are really fond of optimizing their code, and many times optimization has its uses. Still, you should keep in mind Knuth's saying: "Premature optimization is the root of all evil." Before even considering optimization, you should know what to optimize and when. It doesn't help anything to optimize a routine that only takes a percent or two from the total execution time anyway. And there is also a big chance that even if the routine is taking a big portion of total execution time, it may not do it in later phases of development when more stuff is in the game slowing it down. Everything is relative.

Programming Conventions

No Bugs Allowed

Eliminating bugs should usually be your number one priority while programming. If it's not, then you should consider some other career. Do not allow bugs to take over your code and project. They are very hard to get rid of. In one project I worked on we had four programmers trying to reproduce and find one very-hard-to-spot access violation bug for a week. Needless to say, that bug alone cost the company thousands of dollars to fix, and it would have been much cheaper to avoid it in the first place.

Fix bugs as soon as you find them. It's much more efficient that way as you still have better memory of the code you've worked on, and some new features might hide the bug later. Also, fixing bugs early forces you to focus more intently, so that you avoid being "90% ready" for 90% of the actual project duration.

You can also help yourself by making sure your code finds its own bugs by using *design by contract*. *Contracts* in this case means that by specifying behavior exactly, a function and its user make a contract between themselves. If either the user or the function breaks the contract, then an error message should be shown.

In practice, this contract enforcement works by using preconditions, postconditions, and class invariants in your functions to validate everything you are assuming. Be cautious, though, of assuming too much. You should think of a way to check situations where someone uses your code "wrong" too.

Preconditions check the input to the functions; for example, the precondition of sqrt(x) would check that x is greater than or equal to zero. Preconditions are the function's way to tell the caller "if you call me, then the parameters passed to me need to fulfill these requirements."

Postconditions, as the name suggests, check that the function has done what it promised. As you can use the techniques in separate debug build, they don't slow down your game. During development, and maybe even after, you should keep some of the checks active just in case, since that way you have a better chance of spotting the exact location of bugs when your actual clients find them. (Hopefully this doesn't happen, of course, but in practice it will.)

Postconditions and preconditions form a kind of pair of contracts. The function says that if you promise this, I will promise that from the results. Class invariants, on the other hand, specify that the object state is valid. For example, if you have a 2D bounding area class (min,max), you could specify a class invariant that the max corner of the area is always greater than or equal to the minimum corner of the area. If this invariant is violated, then the application user is alerted again.

C++ provides the assert() macro for checking assumptions such as those mentioned above. In some situations, though, you might find it useful to have several different assert macros to provide different levels of debug checking to different builds. This is especially useful on mobile platforms where only very limited resources are available on the actual device, but you still need some way to conveniently check the most critical assumptions on target hardware also.

You might be thinking, why not use assumptions in the middle of the function? Well, of course you can use the assert macro or any other mechanism you wanted for that purpose also, but you should also keep in mind that if you need to check assumptions inside the implementation of a single function, it kind of hints to you that it might be a good idea to split the function into smaller parts. For example, instead of saying that this transform matrix shouldn't have a zero-filled column or row before calculating the inverse transform, you should move the transform itself to its own function that checks that the object (matrix) state is valid before the function is called.

Guidelines

In general, I'm not a big fan of overly strict conventions for every detail. In general, one should be able to trust a programmer's good sense and ability to conform to existing practices just by looking at the old source code. There is also a time and place to avoid even very good guidelines, and too-strict enforcement of guidelines can lead to problems as well. In fact, the guiding principle when making guidelines should be that if there is really no good reason for

some specific convention, then there is probably something wrong with the convention itself. One thing that comes to mind is the so-called, "It looks better that way" convention, which is purely a matter of opinion and not really a good reason for something. Should there be a space after parentheses? Well, if it looks better.

However, more often than not, guidelines can help you to avoid problems and maintain consistency better, among other good things, so I'll introduce a few that might be useful in your project too. I also try to follow my own guidelines and give a reason for each one. At least they have been useful at many companies before, and many individuals working in different companies have ended up with more or less the same set of guidelines. The language of choice is C++, naturally, as it is the language used in practically all game projects.

Header File Layout

The overall reason for this guideline is that maintaining the same layout for all headers makes it easier for different authors working on the same project to find things.

1. The name of the header file should be the same as the class declared in it. This makes it easier for the user to find the correct header file instead of guessing.

2. The header file should start with an include guard with a unique enough name. For example:

```
#ifndef _MYNAMESPACE_MYCLASS_INCLUDED
#define _MYNAMESPACE_MYCLASS_INCLUDED
```

Using namespace name and class name should provide reasonable assurance that the name is unique and can be used as an include guard.

Reason for this specific item: Using include guards is a good practice because it allows the programmer using the header

277

file to include it (indirectly) multiple times without knowing, but still without errors. Of course, including the same file multiple times is still slowing down the compilation a bit, but sometimes the situation just can't be avoided as the user might not know which files are used by the implementation of some library he is using. Both might be using the same files without knowing it.

3. The include guard is followed by include directives #include, starting with the shortest parent path name to the longest path name. For example, #include <io/FileInputStream.h> should precede <lang/String.h> because io is shorter than lang. When parent paths have the same name (e.g., io/FindFile and io/FileInputStream), the names are ordered by the filename length. Files from the same package should follow each other; for example, io/FileInputStream should be included after io/FindFile but before lang/String.

Reason for this specific item: It is easy to see which parent directory or namespace name is shorter than the other. This provides a very quick way to find out if the file you're interested in is included at all.

4. Include directives are followed by forward declarations. Many times pointers, for example, are used in the name only and can be forward declared instead of sucked in by the full header file include. This can greatly help to minimize compile time dependencies in code. In general, if you have only pointers/references to some object in a class interface, you don't need to include the header file and a forward declaration is enough. The preferred order of forward declarations should be the same as the include directives to be consistent, since they are complementary items. For example, if you have included a

String class, you don't need forward declaration, and vice versa.

5. Before the actual class declaration is a comment for the class. All public library header files must be properly documented. The reason for this is that interfaces need to be maintained and probably will be used by other people too, so the documentation requirements for them are higher than for the implementation.

6. Forward declarations are followed by the actual class declaration. There should be only one class declaration in a single file, for multiple reasons:

- Having only one class in a header file makes it easy to find the correct header file — you just include the header file, which has the same name as the class you're looking for.

- By including only the classes you need, you minimize compile time dependencies to other code.

- The code is more readable as the header file is not cluttered up with multiple classes.

- The code is more maintainable because of readability and minimal dependencies.

7. After the class declaration come inline functions. If there are more than a couple of inline functions, it might be a good idea to put them into a separate file with the same class name but with an .inl extension. On the other hand, if you have more than a couple of inline functions or if the inline functions are long, you should ask yourself whether the functions are really good candidates for inlining at all. If you're not sure if something is time critical and it inlined well by the compiler, put the function into the .cpp file.

Preprocessor Usage and Header Files

1. There shouldn't be any preprocessor directives (with the exception of include guards) in any of the public header files. There are multiple reasons for this, but it all boils down to the fact that the header files need to behave the same in various source files when they are included, and using preprocessor directives badly compromises this.

2. Any public header file can be compiled without the requirement to include any other header file before it. This ensures that the header file can be used in various circumstances and doesn't burden the user with its own dependencies.

Source File Layout

1. The base name of the source file should match the header file. In other words, it also matches the class name declared in the header. The reasoning is the same as with header filenames.

2. Include one class at a time in all cases other than simple example and test applications. Files included from the same package follow each other as in header files. This practice makes it easier to see what classes are used and where, making maintenance easier and cutting down dependencies.

3. Many projects use a precompiled header as the first include and some kind of source configuration file as the last included header file. Precompiled headers can be used to collect all of the very rarely changed but frequently used headers, and configuration header files can be used to make some, possibly platform-specific, adjustments before the actual code begins. As an example, I always have a platform-specific <config.h> header file included as the last include file. <config.h> configures memory allocation to use debug versions of the routines when compiling the source code with Microsoft Visual C++7 (Visual Studio.NET 2003).

4. Include the class header file in the class implementation first. This guideline ensures that all header files compile in isolation from other header files, and makes their usage easier since users don't need to think about what other headers should be included. Sometimes this practice might be hard to enforce because of precompiled headers, but you probably shouldn't use precompiled headers in most libraries anyway. Instead of stuffing the precompiled headers, make the dependencies minimal so that you don't need to compile a long time anyway!

5. After the include directives, local declarations follow. Source files rarely have local class declarations (at least they shouldn't!), but usually at least the using directives precede the class implementation to avoid repeating the namespace name all over the place.

6. Local declarations are followed by file scope (static) functions. You might wonder what's the difference between having the functions declared private static inside the class declaration and having them defined in the file scope inside the implementation file. Well, there are some differences that might, or might not, make a difference to you:

- File scope static functions cannot be called outside the file. This means, for example, that you cannot use file scope functions defined in the implementation file from header file inline functions.

- File scope static functions are not visible, dependency-wise, to the outside. This is basically the same issue as the previous item, but this time it's a benefit! This is because file scope functions also do not have any dependencies to the header file, which is not the case with static class functions declared in the header.

- File scope static functions cannot access private members declared in the class, but class scope static functions can. This, again, might or might not be an issue for your purposes. As a general rule, choose file scope static functions if you need them as they have fewer dependencies to the outside than class scope static functions.

7. The actual class implementation. The order of functions should match the class declaration in the header file. This is one of the points that I must admit I have trouble following myself. I do have constructors first, then destructors, followed by normal modifying member functions, non-modifying member functions, and the last static functions, but usually don't sort the functions in any more detail than that.

Class Declarations

Items inside the class declaration should be in the following order to make it easier for the user to find what he or she is looking for:

1. Enumerations inside the class

2. Structures and nested classes inside the class

3. Public variables, if any, make it obvious that they are public

4. Constructors

5. Modifier (non-const) methods

6. Inspectors (const) methods

7. Class functions (static methods)

8. All the previous items for protected access scope

9. Same order for private declarations

You should consider if protected is needed at all. In normal circumstances you don't need it and you should declare the methods as either public or private. Protected members have the danger of weakening data encapsulation through inheritance.

All the same access category member variables should follow each other on consecutive lines, so there is no public/private/public/private jungle inside class declarations.

Member variables should be set in constructors in the same order as they appear in the class declaration, because this makes it easier to see missing initializations. A good compiler will also warn you about incorrect initialization order.

Naming Variables

There are many naming conventions, but you should pick one and stick with it. If you have to change it later on, you'll have to be sure to update all existing code to comply with that standard, which is not an appealing task. So plan the naming conventions to be used in your project before you start. Here are some examples:

- Type names starting with capital letters followed by lowercase. Each new word in the name starts with a capital letter. For example, MyClass, YourBigClass.

- Local variables are all lowercase. For example, myvariable, x.

- Private member variables start with an m_ prefix, followed by a capital letter where every new word starts in the name. For example, m_myMemberVariable and m_x.

- Static member variables start with an sm_ prefix, with the exception of constants, which are all capital letters. The benefit of using sm_ is that it warns about the possible need for synchronization.

- Constants are all capital letters, with the words separated by an underscore. For example, MY_CONSTANT. This makes maintenance and debugging easier, and makes it easier to see what parts of the expressions are constants.

- No str/i/f prefix or other Hungarian notation variations for the following reasons:

1. Member variables should not be used outside the class. Inside, class type prefixes are practically useless.

2. str/i/f doesn't guarantee anything about the type of the variable, and this can lead to problems if people make assumptions about the name. For example, Microsoft seems to have dropped the practice of using the dwVariableName notation; take a look at the new header files in DirectX SDK.

3. Hungarian notation is a relic from a time before strong typing, which makes it much less useful with modern languages like C++ and Java.

4. Using Hungarian notation causes problems and logical inconsistencies when maintenance is needed. See the Win32 SDK, which has some member names prefixed incorrectly as a relic from older SDK versions to avoid introducing incompatibilities between existing source code base files.

- Methods start always with a verb, with the exception of methods that only return information about the object and do not have any arguments. For example, updateSomething(),size(), but getItem(int index) since it has parameters. The reason behind this is that when calling a method you should always be able to see easily and intuitively how it affects the called object.

- This is more a matter of taste, but when declaring pointers to objects you should use Type* x instead of Type *x. The reason is that the pointer is typed as itself, so the pointer start should be an integral part of the type name as well. Whatever you decide, however, always be consistent.

Function Implementation

There are lots of good books written about function design and implementation, but here are the core issues that you should keep in mind while writing functions:

- Do a single clearly defined task in a function. The most common example of functions doing multiple things is C Standard library realloc. As realloc can be used to allocate memory, free memory, and adjust memory size, who needs malloc and free at all? The problem is that the complex overloaded semantics of realloc are very tricky and it's easy to make mistakes while using the function. It's better to make multiple functions in which each does a single clearly defined thing.

- Keep side effects as clearly defined as possible. This is closely related to the previous item.

- Check all assumptions inside functions, even and especially the most obvious ones. This way, when you check assumptions, you can be sure that the mistake is inside the function if it fails.

- Be sure that the function gives the results it promises. This ensures that the bug is not in the function if something goes wrong. The idea is that when everyone checks their assumptions, you catch a situation where something is wrong right away.

- Make sure you pass the arguments to functions in consistent order. The order I've used is:

  - Non-modifiable (in) parameters

  - Modifiable (in/out) parameters, if any (you should avoid these in general)

  - Fully modified parameters (out). In other words, the receivers.

- Avoid return-value overloading. Return-value overloading means that return-value means multiple things. The most common usage of this

pattern is to return a pointer, and if the pointer is 0, then the return value is interpreted as false. This is a very common practice, but it is dangerous because the caller must be aware that the function can return 0. A more explicit convention, such as returning a pointer by using a pointer to a pointer passed to the function and returning only Boolean, might be less ambiguous to the user.

- This last item is more of a style issue, but I consider it so important that I decided to include it here: Opening and closing brackets ({}) should always be in the same column to make it easier to see the flow of code. For example:

```
if (some)
{
    fu();
    bar();
}
```

Additional Reading

Steve Maguire, *Writing Solid Code: Microsoft's Techniques for Writing Bug-Free C Programs*, MS Press, 1993. (One of my favorite programming books; very practical, a classic.)

Bjarne Stroustrup, *The C++ Programming Language, 3rd Ed.*, Addison-Wesley, 2000. (From the original author of C++. Every C++ programmer should have this. Some people consider this book too large, at 910 pages, but I like Stroustrup's writing style so I found it quite effortless to read to the end.)

John Lakos, *Large-Scale C++ Software Design*, Addison-Wesley, 1996. (Really great book; I especially love the discussion about dependencies, which is a topic so often neglected in other programming

books. But for some reason this book is less known to many programmers than the rest of the books included in this list. It should be on every C++ programmer's bookshelf.)

Andrew Koenig, Barbara E. Moo, Ed., *Ruminations on C++: A Decade of Programming Insight and Experience*, Addison-Wesley, 1996. (Covers many C++ concepts in an easy-to-read manner. A very good read.)

Steve McConnell, *Code Complete, 2nd Ed.*, MS Press, 2004. (I actually haven't read this edition, only the first. I included this here since the first edition is good and the second one includes OO programming, so it should be even more useful.)

Chapter 11

Graphics Programming

Core Elements of the Graphics Engine

Programming graphics is fun with today's hardware. You can just say, "Hey, I want 100,000 polygons down here!" and the 3D graphics accelerator does the job. But to draw 100,000 polygons you need to learn to draw one first. Before we go into the actual tutorials, let's take a look at what a graphics engine is made of.

Rendering Context

Before you draw anything you need to have some destination for your drawings. Also, if you think about 3D graphics rendering and accelerators, it's easy to realize that you need some abstraction that represents the graphics device in your computer. The rendering context serves this purpose. The rendering context manages the rendering device state and rendering device-dependent resources like textures and vertex buffers (we'll get back to them later). The rendering state defines, for example, how each vertex or pixel is processed before it's written to the back buffer. The rendering context is mainly used to *create* other objects with it and flip the rendered back buffer to the screen.

Geometry Primitive

To have something visible on screen, you need to have something to draw. A *geometry primitive* represents a unit of this renderable geometry. A geometry primitive can be a triangle, line, or point. And as with most modern hardware, everything is about *batching*; we don't feed the graphics hardware with units of single primitives but instead use *primitive lists*. In its simplest form, a primitive list is just a list of vertex triplets, each of which defines a triangle to be rendered. It can also be a set of polygons, lines, or points. It can be either directly defined by vertices (for example, three vertices form a triangle) or indirectly specified by an index list, which allows the reuse of vertices in multiple polygons or lines to save storage space and provide more efficient rendering. But just having a primitive list isn't enough, since primitives define only the geometry to be rendered. You also need a way to define how you want the geometry of a primitive to be drawn, or what to fill the geometry with. Here a *texture* comes into the picture.

Texture

Having just plain geometry without any surface details is a bit boring, and using several million polygons on surface details (to make the details) is out of the question even for today's advanced hardware. A good compromise is to use a *texture* to give the surface the details it needs. You can, for example, give a surface the appearance of rusted metal, grass, or skin by mapping an image of such material over the geometry. Texture mapping simply stretches an area from a bitmap over your surface at the coordinates you have specified. But as you can imagine, the impressiveness of a simple image over your geometry isn't that great. What's needed is some lighting that will affect the colors of the surface, and that's why you need shaders.

Shader

A shader, or material, describes how a surface and texture should be rendered to screen. The vertex shader takes input of lights and geometry and maybe some shader-specific constants, and gives output

to the pixel shader. The pixel shader takes input from the vertex shader and textures and outputs the actual result on screen. Figure 11-1 illustrates this data flow.

A shader might, for example, tell us that all geometry using this shader should have a colored shiny highlight, like metal. Or the shader might specify that the surfaces are rendered using one texture map and maybe shaded by one point light.

In other words, a shader defines the look of the surface on screen. It requires the application to give to the shader the parameters it needs. Shaders can have almost any parameters you can imagine. For example, a plain diffuse shader might require only the color of the material and the position of a light source. A complex marble shader might require very specific information about the curvature of the marble type currently being rendered. If this explanation of shaders seems confusing, don't worry, it will all become clear later. For now you can just think of a shader as something that draws the textures to the screen and combines the result with lighting. (And actually, that's pretty much exactly what it does.)

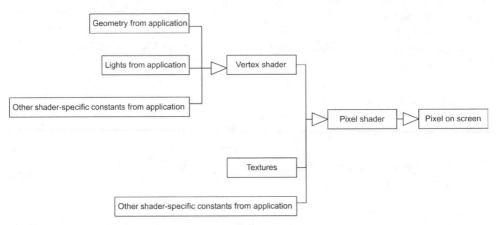

Figure 11-1: Shader data flow

Introduction to the Tutorials

So that's it. You need a rendering context, primitive, texture, and shader. That's what Direct3D and OpenGL provide, right? So, you might be wondering why there is all this fuss about 3D engines. The thing is that you quickly start to realize that you need a lot more than just the bare-bones 3D graphics core to make a game.

For example, instead of moving the points of every object to change their positions on screen, it would be nice to be able to move a camera. And when an object moves, you can't just move the points (as it would quickly explode due to inaccuracies!); you need to give it a transformation frame of reference. You need *much* more to get a single animated 3D character on screen: You need to have file format support for some 3D modeling application so that your team's artists can create the characters. And you need to be able to process

the geometry to be able to render it efficiently, or render it at all. For example, Pixel Shader 1.1 hardware generation shaders require that you have a maximum of about 30 bones, and usually characters have more. And there's a *lot* more to do that I won't go into here.

The point is just that if you're not careful you'll end up making *only* the engine surrounding the game. You'll never make it to the point where you can work on your game at all. This is fine, of course, if you *love* 3D engine development, as I do, but if you want to program games, then making your own engine probably isn't a good way to go. This doesn't mean that the (relatively speaking) "low-level" stuff is not useful to learn. On the contrary; efficient usage of *any* 3D engine requires that you understand what's going on under the hood.

Application Framework for the Tutorials

In all the tutorials in this chapter, we'll be using a simple application framework, which frees us from repetitive and uninteresting routine housekeeping tasks. The framework handles the following responsibilities: the default settings for the application, initialization, the directory structure for environment variables, creation of the application instance, entering a main update/render loop, checks for keypresses, and calling the application instance destructor.

The framework proposes default settings for the application by calling the application implemented function configure() with a reference to a framework:: App::Configuration structure as its

parameter. The application can modify these settings before the framework actually performs the initialization. Usually setting just the name of the application is enough and the other defaults are okay. If needed, however, the following settings can be configured:

- Name of the application main window (config.name)
- Width of the back buffer (config.width)
- Height of the back buffer (config.height)
- Back buffer pixel format, in bits per pixel (config.bits)
- Is full-screen or desktop window used? (config.fullscreen)

● Is stencil buffer required for the application? (config.stencilbuffer)

After making sure the configuration is okay, the framework performs the initialization by first creating the application main window and then the rendering context.

For better maintenance and resource usage you really want to keep your shaders and particles in one place, neatly organized into properly named subdirectories by a usage category. For this reason the framework handles this for you by loading the default set of shaders and particles from the directories pointed to by the SHADERS and PARTICLES environment variables, respectively (you can set environment variables in Windows XP by selecting My Computer | Advanced | Environment Variables). For the actual game you'd of course load the shaders from some local data directory. (All data loading functions allow you to specify shader, particle, and texture directories separately; it's just more convenient to handle it by environment variables during the development process of the game.)

After main window creation, rendering context initialization, and loading the default set of shaders and particles, the framework asks the user application to create its application instance by calling the init() function implemented by the application. The init() function must return an instance implementing App -interface. App is an application instance, something like an object-oriented equivalent of the C language main() function. As a minimum, your class derived from App should implement the update(dt,context) function and nothing

else. The init() function gets the rendering context as a parameter, so you are ready to create the textures, shaders, and geometry in your application constructor. Normally the user-supplied init() function just returns its application instance created with the new operator, so you should perform all your initialization in the application class constructor.

After init(), the framework enters a main update/render loop. During the main loop, the framework measures the elapsed time since the last rendered frame, and asks the application to update itself and render a frame by calling App::update. App::update gets the delta time (in seconds) since the last frame and rendering context, so you can, for example, update your animations based on elapsed time. In general, it's a good idea to base your game update on elapsed time rather than frame rate, since frame rate can vary so much on PCs due to various (uninteresting and rather obvious) reasons that are not dependent on your application.

In addition to the main loop, the framework calls an application when, for example, the main window receives a keypress. In this case, the App::keyDown and App::keyUp virtual functions are called. In addition to these functions, you can also use App::isKeyDown to check for key state, which is handy for reading continuous input like movement.

When the application is closed down, your application instance's destructor is called as you would expect.

Tutorial: Drawing Two Textured Triangles

Before drawing a million polygons to the screen we need to learn to draw one. In this tutorial, and all those following, we'll be using the simple framework introduced in the previous section. In this tutorial you will learn how to:

- Use smart pointers to make resource management less error prone
- Prepare a geometry primitive list ready for rendering
- Initialize a base texture map and shader
- Render the texture mapped primitive list to the back buffer
- Show the back buffer on the screen

At first, this might seem like just a basic example to get you started and really not anything useful in the real world. But this supposition isn't exactly correct, since, as you will see later, the techniques introduced in this tutorial will be used *directly* in a more complicated example later that renders the whole HUD, which you might need in a game. Note that rendering in screen space this way is used because using 3D primitives instead of 2D surfaces is a more effective usage of the hardware, and in architecture levels gives a nice uniform approach to the rendering, which is excellent for us as the users.

Without any more long speeches, let's jump to the code. Open the header file DrawTriangleApp.h from the tutorials\draw_triangle\ directory.

```
#include <framework/App.h>
#include <gr/all.h>
#include <lang/all.h>

class DrawTriangleApp : public framework::App
```

```
{
public:
    DrawTriangleApp(gr::Context* context);
    void update(float dt, gr::Context*
                    context);
private:
    P(gr::Primitive) m_prim;
};
```

The header file is relatively self-explanatory. First, our simple application framework headers are included by including <framework/App.h>. Then all 3D graphics library headers and C++ language support library (lang) headers are included. If you have used Java before, then you might find this library quite familiar looking, as the design of many of the classes are based on java.lang.* classes.

This header file doesn't have any include guards (#ifdef _MYAPP_H ... #define _MYAPP_H ... #endif) because we have only one header and one .cpp file in our simple application.

In the class declaration, the main application class, DrawTriangleApp, is derived from framework::App, and its constructor and update() function declarations are based on the framework conventions as well — both take rendering context as parameters. The application has only one member variable, geometry primitive (class gr::Primitive). Note that the variable is neither a regular pointer nor an object. It is a smart pointer, a reference-counting smart pointer to be exact. Next we look at how these smart pointers are used. If you're familiar with the concept, you can just browse the next section for the main points.

287

Using Smart Pointers to Manage Resources Automatically

As you're familiar with C++ programming, you know that dealing with pointers can sometimes be a hassle, especially if you have multiple pointers to the same object. Also, it's easy to forget to call the delete operator or to call it for the wrong object. There are numerous errors you can easily make, even if you're an experienced programmer. Smart pointers make life easier by keeping count in the object how many times it has been referenced. So when a pointer is assigned to a smart pointer, the smart pointer increments the object's reference count; each time the smart pointer loses the pointer, it decreases the object's reference count, and the object is deleted if the reference count reaches 0. This means in practice that you hardly ever need to call delete manually, which eliminates most of the problems associated with pointers.

Beware of cyclic references though. A cyclic reference appears if A has a pointer to B and B has a pointer to A. For example, GameLevel has a pointer to GameCharacter and GameCharacter has a pointer to GameLevel, which is a quite common scenario. If you convert these pointers to smart pointers, you end up with a cyclical reference, which might not get freed automatically even if you release pointers to both GameLevel and GameCharacter, since both still have pointers to each other. Here are a couple of techniques to solve the problem:

- Use escalation to move responsibility to a higher level. Use a smart pointer only in the higher level "owning" class, in this case GameLevel. This usually works very well since all the objects in

Game Level will be released at the same time as the level, too.

- Move the responsibility to a lower level, in other words *demote* responsibility. So, for example, instead of having two classes dependent on each other, separate the shared component to a new class and make *both* classes dependent on the new one. Voilà! You got rid of cyclic dependency.

- Have a separate destroy() function, which sets smart pointers to 0, releasing objects referenced by them.

Luckily, cyclic references are usually very straightforward and easy to solve by moving the responsibility either higher or lower, but sometimes you can end up accidentally having a pointer *indirectly* without realizing it, and then you have to debug the memory allocations to find the leak. Debugging memory allocation functions, that is debug routines that let you know the source filename and line number where the allocation was made, can help you trace where the leak chain started back to the source.

One thing to keep in mind with cyclic references is that if you end up with them, there *might* be some problem in your software architecture design. In general, it is bad to have classes dependent on each other, because then you have a hard time testing or modifying the classes individually. Any change you make can potentially affect both of the classes. Pretty tricky, so the best thing is to avoid cyclic dependencies in the first place, both in software architecture design and in implementation.

So how do you use smart pointers correctly?

1. First, you use smart pointers when you *store* a pointer to an object.

2. Second, you use smart pointers when you hold *potentially* the last pointer to

the object, for example when you allocate an object in main().

3. Third, you *don't* need to use smart pointers when you give parameters to functions, because functions can assume that the objects are valid until the execution of the function anyway, since *caller* has a reference to the object.

So okay, they are good. But how do we use them in practice, programming wise, in our own applications?

- You include <lang/Object.h> and derive your own class (say, MyClass) from it using public inheritance. In other words, "class MyClass : public lang::Object."

- You declare a smart pointer P(MyClass) and *do not* call delete on it, ever!

- When you declare functions or methods that accept MyClass as a parameter, you just use MyClass*, for efficiency, since the caller already has a valid reference to it. When you *store* a pointer, however, you use a smart pointer declaration, P(MyClass).

For the not-so-gritty details, look at the source code and header files <lang/Ptr.h> and <lang/Object.h>.

This may sound a bit confusing, but it all becomes clear when you look at the code and get a bit used to using smart pointers. After getting used to them, you can't live without them. I can hardly remember the last time I made an error while using smart pointers, and they make my life easier since they release allocated resources safely. And smart pointers do it efficiently too, as resources are deallocated as soon as they are no longer referenced. Okay, now back to the rendering!

Preparing the List of Geometry Primitives

In 3D rendering, performance equals batching. *Batching* means that you give as many triangles to be rendered in a single function call as possible to get the best performance. You also have to remember that 3D accelerators work in parallel to the CPU. This implies that 3D accelerators need their own memory to be able to process the stuff independently of the CPU memory bus, and that the memory has to be allocated efficiently. "Efficiently," in turn, is the same as "not during rendering." Both of these issues lead to the conclusion that to be able to render the most efficiently, you need to allocate geometry primitives on the 3D device's own memory and prepare the memory for rendering beforehand. This section shows how to prepare a list, which in our example contains two triangles forming a textured quad.

Vertex format describes the internal layout of the vertex memory on the 3D device. First, in the application DrawTriangleApp constructor we need to set up the following vertex format for the geometry primitive list:

```
VertexFormat vf;
vf.addTransformedPosition();
vf.addDiffuse ();
vf.addTextureCoordinate(VertexFormat::DF_V2_32);
```

In this case, we specified that we want to use a) vertices transformed to screen space, b) vertex colors, and c) 32-bit float 2-vectors as the data format for the texture coordinates. You can also specify exact data formats for both transformed vertices and diffuse colors if you want, but we just accepted the defaults. Note that not all platforms support all possible vertex formats, so even though the graphics rendering library (gr) interface lets you *suggest* the exact format for the vertices' bit layout, the platform-specific implementation can modify it and choose another compatible format if it needs to for performance reasons. The implementation can also store the vertices either as stride data or as continuous data. Stride data format means that, for example, vertex position components of all vertices can be stored in a single array and all vertex normal components in another array (position0, position1, position2, ..., normal0, normal1, normal2). In continuous data format, all components of a single vertex are stored in the same buffer (position0, normal0, position1, normal1). Beware of counting on an exact bit layout when you deal with vertex data. Luckily, you can easily avoid this bit fiddling by using the setVertexPositions() functions present in the primitive class.

Next, we create the actual primitive list object, which serves as the interface to the memory storage on the actual 3D device:

```
const int VERTS = 4;
const int INDICES = 6;
m_prim = context->createPrimitive(Primitive::
        PRIM_TRI, vf, VERTS, INDICES);
```

Since this primitive list is a 3D device-dependent object, it is managed by the rendering context. We need to create it by calling one of the functions in gr::Context class starting with create. In this function we specify that we want a list of triangle primitives (Primitive::PRIM_TRI) and we want four vertices and an index list of six indices. You can use either indexed or non-indexed primitives, but usually indexed primitives are better since they allow you to save memory for data storage. You might be wondering how, since indices themselves take memory too, but the trick is that indices use very little memory compared to vertices, and usually many triangles share vertices, so using indices helps the 3D device take advantage of that. In addition to memory usage, using indices

is the way to go since they can be more effectively rendered by the 3D devices.

> **Note:**
>
> On the PlayStation 2, you really need to preprocess the indexed triangle lists and use *triangle stripes* instead, but we won't worry about that now.

Note also that we store the returned object to a smart pointer declared in the DrawTriangleApp class, since we need the object later on when doing the rendering.

After creating the primitive list object, it might contain some random garbage data that was present in the 3D device memory, so we need to write all the needed data to the primitive list memory before starting to use the object. But before we write the data, we need to *lock* the object for writing. Remember that the device objects have their own memory, so to be sure the memory is not in use when we access it, we need to lock it before using it. We could do this locking by calling the familiar lock() and unlock() functions on the primitive object, but instead we initialize an auto/stack object of type Primitive::Lock:

```
Primitive::Lock lock(m_prim, Primitive::
        LOCK_WRITE);
```

This lock-handle class works like a smart pointer to the lock; it makes locking/unlocking an automatic process. The lock is automatically freed at the end of the scope, so you don't need to call unlock() or anything else to release the lock. This is even more helpful when you start thinking about error situations, since the code using this lock class is exception-safe and the lock()/unlock() functions aren't if there is even a single piece of code between them that might throw an exception. And remember that even though *your* code doesn't throw an exception, someone else's code might, so it's better to always be exception safe instead of relying on something not throwing them.

After locking, we can write the data to our primitive list, starting from the vertex position data:

```
const int VERTS = 4;
float4 vertpos[VERTS] = {
    float4(10,10,0,1),
    float4(300,10,0,1),
    float4(300,300,0,1),
    float4 (10,300,0,1) };
m_prim->setVertexTransformedPositions(0,
        vertpos, VERTS);
```

The first parameter to the function specifies the first vertex index to set. In this case we want to set all vertices. Notice that even though (X,Y) tell the device pixel where to draw, Z and the homogenous W coordinate are needed for the device to handle possible depth buffering and perspective texture mapping. The coordinates passed to the function form a quadrangle, starting from the top left clockwise, and ending at the bottom left. Note that the coordinate system is the *device coordinate system*, which is to say in screen pixels. The device coordinate system origin (0,0) is in the top-left corner and the (width–1,height–1) coordinate is in the bottom-right corner.

As you already know, texture coordinates are normally used to map a bitmap image to a polygon surface. After the vertex positions we write these texture coordinates to the primitive list for each vertex:

```
float4 vertuv[VERTS] = {
    float4 (0,0,0,0),
    float4 (1,0,0,0),
    float4 (1,1,0,0),
    float4 (0,1,0,0) };
m_prim->setVertexTextureCoordinates(0, 0,
        vertuv, VERTS);
```

Note that now, in addition to the first vertex index, the function also has another argument specifying the texture coordinate layer to be written to. Since we added only one texture coordinate layer

(vf.addTextureCoordinate(VertexFormat::DF_V2_32); in the vertex format creation), we must set this parameter as 0.

The texture coordinate axes are the same as the device coordinates, so the X-axis (or "U-axis," as it is more commonly referred to when speaking about texture coordinates) grows to the right and Y-axis (or "V-axis") grows downward. Texture coordinates, however, are *relative* rather than absolute, so the bottom-right corner is coordinate (1,1) instead of a specific pixel count. This is very convenient for us, since different 3D hardware accelerators might have different requirements for the textures, and the platform might need to scale texture bitmaps to different sizes than what they were originally. Having relative coordinates makes our geometry setup independent of the texture sizes.

Note that our simple texture coordinate usage doesn't result in pixel perfect rendering of the texture image to the screen, since texture coordinates specify the center of the texture pixel in the texture, and we have actually specified the top-left corner of the pixels. To get each texture pixel to correspond exactly to pixels on the device back buffer, we'd need to offset texture coordinates by half of a relative texture pixel, which is to say 1/texture width and 1/texture height, but for the purposes of this tutorial we simply ignore the 0.5 pixel error. (Even though it might be very visible, especially due to the bilinear filtering the 3D accelerator might do while sampling the texture in the drawing process!)

After the texture coordinates, we can relax a bit by setting vertex colors to the primitive:

```
float4 vertcolor[VERTS] = {
    float4 (255,255,255,255),
    float4 (255,255,255,255),
    float4 (255,255,255,255),
```

```
float4 (255,255,255,255) };
m_prim->setVertexDiffuseColors(0, vertcolor,
    VERTS);
```

In this example we set vertex colors as bright white as we just want to get the textured quad without any color modulations. Note that not all shaders require vertex colors, and you should take care that the primitive's vertex format matches the declaration used in the shader file.

The last component to write to the primitive is the index data:

```
int indices[INDICES] = {
    0,1,2,
    0,2,3 };
m_prim->setIndices(0, indices, INDICES);
```

Indices tell the primitive which vertices form which triangle. In this case our four vertices form two triangles: The first triangle consists of vertices (0,1,2), and the second one consists of vertices (0,2,3). Note that we have already benefited from sharing data, since we were able to reuse two vertices from the first triangle in the second one!

In general, less data and more bandwidth equals faster rendering speed. Of course in this particular example, the benefit doesn't make any difference as the rendering setup cost is far greater than rendering two triangles. In practice, you should try to batch your triangle rendering so that you always render at least 2,000 triangles in a single primitive list to gain maximum rendering speed. HUD and other "2D" rendering are exceptions, though usually the number of triangles rendered in a single primitive list is quite small, but on the other hand it doesn't make much difference as we're talking about such a small number of triangles and primitive lists anyway.

Texture and Shader Setup

Textures are 3D device resources as well as primitives, so they need to be created through the rendering context:

```
String datapath = "../../data/images";
P(Shader) tex = context->createTexture(PathName
    (datapath,"rgb_text4b.bmp").toString());
```

In this particular example, we of course already knew the exact filename of the texture, so we could have used the string "../../data/images rgb_text4b.bmp", but usually this is not the case, so I decided to show an example of pathname processing. Texture filenames might, for example, be specified in some scene file format or (for example HUD related) Lua script. On the other hand, for flexibility, we may want to load textures from a separate directory and not always specify the directory name in the script. Using the PathName class we can easily manipulate path names as needed, for example to ask which is the parent directory of a given filename, which is the base name (filename without extension), etc., without requiring error-prone direct manipulation of filename character strings.

The shader setup is only one more line of code than the texture setup:

```
P(Shader) fx = context->createShader(
        "sprite-copy");
fx->setTexture("BASEMAP", tex);
m_prim->setShader(fx);
```

First, we initialize the sprite-copy shader. The shader is very simple; it just copies the texture pixels to the screen and modulates the color by interpolated vertex colors. The shader file itself can be found on the companion CD at shaders\sprite\sprite-copy.fx if you want to take a look at it now, but you don't really need to since we examine shader programming later. "Sprite" shaders are good in this case since we are only using pretransformed (screen space) vertex positions in this example, and sprite shaders don't require us to set up as many parameters as shaders normally do.

Note that we don't need to specify a path for the shader, since the application framework has already loaded the default set of shaders to be used as templates to create new ones. In addition to being convenient, this works as an abstraction since on all platforms separate shaders might not directly match files at all. For example, the shader name might be mapped to a set of fixed rendering pipeline properties instead of a programmable shader FX file of DirectX 9. This is the case on the PlayStation 2, which doesn't have programmable pixel shader hardware, but it does have something similar to vertex shaders, namely its programmable Vector Unit 1. (The PlayStation also has Vector Unit 0, but it's normally used more as a CPU coprocessor to help with vector math.)

Anyway, after loading the shader we set the texture the shader should use, and then set the shader to the geometry primitive list.

Note again the use of smart pointers: Only the gr::Primitive (smart) pointer was stored to the application class; resources of gr::Texture and gr::Shader are managed automatically as the primitive has a reference to the shader and the shader has a reference to the texture. When the primitive is released (at the destruction of DrawTriangleApp class) the (last!) reference to the primitive is released, and when the primitive is released the shader is released, and when the shader is released the texture is released as well... Elegant, convenient, and above all, safe programming.

Rendering a Frame

Since all our 3D device objects have already been set up, there is not much left to do in the actual main loop App::update(float dt, gr::Context* context) method, which is called by the framework in every frame after it has flushed the Win32 message queue. Note that the main loop needs to be abstracted this way since some platforms, such as the PlayStation 2 or Symbian, have no method for flushing messages.

First, we start rendering a scene by creating a Context::RenderScene object:

```
Context::RenderScene rs(context);
```

In general, you should have a single RenderScene object in your main loop. This *exception safe* code ensures that the scene rendering ends at the end of the scope, even if the loop would be exited by a thrown exception.

After beginning the scene, we inform the shader of the primitive that we want to use it to render objects:

```
Shader* shader = m_prim->shader();
int passes = shader->begin();
```

The "passes" value returned by the shader begin() function tells us how many rendering passes are required to render the shader effect on the current hardware platform. You should then call the shader's beginPass(index) function, the primitive's render() function, and then the shader's endPass() function as many times as necessary before ending the rendering with the shader->end() call:

```
for (int i = 0 ; i < passes ; ++i)
{
    shader->beginPass(i);
    m_prim->render();
    shader->endPass();
}
shader->end();
```

Note that there is an even better way of calling the begin()...end() and beginPass(i) ...endPass() functions: You can use Shader::Begin and Shader::Pass helper classes, which call the methods in their constructor and destructor. These classes have the advantage that they provide *exception safety*, which ensures that the corresponding endXXX() method is always called properly even if an exception is thrown.

Now, from our point of view, the primitive has been rendered to the back buffer. (In practice it might take a while before the 3D device actually decides to start rendering, since it works parallel to the CPU.) We end the update by swapping the back buffer to the screen:

```
context->present();
```

That's almost it. Now we have only two "housekeeping" functions to go:

```
void framework::configure(App::Configuration&
                          config)
{
    config.name = "Low Level Rendering Example";
}

App* framework::init(gr::Context* context)
{
    return new DrawTriangleApp(context);
}
```

The first function, framework::configure, modifies the default App::Configuration only by changing the application's main window title to "Low Level Rendering Example." The framework::init function creates our DrawTriangleApp to be managed by the application framework. Now we have a textured triangle on the screen and hopefully a bit of information about what is happening behind the scenes.

Tutorial: Using Transformations

Now that we've covered basic drawing, we move on to transformations. In this tutorial, you will learn to:

- Understand 3D transformation spaces
- Use hierarchical (combined) and inverse transformations
- Set up and use transformations in rendering
- Apply transformations to shaders
- Animate transformations over time

Before getting into the actual code, let's go through some background on transformation spaces, matrices, and what exactly they're made of.

Transformation Spaces

Let's say you have a camera at position (X=0, Y=0, Z=−10), that is, 10 units (pick your favorite distance unit here) behind the world space origin. Don't worry about rotation yet. Now let's assume that you want to know where a cube is located in relation to the camera when the cube is located at the world origin.

Not much to compute of course; if the camera is 10 units behind the origin, then the origin (and the cube) is 10 units in front of the camera. After formalizing this intuitive result we get:

$$P' = P_{obj} - P_{cam} \qquad \text{(object position in camera space)}$$

What you did here is an *inverse transform* (which is only a translation); you transformed something from world space to camera space. Okay, let's flip it the other way around: The cube is at position P_{obj} and its vertex position is V_0 in the cube's own local space. Now we want to know the cube's vertex location in world space, so we calculate it like this:

$$V_{world} = P_{obj} + V_{model}$$ (vertex position in world space)

So far we have assumed that all objects have an identity rotation. That is, the objects (and camera) are facing forward, their Y-axis is up, and their X-axis is pointing right (in a left-handed coordinate system). How much would our equations change if this were not the case?

Transformation with Rotation

From basic trigonometry we remember that the cosine of an angle represents the X-axis position on a unit circle, and the sine is positioned on the Y-axis.

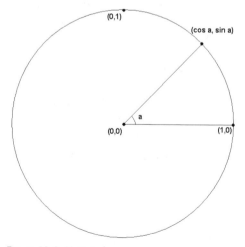

Figure 11-2: Unit circle

Let's assume we want to rotate our vertices on the XZ-plane instead of the XY-plane of the classic unit circle. Of course this changes the equation very little; now we have Y=0 and Z=sin(angle) instead of the other way around.

Here we can make an interesting observation: To know where the vertices of an object are in world space, we don't need to rotate the vertices individually by this angle, but instead we can rotate the model space axes of the object to the world space. So model space is the space where vertex positions are defined originally before applying any transformation to the object. This way we can keep the vertex positions unmodified and compute world vertex positions directly from the axes and the model vertex positions.

Let's say we have rotated our cube about the Y-axis (on the XZ-plane) "angle" degrees. Now the axes of the cube in world space are:

$X' = (\cos(angle), 0, \sin(angle))$

$Y' = (0, 1, 0)$

$Z' = (\cos(90+angle), 0, \sin(90+angle))$

$= (-\sin(angle), 0, \cos(angle))$

The "+90" degrees comes from the fact that when we're rotating only about the Y-axis, the Z-axis moves exactly the same route as the X-axis, but it's 90 degrees ahead (think about the unit circle!). This simplification is just basic trigonometry; since both sine and cosine curves have the same shape, they are just in a different *phase* of the curve with the relation $\cos(angle) = \sin(angle+90)$. Note the usage of angle units: I just keep the angles in degrees here for clarity. When programming, it's best to always keep angles in radians to avoid mixups.

Now that we know the axes of the object in world space, we can combine this rotation with the translation and transform the model vertices to world space:

$$V_{world} = X' * V(x)_{model} + Y' * V(y)_{model} + Z' * V(z)_{model} + P_{obj} \text{ (model-world-transform)}$$

So we multiply the rotated X-axis with the X-coordinate of the vertex and do the same thing with the Y- and Z-axes. This makes sense since we're moving model coordinates *along* the axes and at the end translating with the (world space) position of the object. If rotation is identity (X=(1,0,0), etc.), you get the equation we started with, namely:

$V_{world} = P_{obj} + V_{model}$, since $X' * V(x)_{model} + Y' * V(y)_{model} + Z' * V(z)_{model} = V_{model}$ when $X'=(1,0,0)$, $Y'=(0,1,0)$ and $Z'=(0,0,1)$.

(Try this out and see!)

Using Matrices to Represent Transformations

When you start to think about the stuff you need to do with transformations in a typical game, you quickly see why the transform equation of the previous section doesn't fly as is. Both in graphics and games in general, you frequently need to compute inverse transforms (transform to/from some space) or combine transforms (for example, first transform the vertices to the space of this parent object, *then* transform the vertices to the world space). This can become quite error prone and slow too, since, after all, the combined transform is still a transform and you don't care about the intermediate results, which you're forced to calculate with the previous approach. To overcome these problems we represent the transforms with matrices.

Here is the previous vertex position represented as a homogeneous four-column

vector and the transformation as a 4x4 matrix:

$$\begin{bmatrix} X'(x) & Y'(x) & Z'(x) & P_{obj}(x) \\ X'(y) & Y'(y) & Z'(y) & P_{obj}(y) \\ X'(z) & Y'(z) & Z'(z) & P_{obj}(z) \\ 0 & 0 & 0 & 1 \end{bmatrix} * \begin{bmatrix} V(x) \\ V(y) \\ V(z) \\ 1 \end{bmatrix}$$

You multiply matrices row by column, so the result column vector is exactly the same as with the previous transform equation. The last element will always be 1 with these affine transformations, since we don't apply any perspective projection (yet) before transforming the points to the screen.

Using a matrix to represent this single transform doesn't seem to be much of an improvement, but the benefits become clear when we express more complex transform operations using matrices. Below we represent matrices with M and start with an inverse transform:

$$M_{inverse} = M^{-1}$$

So when we have a transform matrix M, we get the inverse transform by taking the inverse of the matrix. Now let's say that we want to first transform the vertices to parent object space, then to parent's parent, and then to world. We can do this with matrices by first constructing matrices from each object's rotation, and then multiplying the matrices together:

$$M_{total} = M_{parent's \ parent} * M_{parent} * M_{obj}$$

What's even better is that this combined transformation can be used as is, and we can use it instead of doing *three* transformations for vertices. The benefit of all this comes crystal clear when you think about the rendering pipeline and how it transforms vertices:

● Vertices are transformed from object space to parent space, and from parent space to parent's parent's space, until they are in world space.

- From world space the vertices are transformed to camera/view space. Vertex in view space is like transforming the world so that the camera is in the origin.

- The view space vertex is transformed to projection space.

This all can be done with a single matrix-vector multiplication $M_{total} * V_{model}$ as all the matrices can be combined:

$$M_{total} = M_{proj} * (M_{camera})^{-1} * M_{model\text{-}to\text{-}world}$$

Pretty convenient!

In the 3D engine's <math/...> classes all operations work as presented here, so you'd just write the previous equation like this:

```
float4x4 total = proj * camera.inverse() *
    world;
```

And the vertex would be transformed as follows:

```
float4 v1 = total * float4 (x,y,z,1);
```

Or more conveniently:

```
float3 v1 = total.transform(float3(x,y,z));
```

You also don't need to construct rotation matrices, which can be tedious as shown in the previous section on sine and cosine, but rather just say which axis you want to rotate about and by how much. The following example shows the Y-rotation and (1,2,3) translation combined:

```
float3x3 rotation(float3(0,1,0),
Math::toRadians(30.f));
float3 translation(float3 (1,2,3));
float4x4 tm(rotation, translation);
// now tm is ready to transform vertices about
// Y-axis and then translate them by (1,2,3)
```

Note that matrix classes are found in the math library (<math/float4x4.h>, <math/float3x3.h>, <math/float3.h>, <math/float4.h>, ...) and the core math functions are found in the language support library <lang/Math.h>. The float4x4 class also contains a function for setting up a

perspective transform, which is shown in this example of combining transformations:

```
float4x4 proj;
float horzfov = Math::toRadians(90.f);
float frontplane = 0.10f;
float backplane = 10000.f;
float aspectratio = 800.f / 600.f;
proj.setPerspectiveProjection(horzfov,
    frontplane, backplane, aspectratio);
```

This would set up a perspective projection with a 90-degree horizontal field of view, 0.1-unit (meters) front plane distance and 10,000-unit back plane distance, and an aspect ratio of 1.33 (the most common one). When you use this transformation to calculate the actual device coordinates (pixels) of a camera space vertex position, you still need to scale the transformed vector with a reciprocal homogeneous w-coordinate after the projection transform:

```
v1 = proj * v0;
v1 *= 1.f / v1.w;
```

Now v1 is in relative screen space [-1,+1]. To get the actual pixel positions on screen you need to scale the coordinate by half of the viewport size (width/2,height/2) and translate the coordinate origin to viewport center (viewport (x1+x0)/2, viewport (y1+y0)/2). Of course you can formulate this as a transform matrix as well if you want!

Using Transformations in Practice

Now that you know the basic math, let's move on to the source code example. In the tutorials\using_transforms\ directory you will find TransformApp.cpp, which we take a closer look at next. The application is really simple; it animates a square (two triangles) by moving and rotating the triangles across the screen. Although simple, it contains all the basic transformations needed to get 3D graphics to the screen.

First the application sets up the texture and shader. The texture setup is similar to the previous tutorial; it creates the texture from an image file, a 16-color palettized .bmp file to be exact. The shader used in this example is a diffuse shader with texture. For now, you can think of the shader as something that applies lighting to the surface and draws the surface to the screen. We delve into shaders in detail in the next tutorial. The shader application sets up its Diffuse map texture, which modulates the diffuse lighting received by the surface and the diffuse and ambient colors of the surface:

```
// texture setup
P(Texture) tex = context->createTexture
    ("data/rgb.bmp");

// shader setup
P(Shader) fx = context->createShader
    ("diff-tex");
fx->setTexture("BASEMAP", tex);
fx->setVector("AMBIENTC", float4
    (0.1f,0.1f,0.1f,0.1f));
fx->setVector("DIFFUSEC", float4
    (1.f,1.f,1.f,1.f));
```

Next we set up the quad (two triangles) used for rendering. The setup looks a bit similar to the previous tutorial, but this time we're not specifying screen space pixels but *model space* coordinates. First we need to define the data:

```
// geometry primitive data
const int VERTS = 4;
const int INDICES = 6;

float4 vertpos[VERTS] = {
    float4(-100,100,0,1),
    float4(100,100,0,1),
    float4(100,-100,0,1),
    float4(-100,-100,0,1) };

float4 vertnorm[VERTS] = {
    float4(0,0,-1,0),
    float4(0,0,-1,0),
    float4(0,0,-1,0),
    float4(0,0,-1,0) };
```

```
float4 vertuv[VERTS] = {
    float4(0,0,0,0),
    float4(1,0,0,0),
    float4(1,1,0,0),
    float4(0,1,0,0) };

int indices[INDICES] = {
    0,1,2,
    0,2,3 };
```

So we have three components in the vertex format — the vertex *position*, vertex *normal*, and *texture coordinate* (uv). The index list defines how triangles are formed from the vertices.

Now we create the device object using the format we're interested in:

```
// create primitive with our vertex format
VertexFormat vf;
vf.addPosition();
vf.addNormal();
vf.addTextureCoordinate(VertexFormat::DF_V2_32);
m_prim = context->createPrimitive(Primitive::
    PRIM_TRI, vf, VERTS, INDICES);
```

First we add position and normal components, then texture coordinates, and then add the primitive using the vertex format to the rendering context.

Now we have an uninitialized device object, so we need to lock it and copy our data to it:

```
// lock primitive & set data
Primitive::Lock lock(m_prim, Primitive::
    LOCK_WRITE);
m_prim->setVertexPositions(0, vertpos, VERTS);
m_prim->setVertexNormals(0, vertnorm, VERTS);
m_prim->setVertexTextureCoordinates(0, 0,
    vertuv, VERTS);
m_prim->setIndices(0, indices, INDICES);
m_prim->setShader(fx);
```

Now we're done with the prepwork, and can move to the more interesting part of the application, the TransformApp::update() function. In this function, we'll set up all the transforms ready for rendering and render the created primitive using the transforms.

TransformApp::update() starts by setting up a model to world transform. Remember that the benefit of this transform is that by keeping vertices in model space we can move the object freely in the world without the pain of applying movement to each vertex of the object. This has other benefits, since with time the modified vertices would drift away from each other because of floating-point computational inaccuracy. Anyway, the model-to-world transform setup code first updates ongoing time and computes the animated angle from the angle speed (180 degrees, pi, per second):

```
m_time += dt;
    float angle = m_time * Math::PI;
```

Then it computes the world transform by first setting the world transformation matrix translation part on a sine curve based on the animated angle:

```
float3x4 worldtm(1.f);
float movedistance = 100.f;
float x = Math::sin(angle) * movedistance;
worldtm.setTranslation(float3(x,0,0));
```

Over time, the animated position appears to have an oscillating movement on the X-axis that repeats every two seconds (remember, angle speed was 180 degrees/second, so a full circle takes two seconds!). In an actual application, you'd use some 3D modeling/animating package to make the animations you need, but this kind of "debug animation" is frequently useful when you just need to get something moving on screen.

Finally, for the world transform, we set up the rotation part by rotating the object about the Z-axis:

```
// setup rotation in world space
worldtm.setRotation(float3x3(float3(0,0,1),
    angle));
```

The principle is almost the same as with position animation; we create a rotation matrix (3x3) about the Z-axis, rotated by the animated angle.

Now we have a transformation that takes our quadrangle vertices from model space to world space, wherever the object

happens to be. But since we're doing rendering, we usually need things in *camera space*, so we set up the transformation of the camera in world space as well:

```
// set up camera world space transform
float3 camerapos = float3(100,200,-400);
float3x3 camerarot(float3(1,0,0),
    Math::toRadians(30.f));
float3x4 cameraworldtm(camerarot, camerapos);
```

So we first set the camera position's coordinate (100,200,–400) and the rotation to be a bit tilted down toward the object moving along the X-axis. Remember the *trigonometric circle* from high school math when you think about rotations: If you look along the Z-axis, and the X-axis points right and the Y-axis points up, then positive rotation about Z-axis is *counterclockwise* from your point of view.

After we have set up the camera transformation in world space we transform our now-in-world-space object to view (camera) space:

```
// set up view transform, which transforms
// world space to camera space
float3x4 viewtm = cameraworldtm.inverse();
```

Notice how handy matrices are in this context. From *any* camera position and rotation we might have, we can easily get the transformation *to* camera space by inverting the matrix formed from the position and the rotation of the camera in the world space. And using basic matrix algebra, we get the transformation from object model space to camera view space:

```
// calculate transformation from model space to
// camera space
float3x4 modelview = viewtm * worldtm;
```

At this point you should have fallen in love with this elegant and beautiful matrix math! Now that we have our stuff in view space, we would like to view it in *perspective*. To do this, we set up a perspective projection matrix to transform the vertices to homogenous projection space. This space allows

299

Chapter 11

us to perform, for example, polygon clipping without calculating the actual pixel coordinates (which requires division by homogenous w-coordinate and should be avoided if the rendering hardware can do so):

```
// set up view->projection transform
float horzfov = Math::PI/180.f * 90.f;
float farz = 10000.f;
float nearz = 0.10f;
float4x4 projtm;
projtm.setPerspectiveProjection(horzfov, nearz,
    farz, context->aspect());
```

In this particular example, we selected 90 degrees as the *horizontal field of view*, which specifies how much (as angle) of the scene is visible on screen. And as we *don't* want our objects to be squeezed or stretched, we use an *aspect ratio* (ratio of our screen viewport's width and height) to define what exactly the vertical field of view should be. The near clipping plane defines the closest (in camera space Z-distance units) point that can be displayed on screen, and the far plane defines the opposite, the farthest point before it's not displayed at all. Clearly, 0.1 to 10000 is a pretty wide range. You should note, however, that selecting *too* wide a range has a negative side effect: As the Z-buffer has a limited linear accuracy (for example, 16-bit or 32-bit), this means that the part close to the camera can become *very* inaccurate if you select an arbitrarily large far-plane distance or very small near-plane distance. But this is, in general, highly dependent on the application (are you doing a space simulation or an ant action game?) so it's best to try more closely ranged values if visual artifacts occur.

Finally we combine all transformations into a *total transformation*, which transforms model vertices to homogenous projection space:

```
// set up total (model->screen) transform
```

```
// (note: "screen space" in this context is
    platform dependent)
float4x4 totaltm = context->screenTransform() *
    projtm * modelview;
```

There is one trick, as the code's comment suggested: We need to apply any additional rendering context-specific "screen" space transformation before feeding the total transformation to the shader. This is due to the fact that different rendering implementations on different platforms might expect different coordinates as input. For example, the pixel pipeline in Direct3D expects *normalized device coordinates* (coordinates between –1 and 1), but PlayStation 2 shaders might expect coordinates expressed directly in pixels from the user's total transform, so we need to give the platform a chance to express its needs regarding the projection space transform conversion to screen coordinates as well.

Now that we are done with the transformation calculations, we can just set the transformations to the shader and render the primitive using the shader, and end rendering by flipping the back buffer to the screen:

```
// render frame
{
    Context::RenderScene rs(context);
    Shader* fx = m_prim->shader();
    Shader::Begin begin(fx);

    // set up dynamic shader parameters
    fx->setMatrix(Shader::PARAM_TOTALTM,
        totaltm);
    fx->setMatrix(Shader::PARAM_WORLDTM,
        worldtm);
    fx->setMatrix(Shader::PARAM_VIEWTM, viewtm);
    fx->setVector(Shader::PARAM_LIGHTPO,
        float4(camerapos,1.f));
    fx->setVector(Shader::PARAM_LIGHTCO,
        float4(.7f, 1, .7f, 1));

    for (int i = 0 ; i < begin.passes() ; ++i)
    {
        Shader::Pass pass(fx, i);
        m_prim->render();
    }
```

```
}
// flip back buffer
context->present();
```

If the shader stuff seems a bit confusing, don't worry, since we get into that next!

Tutorial: Introduction to Shaders

Exactly what happened in the last tutorial after we applied transformations to the diff-tex shader and rendered the primitive using the shader? In this tutorial we get into the details, and learn about other shaders available in the 3D engine.

From the data flow perspective, we need to separate the two different kinds of shaders. *Vertex shaders* take vertices as input from the application and produce output that is consumed by *pixel shaders*, which produce the final pixel color (among other things on the latest hardware) to the screen. Figure 11-1 shows a data flow diagram. Both shaders consume and produce values interpolated by the hardware. For example, texture coordinates are interpolated between triangle vertices, between pixels on screen, and so forth. In an ideal world, we'd only be interested in calculating values by pixel on screen, so we'd only need pixel shaders. After all, we could move the whole rendering equation to the pixel shader. But in practice we need to use vertex shaders to prepare data in a more convenient form for the pixel shader to process. For example, it would be grossly inefficient to compute the vertex world position for each pixel when we could just compute the positions for the corners and interpolate them. So a good way to look at vertex shaders is as preprocessors for pixel shaders — they calculate *per-vertex* data values, which can be calculated *per pixel* by interpolating between extremes defined by the vertices.

Now let's see what exactly the diff-tex shader used in the previous example did. The diff-tex.fx file in the ka3d\data\shaders\ level directory is the Direct3D effect file that describes the shaders. For now, you can ignore the numerous #ifdef pragmas in the shader file; they are there for reuse of the same shader implementation in other shaders. Now, find the function named vshader in the file:

```
PS_IN vshader(const VS_IN IN)
{
...
}
```

From ka3d\data\shaders\vertexformats\ NormalVertex.fxi you find the VS_IN parameter taken in by the shader. As you can see, VS_IN consists of position, normal, and texture coordinate, as shown here:

```
struct VS_IN
{
    float3 pos      : POSITION;
    float3 normal   : NORMAL;
    float2 uv0      : TEXCOORD0;
};
```

There is also optional data used in skinning, but we're not interested in that now. The point is that the vertex shader assumes some specific vertex layout, and the application needs to conform to it if it wants to use the shader.

Now let's get back to the vshader function. From the previously introduced declaration we can see that it returns the PS_IN structure as a return value:

```
struct PS_IN
{
    float4 pos      : POSITION;
    float4 dif      : COLOR0;
    float2 uv0      : TEXCOORD0;
};
```

This is the data format used by the pixel shader. Since it's only an internal data transfer between the vertex shader and pixel shader (both part of a 3D accelerator), it's not that big a deal for us, since we're not directly manipulating any data accepted by the pixel shader in this example. The actual body of the vshader function is very short; first we copy the texture coordinates and then do the transformations:

```
PS_IN vshader(const VS_IN IN)
{
    PS_IN o;

    o.uv0 = IN.uv0;

    float3 worldpos, worldnormal;
    transformNormalVertex(IN, o.pos, worldpos,
                    worldnormal);
```

We just copy the texture coordinates from the application forward to the pixel shader, or more specifically to the 3D accelerator hardware interpolator, which gives the interpolated texture coordinate values to the pixel shader. Then we compute the homogenous projection space vertex position (revisit the previous tutorial!) and world space normal and position coordinates as well. The transformNormalVertex() function abstracts away details of the vertex transformation. You might be wondering why this is needed since it's only a simple matrix multiplication, but the catch is that we might want to use this shader with animated skinned characters as well, so we isolate the transformation code to a separate function and provide alternative implementations for it, both skinned and non-skinned (the one we're using now) versions.

Lighting the vertex is done next:

```
...
float3 worldlight = normalize
    (LIGHTP0 - worldpos);
float LdotN = saturate(dot(worldlight,
    worldnormal));
o.dif = float4(DIFFUSEC.xyz * LIGHTC0.xyz *
    LdotN, 1);
return o;
```

In this shader code, we first take the world position of the vertex, calculated previously, and compute the vector to light position (LIGHTP0, as set in the application) from it. Then we compute the cosine angle between this (normalized) light vector and the vertex normal. This gives the effect that the vertex receives more lighting when the light source is directly above the vertex. This value needs to be *saturated* between [0,1] so that if the light source is *behind* the polygon using the vertex, the vertex doesn't get lit incorrectly, as plain LdotN would be negative. Finally, we compute the light's diffuse color component by combining this saturated value with the light color (LIGHTC0) set by the application, and the material diffuse color (DIFFUSEC) set by the application as well. This color is fed to the pixel shader.

Here is the pshader function in the same fx file:

```
float4 pshader(PS_IN IN) : COLOR
{
    float4 diftex = tex2D(basetex, IN.uv0);
    float3 dif = diftex.xyz*AMBIENTC.xyz +
        diftex.xyz*IN.dif.xyz;
    return float4(dif, 1);
}
```

This is a lightweight function: First it samples the color from the 2D texture map (our rgb.bmp image) from interpolated coordinates passed in by the vertex shader, then it scales the texture color by the ambient and diffuse colors (computed by the vertex shader) and adds them together as the final output color. Notice that the light source color (LIGHTC0) is a bit greenish, so the polygon is shaded green as well because of the way diffuse light color is combined in the vertex shader.

At the end of the fx files there is a list of *techniques* (or just one technique), which provides multiple different ways to render the same material. The techniques describe which vertex and pixel shader to use, and possibly other parameters needed by the rendering device before actual rendering is done. At run time, the application might evaluate the set of techniques and find the appropriate one for the current hardware. This provides the flexibility needed to cope with the wide range of hardware in the market.

In addition to this diffuse texture shader used in the example, the 3D engine provides a wide array of ready-to-use surface shaders for your use (see data\shaders*.fx). Even though they are not discussed here, their usage is pretty much the same as this basic diff-tex shader, only the vertex format changes according to needs of the vertex shaders.

There are three different vertex formats currently used by the shaders: Lit vertex, Normal vertex, and Tangent vertex, listed in order of increasing complexity. Lit vertex (data\shaders\vertexformats\LitVertex.fxi) contains the vertex color, which is provided directly by the application. Normal vertex (data\shaders\vertexformats\NormalVertex.fxi) provides a vertex normal so that the vertex shader is able to do lighting calculations in the vertex shader. Tangent vertex (data\shaders\vertexformats\TangentVertex.fxi) provides the surface tangent space as well. Surface tangent space is used to do *per-pixel lighting* in surface space. Normal mapping is an example of applying this

technique. Various shaders (*.fx) use different vertex formats, so you need to make sure your data is in the correct format when you initialize the primitives and select shaders for them. If you run into problems, make sure you have Direct3D Debug Runtime selected from the Control Panel and then run the application inside the debugger to see the Direct3D debug output, or use an external debug output viewer such as the DebugView utility from http://www.sysinternals.com/ntw2k/free-ware/debugview.shtml. Direct3D Debug Runtime gives you information if something went wrong with the vertex format setups.

Normally, though, you don't need to worry that much about data formats, as usually your game's geometry data comes from a modeling package like 3ds max or Maya. The data from those packages is *exported* to the file format used by the engine. This conversion process includes converting geometry to a more hardware-friendly format, creating correct vertex formats, and so forth. These tools do the vertex format conversions for you, and you can just load the scene in the 3D engine and render it without knowing specifically which vertex format is in use at what point. But vertex format abstraction only scratches the surface when it comes to the benefits of having a more high-level view of the rendering engine, so next we'll introduce some abstraction to the rendering by introducing transformation hierarchies and scene graphs.

Transformation Hierarchies and Scene Graphs

Matrices are very convenient when it comes to dealing with transformations, but when you start thinking more about real-world situations related to transformations you quickly see how tedious manual transformation management can end up being, even with matrices, since the world is full of various (and complicated!) transformation hierarchies. Earth moves around the Sun, the Moon moves around Earth, a train moves on the ground, in a train a mother pushes her baby around in a stroller. It would be really troublesome for the baby if he wanted to stand up and had to consider his absolute movement starting from the position of the Sun. For the same reasons, hierarchy is your friend when it comes to hiding complexity.

Nodes

So hierarchies represent object relationships. But what kind of objects do we have in a 3D scene? We have already mentioned a few: camera, various geometry primitives, lights, and of course, particle systems, which we'll get into a bit later in detail. But when we start looking into object properties, we notice that they have quite a bit in common. More specifically, all of them have:

- Position
- Rotation
- Scale
- A "parent" object, which defines the frame of reference in which the object's transformation is defined. For example, the baby's parent is technically the stroller (not the mother).

We'll encapsulate this data into *Node*, which serves as the base class for the rest. This is convenient, since by using node abstraction, we can, for example, request a world space transformation of an object deep in the hierarchy, the calculation of which would be very error prone otherwise. Now we can calculate the stroller-riding baby's absolute position in the universe simply by calling baby->worldTransform().translation():

```
float3x4 Node::worldTransform() const
{
    float3x4 worldtm = m_modeltm;
    for (Node* parent = m_parent ;
        parent != 0 ;
        parent = parent->m_parent)
    {
        worldtm = parent->m_modeltm * worldtm;
    }
    return worldtm;
}
```

Note that this function is an iterative implementation that could be (more clearly) recursively expressed as:

```
float3x4 Node::worldTransform() const
{
    if (m_parent != 0)
        return m_parent->worldTransform() *
            m_modeltm;
    else
        return m_modeltm;
}
```

So we calculate world space transformation by applying successive parent frame of reference transformations until no more parents are left. Note the order of multiplications: To transform our object's local transformation to the parent's space, we need to multiply the parent's transformation matrix *before* the object's local transformation matrix. This might seem a bit counterintuitive at first, but remember that matrix multiplication is not commutative (that is, a*b != b*a, in general), and if we want to transform something from A to B to C, then we indeed need to multiply the matrices in order T(C)*T(B)*T(A) to get the correct combined transformation. (Writing the matrix multiplications is left as an exercise for the reader.)

So far so good. Node abstracts transformation hierarchy very nicely. Next we move on to rendering — how do the *primitives* introduced earlier fit into our scene graph?

Meshes and Other Visuals

At first, it would seem like a straightforward design solution to make a geometry primitive list also be a node. But this approach has a couple of problems.

Each primitive list has only a single shader associated with it, so, for example, to represent a character with special shaded hair, we'd need to have multiple primitives to represent the character, as for example, hair would require a separate shader from the rest of the body. To see why this can be a problem, think about moving/rotating the object: We'd need to change the transformation of all the primitives to move the whole character. This problem, however, could be solved by using the transformation hierarchy functionality provided by Node.

The bigger problem is data sharing. Think about a situation such as 1,000 soldiers marching forward on the road. Each is an individual, but we most definitely don't want to duplicate soldier geometry 1,000 times! This would be a requirement if each primitive could have only one transformation associated with it.

The solution to both issues is to leave transformation *out* of the primitive altogether. Instead, we provide a container

node with transformation, called a *Mesh*, that contains a set of geometry primitive lists. This way each geometry primitive can be in multiple Meshes, and be rendered multiple times during the same rendered scene. This also gives nice separation between the rendered geometry and its transformation in the world in general. In addition to being a container of primitives, Mesh provides functionality for setting up dynamic shader parameters, which need to be reset in every frame. These kinds of parameters include, for example, camera and mesh transformation matrices and light parameters. By setting them automatically, the user can render meshes without manually setting rendering constants for each shader.

The Mesh class is a big help in rendering standard primitives, but some visual objects fit poorly to the container concept provided by Mesh. For example, *particle systems* usually only have a single primitive, but they need to be constantly updated in every frame. They could be described as *dynamic* primitives with transformation. Still, they have some things in common with mesh, namely that:

- They can be rendered.
- They have bounding volume in the world.
- They have a shader associated with them.

When rendering, we definitely won't want to handle particle systems differently than meshes. For this purpose, we give them a shared base class, *Visual*, that contains the interface to the shared functionality. In addition to particle systems, other Visual class members include line lists (Lines class), which are very useful for debugging, and Console, which is a class for text rendering.

Lights

Light is another class derived from Node that contains common light properties like color and range, in addition to node transform and parenting properties. In a scene graph, lights are a weak group of objects when you think about modern rendering architecture based on shaders: Alone, the lights do not even cause the scene to be lit! To be precise, they are just input data for the shader, which can either use them or ignore them totally.

Complex shaders, like bump mapping, usually don't support many light sources for performance reasons and pixel shader instruction count limit. In this case, only *key light* is used for the object, and other lights are either approximated or ignored altogether.

Key light can be selected in various ways, depending on the application being developed. The simplest way is to find the closest light source to the object, but sometimes a more proper approximation should be used. For example, in an outdoor daylight environment, the sun probably makes a good candidate for the key light source. Even on a cloudy day, the sun most likely dominates object lighting. For an evening or night environment you might have street lights as light sources. In this case, choosing the closest light source might work well for static objects, but for moving objects it probably doesn't work, since in that case you need a sudden change of light source when you walk from one street light to the next. A much better approximation for this kind of situation is to *weight* light sources and their positions, colors, and other properties, based on the inverse squared distance. Some example C++ source code for calculating position and color of this "imaginary" light source follows.

```cpp
// set up character lighting
LightSorter* lightsorter = m_level->
    lightSorter();
Array<Light*>& lights = lightsorter->getLightsBy
    Distance(position());

float ltweight = 0.f;
float3 ltpos(0,0,0);
float3 ltcolor(0,0,0);

for (int i = 0 ; i < lights.size() ; ++i)
{
    Light* lt0 = lights[i];
    float3 ltpos0 = lt0->worldTrans-
            form().translation();
    float3 ltcolor0 = lt0->color();

    // weight light effect with distance
    // attenuation
    float3 worldlight = ltpos0 - pos;
    float lensqr = worldlight.lengthSquared();
    lensqr *= lensqr;
    if (lensqr > Float::MIN_VALUE)
        worldlight *= 1.f / lensqr;
    float ltweight0 = worldlight.length();

    if (ltweight0 > 0.f)
    {
        ltpos += ltpos0 * ltweight0;
        ltcolor += ltcolor0 * ltweight0;
        ltweight += ltweight0;
    }
}

if (ltweight > Float::MIN_VALUE)
{
    float ltscale = 1.f/ltweight;
    ltpos *= ltscale;
    ltpos *= ltscale;
    m_light->setPosition(ltpos);
}
```

The code above calculates the weighted positions and colors of real light sources based on inverse distance, and normalizes these to the new key light for the object. The effect in practice is that you get smooth transitions between different key lights, and this is what we wanted in the first place. The same technique is used in the game demo provided on the CD to light dynamic objects like the player character Zax.

Simply choosing the closest light source is not very good for static game level lighting either. First of all, many meshes and primitives in levels are large, so picking the "closest" light source has no meaning, since there are multiple light sources close to each level primitive. For example, one primitive in a level might be a whole room, or an even larger area! Level objects also have the nice property that they are *static*, and our closest light source selection doesn't take advantage of that.

Instead, we can compute the base light solution offline, and only add dynamic lighting as an extra component to the level geometry. This way we can, for example, use non-real-time calculation of soft shadows and use a precomputed solution in real time to provide a realistic look. Exactly how we calculate the solution and how we use it is application dependent, but using *radiosity* or other global illumination methods for calculating static lighting are generally good candidates. Radiosity takes into account not only direct lighting but indirect lighting as well, which gives a very realistic look for scenes lit with this technique.

Figure 11-3: Screen shot of real-time scene utilizing light maps computed with radiosity global illumination

The screen shot in Figure 11-3 uses radiosity rendering with light maps. A *light*

map is a technique where light values are stored *per texel* (texture map pixel) in the scene. This can provide very realistic lighting, as an almost infinite amount of computer time can be spent to calculate the lighting solution. For example, Max Payne used this technique for level lighting. In the screen shot, notice how the back of the cube is lit as well, even though there is only one light source. This is due to radiance transfer. In real-time rendering, we can just combine the calculated light map with the texture pixel color by modulation. The pixel shader for doing this could be something like this:

```
float4 lightMapPixelShader(PS_IN IN) : COLOR
{
    float4 texmapvalue = tex2D(basetex, IN.uv0);
    float4 lightmapvalue = tex2D(lighttex,
        IN.uv1);
    return texmapvalue * lightmapvalue;
}
```

Radiosity and other off-line global illumination methods can also be used at the vertex level. This has the benefit that less data is needed — only light color (4 bytes) per vertex — but the negative side is that lighting is much less accurate, as it has only polygon accuracy, and when using light maps the accuracy is per texel. Still, these two methods of using precomputed lighting are not mutually exclusive. Indeed, many games use *both* methods: vertex-based lighting on objects that do not have hard shadow edges and texture-based light maps when more accurate shadows are needed.

Nowadays dynamic lighting has become a more useful approach for level lighting too. Still, precomputed lighting has many advantages; for example, it can simulate radiance transfer effects much more believably, and it can be combined with dynamic lighting too, so you can safely expect precomputed lighting to be used in games for many years to come.

Camera

We're almost done with classes derived from base Node. However, we haven't discussed *Camera* yet. In the previous tutorials, we set up perspective and view transforms manually. Normally, though, this is a very routine operation and would benefit from extra abstraction. Camera can benefit from parenting too; for example, in a racing game, the camera could be parented to the cockpit in the car, providing an inside view. For performance reasons, Camera is also a natural place for render-time temporary buffers and optimizations, since it is the only object that is directly involved with every other object in the scene being rendered. For example, our Camera class provides functionality for *view frustum culling*, which quickly rejects objects outside the screen area.

The Rest of the Scene Graph

We have covered the most important classes of the scene graph used in the engine. The rest of the classes are listed below:

- Console is used for rendering text and HUD graphics like bitmaps to the screen. Console has the familiar printf style function for text rendering, and drawImage to draw textures as regular bitmaps to the screen. Basically, Console could be used to make a 2D game that uses 3D accelerator hardware. Console is part of the scene graph, however, because it can be rendered as part of a 3D scene as well.

- The Dummy class is an invisible box object that is frequently used for such things as marking area-based trigger positions in the game.

- The Lines class is a list of line primitives. Lines are usually used for debug purposes, but they could be used in a game as well, for example as the visual effects of laser gunshots or rain.

- ParticleSystem is a particle system that is usually created from the script description. We cover particle systems in detail later.

- Scene is a class for loading scenes, a hierarchy of nodes, from resource files (such as those exported from 3ds max). Scene also contains some global (shader) parameters common for all nodes in the scene, like fog.

The Class hierarchy of the scene graph and its relationship to primitives, shaders, and textures is shown in Figure 11-4.

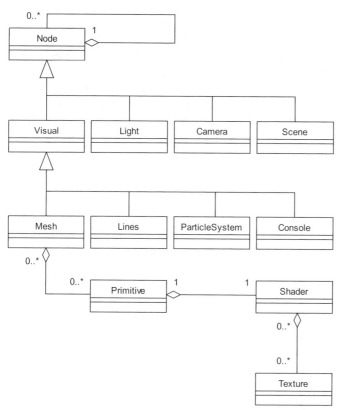

Figure 11-4: Class hierarchy of the scene graph (.hgr and .gr libraries)

Tutorial: Scene Graph Animation Playback

The file tutorials\scene_animation\Scene-AnimApp.cpp is a simple application that loads a scene graph exported from an animated 3ds max scene and then plays back the animation on screen in real time. The application constructor SceneAnimApp is very simple:

```
SceneAnimApp::SceneAnimApp(Context* context) :
    m_time(0)
{
    // load scene file and textures from the
    // same directory
    m_scene = new Scene(context, "data/
        zax.hgr");
    m_camera = m_scene->camera();

    // print object names in hierarchy to debug
    // output
```

```
    m_scene->printHierarchy();
}
```

First, the constructor loads the scene from data\zax.hgr file (hgr stands for "hierarchical graphics") by creating a Scene class instance with the scene filename. The Scene class constructor also accepts texture path, shader path, and particle path as parameters, but we can accept the defaults (empty path strings) in this case, since the textures are in the same directory as the scene file, shaders are preloaded by the framework from the 3D engine default shader directory, and particles are not used in this example.

After loading Scene, the SceneAnimApp constructor requests a camera from the loaded scene. Usually scenes already contain cameras (to provide some meaningful view to the scene), but if the scene doesn't have a camera, the Scene::camera() method would add a default camera to the scene origin, so it's safe to assume that the method returns a valid camera.

Finally, the SceneAnimApp constructor prints the loaded scene graph hierarchy to the debug output. Debug output can be viewed either in the debugger or with some external debug output viewing utility. Here's a copy of the printed hierarchy:

```
data/zax.hgr
    Camera01.Target
    Bip01 Spine
        Bip01 R Thigh
            Bip01 R Calf
                Bip01 R Foot
                    Bip01 R Toe0
                        Bip01 R Toe0Nub
        Bip01 L Thigh
            Bip01 L Calf
                Bip01 L Foot
                    Bip01 L Toe0
                        Bip01 L Toe0Nub
        Bip01 Spine1
            Bip01 Spine2
                Bip01 Neck
                    Bip01 R Clavicle
                        Bip01 R UpperArm
                            Bip01 R ForeArm
                                Bip01 R Hand
                                    Bip01 R Finger3
                                        Bip01 R Finger31
                                            Bip01 R Finger3Nub
                                    Bip01 R Finger2
                                        Bip01 R Finger21
                                            Bip01 R Finger2Nub
                                    Bip01 R Finger1
                                        Bip01 R Finger11
                                            Bip01 R Finger1Nub
                                    Bip01 R Finger0
                                        Bip01 R Finger01
                                            Bip01 R Finger0Nub
                    Bip01 L Clavicle
                        Bip01 L UpperArm
                            Bip01 L ForeArm
                                Bip01 L Hand
                                    Bip01 L Finger3
                                        Bip01 L Finger31
                                            Bip01 L Finger3Nub
                                    Bip01 L Finger2
                                        Bip01 L Finger21
                                            Bip01 L Finger2Nub
                                    Bip01 L Finger1
                                        Bip01 L Finger11
                                            Bip01 L Finger1Nub
```

```
                    Bip01 L Finger0
                      Bip01 L Finger01
                        Bip01 L Finger0Nub
            Bip01 Head
                Bip01 HeadNub
    Bip01
        Bip01 Pelvis
        Bip01 Footsteps
    Omni01
    Camera01
    Zax
```

Most of the objects in the hierarchy are character mesh bones (all objects starting with "Bip01..."). The character mesh in the scene is animated by animating the character skeleton bones and then skinning the mesh over the animated bones. The character has a set of bones, each of which influence some subset of vertices in the mesh. Multiple bones can influence the same vertex, in which case transformation is defined by the weighting influence of the bones. This provides correct bending of such objects as arms and legs, which would otherwise be impossible to animate with rigid objects. In practice, this is how skinning is implemented: The mesh has a list of bones, and each vertex has a few (two to four) bone indices in the list and the weights of each of the indexed bones. Notice the depth of the hierarchy of the character skeleton; for example, finger nubs have 10 parent nodes each! It would be practically impossible to manage such complexity without having proper support of the scene graph.

In addition to mesh bones, the hierarchy contains a point light source (Omni01), a camera (Camera01), the actual mesh (Zax), and the Scene root node named for the scene file, data\zax.hgr.

The SceneAnimApp::update(float dt, Context* context) function is almost as simple:

```
void SceneAnimApp::update(float dt, Context*
    context)
{
    // update animations
    m_time += dt;
    m_scene->applyAnimations(m_time, dt);

    // render frame
    {
        Context::RenderScene rs(context);
        m_camera->render(context);
    }

    // flip back buffer
    context->present();
}
```

First we update the animation time by adding delta time (seconds). Then we set scene keyframed animations to the specified time. Note that the Scene::applyAnimations function takes both absolute time and delta time, since some animations might not be based on absolute timing, such as particle effects animations. Let's take a closer look at Scene::applyAnimations():

```
void Scene::applyAnimations(float time, float dt)
{
    // update key frame animations
    if (m_transformAnims != 0)
    {
        float3x4 tm;
        for (Node* node = next() ; node != 0 ; node = node->next())
        {
            String name = node->name();
            TransformAnimation* tmanim = m_transformAnims->get(name);
            if (tmanim != 0)
            {
                tmanim->eval(time, &tm);
                node->setTransform(tm);
            }
        }
    }

    // update particles
    for (Node* node = next() ; node != 0 ; node = node->next())
    {
        ParticleSystem* ps = dynamic_cast<ParticleSystem*>(node);
        if (ps)
            ps->update(dt);
    }
}
```

First, the function iterates through the scene graph without recursion by using the Node::next() function, which returns the "next" node in the hierarchy in child-first-then-siblings order. For each node, the function requests TransformAnimation from TransformAnimationSet, a hash table containing all animations in the scene file. You might be wondering why animations are kept separate from nodes. The reason is simple: There is no simple relationship between animations and nodes. For example, you might have a single scene file that contains the character mesh, but multiple animation scene files from which to load animations. By keeping animations and nodes totally separate, we can keep memory usage close to optimal by loading *only* animations from the animation scene files.

After getting TransformAnimation for the node by name, its value, a transformation matrix, is evaluated at the given time by calling TransformAnimation::eval with time and output matrices as arguments. Finally, the transform animation is set to the node by calling Node::setTransform, which completes the keyframed animation playback implementation as done by Scene::applyAnimations.

After keyframed animation playback, Scene::applyAnimations also updates particle systems whose updates are based on delta time, but we don't get into particle systems updating here since an entire section is devoted to them later in this chapter.

After animation and time update, SceneAnimApp::update continues by rendering the frame to the rendering context. This is done by instancing the Context::RenderScene class and calling the Camera::render(context) function. In a more complex example, we might have multiple rendering *pipes*, which perform multi-pass rendering. For example, the game demo supplied on the companion CD uses five rendering passes:

1. Scene is rendered normally.

2. Scene is rendered by blending in fog color.

3. Scene glow effect is rendered to the second render target, glow is blurred, and blur is added to the top of the fogged scene.

4. Particle systems and other sprites are rendered.

5. HUD is rendered on top.

Multi-pass rendering is achieved by using simple classes derived from the Pipe base class and their common shared setup class, PipeSetup. But at the core of these classes, Camera::render is still used to do the actual work.

After the scene has been rendered and rendering ended (at the destruction of the Context::RenderScene object), the results

are shown on screen at the end of SceneAnimApp::update() by calling the Context::present() function. This either flips or copies the back buffer to screen, depending on whether we are in desktop window mode or full-screen window mode.

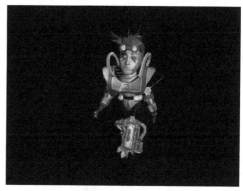

Figure 11-5: Scene graph animation playback tutorial

Tutorial: Transformation Hierarchies and Parenting

In this tutorial we load objects from one scene file, but we construct the hierarchy and animate the objects manually. This is closer to an actual in-game scenario, since normally you most likely do a lot more than just play one big animation (with the exception of cut scenes, perhaps).

First, in the application constructor HierarchyApp we load up the resources we'll be using for the rest of the tutorial:

```
HierarchyApp::HierarchyApp(Context* context) :
   m_time(0)
{
   // get resources
   m_scene = new Scene(context, "data/
                       space.hgr");
   m_camera = m_scene->camera();
   m_sun = m_scene->getNodeByName("Sun");
   m_earth = m_scene->getNodeByName("Earth");
   m_moon = m_scene->getNodeByName("Moon");
```

Figure 11-6: Earth is parented to the Sun and the Moon is parented to Earth.

So we first load the scene, and then find Sun, Earth, and Moon objects from the scene by name. After this, we'll set up the hierarchies:

```
// set up some hierarchies (note: this hierarchy
// could also be made already in 3ds max, but we
// do it here just to show how it is done)
m_sun->linkTo(m_scene);
```

```
m_earth->linkTo(m_sun);
m_moon->linkTo(m_earth);
```

So Earth is a child of Sun, and Moon is a child of Earth. We also want Sun to actually light up the other objects, so we'll add a light source to the scene as well and parent it to Sun:

```
// parent simple point light to Sun
P(Light) lt = new Light;
lt->setColor(float3(1,1,0));
lt->linkTo(m_sun);
```

Now we're almost done with the scene setup, but we still need to initialize the camera a bit farther away from the action:

```
// put camera looking at Sun
// (don't try this at home)
m_camera->setPosition(float3(2,5,-16));
m_camera->lookAt(m_sun);
```

In 3ds max, we have applied the bump-glow.fx shader to Sun, so we need to set up the rendering pipeline that supports this effect as well. Normally, calling Camera::render is like a shortcut for using the DefaultPipe rendering pipeline, but now since we need another pipe as well, we create this DefaultPipe explicitly along with GlowPipe and PipeSetup. PipeSetup contains the shared rendering setup code (frustum culling, etc.), which needs to be done only once for all pipes to be used in rendering. The actual setup code is very simple:

```
// set up extra rendering pipeline for glow
m_pipeSetup = new PipeSetup(context);
m_defaultPipe = new DefaultPipe(m_pipeSetup);
m_glowPipe = new GlowPipe(m_pipeSetup);
```

HierarchyApp::update(), called every frame while the sample is active, starts by updating time as the previous samples did. Then it sets the transformations of the Sun, Earth, and Moon objects:

```
// put Sun to center and rotate it about Y-axis
float sunangle = m_time * Math::toRadians(45.f);
m_sun->setPosition(float3(0,0,0));
```

```
m_sun->setRotation(float3x3(float3(0,1,0),
                            sunangle));
```

```
// put Earth 25 units away from Sun and rotate
// it twice as fast
float earthangle = m_time * Math::
        toRadians(90.f);
m_earth->setPosition(float3(25,0,0));
m_earth->setRotation(float3x3(float3(0,1,0),
        earthangle));
```

```
// put Moon 10 units away from Earth and rotate
// it twice as fast
float moonangle = m_time * Math::
        toRadians(180.f);
m_earth->setPosition(float3(10,0,0));
m_earth->setRotation(float3x3(float3(0,1,0),
        moonangle));
```

Notice that each object is set to a *constant* position, but due to the rotation of their parents, the objects move in world space. Very convenient for us, as this way we can make complex animations with simple code.

Finally, we render the pipelines to the default render target (which is the rendering context) and flip the back buffer to the screen:

```
// render frame
{
    Context::RenderScene rs(context);
    m_pipeSetup->setup(m_camera);
    m_defaultPipe->render(0, context, m_scene,
                          m_camera);
    m_glowPipe->render(0, context, m_scene,
                       m_camera);
}
```

```
// flip back buffer
context->present();
```

You should experiment a bit here. You can, for example, try to disable glow effect by commenting out line 81, m_glowPipe->render(), which actually renders the glow effect.

Glow Post-Processing Effect Implementation Details

How exactly is the glow effect done? It's actually relatively simple. Take a look at the GlowPipe::render() implementation in hgr/GlowPipe.cpp.

First the scene is rendered to a texture using the GLOW technique as defined by the shaders used in the scene:

```
// render scene to texture
context->setRenderTarget(m_rtt);
context->clear();
setup->setTechnique("GLOW");
camera->render(context, 0, 100, setup->visuals,
        setup->priorities, &setup->lights);
```

This technique makes non-glowing objects opaque black (so that nonglowing objects block the glow from objects farther away), and the glow color is scaled by the glow strength for glowing objects. Glow color comes from glow texture, and glow strength comes from the alpha channel of the Normal map. Note that the alpha channel of the base map cannot be used since it's already in use for controlling "glossiness" of the specular highlight in the bump-glow.fx shader:

```
half4 psGlow(PS_IN IN) : COLOR
{
    half4 colorMap = tex2D(colorTex, IN.uv0);
    half4 N = tex2D(normalTex, IN.uv1);
    half3 c = colorMap.xyz * N.w;
    return half4(c, 1);
}
```

Now that we have the glow rendered to a render target texture, we use it as the source texture for blurring. Actual blurring is done by two pixel shaders, which sample four neighboring texels each and blend them by weight to the final color:

```
half4 psBlur0(PS_IN p) : COLOR
{
    half3
    c =  tex2D(basetex, p.uv0).xyz * BLUR_BRIGHTNESS * 0.165256;
    c += tex2D(basetex, p.uv1).xyz * BLUR_BRIGHTNESS * 0.160336;
    c += tex2D(basetex, p.uv2).xyz * BLUR_BRIGHTNESS * 0.15093;
    c += tex2D(basetex, p.uv3).xyz * BLUR_BRIGHTNESS * 0.137845;
    return float4(c, 1);
}

half4 psBlur1(PS_IN p) : COLOR
{
    half3
    c =  tex2D(basetex, p.uv0).xyz * BLUR_BRIGHTNESS * 0.122128;
    c += tex2D(basetex, p.uv1).xyz * BLUR_BRIGHTNESS * 0.10499;
    c += tex2D(basetex, p.uv2).xyz * BLUR_BRIGHTNESS * 0.0875721;
    c += tex2D(basetex, p.uv3).xyz * BLUR_BRIGHTNESS * 0.0708685;
    return float4(c, 1);
}
```

Weights have been calculated offline with a Gauss curve to provide a smooth shape for the blurring. Due to Pixel Shader 1.1 hardware limitations (we want to remain compatible with GF3- and GF4-generation 3D accelerators), we need to do the blurring separately in horizontal and vertical directions, and both twice since we want to use eight samples per direction and we can use only four texture samples in one pass. This causes the blur rendering to be done eight times at the end! Luckily this is a relatively lightweight operation, since we're only rendering a single overlay quad from one texture to another:

```
// horizontal blur (to texture)
context->setRenderTarget(m_rttBlurH);
renderOverlay(m_overlay, m_blurH, m_rtt);

// vertical blur (to texture)
context->setRenderTarget(m_rttNewBlur);
renderOverlay(m_overlay, m_blurV, m_rttBlurH);
```

After the glow has been blurred to both directions, blur from the previous rendered frame is combined with the current one. Combining is done by the trail pixel shader, which multiplies both colors of the new blurred glow and the glow of the previous frame by constant coefficients and adds them together:

```
// combine faded old blur to the new blur (to
// texture)
context->setRenderTarget(m_rttBlur);
m_trail->setTexture("BASEMAP1", m_rttNewBlur);
m_trail->setTexture("BASEMAP2", m_rttOldBlur);
renderOverlay(m_overlay, m_trail);
```

The trail pixel shader code is as follows:

```
half4 pshader(PS_IN p) : COLOR
{
    half4 c1 = tex2D(baseTex1, p.uv0);
    half4 c2 = tex2D(baseTex2, p.uv1);
    return c1*LEVEL1 + c2*LEVEL2;
}
```

This causes the nice motion blur effect in which the old glow slowly fades away over multiple rendered frames.

Finally, the combined blur is combined with the normally rendered blur:

```
// add blur to actual target
context->setRenderTarget(target);
renderOverlay(m_overlay, m_add, m_rttBlur);
```

The combining is done simply by returning the texture color from the pixel shader:

```
half4 pshader(PS_IN p) : COLOR
{
    return tex2D(basetex, p.uv0);
}
```

and enabling additive blending in the technique definition at the end of the pp-add.fx file:

```
technique Default
{
    pass P0x
    {
        VertexShader = compile vs_1_1 vshader();
        PixelShader = compile ps_1_1 pshader();
        CullMode = NONE;

        SrcBlend = ONE;
        DestBlend = ONE;
        AlphaBlendEnable = TRUE;

        ZWriteEnable = FALSE;
        ZEnable = FALSE;
    }
}
```

At the end of the GlowPipe::render() function, the new blur texture is swapped with the old one so the new blur will become the old blur in the next frame's blur rendering.

Tutorial: Character Animation

In this more advanced tutorial we take a look at a character animation system. What is a character animation system exactly? We have already shown you how to play animations, right? Well, when you have a character with multiple animations the issue is a bit trickier. Consider, for example, a simple walking forward movement:

1. First, character is standing still.

2. Character starts walking forward, so we need an animation *transition* from standing to walking.

3. While character is walking, we need to move the character's position in the game world. However, we *cannot* simply set the linear velocity for the movement, because most movements like walking are not exactly linear, so using constant velocity would cause slipping of the feet, which looks bad. To solve this problem we'd need to *extract the movement speed* from the animation position keyframes.

4. When the character stops, we need to transition again to the standing animation. This transition needs to take into account that the character is slowing down, so we need to make a transition for the speed as well.

This example should convince you that it's not exactly a walk in the park to implement something as simple as an animated character walking. So how do we tackle this problem in a more general case?

First we need to think about the *states* of the character. These states might match the animation list, but not necessarily. For example you might use a single *idle* state and have multiple animations associated with it. In our case, however, we decide to map our character animations directly to states and define the CharacterAnimationApp class declaration enum State:

```
enum State
{
    STATE_STAND,
    STATE_WALK_FORWARD,
    STATE_STEP_LEFT,
    STATE_STEP_RIGHT,
    STATE_JUMP_UP,
    STATE_JUMP_OUT,
    STATE_IDLE1,
    STATE_IDLE2,
    STATE_COUNT
};
```

As we have direct one-to-one mapping between states and animations, we have direct array indexing between State and TransformAnimationSet associated with each state. We initialize the character mesh and the animations in the CharacterAnimationApp constructor:

317

```
CharacterAnimationApp::CharacterAnimationApp(Context* context) :
    m_time(0),
    m_state(STATE_STAND),
    m_transitionState(TRANSITION_NONE),
    m_transitionTarget(STATE_STAND),
    m_transitionTime(0),
    m_transitionStart(0),
    m_transitionLength(0),
    m_idleAnimIndex(1)
{
    // set up scene, key light, and camera
    m_scene = new Scene;
    P(Light) lt = new Light;
    lt->linkTo(m_scene);
    lt->setPosition(float3(0,3,0));
    m_camera = new Camera;
    m_camera->linkTo(m_scene);

    // set up character mesh
    m_character = new Scene(context, "data/mesh/zax_mesh.hgr");
    m_character->linkTo(m_scene);

    // load character animations
    m_anims[STATE_STAND] =
    loadCharacterAnimation(context, "data/anim/idle_stand.hgr");

    m_anims[STATE_WALK_FORWARD] =
    loadCharacterAnimation(context, "data/anim/walk_frwd.hgr");

    m_anims[STATE_JUMP_UP] =
    loadCharacterAnimation(context, "data/anim/jump_up.hgr",
        TransformAnimation::BEHAVIOUR_STOP);

    m_anims[STATE_JUMP_OUT] =
    loadCharacterAnimation(context, "data/anim/jump_out.hgr",
        TransformAnimation::BEHAVIOUR_STOP);

    m_anims[STATE_STEP_LEFT] =
    loadCharacterAnimation(context, "data/anim/sidestep_left.hgr",
        TransformAnimation::BEHAVIOUR_STOP);

    m_anims[STATE_STEP_RIGHT] =
    loadCharacterAnimation(context, "data/anim/sidestep_right.hgr",
        TransformAnimation::BEHAVIOUR_STOP);

    m_anims[STATE_IDLE1] =
    loadCharacterAnimation(context, "data/anim/idle_look_around.hgr");

    m_anims[STATE_IDLE2] =
    loadCharacterAnimation(context, "data/anim/idle_stretch.hgr");

    // set up debug line grid
    P(Lines) linegrid = createXZGrid(context, 30.f, 1.f);
    linegrid->linkTo(m_scene);

    // set up rendering pipelines
```

```
m_pipeSetup = new PipeSetup(context);
m_defaultPipe = new DefaultPipe(m_pipeSetup);
m_glowPipe = new GlowPipe(m_pipeSetup);
}
```

In loadCharacterAnimation, we first load the animation file, then make sure it is aligned correctly to the character, and finally scale inches to meters. Although inches are the most natural unit to use when working with characters in 3ds max, we want to keep everything in the metric system for consistency. The alignment check is done by checking the direction of the Bip01 bone, which is used in 3ds max as the base node of the character skeleton. This alignment check is, of course, not a requirement if you have uniform animation data:

```
P(TransformAnimationSet) CharacterAnimationApp::loadCharacterAnimation(
    Context* context, const String& filename,
    TransformAnimation::BehaviourType endbehaviour)
{
    // load animation set
    P(Scene) scene = new Scene(context, filename);
    P(TransformAnimationSet) animset = scene->transformAnimations();
    assert(animset != 0);

    // make sure root bone Bip01 points forward
    TransformAnimation* anim = animset->get("Bip01");
    assert(anim);
    float3x4 tm;
    anim->eval(0.f, &tm);
    if (tm.rotation().getColumn(0).z > 0.f)
        animset->rotate(m_character, float3x3(float3(0,1,0), Math::PI));

    // character animations have been created in inch units
    // so scale them to metric system
    const float INCH_M = 0.02540000508f;
    animset->scale(m_character, float3(1,1,1)*INCH_M);

    animset->setEndBehaviour(endbehaviour);
    return animset;
}
```

The default end behavior for an animation is "repeat." The default is good for animations like walking and running, which definitely need to repeat after ending. Some animations, such as jump and sidestep, specifically require that they are not repeated automatically, so we need to let the animation system know this by setting the TransformationAnimationSet end behavior explicitly.

So far so good; we now have character states defined and a correctly aligned animation associated with each state. Next we need to think about animation and state transitions.

We define two transition modes, namely none and blending. None is used when only one animation is playing, and blending is used when two animations are playing. In a general case, we might have n animations blending at the same time, since the blend target state might not be achieved before the next blend starts (for example, the user might be tapping the left and right buttons quickly), but we can exclude this case by agreeing that no new transitions can start before the old transition is done. This might seem restricting, but in practice blending n arbitrary animations would lead to bad visual artifacts anyway, since, for example, we couldn't be sure that the hand doesn't intersect with the body when we are animating the hand movement using multiple source animations. The transition mode is used to select active animations at the start of the CharacterAnimationApp::animateCharacter function:

```
void CharacterAnimationApp::animateCharacter(float dt)
{
    m_time += dt;
    m_transitionTime += dt;

    // select active animations
    TransformAnimationSet* animlist[2] = {0,0};
    float animweights[2] = {0,0};
    float animtimes[2] = {0,0};
    int animsets = 0;
    switch (m_transitionState)
    {
    case TRANSITION_NONE:
        animlist[animsets] = getAnimation(m_state);
        animweights[animsets] = 1.f;
        animtimes[animsets] = m_time;
        animsets = 1;
        break;

    case TRANSITION_BLEND:
        animlist[animsets+1] = getAnimation(m_transitionTarget);
        animlist[animsets] = getAnimation(m_state);

        animweights[animsets+1] = (m_transitionTime - m_transitionStart) / m_transitionLength ;
        animweights[animsets] = 1.f - animweights[animsets+1];

        animtimes[animsets+1] = m_transitionTime;
        animtimes[animsets] = m_time;

        animsets = 2;

        if (m_transitionTime >= m_transitionStart+m_transitionLength)
        {
            Debug::printf("Transition done: %s (t=%g)\n",
                toString(m_transitionTarget), m_transitionTime);

            m_state = m_transitionTarget;
            m_time = m_transitionTime;
            m_transitionState = TRANSITION_NONE;
        }
        break;
    }
```

The TRANSITION_NONE case is easy; we just call getAnimation(state), which returns animation directly from the array indexed by character state. We could have also used the m_anims array directly, but getAnimation() has some error checking functionality (namely, it checks that the animation has been defined), so we use that function instead. In the TRANSITION_NONE state, the animation weight is naturally 1 (there is only a single animation), and its time is how long the state has been active.

In TRANSITION_BLEND, the situation is not much more complicated. We blend using linear interpolation between two animations, based on how long the transition is and what part of the transition is still left. When a transition starts, the old animation is fully in effect and the weight of the new animation (m_transitionTarget) is 0. When transition reaches its end, m_transitionTarget animation weight has reached 1. When the transition has reached its end, transition target is set as the new active state (including state time), and transition mode reverts back to TRANSITION_NONE, ready for the next transition.

After we know the active animation sets and their weights, we can apply them to the nodes:

```
// update node transforms from animations
for (Node* node = m_character ; node != 0 ;
        node = node->next())
    TransformAnimationSet::blend(animlist,
        animtimes, animweights, animsets, node);
```

TransformAnimationSet::blend takes a list of animation sets, their animation times, blending weights, number of animation sets in the lists, and the node to which to apply the blended output. Note that this function performs *n* animation blending, so it is not limited to the two animation sets used here, if for some reason we would feel the need to blend more animations at some point.

Next we calculate how much we should actually move the character in the world based on the animation. This is done by calculating the Bip01 bone movement velocity from the distance moved between successive keyframes. We need to weight this value as well, since we might have multiple animation sets in a transition:

```
// calculate character speed from animation of
// Bip01 bone
float3 localvelocity(0,0,0);
Node* bipnode = m_character->getNodeByName
        ("Bip01");
assert(bipnode);
for (int i = 0 ; i < animsets ; ++i)
{
    TransformAnimation* a = (*animlist[i])
            [ bipnode->name() ];
    if (a != 0)
    {
        float weight = animweights[i];
        localvelocity +=
            a->getLinearVelocity(animtimes[i])
                * weight;
    }
}
```

Note that without this movement speed weighting, the character's feet would slip due to incorrect velocity during character state transitions.

Now that we know the velocity, we need to negate the effect of the moving character in the mesh by moving all top-level nodes in the character scene with negative offset calculated from Bip01 position:

```
// compensate movement extraction from Bip01
// node by translating top-level nodes
const float biplevel = bipnode->position().y +
        .01f;
float3 pos = -bipnode->position();
pos.y += biplevel;
for (Node* n = m_character->firstChild() ;
        n != 0 ;
        n = m_character->getNextChild(n))
{
    n->setPosition(n->position() + pos);
}
```

This causes the character mesh to effectively stand still when we eventually apply the movement in the game world. If we didn't do this, then the character would be moved *twice*. We really need to keep the mesh in the center of the game world object anyway, since otherwise we would have a hard time keeping track of correct game object positions; for example, while doing collision checking.

Next, since we don't have any collision checking in this example, we keep the character object on the ground if he's not jumping:

```
// make sure we're on the ground if not jumping
if (!isJump(m_state) &&
!isJump(m_transitionTarget))
{
    float3 pos = m_character->position();
    pos.y = 0.f;
    m_character->setPosition(pos);
}
```

When later in the actual game demo we have collision checking working, things don't get much more complicated since we have kept the character mesh in the origin of the game object local space. This way we can just add character world collision checking using a capped cylinder in place of the character and map that cylinder position directly to the character mesh position.

Next, we'll rotate the character 90 degrees/second based on user input:

```
// update character rotation
float3x3 rot = m_character->rotation();
float angle = Math::PI * dt * .5f;
if (isKeyDown(KEY_LEFT))
    rot = rot * float3x3(float3(0,1,0),-angle);
if (isKeyDown(KEY_RIGHT))
    rot = rot * float3x3(float3(0,1,0),angle);
```

In an actual game, we'd probably add turning left/right as animation states as well, but here we simply rotate the character.

Next we make sure the character doesn't fall on his nose while jumping and walking around; in other words, the character rotation Y-axis points up:

```
// orthonormalize rotation so that character
// doesn't tilt
```

```
float3 xaxis = rot.getColumn(0);
float3 yaxis = rot.getColumn(1);
xaxis.y = 0.f;
yaxis.x = 0.f;
yaxis.z = 0.f;
rot.setColumn(0, xaxis);
rot.setColumn(1, yaxis);
rot = rot.orthonormalize();
m_character->setRotation(rot);
```

This is very important to remember, since even though the character would be perfectly aligned upward in the animations, calculations can drift pretty quickly due to floating-point inaccuracy issues.

Then we update the character position in the world based on the velocity we calculated from the animation data earlier:

```
// update character position by world space
// linear velocity
float3 worldvelocity = rot.rotate
        (localvelocity);
worldvelocity.y = 0.f;
m_character->setPosition(m_character->position()
                    + worldvelocity*dt);
```

Next we evaluate the possible new target state and trigger transition blending if the target has changed:

```
// update character state
if (TRANSITION_NONE == m_transitionState)
{
    evaluateTransitionTarget();

    // start transition if changed
    if (m_transitionTarget != m_state)
    {
        Debug::printf("%s -> %s (t=%g)\n",
                    toString(m_state),
                toString(m_transitionTarget),
                    m_time);

        m_transitionStart = m_time;
        if (needsTimeReset(m_transitionTarget))
            m_transitionStart = 0.f;

        m_transitionLength = 0.30f;
        m_transitionTime = m_transitionStart;
        m_transitionState = TRANSITION_BLEND;
    }
}
```

Notice that some target states require a time reset; for example, when you step left the stepping animation always needs to start from the beginning. It's equally important that the time is *not* reset for some states, like when you transition between walking and running; it would look very weird if the feet went to the default pose every time a transition is done.

Actual target state selection is done by evaluateTransitionTarget(). The function uses the current character state and user input to select the desired target character state in the current situation:

```
void CharacterAnimationApp::evaluateTransitionTarget()
{
    m_transitionTarget = m_state;

    if (STATE_WALK_FORWARD == m_state)
    {
        // walk state update
        if (!isKeyDown(KEY_UP) && !isKeyDown(KEY_W))
            m_transitionTarget = STATE_STAND;
        if (isKeyDown(KEY_SPACE))
            m_transitionTarget = STATE_JUMP_OUT;
        if (isKeyDown(KEY_A))
            m_transitionTarget = STATE_STEP_LEFT;
        if (isKeyDown(KEY_D))
            m_transitionTarget = STATE_STEP_RIGHT;
    }
    else if (STATE_STAND == m_state || isIdle(m_state))
    {
        // trigger new idle animation if more than 4 seconds elapsed
        if (m_transitionTime-m_transitionStart > 4.f && isAnimationEnd(0))
        {
            m_transitionTarget = selectIdle();
        }
        // idle state update
        if (isKeyDown(KEY_UP) || isKeyDown(KEY_W))
            m_transitionTarget = STATE_WALK_FORWARD;
        if (isKeyDown(KEY_SPACE))
            m_transitionTarget = STATE_JUMP_UP;
        if (isKeyDown(KEY_A))
            m_transitionTarget = STATE_STEP_LEFT;
        if (isKeyDown(KEY_D))
            m_transitionTarget = STATE_STEP_RIGHT;
    }
    else if (isJump(m_state))
    {
        // jump state update
        if (isAnimationEnd(0.1f)) // state re-evaluation needed?
            m_transitionTarget = STATE_STAND;
    }
    else if (isStep(m_state))
    {
        // step state update
        if (isAnimationEnd(0.3f)) // state re-evaluation needed?
            m_transitionTarget = STATE_STAND;
    }
}
```

Now that we're done animating the character, let's take a look at how to animate the camera with the animateCamera() function:

```
void CharacterAnimationApp::animateCamera
    (float dt)
{
    // update camera position based on character
    // transform
    float3x4 targettm = m_character->
        transform();
    float3 cameradistv(0.f, 2.5f, 3.f);
    m_camera->setPosition(targettm.transform
        (cameradistv));
    m_camera->lookAt(targettm.translation() +
        float3(0,1.5f,0));
```

This provides the basic following movement for the camera. First the camera is set to a position (0,2.5,3) relative to the character transformation, then the camera is tilted so that it points toward the character's head, which is about 1.5m above the feet. Next we handle the idle state special camera angle, and we're done:

```
// set idle camera position
if (isIdle(m_state) && m_state != STATE_STAND)
{
    m_camera->setPosition(targettm.transform
        (float3(0,0.2f,-2)));
    m_camera->lookAt(targettm.transform
        (float3(0,1.5f,0)));
}
```

That's it! There are a couple more helper functions, which we haven't taken a look at, but we can ignore them here since their function is relatively self-evident and they don't have much to do with character animation anyway. For example, createXZGrid creates the debug line grid shown below the character's feet. At this point you should start playing around with the example application. When you feel more comfortable with the source code and how it works, you could try to add new animations to the application — there are plenty of them on the companion CD.

Separate Upper Body Animation, Aiming, and Shooting

In the game demo on the companion CD, we'll add a couple more features to the character animation system presented here. Most importantly, we add separate *upper body animation*, which is quite like the body animation state but applies only to the upper body of the character. We need this kind of separate upper body state because, for example, aiming and shooting require that the character can perform other activities at the same time, such as the character walking and running while shooting. Notice that you cannot escape this requirement by using a complete "shooting and walking" animation, because you cannot know when the player wants to shoot or aim, and the cycle of that animation does not match the walking animation.

Luckily this complication does not make things much more difficult. We just need to keep track of the upper body state and only apply related animations to it, like this:

```
// apply upper body animation
Node* bipspine1 = m_root->getNodeByName
    ("Bip01 Spine1");
for (Node* node = m_root ; node != 0 ; node =
    node->next())
{
    if (node->hasParent(bipspine1))
    {
        TransformAnimationSet::blend(anims,
            upperanimtimes, upperanimweights,
            animsets, node);
    }
}
```

The code above applies the specified animation set only to the bones that are children or grandchildren of Bip01 Spine1. Notice that we detect a specific bone part of the upper body by comparing it to the root of the upper body, usually Bip01 Spine1 in 3ds max models.

There is one additional complexity with upper body animation implementation: We need to take into account that the character can potentially be aiming or shooting upward or downward. This can be handled by keeping separate sets of up/front/down animations, and then blending between them accordingly. First, we calculate the blend between front and up/down animation from the character aim pitch angle (in radians, limited to a range of [–1,1] to prevent extreme tilting):

```
// find out blend between up/front/down
float pitch = InterpolationUtil::clamp(m_pitch,
            -1.f, 1.f);
float u1 = Math::abs(pitch);
float u0 = 1.f - u1;
```

In this example, u0 is the weight of the "front" animation and u1 is the weight of the up/down animation. Now, let's assume that we are performing a shooting animation. We calculate the blend between animation sets:

```
float upperanimweights[4];
float upperanimtimes[4];
TransformAnimationSet* anims[4];
int animsets = 0;

anims[0] = m_upperBodyAnims[UPPERBODY_SHOOT]
        [VERT_FRONT];
upperanimweights[0] = u0;
upperanimtimes[0] = animtime;
++animsets;

if (m_pitch < 0)
    anims[1] = m_upperBodyAnims[UPPERBODY_SHOOT]
            [VERT_UP];
else
    anims[1] = m_upperBodyAnims[UPPERBODY_SHOOT]
            [VERT_DOWN];
++animsets;
```

This way the character is aiming or shooting up/down according to his pitch angle. This naturally isn't too accurate when it comes to aiming with an actual weapon, so we could improve the aiming by aligning the weapon to the aim target.

```
float3x4 tm = handtm;
float3 aimz = normalize (target - handtm.trans-
            lation()));
float3 weaponz = -handtm.getColumn(0);
float angle = Math::acos(dot (weaponz,aimz));
if (Math::abs(angle) > 0.001f)
{
    float3x3 rot(normalize(cross(weaponz,aimz)),
            angle);
    tm.setRotation(rot * tm.rotation());
}
```

Note the local transformation spaces in the above code example: It is assumed that the hand's (holding weapon) local space X-axis points to the opposite direction of the weapon aiming direction. For example, if you'd be aiming along world Z-axis, your hand's local coordinate space X-axis would point along the direction of the world's negative Z-axis. This convention is set by 3ds max/Character Studio coordinate axis conventions. The practical effect of all this coordinate hassle is that usually you need to draw some debug lines to find out which axis points where in node hierarchies coming from some 3D content authoring tool. The actual alignment above is done by computing the angle between the ideal aiming direction (aimz) and the actual weapon direction (weaponz), and then rotating the weapon by that angle in the right direction.

Tutorial: Rigid Body Physics Simulation

You might be wondering why we have a physics simulation in a graphics tutorial. Well, one way to look at physics is as a tool for animation, or for those who majored in physics, animation can demonstrate physics properties.

Especially in simulations, unexpected things happen. In that case it's very useful to be able to see some run-time text on the screen that lets us know what's going on, so we also take a look at the methods available in the engine for that purpose.

Simulation Basics

A simulation *world* is a container for rigid *bodies* and *joints* (or *constrains*). A rigid body is the actual object being simulated, and a *joint* limits relative movement between bodies. Rigid bodies have the following properties that change over time:

- Position (three-vector)
- Linear velocity (three-vector)
- Orientation (3x3 rotation matrix)
- Angular velocity (three-vector)

And the following constant properties:

- Mass
- Center of mass (in body's local coordinate space)
- Inertia matrix (distribution of mass in the body, in local space)

Note that rigid bodies do *not* have geometry. Instead, the simulator asks for *contacts* from the collision system. *Collision space* contains a set of *geometry* objects. Geometry objects do not know anything about the *simulation world*. Geometry objects' only functionality is to resolve collisions and contacts between other objects. This approach allows independence of the

simulator from the used collision system. We have only one kind of body, but we might have any number of geometry object types. For example:

- Sphere
- Box
- Capped cylinder (capsule)
- Cylinder
- Plane
- Ray
- Triangle mesh

Luckily the user doesn't need to implement each type of collision check that is needed. Since any geometry can potentially collide with any geometry user defines, the collision checking library could need to implement 6! (720) different types of collision checks with the geometry object types listed above!

In addition to rigid bodies, the simulation world has *joints*. A joint is a relationship between two or more bodies — it *constrains* movement between the bodies. The simulator works by trying to satisfy these constraints. There can be various constraints, for example:

- A ball joint connects two bodies so that one works as a "socket" and the other as a ball.
- A hinge joint connects two bodies like a door is connected to a wall (except that in this case the wall isn't necessarily stationary).
- A slider joint connects two bodies so that they can slide along a common slider axis shared by the bodies.
- A contact joint prevents two bodies from penetrating each other.

Okay, now we have defined world, body, joint, space, and geometry. The actual simulation setup for 3D rendering is done in the following way:

1. Load (or otherwise construct) a visual 3D scene.

2. Create a dynamics world.

3. Create rigid body geometry objects in the world from each object in the visual scene, for example by creating a rigid body with box geometry from the mesh's bounding box. (You probably want to use some tag to indicate which mesh to use as the source for the rigid body, since usually not *all* visual objects are simulated.)

4. Set state (position, rotation, etc.) of the rigid bodies from the visual mesh transformations.

5. Create and attach joints (if any) to the bodies.

6. Set the parameters of all joints.

7. Create a joint group to hold (temporary) contact joints.

And the main loop goes like this:

1. Apply forces to the bodies (if any).

2. Adjust the joints' parameters (if any).

3. Do collision detection.

4. Collect contacts from the collision detection system to the contact joint group.

5. Do a simulation step.

6. Remove all contacts from the contact joint group.

7. Update the visual meshes' transformations from rigid body transformations.

8. Render the visual meshes.

Text Rendering (Debug Info and In-game HUD)

Everyone is familiar with printf function usage. In graphics applications, we have the hgr::Console class in the 3D engine and its Console::printf function, which is almost as simple to use. The only difference from the standard printf is that with Console you need to flush the text by rendering the console to make the output visible.

Let's take a look at the source code tutorials\physics_simulation directory. Before initializing the simulation, we initialize a text rendering console in the PhysicsApp constructor:

```
// create text output console (using Comic Sans
// MS font)
m_console = new Console(context,
    context->createTexture("data/comic_
    sans_ms_20x23.png"), 20, 23);
```

The code creates the hgr::Console object, using the specified comic_sans_ms_20x23.png texture. Texture itself is fairly simple; it's a 16x16 table of ASCII characters. The constructor also takes in individual character widths and heights so that it can calculate where each character bitmap can be found. For example, the ASCII code for the letter A is 0x41, which means that the character bitmap is second from the left in the fourth row. This code might look ugly to you from an internationalization viewpoint, but in fact the Console supports the full range of Unicode characters. You can add to Console any number of this type of *character pages*, which define a 16x16 set of characters. If, for example, you need Unicode code points in the range of 0x1000 to 0x1100, you could add fonts from character page number 32, which would contain the specified 16x16 set. Strings themselves are treated as UTF-8 encoded, so the full Unicode code point range is available for use.

Text rendering is, of course, useful for such things as creating a game UI, but it is also useful for debug purposes. For example, to keep your simulations performance-friendly, you should always try to keep the number of enabled bodies (*enabled* means that they are participating in the simulation) as low as possible. So it's very useful to know how many active bodies you have running all the time. This kind of information doesn't really fit into a debug log, since log files and outputs are usually viewed only after something has gone wrong. And you most definitely don't want to swamp your log file by dumping information in every frame anyway! Having debug output directly on the screen, for example over the game HUD, is much more useful.

Actual text rendering is done in the PhysicsApp::renderDebugInfo() function. First, the text console position is set to the top-left corner of the screen, then the text lines are printed using the familiar-looking printf() syntax statements:

```
void PhysicsApp::renderDebugInfo(Context* con-
text, float fps)
{
    // set text console origin to top-left
    // corner
    m_console->setPosition(float3(0,0,0));

    // show UI
    m_console->printf("F5 resets\n");

    // show number of active bodies in
    // simulation
    m_console->printf("active bodies: %d\n",
            m_world->enabledBodies());
```

Notice that you can also change the origin of the console later, since the text itself is not rendered to the screen until Console::render is called. But before that, we print some function performance profiling statistics (function name, % of used execution time, and call count):

```
// render info about profiled blocks
for (int i = 0 ; i < Profile::blocks() ; ++i)
```

```
{
    m_console->printf("%-16s = %5.1f %%
            (x%d)\n", Profile::getName(i),
            Profile::getPercent(i),
            Profile::getCount(i));
}
Profile::reset();
```

By adding a PROFILE(functionName) macro to the start of a function (see the following PhysicsApp::simulate() implementation), we get performance statistics of that function recorded by our profiler. The macro records the number of times the block was executed and the time spent executing it. Profile::getPercent() is scaled by the time spent in whole frame, which is to say the time spent between Profile::begin-Frame() and Profile::endFrame() calls. You probably still want to use some external full profiling tool like Intel VTune or AMD CodeAnalyst every now and then (for example, to get a call graph), but this simple and lightweight profiler can give you useful run-time information about your code performance without causing much overhead.

Simulation in Practice

Now let's move on to the actual simulation code. This tutorial shows you how to make a simple simulation from a scene created in 3ds max as outlined in the section called "Simulation Basics."

PhysicsApp constructors call restart(). The same function also is used when the user presses F5 to reset the simulation. This is convenient since by sharing the init and reset code, we can make sure that *both* features work properly. The function itself is very simple:

```
void PhysicsApp::restart()
{
    // (re)start time
    m_time = 0.f;

    // (re)load scene to be simulated
```

```
m_scene = new Scene(m_context, "data/
                      scene.hgr");
m_camera = m_scene->camera();

// (re)start simulation
initSim();
}
```

First time is reset, then the scene is loaded, and finally the simulation world is initialized. The initSim() function starts by removing old objects (if the application was already initialized) and creates the simulation world and space:

```
void PhysicsApp::initSim()
{
    m_objects.clear();
    m_world = new ODEWorld;
```

ODEWorld is a simple wrapper that combines the simulation world and main collision space. The ODEWorld constructor also sets the most commonly needed default values for our simulation; for example, gravity is set as −9.8 (m/s²) along the world space Y-axis. You can change gravity with ODEWorld::setGravity() later if you want; for example, if your game is happening on the Moon's surface, your gravity would need to be less than the default.

After adjusting the parameters we loop through the loaded scene nodes and find meshes:

```
// create simulation objects from meshes
for (Node* node = m_scene ; node != 0 ;
       node = node->next())
{
    Mesh* mesh = dynamic_cast<Mesh*>(node);
    if (mesh)
    {
```

Now we should take a break and think about the simulation a bit. Do we want to simulate all meshes we find from the scene? Most definitely not, since in a real game most geometry would actually be *level geometry*, which can be considered to have such a large mass that it is immovable. We also don't want to create these kinds of

ultra high mass bodies in the simulator for numerical accuracy reasons. Instead, we create *only* collision geometry for static level geometry, and leave it without actual simulated rigid bodies. This way level geometry affects the collisions of other simulated objects, but doesn't move by itself. Convenient.

Next we parse the simulation options from the user property string of the mesh. The user property string is an object-specific text field, which can contain, for example, settings that don't necessarily make any difference to the graphics rendering code:

```
// parse properties (from 'User Defined
// Properties' text field)
String props = m_scene->userProperties()->get
                  (mesh->name());
ODEObject::GeomType geomtype;

ODEObject::MassType masstype;
float mass;
ODEObject::parseProperties(mesh, props,
          &geomtype, &masstype, &mass);
```

First, GeomType is parsed from the Physics=$<x>$ property, where $<x>$ is either a box, sphere, or trimesh. Then MassType is parsed. It receives the value MASS_INFINITE if the mass=$<x>$ and density=$<x>$ properties are missing; otherwise, it is either MASS_DENSITY or MASS_TOTAL, depending on whether total mass was set using Mass=$<x>$ or relative mass was set using the Density=$<x>$ property. This kind of user text string property usage may look like a bit of a hack, but this way new properties can easily be introduced without making any changes in the interfaces or breaking backward compatibility. Besides, a lot of the values we want to cover are by nature scriptable-like, so user property parsing is fine for that purpose.

After parsing rigid body properties, we make sure that it is no longer animated:

```
// remove from animation set
m_scene->transformAnimations()->remove
        (mesh->name());
```

Finally, we create ODEObject, a wrapper for both the body and its geometry, using parsed properties and add it to the list of all simulated objects:

```
// create rigid body with these properties
P(ODEObject) obj = new ODEObject(m_world->
    world(), m_world->space(), mesh, geomtype,
    masstype, mass);
m_objects.add(obj);
```

The ODEObject class uses the mesh's bounding volume and triangle information to calculate requested rigid body objects for the simulation. ODEObject also takes care of mapping transformations between visual meshes and simulated rigid bodies.

Now we're done with the initialization and we can move on to the update(). First we start measuring the elapsed time of the update, and then update the cumulative time:

```
void PhysicsApp::update(float dt, Context*
    context)
{
    Profile::beginFrame();

    // update time
    float fps = 1.f / dt;
    float fixdt = 1.f / 100.f; // simulate
        // physics at 100Hz
    if (isKeyDown(KEY_F4))
    {
        dt *= .2f;
        fixdt *= .2f;
    }
    m_timeToUpdate += dt;
```

Next, we'll update all keyframed animations in the scene (in this 3ds max scene we happen to have none), update the simulation by using fixed update time, render the frame to the back buffer, swap the back buffer to the screen, and end frame timing:

```
    m_scene->applyAnimations(m_timeToUpdate,
            dt);
    simulate(fixdt);
    render(context, fps);
    swapBackBuffer(context);

    Profile::endFrame();
}
```

Now let's look at the details. First the simulate() function:

```
void PhysicsApp::simulate(float dt)
{
    PROFILE(simulation);

    // update simulation at fixed interval
    for (; m_timeToUpdate > dt ; m_timeToUpdate
            -= dt)
        m_world->step(dt, 0);

    // get visual object positions from the
    // rigid bodies
    for (int i = 0 ; i < m_objects.size() ; ++i)
        m_objects[i]->updateVisualTransform();
}
```

First we stepped the rigid body simulation by the given fixed update interval (0.01 seconds), and then updated the visual object transformations based on the simulated objects' transformations. Quite straightforward. Notice, however, that we cannot simply copy the transform between the rigid body and the visual body, since the visual mesh might, for example, have scaling or a non-center-of-mass pivot point. Of course you can always *avoid* such geometry in the modeling application in the first place, but updateVisualTransform() already handles transformation conversions without special cases or restricting the artists.

Notice that you should almost always modify transformation of the simulated objects by applying forces and impulses to the rigid bodies and not by modifying rigid body positions and velocities directly, since it might have undesirable and unexpected effects in the stability of the simulation.

Inside ODEWorld::step

What exactly happens inside ODEWorld::step()? Let's find out. In ODEWorld.cpp you can find this example of the function:

```
void ODEWorld::step(float dt, ODECollisionInter-
                    face* checker)
{
    // use default collision checker if needed
    ODEDefaultCollisionChecker defaultcollision-
                    checker;
    if (!checker)
        checker = &defaultcollisionchecker;
    // collect contacts
    dJointGroupEmpty(m_contacts);
    CollisionCallbackProxyData data;
    data.world = this;
    data.checker = checker;
    dSpaceCollide(m_space, &data,
                    collisionCallbackProxy);
    // simulate step
    dWorldQuickStep(m_world, dt);
}
```

Note that all functions starting with a lowercase "d" are Open Dynamics Engine (ODE) functions. ODE is used by the ODEWorld and ODEObject implementation.

First, as we pass null ODECollisionInterface* to the step function, we select ODEDefaultCollisionChecker as the active collision interface.

Then we collect all contact joints from the collision space by clearing old contacts and calling dSpaceCollide. Space collide determines which geometry objects are close to each other and calls (indirectly) our callback interface ODECollisionInterface*, which we defaulted to ODEDefaultCollisionChecker. ODEDefaultCollisionChecker has only one function, checkCollisions:

```
int ODEDefaultCollisionChecker::checkCol-
            lisions(dGeomID o1, dGeomID o2,
    dContact* contacts, int maxcontacts)
{
    // get geometric properties of contacts
    int numc = dCollide(o1, o2, maxcontacts,
        &contacts[0].geom, sizeof(contacts[0]));
    // set contact non-geometric parameters
    for (int i = 0; i < numc ; ++i)
```

```
    {
        contacts[i].surface.mode =
            dContactBounce | dContactSoftCFM;
        contacts[i].surface.mu = dInfinity;
        contacts[i].surface.mu2 = 0.f;
        contacts[i].surface.bounce = 0.1f;
        contacts[i].surface.bounce_vel = 0.1f;
        contacts[i].surface.soft_cfm = 0.0001f;
    }

    return numc;
}
```

checkCollisions() gets both geometry objects that can potentially collide and a buffer to receive the contacts/collisions if there are any. The actual geometry object type-dependent contact check is done with a call to dCollide. After determining the contacts, we process them by setting the surface properties. For example, we set friction (mu field) to infinity, and specify that soft constraint force mixing should be used. If you run into stability problems (suddenly some object jumps into the sky!) with your simulation, the first thing you should try is increasing the CFM coefficient.

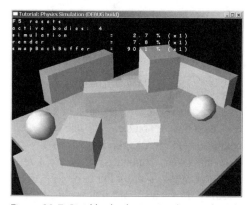

Figure 11-7: Rigid body physics simulation of a 3ds max scene and performance profiling information

Now back to ODEWorld::step(). After all contacts have been collected, the simulation step is taken by a call to dWorld-QuickStep(), and we're done.

Particle Effects

Particle effects are an old but still useful trick. Sometimes it's funny how relatively simple particle effects can still wow even experienced viewers. One third-person action game I worked on a few years ago was heavily hyped about gameplay, etc., when all we had was a couple of cool particle effects with a slow motion effect. That's a good example of how far they can take you!

First we'll take a quick look at basic Newtonian mechanics, which form the groundwork for the particle simulations. Then the concept of *domain* is introduced, which is used to define random variable distributions for various values used in simulations. After the basics are covered, we get into the actual properties of particles, emitters, and systems. Last, but not least, we step through a few particle systems to show how the particle systems are built in practice.

About Particles, Emitters, and Systems

Before we start with the simulations, it's good to clarify exactly what we mean by particles, emitters, and systems.

A *particle* is the smallest unit of a simulation, a point-like object. A particle has position, velocity, image, color, transparency, and other properties, which we'll get into later in this section.

An *emitter* is a set of particles. Emitters have their own properties too, like emission rate, maximum particle count, and emission stop time.

And as you might have guessed, a *system* is a set of emitters. A system has properties such as the number of emissions per second. Now you may be wondering why

you have this "system" level in particle simulations at all. Couldn't we just use emitters directly, and maybe launch multiple particle emitters from the application if needed? Of course we could, and many games do just that, but then we'd lose a lot of expression power from our particle systems engine. The neat thing with having the system level is that, you can coordinate more accurately how you want multiple, seemingly independent emissions to behave. To make this more clear, think about how rain splashes on the ground. You can, of course, look at raindrops as independent effects, but when you look at the system as a whole you can specify things like the rate of splashes to match the rate of raindrops falling down. This is very convenient and helps you to build more impressive systems more easily. Now let's move on to the simulation basics.

Particle Simulation

What makes particles such nice objects to simulate is that they are so simple. Particles are just points in space after all. The simulation loop goes like this:

1. Create new particles by elapsed time.

2. Assign initial properties to new particles.

3. Remove old (dead) particles.

4. Simulate all particles, and update their velocities and positions.

5. Transform and render the particles to the screen.

From high school physics classes we know Newton's laws of motion:

- Every object in a state of uniform motion tends to remain in that state of motion unless an external force is applied to it.

- The relationship between an object's mass m, its acceleration a, and the applied force F is $F = ma$.

- For every action there is an equal and opposite reaction.

The first law hints at how the simulation should work — by applying forces to particles. The second law in turn gives us a starting point for the simulation. First, we'll pick a force that we want to apply for particles. In this case we pick gravity, $G = mg$, since it's pretty hard to try to avoid it. The constant g is the familiar 9.8 m/s². Putting the gravity G equation in the place of F in the equation gives us:

$$mg = ma$$

Now, since the mass is a constant larger than 0, we can divide the equation by m and get the equation for acceleration, a = g. This is not a surprise, but it's a nice result since it tells us that acceleration is not dependent on mass when we simulate gravity, so we can drop the mass from our particle simulation altogether. By integrating the acceleration over time we get the familiar equation of velocity:

$$v = a * t + v_0$$

Now we make another observation: We don't have to be concerned with an arbitrary point of simulation in time since we update the simulation in each frame. What we are doing implicitly is in fact integrating the state of the simulation over time each time we update a frame in the game (or whatever real-time rendering application we have). This gives us a nice update equation when we know that time since the last update is dt:

$$v = a * dt \Rightarrow v = v_0 + a * dt$$

And position is updated naturally with the velocity with the following familiar equation:

$$p = v * dt \Rightarrow p = p_0 + v * dt$$

So now we're done with the particle simulation. If we have forces affecting particles that do not depend on mass, then we'd take the masses of particles into account. But it wouldn't make the simulation much more complex either, since we can get the acceleration from force by dividing the force by particle mass.

Note that all these equations only had scalars in them. But the equations are precisely the same when vectors are involved, so you can just replace F with vector F, a with vector a, and v with vector V to get vector equations.

Concept of Domains

The particle system engine is heavily based on the concept of *domains*. It is a bit of an abstract concept, but understanding it is essential for effective usage of particle systems. Once you understand it, though, using particle systems becomes very intuitive and orthogonal, as nearly all properties of particle systems are simply defined by setting appropriate value domains for each property.

Domains are source value ranges for various random values needed by particle systems. Domains can be sources for scalar values and 2D and 3D vectors used in the simulation. Let's clarify this further.

Say that some particle effect has a particle initial position domain set as "Sphere with radius 4," which means that the initial positions of new particles are randomized inside a sphere that has a radius of 4. If the particle initial velocity domain is set as Point (–50,0,0), then all particles have an initial velocity of –50 along the negative

X-axis. The position domain is very straightforward, since it's literally the position in space where the particles are born. The velocity domain means the space where the tip of the velocity vectors will be when their start point is at the origin. For example, unit sphere velocity domain means that particles get random speed in range (0,1) to random direction.

It is easy to make pretty much any kind of particle effect with various domains. For example, rain could be made by setting a flat 100x100 position box to 50 meters above the ground with Box(−100,50,−100, 100,50,100) and then setting velocity at Point(0,−20,0) and at Gravity=−9.8. In this case, the particles would be born on that flat 100x100 box 50m above the ground and their initial velocity would be 20m/s downward with an acceleration of $9.8m/s^2$. In addition, particle sprite elasticity could be set above 0 (say, to 0.1) to cause the particle bitmap to stretch along the movement speed, which also works very well with effects like sparks.

Particle Properties

When particles are created, they are assigned properties from various different domains, which is to say random value distributions. A description of each of these properties and how they are used in the particle effect system follows. The most obvious of these are particle position and velocity, so we start with those.

Particle start position specifies the volume in space where the initial particle positions are randomized. Note that this position is specified in local space, which means that it might be also affected by the parent object position if the particle system is parented to some object in a 3D scene (as they usually are). For example, gunfire flame might be parented to the barrel of the gun, so its position is defined relative to the barrel transformation frame of reference. The most common particle position domains are sphere and box volumes, which are very simple and intuitive to use, but don't limit your imagination to these; triangle or rectangle position sources could be used to create effects like energy shields with complex shapes.

Particle start velocity is a 3D domain that describes the direction and length of the initial particle velocities. For example, rain might have a constant velocity downward (for example, Point(0,−20,0) domain), and a gun blast might have a velocity sphere or cylinder somewhere farther away from the origin, which would create a directed blast with some minor variation as well. This vector is also specified in local space, so the direction in world space might be affected by any parent object.

Particle life time is a 1D domain that specifies how long the particle exists in the simulation before it is removed. Usually a Range(a,b) domain is used for this purpose to make it appear more natural since we don't want particles to always die at the same time. You can also use this value to optimize a simulation; for example, there is no point in simulating raindrops after they have gone through the ground plane.

Particle start size specifies the initial radius (half of width/height) of particles when they are created in the simulation. The engine doesn't force any specific units, but you can consider it to be meters or inches if you want. Range domain types can be used to introduce variation to the simulation; for example, Range(1,2) means that particle sizes are randomized between 1 and 2 meters in size.

Particle end size uses the same units as particle start size, and it's normally employed to simulate particles getting smaller when their end of life approaches. Of course, you can use it for more interesting purposes, such as gas particles that might become larger (and fade out) when they grow older.

Particle start alpha is a domain that defines the initial constant alpha of the particles when they are created. Exact usage of the alpha is shader dependent, but normally (both with additive and alpha shaders) alpha means constant transparency, so that when alpha=0.5, the particle is half transparent, and when alpha=1, the particle is fully opaque. Note that this constant transparency is combined with particle texture (animation) transparency, so in the end particles might be more transparent than what the constant transparency level specifies alone.

Particle end alpha is the same kind of 1D domain as particle start alpha but for the end of the particle's life. Normally this property is used to fade particles to black at the end of simulations, but try it the other way around too; you might be able to create interesting effects that way! In general, the best way to learn how to use the particle simulation parameters is to play with the particle effects and boldly try combinations that no man has tried before.

Particle start color is an (R,G,B) domain that defines the initial color of the particle. It is multiplicatively, at least by default particle sprite shaders, combined with particle texture color. For example, if the texture color is white (1,1,1) and the particle color is red (1,0,0), then you get a red (1,0,0) texture, since (1*1, 1*0, 1*0) = (1,0,0). But watch the color combinations carefully, since, for example, having a red (1,0,0) texture and a green (0,1,0) particle color results in a totally black end result because of combining! Be sure to check for this if

you don't see anything on the screen when you're playing with the effects.

Particle end color (R,G,B) defines the color just before the particle system is removed from the simulation. A conventional usage includes fire, which might have more of a blue tone at the end of the life of each particle, but is more red/yellow at the start. If you want to get wild you can create pretty hallucinogenic effects by randomizing start and end colors.

Particle sprite elasticity requires a bit longer explanation. Sometimes when a particle moves really fast, it needs to be stretched in the direction of movement to create a realistic-looking effect. This 1D domain can be used for that, since it specifies how much the particle velocity affects the shape of the particle. An obvious usage for this property is when you make sparks, rain, and other similar velocity-oriented effects. Normally values between 0 and 0.2 are okay, but out-of-range values could be used in some special cases. Trial and error is the best way to learn its use. Note that particle elasticity is a mutually exclusive property with particle sprite rotation, which is introduced next.

Particle sprite start rotation is the angle at which the particle is initially rotated on screen. For example, having the particle sprite rotation domain set as Range(–90,90) says that particles can be rotated anywhere between +–90 degrees in either direction. If the sprite rotation speed parameter (described next) is set to Constant(0), then the particle will also stay in that pose.

Particle sprite start rotation speed can be used to create various good-looking gas, smoke, and haze effects when combined with big semi-transparent, multiplicative sprite bitmaps. Units are degrees per second, so setting sprite start rotation as Constant(360) means that the particle sprite will be rotating on the screen one full time around a second.

Particle sprite end rotation speed is an orthogonal value to particle end alpha and end color in a sense that it gives the particle rotation speed at the end of the particle's life. It is normally used to slow down particles toward the end of their life.

Texture name is the bitmap filename to use to render particles with. Texture is combined with possible alpha and color values multiplicatively, so that if, for example, the texture alpha channel is 50% and constant alpha is set to 50%, then the end result alpha will be 25%. The same combining is used with colors. This behavior can be changed by using a custom shader to render particles. Basically the shader is not bound in how it uses the parameters, it's just that the default sprite shaders use the parameters as described here. And of course if you don't use the parameters in an intuitive way, it might be confusing for the user to apply the shader.

Texture frame count specifies how many images are "embedded" in the bitmap using n*m grid. For example, if you have a texture size of 256x256 and you specify the texture frame count as 16, then you should have 4x4 textures of 64x64 size in the texture image. This is basically the same as having multiple images in a sequence, such as img0001.bmp, img0002.bmp, etc., but it's more effective as no rendering state changes are required when rendering the particle images.

Texture animation type specifies the logic of selecting each frame used to render each particle. Available options in the engine are selection by simple playback loop, selection by life phase, and random frame selection. Simple playback loop means that texture animation frames are used one after another using a constant frame change rate

(described below), and when the last frame is reached, then the next one will be the first texture frame again. Selection by life phase means that when the particle is born it uses the first texture frame, just before it's removed it will be using the last frame, and during its life it uses all the frames between those. Selection by random randomly selects the frame to be used. This might not seem too useful at first, but it can be used to create nice fire effects when you use random frames from a set of flame images. The output can be quite impressive when you have a lot of flames overlapping each other as used in games like Max Payne, for example.

Texture frame rate is in units of number of frames per second and says how often the image used to render each particle is changed. In some frame selection logics the frame rate might not be affected at all. For example, if the frame is picked by the particle's life phase, then the displayed frame will be independent of frame rate. Note also that each particle is unique and its image changes independently of any other.

Texture view type describes how the particle sprites are rendered with relation to the camera. To be more precise, the parameter selects which direction is considered "up" by the particles. This property might seem a bit confusing, but this example should clarify it a bit: If particles consider the "up" direction to be the same as the camera up direction, then their bitmap's direction is *always* the same as the camera up direction, independent of camera rotation. This is generally okay behavior, but for slowly moving big particles it might look funny because they'll seem to rotate along with the camera Z- (look-at) axis. The other option is to select the particle "up" direction from the world space Y-axis direction. In that case, particle rotation is more independent from the camera's rotation, but problems arise if you look at particles more or less along the world space Y-axis. In that case, particles seem to rotate along their axes very rapidly since the world Y-axis direction can change very rapidly in camera space. But don't worry if you don't completely understand the description above, since both of these situations are fairly special cases that rarely occur in a normal game environment.

Shader specifies exactly how the various particle parameters are used to render the particles. For example, particles might be rendered using additive blending (sprite-add shader) or alpha blending (sprite-alpha shader). In general, additive blending creates better "halo" type lighting effects and alpha blending is more suitable for transparent effects like smoke and haze.

Emitter Properties

Emission property domains closely resemble particle properties, which is good in that we don't need to repeat the lengthy list here. There are a few differences though.

Emission position is a domain that specifies the pivot point for an emission. Normally this is the origin Point(0,0,0), but occasionally some other range is useful. For example, you can create multiple rain splash particles by creating new emissions inside a random box that covers the area that is being rained on.

Emission max particles sets the limit of how many particles there can be in a single emission. Be careful with this parameter if you have multiple simultaneous emissions, since the number of particles can quickly become huge!

Emission rate describes how often new particles are added to the emission as the rate of particles/second. If the maximum count of particles is reached, then existing particles are removed with the kill mode logic as described next.

Emission kill limit specifies how particles are removed from the system when the maximum limit is reached. Options in the engine are None, Oldest, and Random. None means that when the maximum number of particles is reached, no more particles are added, but also that no existing particles are removed before they are removed naturally (by dying of old age). Using Oldest as the kill logic means that when a new particle needs to be added, the oldest one is removed. Random kill removes some random existing particle when adding a new one.

Emission life time sets the time when the emission is removed from the particle system. *Emission stop time*, on the other hand, defines when the emitter stops launching new particles. It is useful to separate the two because otherwise you might experience sudden vanishing of particles at the end of emission life time, because individual particles belonging to an emission are removed along with the emission. A separate emission stop time enables you to stop emitting new particles a bit before the emission itself is removed.

System Properties

System-wide properties are used to configure how emissions behave in the system. The emissions' relationship with the system is more or less the same as the particles have with their emission source. There are only a few system properties:

System rate specifies the number of new emissions per second that are added to the system.

System stop time sets the time when no new emissions are created. The behavior and usage are similar to the emission stop time described above.

System max emissions is the maximum number of simultaneous emissions in the system.

System kill limit specifies how the emission count limit is maintained. Emissions can be left alone (so that no new emissions are created when maximum count is reached), removed by age, or removed randomly.

Particle Effect Examples

Now we're pretty much done with particle effect properties. The list of properties might have seemed a bit overwhelming at first, but luckily you don't need to learn every possible parameter to make cool effects. The best way to get started is to take some existing (and working) effect as a base and modify it. Change only one or two parameters at a time so you see clearly how your changes affect the simulation. It's also good to use some "real" context, like a game level as a background, when you design your effect. This way you have a better chance of fitting the effect into the mood of the level. After all, none of the effects exist in isolation from the rest of the game (hopefully!). Next we'll design a few effects and see how they work.

Figure 11-8: Fire and rain particle effects

Fire Particle Effect

This example shows only the particle system .prt file and the comments. The actual playback code can be found in the section called "Playing Particle Effects in the 3D Engine." Anyway, now into the fire! The particle system files start with the documentation and helper functions, so we skip directly to the system properties on line 94.

Fire System Properties

```
SystemMaxEmissions = 1
```

This sets the maximum number of simultaneous emissions. Since we're modeling fire, we have only one emission, but if, for example, we were modeling rain splashes, we could have up to 100 emissions active at the same time (as raindrops hit the ground, each would require a new emission).

```
SystemLimitKill = "NONE"
```

SystemLimitKill describes how the emission limit is maintained. NONE specifies that when the limit is reached, no old emissions are removed before free space becomes available by natural removal. OLDEST specifies that the oldest emission should be removed to make room for a new emission. RANDOM removes a random emission if the maximum limit is reached.

```
SystemRate = Constant(100)
```

SystemRate is the number of new emissions/second. Even though we only have one simultaneous emission, we still use a high number because we want the emission to be lit up quickly.

```
SystemStopTime = Infinity()
```

This describes when the whole system should stop new emissions. Infinity() keeps it alive as long as the object exists in the application.

```
SystemLifeTime = Infinity()
```

This is the time limit when all remaining emissions are removed from the system and the system deactivates itself.

Fire Emission Properties

Next we move on to the properties of a single emission. Remember that a system consists of emissions, which in turn consists of particles. We find familiar looking parameters here:

```
-- Maximum number of particles simultaneously
EmissionMaxParticles = 150

-- How max particle limit is maintained:
-- kill NONE, OLDEST, RANDOM
EmissionLimitKill = "NONE"

-- Emission rate, particles/second
EmissionRate = Range(250,300)

-- Time after no more new particles are emitted
EmissionStopTime = Infinity()

-- Lifetime of particle emitter
EmissionLifeTime = Infinity()
```

Note that EmissionRate is set quite high so that the fire looks aggressive as new particles are frequently born. Otherwise the parameters are very similar to the system parameters, but this time they affect particles instead of emissions. The last parameter is different, however; it describes the position of an individual emission in the system:

```
-- Pivot point for the emissions
EmissionPosition = Point(0,0,0)
```

For the fire we use the system origin, but if, for example, we were making rain, we could say that emissions are born on a flat "sky" box above the ground, like Box(-50,30,-50, 50,30,50), which would cause raindrop emissions to cover a larger 100x100 area from 30 units above the ground.

Fire Particle Properties

Finally we move to the properties of individual particles. First we define particle life time as short, as individual flames don't exist that long:

```
-- Particle life time in seconds
ParticleLifeTime = Range(0.5,2)
```

Then we specify that the particle system doesn't need to be updated if it's not visible for a long time:

```
-- If true then particles are updated even
-- though they are not visible.
-- Note: Normally this should be set to false
ParticleUpdateAlways = false
```

Then we give particles a random position inside a 2-unit radius sphere, 2 units above the ground, to simulate the effect that some flames aren't created in the center of the fire:

```
-- Volume in which the particles are born
ParticleStartPosition = Sphere(0,2,0, 0,2)
```

As we're still aiming for aggressive fire, we set the initial velocity for individual particles quite high up the Y-axis:

```
ParticleStartVelocity = Sphere(0,22,0, 3,5)
```

So the particle's initial velocity vectors get randomized inside a 3- to 5-meter (hollow) sphere 22 units above the ground. This gives an almost direct upward movement but with some variation to keep the flames more interesting.

Next, we define ranges for particle sprite world space size, color, and transparency over time:

```
-- Start size of particle
ParticleStartSize = Range(3,7)

-- Life time end size of particle
ParticleEndSize = Range(3,7)

-- Start color (R,G,B in range 0-1) of particle
ParticleStartColor = Box(1,1,1, 1,1,1)

-- End color (R,G,B in range 0-1) of particle
ParticleEndColor = Box(1,1,1, 1,1,1)
```

```
-- Start opacity of particle
ParticleStartAlpha = Constant(1)

-- End opacity of particle
ParticleEndAlpha = Constant(0)
```

And this time we don't use the sprite elasticity property, but give some initial spin that fades away over time:

```
-- Particle sprite elasticity wrt particle
-- velocity, set Constant(0) to disable
-- (note that elasticity and rotation are
-- mutually exclusive)
ParticleSpriteElasticity = Constant(0)

-- Particle sprite initial rotation (degrees)
-- (note that elasticity and rotation are
-- mutually exclusive)
ParticleSpriteRotation = Range(0,360)

-- Particle sprite initial rotation speed
-- (degrees/sec)
ParticleSpriteStartRotationSpeed =
Range(-360,360)

-- Particle sprite end rotation speed
-- (degrees/sec)
ParticleSpriteEndRotationSpeed = Constant(0)
```

Note that "elasticity" means how much an individual particle's current velocity affects its shape. Elasticity is very handy for modeling such things as sparks, raindrops, or other fast-moving particles that are affected by their movement direction.

Fire Bitmap Properties

We animate the fire bitmap over time, so that each of the 16 frames embedded in a single bitmap is used when the particle is a certain age. This gives us the effect that older particles can be recognized by appearance:

```
-- Texture bitmap
Texture = "textures/fire1.bmp"

-- Number of frames embedded in texture
-- (nxn grid)
TextureFrames = 16

-- Method of selecting which frame to display:
-- LOOP plays back animation in constant frame
```

```
-- rate (TextureFramerate)
-- LIFE starts from first frame and gradually
-- animates until end of life
-- RANDOM selects random frame in interval
-- defined by TextureFramerate
TextureAnimation = "LIFE"
```

Finally, we select the shader that should be used to render the particles. In this case the sprite-add shader works best, since we want fire to cause a "brightness" effect as well, and the additive shader fakes that nicely. This happens because the pixel colors of the fire bitmap are *added* by the shader over the old pixel colors in the frame buffer.

Playing Particle Effects in the 3D Engine

Playing particle effects in the engine is nearly trivial. You just need to supply the ParticleSystem constructor with the rendering context and the filename of the particle system, and then call the ParticleSystem::update(dt) function in every frame to keep the particles moving.

Note that you can, for example, link particle systems to a node hierarchy to animate them along another scene. For example, you could attach a particle to the head of a torch, and when the player carries the torch around the particle effect moves along with it.

Below (from tutorials\particle_rendering\ParticleApp.cpp) is a fully working example of rendering a single particle system on the screen:

```
ParticleApp::ParticleApp(Context* context)
{
    // scene setup
    m_scene = new Scene;

    // particle system setup
    m_particleSystem = new ParticleSystem
            (context, "data/fire.prt");
    m_particleSystem->linkTo(m_scene);
```

```
// camera setup
m_camera = new Camera;
m_camera->linkTo(m_scene);
m_camera->setPosition(float3(0,3,-20));
m_camera->lookAt(m_particleSystem);
}

void ParticleApp::update(float dt, Context*
    context)
{
    // update particles
```

```
m_particleSystem->update(dt);

// render frame
{
    Context::RenderScene rs(context);
    m_camera->render(context);
}

// flip back buffer
context->present();
}
```

Additional Reading

Graphics programming requires a solid understanding of the basics of (linear) algebra and trigonometry. So in addition to the following books, dig up those high school, college, and university-level books again if you have let yourself become a bit rusty on the topics.

Alan H. Watt, *3D Computer Graphics, 3rd Ed.*, Addison-Wesley, 2000. (A modern introduction of a wide array of topics related to computer graphics. A very good read.)

James D. Foley, et al., *Computer Graphics: Principles and Practice in C, 2nd Edition*, Addison-Wesley, 1995. (A classic, but I prefer Watt's book since it focuses on 3D.)

Alan Watt and Mark Watt, *Advanced Animation and Rendering Techniques: Theory and Practice*, Addison-Wesley, 1992. (A very good book, but you probably don't need both if you already have *3D Computer Graphics* by the same author.)

Tomas Akenine-Möller and Eric Haines, *Real-time Rendering, 2nd Ed.*, AK Peters, 2002. (Another good book about 3D computer graphics. Very up to date and numerous topics covered, including collision detection. See also the book's web site at www.realtimerendering.com for a nice collection of links. Very useful even if you don't have the book!)

Wolfgang F. Engel (editor), *ShaderX²: Introductions and Tutorials with DirectX 9*, Wordware Publishing, 2004. (I haven't actually read this book, so take my recommendation with a reservation, but since there are so few books about using HLSL in shader programming, I decided to include this one.)

Thomas H. Cormen, et al., *Introduction to Algorithms, 2nd Ed.*, MIT Press, 2001. (If you don't know the difference between $O(n)$ and $O(n^2)$, then you're in trouble. Basic knowledge of algorithms is essential for anyone working on computer graphics programming, and this book gives a nice introduction to the topic. Heavy read though, 1180 pages, but at least you get a lot of bang for your buck.)

Collision Checking

Introduction

The primary function of collision checking is to find *contacts* between objects. But collision checking has other useful purposes too, for example you might do object *occlusion culling*, meaning that you find the objects that are occluded by others, based on your collision system. Or you could *trigger* events based on collisions, so that you place a trigger object in the world that the player can collide against and associate with it some event, such as a player getting a new inventory item. Collisions can also assist something like a chase camera implementation. A camera might probe the environment using the collision system to find a suitable distance to steer away from walls. AI could use collisions as well to find out whether or not an enemy (player) is visible. When shooting with a weapon, the collision system could be used to check the line of fire.

Simplifying the Problem

As always, you should aim for simplicity. When you start considering how collisions should be handled in your game, whether your game is 2D or 3D, you should consider the detail level you're dealing with. For example, you can usually get away with using simpler shapes for collision checking rather than dealing with the raw polygon level. Sometimes you can even collapse the collision check to 2D, as in many racing games, instead of computing full 3D collisions. Let's take a look at a couple of simplification examples below.

Character Collisions

A character's collision shape could be modeled as two spheres with a cylinder in between (in other words, forming a capsule), as shown in Figure 12-1. So instead of a character "walking" in a game level, you have a moving capsule. This may sound like a crude approximation of a complex human being, but it actually has many desirable properties:

- The character can *always* turn around and back up. This property relates to the symmetry of the capsule shape. If you have, for example, a character consisting of multiple asymmetrical parts, you could walk in some narrow corridor and be stuck there forever if there wasn't space to turn around and walk back! Symmetry helps to always keep the character in a valid position.

- The character can walk (or more properly, slide) up stairs or against walls and other characters, without handling these as special cases. Since the character is a convex and round shape, it rarely gets stuck on anything, and that in turn helps to keep the gameplay smooth. Nothing is more annoying than getting your hero stuck on a simple obstacle. The bottom sphere especially helps with varying heights in game levels, as you can step up on non-continuous level geometry (imagine, for example, pushing a big beach ball against stairs).

- Computational efficiency and complexity is improved. The fewer moving parts you have, the more efficient it is. By approximating a complex character with a simple shape like a capsule, you gain a lot, obviously.

- Simple shapes give you a better chance of making your simulation more robust in terms of simulation errors. Collisions can get (surprisingly) tricky when it comes to low-level numerical accuracies, and any simplification works in your favor.

In addition to characters, this simplified approach works well for many other objects:

- Camera collisions can be modeled with a moving sphere.

- Bullet collisions can be modeled with a simple moving point (e.g., a ray).

- Event triggers, like in-game cut scenes, can be modeled with (stationary) boxes or spheres.

- Environmental sounds can be modeled as spheres or boxes as well. (A sphere is a more natural choice for sound, but a box often gives more control to level designers.)

Vehicle Collisions

Vehicles, such as cars, consist of parts. Even though the shape itself is complex, its parts are probably not. For example, a car could be represented simply by spheres for the tires and a box as the body. Most car games use some variation of this approach.

The racing track could also be represented by a simpler form, such as a 2D *height field* that would provide fast access to information about where the car tires might be colliding.

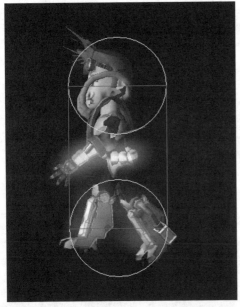

Figure 12-1: Modeling character collisions with two spheres and a cylinder

Different Views and Detail Levels in Collision Space

An object doesn't have to use the same collision assembly for all collision checks. Often you can make easy and non-restricting assumptions that help you eliminate many collision calculations in the first place.

Continuing with the vehicle example, you might use spheres as tires to collide with the ground, but use *only* the body box to collide with other cars, based on the assumption that tires are always below the car and you can't drive over other cars.

In practice, the above example can be generalized by defining collision *object categories* and *collision flags* for each object. The collision category defines the flag type for the object. Collision flags express all the flag types of the objects (OR together) that can be collided against. Then you can simply use a binary AND (&) of category and flag to check if two objects can be collided against. The game demo supplied with this book uses the same approach to limit the number of collision checks needed.

When it comes to simplifying character collisions, you might use a capsule to check collisions against level geometry, but bullets probably need a more detailed approach. Maybe not polygon level, though. For example, when you know that a bullet trajectory (line segment) collides against the character capsule, you could do a more detailed collision check against the character's bone bounding boxes. You can extend this level of detail usage in collision checks to other applications too.

You also might decide beforehand with the level designers that they don't do any "sharp" level geometry in the height range between the character's shoulders and knees. This assumption would help you to eliminate middle body cylinder collisions (against the level), and you just use the two spheres, saving computation cost, while bullets would still use the original capsule as the initial collision check bounding shape.

The above examples give different views of collision space, but they are also examples of a more general idea of limiting possibilities, which works in application fields beyond collisions and game development. In the real world, everything is infinitely complex. You absolutely *need* to make assumptions and simplifications to manage the complexity. The more you can limit them, the better, since that way you end up with a simpler problem to solve.

Checking Collisions against Level Geometry

Game levels are often impossible to represent with simple shapes. They are just too complex and action happens *inside* a level, which suggests that you probably need multiple simple shapes to represent it. This is not that bad of a problem, however, as we have already managed to simplify the other colliding shape (the character), and the level never collides with itself.

Still, we need an efficient method to determine which level polygons the simplified character shape can potentially collide with. A level can consist of hundreds of thousands of polygons, and checking each of them would be insanely expensive performance wise. In many game types you can make assumptions that work in your favor for this task. In racing games, for example, the track is usually quite linear and the world is relatively flat, even in 3D games. You can use this assumption to *divide* your world into a grid of blocks, basically a 2D map of the track. Using this map you can quickly find out, based on your car's position indexed to the map, where in the world you happen to be now and which objects or polygons are potentially collidable. Note that the same approach works for simplifying graphics rendering of the game world.

Even if you're developing a more complex third-person game, you can still approach the problem from the same perspective. You still have many choices to divide and conquer the world. For example, you can divide the world by partitioning it recursively until you end up with manageable portions of the world. Examples of this partition approach are BSP tree, OBB tree, AABB tree, and octree. A brief introduction to each of these techniques follows.

BSP Tree

BSP tree (binary space partition) is a good example of the *divide and conquer* approach of solving the problem of collision detection. The idea is that instead of checking collisions against individual triangles right from the start, you check collision against a *plane* that divides the triangles into two halves. If you are on one side of the plane, you can totally ignore checking the triangles on the other side of the plane. When you do this recursively, you end up with O(log n) checks instead of O(n). (Think about a tree diagram on a piece of paper; you can see that each of the plane checks can halve the number of potential triangle checks left.) For example, with 100,000 polygons you could end up with ~17 checks instead of 100,000. Quite effective! Of course in cases when your colliding object is *crossing* the partitioning plane in the tree, you need to check both halves, which increases the number of checks needed a bit.

OBB Tree

OBB tree (oriented bounding box) uses the same divide and conquer principle, but this time you use bounding boxes instead of planes to divide the polygons into groups recursively. You build the tree using either the bottom-to-top or top-to-bottom approach. In the first approach you start with a bounding box representing a single triangle. Then you pick a triangle near it and compute a higher-level bounding box consisting of both triangles. After this you pick two of these higher-level bounding boxes and combine them, recursively... At the end, you have a complete tree consisting of bounding boxes. When doing the collision checking, you start with the top-level bounding box:

1. Check collisions against the bounding box. If you don't collide with it, exit early and report that there are no collisions.

2. Otherwise, recursively check the children until you find either the colliding polygons or you determine that the bounding box doesn't collide with our collision object.

As you can see, basically the only difference in this algorithm from BSP tree is that you check against bounding boxes instead of partitioning planes.

AABB Tree

AABB tree (axis-aligned bounding box) is similar to OBB tree, but this time we use only axis-aligned bounding boxes. The boxes are, generally speaking, more loose than in OBB tree, but the benefit of having the boxes axis aligned is that they require less storage space and they are faster to check against. Instead of doing a more complex OBB-sphere test, for example, you could do simple comparison of sphere

center +– radius and AA-box coordinates. Construction and collision checking using the tree works otherwise the same as in OBB trees.

Octree

In octree, the world is partitioned as well, but this time it is divided into eight *octants*:

1. X+, Y+, Z+ (on the positive side of center point X-axis, the positive side of Y-axis, the positive side of Z-axis)
2. X+, Y+, Z–
3. X+, Y–, Z+
4. X+, Y–, Z–
5. X–, Y+, Z+
6. X–, Y+, Z–
7. X–, Y–, Z+
8. X–, Y–, Z–

By using similar simple coordinate comparisons as with axis-aligned boxes, you can quickly test in which octant (or octants) your object is located. Then you recursively check the specified octants until you reach the polygon level and you can check against individual triangles.

Colliding a Moving Sphere against a Moving Triangle

Octree, BSP tree, AABB tree, and OBB tree are just optimization techniques — they don't give you exact collision information. At the end you still have your collision shape, like a sphere, and the triangle you need to test against. In this section we take a look at the details of determining the exact collision information between a moving sphere and a moving triangle, which could be the case, for example, when the character bottom collision sphere collides

with the level. As with more high-level collision checks, we start by simplifying the problem.

First we combine the movements of the objects. If D_S and D_T are the movements of the sphere and the triangle, respectively, we can express the combined movement D as $D = D_S - D_T$ and treat the triangle as a stationary object. Note that this simplification ignores a possible rotation of the triangle, but that is usually not a problem, as rotation can be approximated by linear movement if the time interval is small enough.

Next we divide the moving sphere-triangle collision check to subproblems, which are easier to solve. We do this by considering each part of the triangle individually and possible collision scenarios against it. The triangle consists of:

- Vertices (three) at the corners
- Edge line segments (three), which are between vertices
- A polygon face, which is an area between edge line segments

Now we can simplify the collision check by considering movement of the sphere against each of these parts in turn.

Colliding against vertices is easy. We can *reverse* the collision check and consider movement of a point (vertex) against the sphere by movement –D. Movement of a point forms a line segment, and solving line segment vs. sphere intersection is just high school algebra: We just need to form equations of line and distance to the sphere, and then replace the point in the distance equation by the point expressed by the line equation. This results in a quadratic equation, which we solve. If we get a root in range (0,1), then we have a collision.

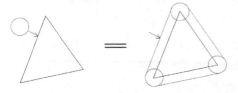

Figure 12-2: Reversing moving sphere vs. triangle check to moving point vs. extruded triangle

Testing the movement of a sphere against the interior face of the triangle seems like a harder problem at first, but this time we're able to simplify the problem by making an interesting observation: If the sphere collides (first) with the interior face, then the colliding point *must* be the one that is closest to the plane defined by triangle, and the closest point is the one farthest away from the sphere center toward the polygon plane. This observation allows us to simplify the check in the following way:

1. Solve the intersection of the line segment (sphere movement) and the plane by solving equation N_{plane} dot $(P_0 + D*t) == 0$, where N is the plane normal, P_0 is the sphere center at the start of movement, and D is the total movement. If solved t is in the range (0,1), then we have an intersection on the plane.

2. If we have an intersection, then check if the intersection point is inside the triangle.

Now we just need to test if the point is inside the triangle. That we can do by using a vector cross product and the information about the point order of the triangle. Remember that if we calculate a cross product of two vectors, we get a vector that is normal to the plane defined by these two vectors. By using a face normal (computed by (p2–p0) cross (p1–p0) if needed) and edge vectors, you can find the *edge plane*, the plane that is formed by the edge vector and face normal. If the point is inside all the edge planes, then the point is also inside the triangle face. Note that this is not the fastest way to do a point-in-polygon check, but it does work.

Now that we have found all the collisions between the moving sphere, triangle vertices, and the triangle face, we have only triangle edges left to check. This is the trickiest part of the triangle check. We solve the issue by using the Minkowski sum of the line and sphere vector spaces; in other words, we *extrude* or *fatten* the line by the sphere radius so that it becomes a capsule, and we reduce the sphere radius by the same amount. This reduction leaves us a capsule and a moving point. Since we have already checked collisions against the capsule end caps (vertices), we only need to check collisions of a moving point and an open cylinder defined by edge line segments and the sphere radius. Figure 12-2 illustrates this extrusion.

We tackle the line/cylinder collision check by simplifying it, as usual, until we end up with an easy-to-solve equation:

1. First, we set up *cylinder space*, which has the origin at the start of the cylinder and one axis (say, Z) along the cylinder axis. In matrix terms, we generate an *orthonormal basis* about the cylinder axis, which is to say that all cylinder space axes are perpendicular to each other and each axis is unit length. (Note that the math::float3x3 matrix class has a generateOrthonormalBasisFromZ() function that is suitable for this purpose.)

2. Then we transform the line segment to this cylinder space using an inverse transform.

3. Next we *clip* the line segment to the range of the cylinder, so that we're left with a line that has both end points between Z = 0 and Z = cylinder length. If the length of this clipped line is 0, then we know that the line cannot intersect the cylinder. The clipping is done the same way as calculating the intersection of a line and a plane.

4. After this, we can ignore Z altogether, since we know that the cylinder is symmetrical along its local Z-axis and both end points of the line to be tested are inside the Z=(0,length).

5. Now we have reduced the 3D line/cylinder test to 2D line vs. origin centered circle test, which can be solved by replacing the 2D line (on the XZ-plane) equation with a 2D distance-to-origin (on the XZ-plane as well) equation.

By solving the resulting quadratic equation we have also solved all collisions between the moving sphere and moving triangle!

Collision Checking between Objects

At the risk of repeating myself, we start by dividing and simplifying the problem: First we divide the problem of checking collisions between two objects to narrow-phase and broad-phase collision checking. In *narrow-phase* collision checking we want to find out if two nearby objects collide. In *broad-phase* collision checking we find out if two objects are nearby in the first place.

Narrow-phase Collision Detection

We start with narrow-phase collision detection. We've already dealt with a couple of narrow-phase collision detection examples. Next we consider collisions between two characters, represented by two capsules as before.

First, we make the assumption that the character capsules are always aligned to the world space up (Y) direction. We want to keep our character standing, at least collision shape wise, after all. Even if our character is able to duck or crawl, we don't want to handle this by rotating the collision shape, but instead we would probably use a collision shape better suited for the movement.

Next, we assume that if the characters are colliding at either of the capsule caps, then they are colliding at the middle cylinder as well, so we can check only the middle cylinders for collisions. Technically, this assumption might be incorrect, but since characters shouldn't be able to jump on top of each other anyway, we should be fine with this.

Now we have two Y-aligned cylinders to check. By looking along the Y-axis, we can find if the cylinders collide by first checking if their ranges overlap along the Y-axis, and then checking if the distances on the XZ-plane are less than r_1+r_2. (Another way to look at this check is that we extrude the second cylinder by the radius of the first one.) If both checks are true, the characters collide with each other.

Note that if we want to be able to collide against characters and other objects smoothly instead of getting stuck to them, we want objects to *slide* against each other. We can achieve this by eliminating object velocity against the contact plane normal. The contact plane in character-character collisions is directly along the vector between the XZ-plane character center points, $N=normalize(A_{xz\_}B_{xz})$. When we have this normal N, we can eliminate the velocity of A against it by subtracting the velocity component from the normal, $V = V - (V \cdot N)*N$. This way the character gets left with a velocity that doesn't collide with

the other object, which allows smooth movement in the next update as well.

Broad-phase Collision Detection

When we have a bunch of objects, the easiest way of testing collisions between them is to test every single one against every other object. This might be fine for a few objects, but the performance may suffer with the number of collision tests and time required by this basic broad-phase algorithm $O(n^2)$. Luckily we can do better. Take a look at the examples below.

Using a *hash table*, we take advantage of the fact that even though there might be many objects in the world, they are usually not clustered too closely. A hash table divides the world into *buckets* along some of the world axes. (If, for example, our world is relatively flat in the world Y-direction and most objects move close to the XZ-plane, there's no need to make a separate hash table for the Y-axis.) Each object in the world is at least in one bucket in each hash table. To find out which objects can potentially collide with each other, we only need to check which objects are sharing the same buckets. As a single element can be accessed in a hash table in constant time, the expected time requirement of this algorithm is $O(n)$.

Coordinate sorting is another approach to the same problem, which has a good expected time requirement. In this algorithm, we keep objects' world space axis-aligned bounding boxes minimum and maximum coordinates sorted along X-, Y- and Z-axes, with each axis in its own list. By reading these lists we can quickly find out if two objects overlap: If object A minimum coordinates are larger than object B maximum coordinates, the objects cannot collide with each other. Sorting itself has a time requirement of O(n log n), but keeping the lists sorted has an expected time requirement of O(n).

Additional Reading

The subject of collision checking also requires a solid understanding of the basics in (linear) algebra and trigonometry. So dig up those high school, college, and university-level books again if you have let yourself become a bit rusty on the topics.

Tomas Akenine-Möller and Eric Haines, *Real-time Rendering, 2nd Ed.*, AK Peters, 2002. (Very nice book mainly about computer graphics, but includes chapters about collision detection and intersection calculations too. See the book's web site at www.realtime-rendering.com for a list of collision detection links. The site also contains a useful table of various intersection testing methods —www.realtimerendering.com/int/.)

Mark De Berg, et al., *Computational Geometry, 2nd Ed.*, Springer-Verlag, 2000. (A good textbook about algorithms related to computational geometry. User-friendly pseudocode included illustrates the algorithms explained.)

For a large list of papers, see *Collision Detection and Proximity Queries* at the web site of the UNC Gamma Research Group at http://www.cs.unc.edu/~geom/papers/subject.shtml#COLLISION.

Chapter 13

Making Your Game Scriptable

Introduction

Scripting can reduce your workload immensely and make the overall game development workflow much smoother. Instead of seeing the results in the game after new builds, the artists can prototype and try the new content in the game real-time while they are developing it. Programmers are freed from routine content modification work and can focus on actual features.

Lua Basics

Lua is a small language especially well suited for extending C/C++ applications to be scriptable. Its origins are in a data definition language designed in 1993 for automating the task of data input to simulations in the Brazilian oil industry, but it has been used in numerous games in recent years. Lua has a number of qualities that make it suitable for game development:

- Lua is very small. The whole source take about 250 KB, and run-time overhead is less than 70 KB.

- Lua is very easy to learn. In practice you can learn the language and start using it effectively in less than a day.

- Lua is easy to integrate. With the C++ wrapper I introduce later, the integration is trivial.

- Lua is very portable. Only a few standard ANSI C library functions are used.

First I'll introduce the language itself. It is also useful to know the basics of the low-level Lua interface if you run into problems, so I'll go through it quickly before getting into the high-level C++ wrapper.

Lexical Conventions of Lua

Lua's lexical conventions closely match most other common languages. Identifiers and key words are case sensitive. Identifiers need to begin with an alphabetic character or underscore and any alphanumeric character can follow. Only single-line comments are supported, and comments start with -- (two dashes). String literals can be created with the C-like double quote (" ") pair and contain escape sequences like \ n (new line). Lua also supports multi-line string literals in the form of the double square bracket ([[ ]]) pair, for example:

```
a = [[ this is a
    multiline string
    literal ]]
```

String literals created with the [[ ]] pair can span multiple lines, but escape sequences are not expanded inside the pair.

To conform to Unix scripting conventions, if *chunk* starts with the # character, the first line is skipped. A chunk is the unit of execution in Lua — more about chunks in the section called "Statements."

Types and Values

Lua is a dynamically typed language, as most scripting languages are. Basic types in Lua are nil, Boolean, number, string, table, function, and userdata.

Boolean and number have value semantics. Strings have internally referenced semantics, but strings are immutable, so they actually appear to the user as having value semantics. Nil is a special type that roughly matches the C NULL value. Function instantiations, or *closures*, are first-class variables in Lua and they have reference copy semantics, as well as tables and userdata.

Lua relies heavily on associative arrays, which can be accessed by any type except nil. Associative arrays are implemented with the *table* type in Lua. Tables can also be heterogeneous; they can contain values of all types except nil. Tables are the only data structuring mechanism in Lua. In addition to named record access using array["name"], Lua provides syntactic sugar array.name and iteration over table elements using next(array,key), which returns the key and value of the next array element.

Userdata is a special data type that can only be modified from C code. This guarantees integrity when extending C applications by scripting, as the scripts cannot modify the value of userdata. Userdata has reference semantics, as well as tables and functions. *Metatables* can be used to define operations on userdata values, which allows Lua to be extended with custom types. Every table has a metatable, which defines the behavior of the original table. For example, for addition, Lua calls the __add member of the metatable.

Lua is not an object-oriented language, but it does support object-oriented programming by the usage of tables. Lua tables can contain associations to functions and the table itself can be passed as a first parameter to the function by using a colon (:) operator. For example, a:f() calls function f of table a and passes the table as an argument to the function.

Lua provides *type coercion* between strings and numbers at run time. This is applied so that any arithmetic operation tries to convert a string to number. Also when a string is expected, a number is converted to a string automatically.

Statements

As Lua was intended for extending applications, it has no concept of a main() function. The basic unit of execution is a *chunk*. A chunk is a sequence of Lua statements, which is optionally followed by a semicolon. Chunks are interpreted as anonymous functions, so chunks can have local variables and can return values.

In addition to the traditional assignment, Lua supports assignment of multiple values. For example a,b,c = 1,2,3 assigns a = 1, b = 2, and c = 3. Parameters to assignment are evaluated applicatively, so that x,y = y,x performs the swap operation correctly between x and y.

Lua has control structures similar to other common imperative languages. For example, the following code prints odd positive numbers less than 100:

```lua
local n = 1
local odd = true
while n < 100 do
  if odd then
    print(n)
  end
  odd = not odd
  n = n + 1
end
```

In addition to while, Lua has repeat and for loops. Repeat has the form:

```lua
repeat block until exp
```

The for loop has two forms, numerical and generic. The numeric form is:

```lua
for i=first,increment,last do block end
```

The generic form is:

```lua
for v1,...,vn in explist do block end
```

The generic for form is shorthand for the code below. Note that v1, v2..., vn are all locals inside the for loop.

```lua
do
  local _f, _s, v1 = explist
  local v2, ... , vn
  while true do
    v1, ..., vn = _f(_s, v1)
    if v1 == nil then break end
    block
  end
end
```

Lua also has return and break statements. Return is used to return a value from a code block, and break is used to break an iteration inside the loop. Lua's return statement supports multiple return values. The other difference from C language return semantics is that return and break can only be executed as the last statement of their (inner) blocks.

Expressions

Lua expressions are similar to C expressions. In arithmetic operators, the main difference is the power operator $^\wedge$, which is only present as the pow standard library function in C. Relational operators are also similar to C, with the difference of inequality, which is $\sim=$ in Lua. Logical operators are expressed in written form: and, not, or. Booleans are true and false, but they are a quite recent addition to Lua and so nil is still considered false in versions preceding Lua 5.0.

String concatenation is done with the double period (..) operator. Due to coercion rules, numbers can be concatenated to strings with this as well.

Precedence order in Lua is similar to other common languages like C. Concatenation comes after arithmetic but before relational operators.

Functions

Lua functions are first-class variables with reference copy semantics. A function is defined by:

```
function f(parameters)
    ...
end
```

This is actually syntactic sugar for:

```
f = function(parameters)
    ...
end
```

which more properly shows what is happening when Lua executes the definition. When Lua executes a function definition, the function is closed. Different function instances, or closures, can have different running environments, if they refer to parent block local variables. For example,

```
f = function(a, b)
    return function() a+b end
end
```

creates a function that returns the value of a+b at the time when function f was called. As introduced in the "Statements" section, functions can return multiple values using return with multiple parameters separated by commas. As the previous example suggested, Lua also supports anonymous and non-global functions. A variable number of arguments is supported by defaulting all arguments to nil. Lua also supports proper tail recursion; in other words, recursion at the end of the function reuses the same stack space for the call, so that tail recursion can have unlimited depth.

Lua and C/C++ Integration

Lua can be used as a language for operating system scripting, but the main focus of Lua usage has always been *enhancing* applications with scripting. This section describes the basics of Lua and C/C++ integration, with an introduction to the core Lua library C language interface, C++ techniques to make Lua usage more convenient and less error prone, the usage of the C++ wrapper, using Lua scripts for data definition, and making function calls with Lua script.

Lua C Interface

One of the many attractive points of Lua is that it is easy to get started using it. Lua implementation is fully reentrant, which means that it has no global variables. The Lua library state is contained in lua_State, which is initialized and deinitialized by calling lua_open and lua_close, respectively. Script compilation can be done by simply calling lua_dofile with the Lua state and

name of the script file as parameters. So far so good. Unfortunately, things get a bit more complicated when we start calling functions defined in Lua scripts, and even more complicated when we want Lua scripts to be able to call our functions.

Calling functions defined in Lua scripts is heavily based on the manipulation of the Lua virtual stack. The Lua virtual stack is used to pass values to and from C. Assume, for example, that the programmer wants to call a Lua script function that is an entry in a Lua hash table. This is a very common scenario in Lua usage, as tables are used frequently as roughly corresponding to objects in C++, so table functions correspond to C++ methods as well. To achieve this relatively simple operation, the programmer needs to:

1. Push the table reference to the Lua virtual stack.

2. Push the hash table key (the function name) to the Lua virtual stack with lua_pushstring.

3. Call the Lua C interface lua_gettable function with the correct Lua virtual stack index, which specifies where to find the table in which the hash table entry, defined by the previously pushed key, is located. In this case the correct index is –2, which means that the table to be used in this operation is the second element from the top of the stack backward.

4. Push any function parameters, for example a number, to the Lua virtual stack with lua_pushnumber. Arguments are passed to the stack in direct order, which means that the first argument to the function needs to be pushed to the virtual stack first as well.

5. Execute the actual script function by calling the lua_call function with the correct number of parameters. Note that function arguments are not type checked; you need to check the argument types yourself if you want to be sure that the programmer didn't pass incorrect arguments to the Lua virtual stack, say, by calling lua_pushstring when he should have called lua_pushnumber.

6. After the function has been executed by the Lua interpreter, the parameters returned by the Lua function are returned to the Lua virtual stack.

7. Parameters are not type checked either, so the programmer needs to verify types manually, for example, by calling lua_isnumber for each returned number parameter.

8. The programmer needs to retrieve the parameters, for example, by calling lua_tonumber with the correct index to retrieve the actual return value.

9. At the end, the programmer needs to clear the returned values from the Lua virtual stack by calling lua_pop(n).

Here is the same process as C code:

```
lua_getref(luastate, table);
lua_pushstring(luastate, "myfunc");
if (!lua_istable(luastate,-2))
  error("invalid table reference");
lua_gettable(luastate, -2);
lua_pushnumber(luastate, x);
if (!lua_istable(luastate,-2))
  error("cannot call non-function");
lua_call(luastate, 1, 1);
if (!lua_isnumber(luastate,-1))
  error("function myfunc didn't return number");
float returnval = lua_tonumber(luastate, -1);
lua_pop(luastate, 1);
```

The mechanics of Lua usage are similar when we want to be able to allow Lua scripts to call our C functions. C functions need to have a declaration of:

```
int scriptableCFunction(lua_State* luastate);
```

to be able to be called from a Lua script. Arguments are again received in direct order, and return values are sent to the top of the stack in direct order as well. The actual return value integer represents the number of return values left at the top of the stack.

Needless to say, programming Lua this way is tedious and highly error prone. For example, the programmer might accidentally call a wrong table by using an index that is off by one, which is an easy mistake to make. Even the Lua 5.0 reference manual suggests using macros or some other high-level mechanism for actual Lua library usage.

C++ Techniques for Lua Integration

Luckily, C++ provides mechanisms to make Lua usage effortless in actual applications. Initialization and script compilation is already straightforward with the Lua C API, but stack management was the problem in the examples shown earlier. Lua virtual stack management can be made considerably easier to use with modern C++ features.

Obviously, the first place to start when abstracting Lua virtual stack usage is the Lua hash table type, which is in heavy use especially when using Lua tables as C++ object counterparts. In my Lua C++ wrapper this abstraction was done with the C++ class LuaTable. LuaTable provided basic table operations like setString, setNumber, and so on, to avoid burdening the application programmer with Lua low-level stack management. This makes Lua table usage quite simple. So instead of writing the following:

```
lua_getref(luastate, table);
lua_pushstring(luastate, "mystring");
if (!lua_istable(luastate,-2))
  error("invalid table");
lua_gettable(luastate, -2);
if (!lua_isstring(luastate,-1))
  error("variable is not string");
char mystring[ENOUGH_SPACE];
strcpy(mystring, lua_tostring(luastate,-1));
lua_pop(luastate, 2);
```

The programmer can simply write:

```
String mystring = table.getString("mystring");
```

without having to be concerned with Lua virtual stack management details.

A more difficult target for abstraction is the function calls. If we look at the calls made from C++ to Lua scripts, we see that the only things that differ between calls are:

- Name of the Lua script function to be called

- Number of parameters given to the function

- Type of each parameter

- Optional return value and its type

Name-based calling of a Lua script function is easy to abstract. It can simply be done in a similar fashion as the table and string usage example shown earlier. For example, table.call("myfunc"); could be a simple call to a Lua script function without parameters or return values.

The number of function arguments and their types are a bit more difficult. The argument types can be abstracted by providing overloaded functions to push values to the Lua virtual stack, so that the programmer does not need to know the actual types pushed as Lua function parameters. The number of arguments can be abstracted by providing overloaded versions of the previously introduced call abstraction for the different number of parameters, say, from zero to 10 parameters. Now we can type table.call("myfunc",123,"hello"); without virtual stack management issues.

Receiving function calls from Lua is the hardest task. Ideally, we'd like to write a C++ function as is and then just register it to Lua by making a simple call like luastate->registerFunction("myfunc", myfunc);. This can be achieved by making registerFunction a template function that has the function type F as a template parameter. Clearly, at the time registerFunction is called, the compiler knows the declaration of the function parameter. This type can be used to form a new template function with the same calling convention as a regular Lua C function. This function in turn knows F, and can forward the function call to the correct function. This template magic might sound a bit confusing, but luckily the usage is easy. Now let's move on to the actual C++ wrapper usage.

Introduction to the C++ Wrapper for Lua

A Lua wrapper consists of three classes (LuaState, LuaTable, LuaObject) and an exception class (LuaException) thrown when something goes wrong. You use the wrapper by deriving your own (script-enabled) classes from LuaObject. At run time you need to create LuaState and register scriptable functions in each LuaObject derived class instance, and you're done. I'll go through every step in detail below.

LuaState, as the name implies, is a C++ wrapper for the low-level lua_State class, which is the heart of Lua. LuaState acts as a virtual machine for the script code. For example, each LuaState has its own global namespace. LuaState is actually only a thin wrapper around lua_State; LuaState's main responsibilities are to provide exception-based error handling support when using Lua. The LuaTable and LuaObject classes are more interesting, and are discussed in the next sections.

Using Lua Scripts for Data Definition

LuaTable is, as the name suggests, a handle to a Lua table. LuaTable simplifies a great deal of Lua table usage. You can query and set properties of tables, even members, which are also tables. For example, the following code shows how you create a LuaState and then a Lua table to the state (virtual machine) and set the table's myVariable as 123.456:

```
LuaState lua;
LuaTable tab(&lua);
tab.setNumber("myVariable", 123.456f);
```

You can also easily use nested tables, which are very common in Lua scripts. For example, to create a nested table "position" to a previously introduced table and set the position table as {x=1, y=2, z=3}, you could do the following:

```
LuaTable postab(&lua);
postab.setNumber("x", 1);
postab.setNumber("y", 2);
postab.setNumber("z", 3);
tab.setTable("position", postab);
```

But this isn't very interesting, so let's show how you actually let the user define the position table values inside script. In the following code snippet we compile a script called testscript.lua and let it define the values for the position table, which we just read back to the application. Below is the Lua script, followed by the associated C++ code.

```
-- testscript.lua:
position = {x=1, y=2, z=3}
```

And the associated C++ code:

```
LuaState lua;
LuaTable tab(&lua);

FileInputStream in("testscript.lua");
lua.compile(&in, in.available(), "testtab",
            &tab);

LuaTable pos = tab.getTable("position");
printf("pos = {x=%g, ...}", pos.getNumber("x"));
```

Take a look at the above source code again: Lua script is compiled using an empty "tab" table as a running *environment* for the script. That means in practice that all assignments assign values to our table members. This way the scripts can work more or less in the same way as C++ constructors. C++ code reflects this; notice that the tab table is passed to the compile function as the last argument. Then when we read the variable, we first ask the table named "position" from our tab table handle. After we have a handle to the "position" nested table in tab, we can just simply ask for the members x, y, and z from it. Convenient, yes, but being able to make function calls from script to C++ code and vice versa is even more useful, and we get into

359

that next with an introduction to the LuaObject class.

Making Function Calls to and from Lua Script

LuaObject is the glue between your class and Lua scripts. You use the class by deriving your own class from it, register functions, and compile script associated with the object. After registering the functions, Lua script can call your C++ code. Script functions defined in the Lua script can also be called directly from C++ code.

As an example, let's declare a class called MyMonster. MyMonster has the name defined in the Lua side and the 2D position defined in the C++ side (which is a very reasonable scenario). C++ provides member functions for the script, which the script can use to access and modify the position. The script doesn't need to provide services for C++ code, as C++ code can just read the variable set by the script. But first, we declare our MyMonster class:

```
class MyMonster :
    public LuaObject
{
public:
    MyMonster(LuaState* lua);

    void setPosition(float x, float y);

    float positionX() const;
    float positionY() const;

private:
    float m_x;
    float m_y;
};
```

Nothing really special there; it's just like any C++ class. Notice especially that setPosition, positionX, and positionY are regular C++ functions, which can be used as is in the C++ code as well. But what makes a difference is the implementation of the MyMonster constructor:

```
MyMonster::MyMonster(LuaState* lua) :
    LuaObject(lua)
{
    registerMethod("setPosition", this,
        &MyMonster::setPosition);
    registerMethod("positionX", this,
        &MyMonster::positionX);
    registerMethod("positionY", this,
        &MyMonster::positionY);
}
```

Here we register the methods of the class to the Lua object, so that they can be used as is in the Lua script as well. The script could look something like this:

```
setPosition(1, -3)
trace("created monster, position:")
trace("x=" .. positionX() .. ",
        y=" .. positionY())
```

The second line just prints the monster position to the debug output. Note that it calls the C++ functions positionX() and positionY() to retrieve the position of the monster, and notice also that no special boilerplate code was needed to make the function calls. Couldn't get much simpler, eh?

Still, even after all this abstraction, low-level Lua knowledge is useful. For example, you might need to handle a variable number of arguments or have some other special situation. In that case, you need to use LuaState directly for handling arguments. For this purpose, there is a separate, more low-level method registering function called registerLuaMethod, which uses a fixed function calling convention. It does not handle arbitrary arguments but always assumes LuaState* as the single and only argument. The parameters to this function are passed on top of the Lua stack, which is the same convention Lua uses to call C functions too. The return value should say how many values should be popped from the stack, so registerLua-Method supports an arbitrary number of return values as well. Below is an example function implementation using registerLua-Method conventions of a function, which sums all its arguments together.

```
int MyClass::sum(LuaState* lua)
{
    // number of arguments to sum
    int count = lua->top();
    // get numbers from top of Lua stack
    float sum = 0.f;
    for (int i = 1 ; i <= count ; ++i)
        sum += lua->toNumber(i);
    // push result to the top
    lua->pushNumber(sum);
    // inform Lua to expect one return value
    return 1;
}
```

Additional Reading

R. Ierusalimschy, L. H. de Figueiredo, W. Celes, *Lua 5.0 Reference Manual*, Technical Report MCC-14/03, PUC-Rio, 2003. (Everything you need to know about Lua. Can be found at www.lua.org/manual as well.)

Michael L. Scott, *Programming Language Pragmatics*, Morgan Kaufmann, 2000. (Maybe a bit of a heavy read, but a good textbook or reference about the fundamental concepts behind programming languages. And the book covers *many* programming languages too.)

Chapter 14

Using Triggers and State Machines

Overview

Now that we know how to draw graphics, handle collisions, and make things scriptable, we're ready to move on to interaction in the game world. In this chapter, we introduce the key concepts to enable interaction: triggers and finite state machines (FSMs). Together, they help us to build complex worlds by using simple constructions. As the two are commonly used together, we introduce both of them here. First, we start with triggers.

Triggers

Remember the basic character animation system we did in one of the graphics animation tutorials? Now imagine that you add gameplay functionality to the same piece of code, such as inventory, aiming, health, weapons, ammo, and so forth, and then think about the player character moving in a level. In a typical game you could, for example, open doors, pick up items, talk to non-player characters, use explosives to make your way through obstacles, etc. Obviously you have numerous choices. It is clear in this context that you, as a programmer and system designer, absolutely need to move most of the gameplay complexity to somewhere other than in the player class. The world is a good candidate. This is where triggers come into play.

Trigger Properties

A *trigger*, as the name suggests, is a passive object until some other game object *signals* the trigger, in other words activates it. Triggers usually have some volume, like a box or sphere, that defines the range in which the trigger can be activated. An activator object can be a player character, AI, bullet, camera, or any other game object. Different triggers can listen for different sets of activator objects. For example, we probably don't want cut scenes to be activated unless it's by the player's character arriving at a particular site, but a booby trap or mine could be activated by anyone.

A trigger can be activated only once when an object enters the space of the trigger, or it can be activated continuously when an object is in the range of the trigger. A one-shot trigger could be something like an item that is picked up (the item is not there anymore after it has been picked up) and a continuous trigger could be something like lava, which causes damage to the player for the entire time the player is walking on it.

Note that here we do not equate triggers and events given to the game objects. A trigger might or might not give some feedback to the object that triggered it. For example, when a character "opens" a door by walking toward it, the character itself doesn't necessarily need to know anything about the door being opened. (The character collides *first* with the open-door trigger, which opens the door, so the character never actually knows that the door is there!)

Triggers do not have to be predefined to some specific location or area. For example, the characters in a game could cause continuous walking sound triggers to be emitted while they walk. This sound trigger would inform enemies in the trigger area about itself. Other characters can then react to this sound trigger, which could cause a guard to be alarmed. Triggers can also be based on timers or other properties that are needed in a specific game. Basically, any event in the game can cause a trigger to be created or signaled, and often triggers provide very elegant and general-purpose design solutions.

Trigger Integration into the Game Engine

Triggers use the collision system of the game as if they were game objects. The difference is that even though triggers are collided against, they do not use the collision information to provide any kind of collision response to either of the objects, but they view the collision only as a potential activation signal.

As triggers are very small and specialized systems (for example, one trigger could just call one damage(x) function to give damage to the player), they are ideal candidates for scripting. Like any other objects, they need an *initialization* function to set up their state. They also need *signal* functions for different types of objects they want to be aware of. For example, signalPlayer(player) could be a function that gets called when the player is in the range of the trigger, signalPlayerEnter(player) could be called only when the player enters the range, and signalPlayerExit(player) could be called when the player leaves the trigger range. What different triggers do in each of these functions is specific to the game. For example, in a platformer game, a coin trigger might just increment the number of coins collected and remove the coin mesh from the game level.

It is good to derive the actual trigger volume from some graphics property so that it's more intuitive for level designers to place the triggers. Most modeling packages provide some kind of *dummy objects* or *dummy boxes*, which you can use to associate a simple volume for the trigger.

You can also specify the used trigger script in the modeling package, for example, by using *user property strings*, which are available in most packages. A user property string is a piece of text that you can associate with a single object like the dummy object or box. The property to add a trigger could be something like Trigger=coin_trigger, or whichever trigger you want to create. Other options for user property strings are name tags (naming the object so that it has Trigger=coin_trigger in its name), or systematic naming conventions, like coin01, coin02, etc. Of course, another option is to implement a dedicated trigger object as a plug-in for your modeling package.

Trigger System Performance

In addition to moving complexity from the game objects to small manageable scripts, triggers are efficient performance wise, as they do not require continuous checking from the objects. Instead of player character code actively looping through all doors in the game level for nearby doors it could open, a player-aware trigger is signaled when a player is nearby and the trigger (script) opens the door in front of the player. As triggers use the same collision system as other objects, *all* triggers can be handled $O(n)$ time instead of $O(n^2)$, which would be necessary if all objects were to check the triggers separately.

Example: Collecting and Using Items with Fake Inventory

Now let's take a look at a practical example of using triggers in game. In all first- and third-person games you can find new items, use them for various purposes, and so on. What is not so clear is that you don't necessarily need *any* kind of inventory system to implement this functionality with triggers.

Think about the case of a locked door. To open the door, the player would need a key for that door. The first solution that comes to mind is that the character would have an inventory, and when the character finds a key, the key is put into the inventory. When the character goes to the door, determining which key fits that door is based on some object identification match. This solution might match real life quite closely, but the solution is unnecessarily complex.

Instead, with triggers, there is no need for things like keys or, for that matter, inventory. First, instead of having a key object on the ground, we have a simple trigger. When the character "picks up the key," the trigger gets signaled. The trigger then "unlocks" the door as soon as the signal occurs. In addition to modifying the door object state, the trigger adds a small key icon to the game HUD. After this, the trigger can remove itself. Now, the next time the player reaches the door, the door opens because the player is carrying the key! When a door is opened, the door removes the key icon from the game HUD. So we gave the player the illusion of keys, locks, inventory, and unlocking without any of the above actually existing in the first place!

Another example of fake inventory could be a platformer style game in which you need to collect coins. Instead of actually having coins in the player character inventory, you would have *coin triggers* in the level that simply remove the coin mesh from the level and increment some global count of collected coins when the player character collides with the coin trigger. The HUD displays some symbolic coin icon and the number of coins collected without the player character object knowing anything about coins or their usage. This way, triggers provide very scalable systems for handling all kinds of inventories without adding any complexity to a probably already complex player character system.

Example: Storytelling with Triggers

Triggers are often used to give the game a more cinematic look and feel. They can be used to associate cinematic events to either gameplay or location. The simplest example is a cut-scene playback that is triggered when the player arrives in a new area. For example, a camera might pan around the scenery and show the general mood of the new area. But triggers go beyond that, and indeed, it's often better to put storytelling *inside* the game instead of having separate cut scenes.

Imagine that the player encounters an enemy mobster and shoots toward the enemy. The enemy has placed a gunshot listener trigger near himself, which makes the enemy drop any weapon and run away when it's signaled. The player is definitely impressed by this "intelligence"!

The same enemy might be scripted to run to some specific location, like a dead end, and become entrapped. This situation can also be made with triggers. You might, for example, make the enemy run forward until it reaches the dead end trigger, which makes the enemy stop and duck in fear. You can implement this multiple ways, though, and it may be better to have a more general system for path finding.

Anyway, now the enemy is shaking in fear, and creates a gun aim trigger that detects the player's gun pointing at the enemy. If the player stands next to the enemy and points the gun toward him, the trigger informs the enemy that it should give some important hint. Or the trigger could just ask game HUD to display "Please don't shoot me, you can find the magic mushroom downstairs." on screen. This makes the player really feel like he's in the game, as "everything" seems to interact with his actions.

Example: Time-based Objectives

Usually time-limited tasks don't work that great gameplay wise, except maybe in a platformer game. Imagine this scenario:

You have a pad on the floor that activates when the player character jumps on it. In another room, there is another pad that must be jumped on before five seconds has elapsed from the jump on the first pad. If the player reaches the second pad in time, he will be awarded a new weapon. As these events are happening, you want to display a running counter on the game HUD to inform the player about the elapsing time.

This can be implemented with triggers like this: First, there is an area trigger at the location of the first pad. Note that there *isn't* an active trigger at the area of the second pad at this time, but a disabled one. After the player collides with the first pad trigger (note that there isn't any collision response, of course), the trigger signal script enables the other pad trigger and creates a timer trigger. This timer trigger requires continuous updating, and after one second has elapsed, it decreases its count. After reaching zero, the timer trigger disables the second pad trigger again. The second pad trigger, on the other hand, does nothing unless the player signals it by colliding with it. This signal then awards the player with the new weapon and disables both itself and the first initiating trigger so that the player cannot use the same mechanism to get multiple weapons.

Trigger Script Error Handling

Note that the above description has several potential scripting bugs. What happens when the timer reaches zero after the player has reached the second trigger? In this case the second pad trigger has already been removed and the timer trigger tries to remove it again, resulting in a potential crash. There are several solutions to this issue, but one is to use defensive programming when providing the interface for scripts. In this case, the second removal attempt wouldn't do any harm if the remove command checks if the trigger exists. Usually error messages are better choices than hiding bugs with defensive programming, but level scripts are often at least modified by non-programmers, so it's better to be on the safe side with error handling, at least when you ship the game. It's very annoying for the user to get stuck in a game due to any error, and that includes script errors as well. This doesn't mean that error conditions shouldn't still be noticed and logged for later reviewing.

The second potential problem in the example comes from the fact that the player can collide with the first trigger multiple times, but we don't want to give the player multiple weapons or multiple counters. The solution is that the first trigger must disable itself when the timer and the second trigger are activated and vice versa.

Basically there is no difference whether you deactivate or remove the first trigger, but usually it's better to use deactivation, since removal might cause crashes if someone tries to refer to a nonexistent trigger. Problems caused by incorrect usage of deactivated triggers are hopefully less fatal.

Example: Opening a Door with Explosives

In this example, we give a character in our game an exciting task: Find explosives, set up explosives against a locked door, and blow the door up. Everything is done using simple triggers.

First, our player character tries to open a door (walks toward it as usual). There is a trigger next to the door that displays the text "It seems locked and too heavy to be kicked in. Maybe I can find some explosives." on the screen HUD. Now the player guesses that he should find some explosives, probably in another room. Note that this door trigger also activates the explosives pickup trigger, since we don't want the character to be able to pick up the explosives before he knows that he needs them. In general, the player shouldn't be able to solve problems before he encounters them!

Now our character reaches the explosives. As in the key/locked door example, the explosives trigger adds a small HUD icon showing that the character has the explosives, activates the explosion setup trigger next to the heavy locked door, and deactivates the trigger that displayed the "It seems locked..." comment.

Now the character approaches the door again, this time with explosives. As the explosion setup trigger has been activated, the player signals the trigger when he walks toward the door. Now the explosion setup trigger signal function adds a cartridge of explosives to the door mesh and sets a timer trigger of five seconds. The player (hopefully!) moves away from the door. After the timer trigger has elapsed, the trigger removes itself and starts a cut scene showing the exploding door, with cool explosion particle effects, rigid body physics for the flying door, and smoke particle systems attached to the door after the event. And all this can be done with very simple trigger scripts as described above.

Finite State Machines (FSMs)

In some of the previous trigger examples, we constructed finite state machines (FSMs) without even realizing it. In the example where we had time-based objectives, we ended up wondering whether we had covered all the special cases and potential error scenarios. This showed the need for some level of formalization of a state machine to handle the increasing complexity. In this section, we take a look at this formalization and go through some state machine examples.

Formally, a finite state machine consists of:

- A finite set of states, often denoted as Q
- A finite set of input symbols
- A transition function, which takes as arguments a state and an input symbol and returns a state
- A start state, which belongs to state set Q

In addition, we might associate *actions* to be executed in state transitions and state entering or exit.

These kinds of finite state machines are widely used in game development, and for a good reason: They work well in a wide variety of contexts and they are very easy to program.

The simplest (and most efficient) incarnation of FSM is the familiar switch statement. It has a set of states, an input symbol, a transition function that is implicitly defined by cases, and a start state that is the initial value of the input variable.

For example, FSMs can be used in character animation systems to add interactivity to levels, make interactive tutorials, set up working machinery on levels, and even AI. In fact, traditionally action/adventure game

AI has been solely based on state machines. Especially from a cinematic gaming perspective, state machines pose very desirable qualities for an AI player. Often the desire is for the AI player to behave more like a scripted sequence than have true "intelligence." It's more important to give the player an illusion of intelligence than have any actual intelligence in the agent.

You probably want to use some higher-level abstraction than switch statements in your game state machines most of the time, but since the abstraction is pretty much case dependent (many times the switch statement is just fine), we won't go into that here. Instead, let's take a look at practical state machines at work.

Example: An On-Off Switch

One of the simplest finite state machines you can find in games is an *on-off switch*. It consists of two states, ON and OFF, its initial state being ON. Inputs are TURNON and TURNOFF and the transition function goes as follows:

Input	Current State	New State
TURNON	OFF	ON
TURNOFF	ON	OFF
TURNOFF	OFF	OFF
TURNON	ON	ON

Notice how it helps to formulate the state machine as a table so you can easily see which input/state combinations have not yet been considered in the transition function. This also shows the burden of state machines: You *always* need to consider which state transitions are valid with different state/input combinations. You'll become very much aware of this when you start working on your game's character animation system, which has numerous states to be considered. Having everything explicitly defined like this helps to assure you that the system implementation also works in practice, and no special case is left unnoticed.

State machines are closely linked to triggers. Often triggers provide input to state machines, and state machines use triggers as well. For example, our on-off switch might have a player use trigger in front of it, which informs the player that the *use* action is available at that location. When the player uses the trigger, the trigger signals the associated FSM that the switch has been toggled.

All this might sound like overkill for a simple switch, but a bit of formalization overhead more than pays off in more complex scenarios where you don't see the "big picture" as clearly when it comes to states and transitions. Even in this on-off switch case, an easy error would have been to not notice how the "enable" input can be applied independently of the on-off switch state, even though it has no effect when the switch is already on.

Example: Breakable Objects

In this example, we take a look at a bit more complex combination of triggers and state machine. We define a *breakable object* state machine consisting of three states: INTACT, DAMAGED, and BROKEN. The state machine accepts only one input, HIT, which is triggered when a bullet hits the object. The initial state is INTACT. The associated transition function is:

Input	Current State	New State
HIT	INTACT	DAMAGED
HIT	DAMAGED	BROKEN
HIT	BROKEN	BROKEN

The transition function ended up being very simple. We associate the following actions with the transitions INTACT->DAMAGED and DAMAGED->BROKEN:

1. Hide the mesh associated with the previous state (for example, crate_intact).

2. Unhide the mesh associated with the new state (for example, crate_damaged).

3. Play the particle effect "smoke."

4. Play the sound "crash."

So each time the state machine goes from one state to another, the particle effect and sound are played back and the mesh is changed to a more damaged unit.

Connectivity to the outside world can also be done with triggers. We add a bullet trigger in the location of a breakable object, which listens to hitting bullets and translates these signals to input to the FSM. Then we associate intact/damaged/broken object mesh versions (like crate_intact, crate_damaged, crate_broken) with the state machine, so that it can change them accordingly in its transition function. All this is easiest to do with a simple script. We can even embed the state machine into the trigger, and have only one (trigger) Lua script associated with the crate objects:

```
function init()
    setMesh("crate_intact")
    stateFunc = stateIntact
end

function transition()
    playParticle("smoke")
    playSound("crash")
end

function stateIntact()
    transitionEffect()
    setMesh("crate_damaged")
    stateFunc = stateDamaged
end

function stateDamaged()
    transitionEffect()
```

```
    setMesh("crate_broken")
    stateFunc = stateBroken
end

function stateBroken()
    -- nothing to do
end

-- called when bullet hits the trigger box
function signalBullet()
    stateFunc()
end
```

Example: Two-floor Elevator with Closed Car

In this slightly more complex example we take a look at how to build an elevator. Our elevator is comprised of the following parts:

- Elevator car
- Elevator door
- Elevator finite state machine
- Elevator request push button outside the elevator, on both floors
- Elevator up/down push button inside the elevator car

For simplicity, we agree that there are only two floors. It wouldn't be much more complicated if we had multiple floors, but we'd need to consider multiple inputs and revise a strategy for the elevator for how it should move when multiple requests are initiated. (One possible strategy could be that it tries to keep going in the same direction as long as possible.)

Anyway, let's first consider the states of our elevator and try the following set of states:

- Waiting upstairs, doors closed (UP_CLOSED)
- Waiting downstairs, doors closed (DOWN_CLOSED)
- Waiting upstairs, doors open (UP_OPEN)
- Waiting downstairs, doors open (DOWN_OPEN)
- Upstairs reached (UP_REACHED)
- Downstairs reached (DOWN_REACHED)
- Doors opening upstairs (UP_OPENING)
- Doors opening downstairs (DOWN_OPENING)
- Doors closing upstairs (UP_CLOSING)
- Doors closing downstairs (DOWN_CLOSING)
- Going up (GOING_UP)
- Going down (GOING_DOWN)

Surprisingly many. Next, the possible inputs:

- Request elevator downstairs (REQ_DOWN)
- Request elevator upstairs (REQ_UP)
- Push elevator button inside the elevator car (BUTTON)
- Empty input (NO_INPUT)

So now we have the states and the input. Notice that we allow *empty transitions* in this state machine, since it's likely to be the most common input in a less busy area.

Let's assume the start state is that the elevator is downstairs, its doors closed. The only thing we're missing is the transition function. The transition function maps state and input to the next state, so we need all combinations of states and inputs to define it completely. This means that the transition function has 12*4 = 48 possibilities!

This shows the need to keep your machines as simple as possible; otherwise, you quickly end up with a combination explosion. Listing the transition function explicitly helps you to avoid surprises, which is always good, since otherwise you might end up with some mysterious script crash caused by an unexpected state when the player does something "wrong." Our first try with the transition function goes as follows:

Input	Current State	New State
REQ_DOWN	UP_CLOSED	GOING_DOWN
REQ_UP	UP_CLOSED	UP_OPENING
BUTTON	UP_CLOSED	GOING_DOWN
NO_INPUT	UP_CLOSED	UP_CLOSED
REQ_DOWN	DOWN_CLOSED	DOWN_OPENING
REQ_UP	DOWN_CLOSED	GOING_UP
BUTTON	DOWN_CLOSED	GOING_UP
NO_INPUT	DOWN_CLOSED	DOWN_CLOSED
REQ_DOWN	UP_OPEN	UP_CLOSING
REQ_UP	UP_OPEN	UP_OPEN
BUTTON	UP_OPEN	UP_CLOSING
NO_INPUT	UP_OPEN	UP_OPEN
REQ_DOWN	DOWN_OPEN	DOWN_OPEN
REQ_UP	DOWN_OPEN	DOWN_CLOSING
BUTTON	DOWN_OPEN	DOWN_CLOSING
NO_INPUT	DOWN_OPEN	DOWN_OPEN
REQ_DOWN	UP_REACHED	(delay input)
REQ_UP	UP_REACHED	(delay input)
BUTTON	UP_REACHED	(delay input)
NO_INPUT	UP_REACHED	UP_OPENING
REQ_DOWN	DOWN_REACHED	(delay input)
REQ_UP	DOWN_REACHED	(delay input)
BUTTON	DOWN_REACHED	(delay input)
NO_INPUT	DOWN_REACHED	DOWN_OPENING
REQ_DOWN	UP_OPENING	(delay input)
REQ_UP	UP_OPENING	(delay input)
BUTTON	UP_OPENING	(delay input)
NO_INPUT	UP_OPENING	UP_OPEN
REQ_DOWN	DOWN_OPENING	(delay input)
REQ_UP	DOWN_OPENING	(delay input)
BUTTON	DOWN_OPENING	(delay input)
NO_INPUT	DOWN_OPENING	DOWN_OPEN
REQ_DOWN	UP_CLOSING	(delay input)
REQ_UP	UP_CLOSING	(delay input)
BUTTON	UP_CLOSING	(delay input)

Input	Current State	New State
NO_INPUT	UP_CLOSING	UP_CLOSED
REQ_DOWN	DOWN_CLOSING	(delay input)
REQ_UP	DOWN_CLOSING	(delay input)
BUTTON	DOWN_CLOSING	(delay input)
NO_INPUT	DOWN_CLOSING	DOWN_CLOSED
REQ_DOWN	GOING_UP	(delay input)
REQ_UP	GOING_UP	(delay input)
BUTTON	GOING_UP	(delay input)
NO_INPUT	GOING_UP	UP_REACHED
REQ_DOWN	GOING_DOWN	(delay input)
REQ_UP	GOING_DOWN	(delay input)
BUTTON	GOING_DOWN	(delay input)
NO_INPUT	GOING_DOWN	DOWN_REACHED

Let's try to simplify this construction a bit. The problem we seem to be facing is that we don't have a "command queue" in our state machines, and we need to code a long sequence of commands to go downstairs from the upstairs-and-door-open state. We also see that most of the states in our elevator FSM abstraction ended up ignoring or delaying input altogether, which is not a very useful functionality to code as states.

To cure these issues we'll reconstruct our state machine as follows: We model all opening/closing/going states as *transitions* ("arcs" in the state diagram) instead of states, and decide that transitions are *uninterruptible* by any input. Next, we cut down empty transitions from our state machine. This way we end up with the following transition function:

Input	State	Transition	New State
REQ_UP	UP_OPEN	NONE	UP_OPEN
REQ_DOWN	UP_OPEN	CLOSE+DOWN+OPEN	DOWN_OPEN
BUTTON	UP_OPEN	CLOSE+DOWN+OPEN	DOWN_OPEN
NO_INPUT	UP_OPEN	NONE	UP_OPEN
REQ_UP	DOWN_OPEN	CLOSE+UP+OPEN	UP_OPEN
REQ_DOWN	DOWN_OPEN	NONE	DOWN_OPEN
BUTTON	DOWN_OPEN	CLOSE+UP+OPEN	UP_OPEN
NO_INPUT	DOWN_OPEN	NONE	DOWN_OPEN

Now this looks better. We ended up with three transitions (including an empty transition) and only two states. Notice that at the same time we also eliminated the need

for UP/DOWN_CLOSED states as well. The only price we pay is that transitions become more complex, but at least in this case it more than pays off in terms of simplicity. Next we need to take a look at the other aspects of in-game integration.

Usage of triggers in this case is straightforward: We need one of the previously discussed player-use triggers on each floor, next to the call button. When the player uses the trigger, the trigger is signaled and the FSM gets input as REQ_UP or REQ_DOWN, depending on which of the triggers was signaled. One trigger is also needed inside the elevator car. It will, when signaled, give BUTTON input to the FSM.

The next question is the animation of transitions. As we simplified the whole state machine, now we can model the whole transition as a single sequence. But we can also note that the second transition is a *mirror* of the first one, so we need only one animation. The animation starts with the downstairs doors open, then the doors close, and the car moves upstairs. Finally, the doors open upstairs. This animation works for both CLOSE+DOWN+OPEN and CLOSE+UP+OPEN transitions when played back in two directions.

One issue left is the elevator movement and how that integrates into our game world. We realize that there might be objects in the elevators, which complicates issues a bit.

Luckily we have options: 1) Add, for example, a *slider joint* to our elevator car, define the maximum force and desired velocity, and actually simulate the movement of the elevator car. 2) We find out which objects are in the elevator, and apply force to each of the objects to make them move at the same speed with the elevator animation.

This time we choose the second option, since the elevator car object can determine all current contacts with the collision system, and this way we don't need to worry about where the car animation actually

moves the elevator, nor whether it makes sense physically, for that matter.

Now we're almost done. The only thing we still need to consider is if something is between the doors when they close. We handle this special case by deciding that any transition is *reversed* if any collisions occur. For example, if there is an object between the doors when they close downstairs, the elevator returns to the DOWN_OPEN state. This should work fine as long as we ignore small objects. (You definitely don't want your elevator to get stuck because of a bullet on the ground!)

Example: Enemy Guard Robot AI

Some people disagree about whether finite state machine-based agents should be considered AI agents at all. Well, maybe FSMs do not have much in common with modern AI research, but if we regard as AI *anything* that looks like it behaves intelligently to the player, then FSMs can definitely be used to make a good AI player.

We need to make some assumptions here to reduce the scope of this section. We will focus only on the enemy guard robot in first- or third-person games, which in our case means that the enemy is mainly interested in getting the player killed. It does not do laundry, communicate with other robots, eat, or do anything else.

The enemy robot does potentially only the following things, one at a time:

- *Idling* on the patrol path, recharging his batteries by enjoying the sunlight
- *Patrolling* around his path
- *Combat*. In combat mode, the robot tries to fight the player character.
- *Fleeing* when the battle isn't going well

- *Searching* for the player when he tries to hide during combat

This clearly shows the need for multiple levels of finite state machines. If we tried to model *everything* in a one-state machine, it'd be huge (and completely unmaintainable!).

Instead, we have one *behavioral* state machine, with states from the list above. Each of the states in this high-level machine can contain multiple substates, which perform smaller subtasks. The behavioral state machine selects the transitions based on what the robot sees, hears, feels, and guesses. For example, if the player walks into the field of view of the robot, then the robot likely transitions to the combat mode, regardless of its previous behavioral state. The easiest way to model these perceived inputs is to use a collision system to trace the line of sight and to use ranges for other inputs such as hearing sounds.

Anyway, now we assume that the robot has noticed the player, one way or another, and the robot decides to transition to the combat state. The combat state might consist of the following available strategies:

- *Camp/ambush* player behind corner
- *Shoot* and *strafe* at the same time
- *Kamikaze* approach by running and shooting toward player
- *Flee and shoot* at the same time

Each of these might also be implemented with state machines, but they interact with the high-level behavioral state machine only indirectly, as the combat state changes to something else, e.g., searching.

Patrolling can also be implemented in multiple ways. You can instruct the robot to move directly with the Logo programming language turtle graphics style "walk forward 5 meters" commands, or you can define patrolling paths as curves in the

modeling software, which makes complicated path building less of a pain. These curves can then be deconstructed to a list of points that are followed by the robot. In pseudocode:

```
MyPatrol::MyPatrol ()
{
    m_index = 0;
}

void MyPatrol ::update()
{
    if (hasReachedThePoint(m_index))
    {
        // go to next point
        m_index = (m_index+1) % pointcount;
    }
    else
    {
        float3 direction = (getPoint(m_index) -
            m_position).normalize();
        walkTo (direction);
    }
}
```

Okay, so now the robot knows how to follow the path. More complex paths, like forking ones, could be created by preprocessing path curves and finding out where they intersect on the XZ-plane. Basically, only the intersection points would require more complex handling; the robot would need to select the path where it goes next. As this doesn't bring much extra value to our pseudocode we leave this as an exercise to the reader.

Still, this doesn't mean that straightforward goto(x,z) style movement commands wouldn't have their place. For example, during combat the robot definitely needs to abandon its post and head toward the player or some other location, maybe the nearest place to hide.

The places to hide could be modeled as dummy objects in the level that mark safe spots. When the robot ends up in combat, it could, if needed, find the nearest safe spot and head toward it. There is one potential complication, since the concept of a safe spot might be quite dependent upon which direction you look at the combat situation. The robot might try to analyze the scenario by building some estimate of a firing direction, and base his decisions about the best safe spots on that. Each safe spot in turn would store information about the direction of the spot, for example, the safe spot would be safe to the positive X-axis, but not toward the negative X-axis. By using this information, navigation of the robot during battle might seem to look quite sophisticated, even though it was simply based on predefined safe spots and their valuation function during combat.

Fleeing of the robot during battle could be implemented using the patrolling paths as well. Initial fleeing in the combat, when the robot is not on the path, would need to start by looking for a direct route to some patrolling path. If multiple direct routes to patrolling paths were found, the robot would need to decide which of them leads to a safe place quickly. This could be based on ray tracing the line of sight from the enemy to the robot and checking when the robot reaches a hiding place whether a specified patrol path could be used to escape.

You could also spend multiple AI update cycles to optimize the path to the safe place. This would look to the player as if the AI were puzzled for some time, which again increases its illusion of intelligence.

And remember that it's not always a bad thing to make wrong decisions, since to err is human, and to err during fierce battle (with its high stress levels) is even more human. And looking human is good, especially for a computer game AI.

Additional Reading

Steve Rabin (editor), *AI Game Programming Wisdom*, Charles River Media, 2002. (Contains articles related to finite state machines, triggers, and AI. A good book in general.)

Sunbir Gill, "Visual Finite State Machine AI Systems," *Game Developer Magazine*, Nov. 2004. (A nice article about importing AI state machines directly from the Visio diagram drawing tool to the game code. The article can also be found at the Gamasutra web site, http://www.gamasutra.com/features/20041118/gill_01.shtml.)

Stuart J. Russell, Peter Norvig, *Artificial Intelligence: A Modern Approach, 2nd Ed.*, Prentice Hall, 2002. (A good introductory book about a wide variety of AI techniques. Not really from a game developer's perspective, but the book includes many game-like examples as well.)

John E. Hopcroft, Rajeev Motwani, and Jeffrey D. Ullman, *Introduction to Automata Theory, Languages and Computation, 2nd Ed.*, Addison-Wesley, 2001. (A good basic textbook about the theory of computation. Related to this chapter because it contains a nice introduction to deterministic finite automata, and teaches you to construct and handle them.)

Chapter 15

Game Framework Design

More often than not, software architectures suitable for games have many similarities. In this chapter we look at design primarily from the perspective of a first- or third-person action game, but we also discuss how design applies to some other game genres. The chapter is a very quick introduction to software design, but you have to start somewhere, and at least you shouldn't be bored while waiting to get into actual coding! And *any* effort spent on software design is definitely better than the code-and-fix approach.

Analyzing Software Requirements

As making games isn't really that radically different from other software development, it's not surprising that many of the same approaches that work well for traditional software engineering work well for games too.

A good approach for getting started with game software architecture design is to first make an informal textual description of the game (or a proper design document) and then explicitly cut "marketing" talk and unnecessary features out of it before continuing with the design. Unfortunately, many game design documents are unnecessarily long because they end up being a kind of mix between design documents and marketing material, so you probably don't want to use them directly.

The design document might also be written by people without any programming background, which may result in unnecessarily complex features if they don't think about the concepts and needs behind the descriptions. That's why it's a good idea to keep the design document as separate from the implementation as possible, so that the design document describes only *what* and not *how*.

The bad thing about a long design document is that no one reads it or keeps it up to date. For example, in one project I worked on, the design document of the game was 100+ pages. When I asked the programmers how many of them had read the design document, it turned out that none had. The reason: The document was overly wordy, and it was quite difficult to pick actual feature descriptions from it. When the design document sounds like marketing material without much information, you get bored and stop reading before even reaching the actual features.

Anyway, after you have a very condensed, no-nonsense description of the game, you can start gathering verbs and nouns from it. This is an old and simple approach, but it works quite well in practice. A noun in this case is a potential class or object and a verb is a potential functionality or action for some object. In practice, it's often easier to find objects first, and only then think about responsibilities and how they should be assigned to the objects.

Let's see how this would work for our game demo. From our game description, or from descriptions of other third- or first-person games, we could end up with an initial object list that looks something like this:

- Level
- Start point
- Vehicle
- Player character
- Enemy
- Friendly character
- Laser pistol
- Crate
- Barrel
- Moving pad
- Health power-up
- Coin
- Bullet
- Ammo
- Shell
- Cut scene
- HUD

Notice that the list isn't radically different from, for example, a racing game's list. The level would be a track, the characters' cars, other racing cars, and so forth.

Designing the Class Architecture

Now that we have the initial object list, we can start categorizing these objects and determining the relationships between them. There are a number of relationships to consider, for example:

- Does the object consist of other objects?
- Are the lifetimes of two objects dependent on each other?
- Does the object use some other objects?
- Which other objects use this object?
- Is this object type a special case of some other, more general type?

Let's see how this works in practice with our object list. We start with the level, since all action happens in it.

First, we note that the level definitely needs to be a class in the game; we call it GameLevel. Next, we note that all player character and other game objects are *contained* in the level. This doesn't necessarily

mean that the objects' lifetimes are dependent on the lifetime of the level, since in this case a player character can move to and from levels. So we model this relationship as an *aggregation*; destroying the level does not necessarily destroy the objects inside the level. Now we can start to categorize various objects in the level.

Both the player and enemies are *characters*, sharing most of the same functionality, so they can have a shared base class, GameCharacter. Note that we use the "Game" prefix to avoid confusing a class named "character" with the word "character" in a text string.

Start point can be just a simple property of the level, so we don't make it its own class. If in doubt, it's usually better to have each object in its own class, but in this case we have only a simple matrix representing the start point, so we can leave the class out as unnecessary implementation burden.

Vehicle, on the other hand, is very much its own class. Vehicles in turn probably consist of many other objects, like tires and body. Still, vehicles also share some properties with characters, such as positions and velocity in the level.

So we make this concept of *game object* a generalization, GameObject. This is natural since all game objects are in the level. They have position, rotation, and velocity and they can move around in the level and collide with other game objects. Much of this functionality can be shared between various objects like characters, cameras, and vehicles.

Next, we consider the laser pistol. We can immediately generalize this as a weapon. When considering weapons, we have to consider two different things: how they are represented when they are in the level and how they operate when a GameCharacter uses them. We decide to represent a weapon that can be picked up by placing a trigger (GameTrigger) on the weapon's position. This trigger then adds the weapon to the character (inventory), which collides with the trigger. Game-Weapon is still a GameObject as well, since it has position and other similar properties when it's not in any character's possession.

Health power-up, coin, and ammo are also specializations of more general location-based GameTriggers, with an additional mesh. We place a trigger and some mesh representing the health power-up on the level. For this specialization, however, we can do without adding any class to our framework, since we have scripting support and the power-up is sufficiently simple to not require any custom

C++ code or separate handling. Each of these pick-up types will just have their own script associated with GameTrigger objects.

Crate, barrel, and moving pad share many properties. All have geometry, they can be considered part of the level, characters can stand on top of them, and they are either simulated by physics or animated by keyframes. We generalize them as GameDynamicObjects, which in turn is a specialization of GameObject.

We also add a class for GameCamera. This might seem unnecessary, as we already have a camera class in the engine, but GameCamera has very meaningful functionality: It controls the logic of how the camera follows the player character in the game. This is by nature very game specific, so we also need to have the class in the game instead of just in the 3D graphics engine. GameCamera can also contain scripting functionality specific to the game.

GameHUD, on the other hand, is a completely separate class from the main GameObject hierarchy. It has no position in the level, and it is not contained within GameLevel either. However, as it is desirable to have a scriptable HUD, we probably want to derive it from LuaObject. The GameObject should be derived from it too to provide scripting support to all game objects.

Figure 15-1 shows these relationships using UML (Unified Modeling Language) notation for class diagrams, which is relatively standard notation in software design. A basic reference for the UML class diagram notation can be found in Figure 15-2.

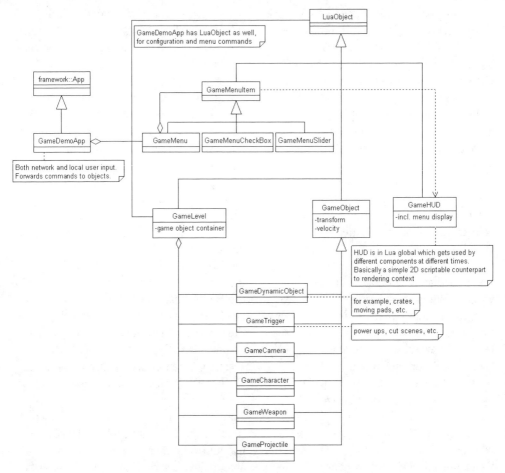

Figure 15-1: Visualizing class relationships using UML class diagram notation

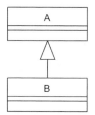

Generalization. A is base class of B

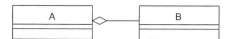

Aggregation. B is part of A, but destroying A doesn't
necessarily destroy B (think of A having a pointer to B)

Composition. B is part of A, and destroying A always
destroys B (think of B as a member of A)

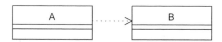

Dependency. A is dependent on B

Figure 15-2: Basic UML class diagram notation

Additional Reading

Craig Larman, *Applying UML and Patterns*, Prentice Hall, 1997. (Easy-to-read and practical book about UML and its usage.)

Erich Gamma, et al., *Design Patterns*, Addison-Wesley, 1995. (A classic book about reusable patterns in software development. The book lists common software design patterns systematically and explicitly, and in an easy-to-read manner.)

Grady Booch, *Object-Oriented Analysis and Design with Applications, 2nd Ed.*, Addison-Wesley, 1993. (May be a bit academic, but still a good introductory book about OOAD.)

Roger S. Pressman, *Software Engineering, A Practitioner's Approach, 5th Ed.*, McGraw-Hill, 2000. (Contains a lot of stuff about various topics related to software engineering, including object-oriented analysis and design.)

Chapter 16

Game Demo Technical Document

Now it's time to put the various pieces together. In this chapter we make a basic technical document for our game demo. While a game design document answers the question "what," the technical document should answer the question "how." So the document is written mainly for the producer and programmers new to the project. Even though the producer wouldn't understand everything, he can be sure that the technical issues have been thought out beforehand.

Note that the concept of "technical document" in game development is usually a bit loose. If you want to map the term to more standard software engineering terminology, the technical document is something between a *requirements specification* and a *technical specification*. A game design document is usually more like a requirements specification, but the line isn't always that clear. Anyway, how you structure the document is up to you; the main thing is that you think about the stuff needed to make the game.

Even with a relatively small project, it's best to start with specifying the scope and requirements explicitly. Otherwise, you might end up noticing that the small project wasn't so small after all.

Limiting Features

Before writing down how the features of the game are made, consider whether each of the features is really needed. What is a good feature made of anyway?

- The feature is easy to understand.
- The feature has solid reason for being.
- The feature is easy to design into the overall architecture.
- The feature is easy to implement.
- The implementation works in all cases needed.
- The implementation can be done efficiently.

So in other words, the best feature is the one that you don't do at all, but unfortunately that's not always an option. Still, it's a good idea to cut down as many features as you can before you start planning how to implement them.

Hardware Requirements

There is one problem when you plan hardware requirements for a game demo. If the game we're talking about is a normal PC game, it will be in shops after about two years. But the demo might still be evaluated by potential publishers with relatively low-end machines. So adjusting between current system requirements and future users' computers might require some balancing. You might want to provide at least an option for lower detail level and legacy shaders, which also work on lower-end hardware.

In our case, luckily, we're making a demo for the book. The book's audience will be using the demo in a couple of months, so we don't want to go overboard with system requirements and put off potential readers. Also, the readers of the book will be future developers, so they'll likely have a quite decent 3D adapter, which makes things easier for us.

Basic Technical Document

Target Platform

The demo should work well on a 2+ GHz PC with 256 MB memory and a modern 3D accelerator with 128 MB of memory and pixel shader support.

Because of our limited testing possibilities we can promise only that the demo included with this book works on Windows XP. DirectX 9.0c must be installed before the demo.

All 3D accelerators with at least Pixel Shader 1.1 level hardware are basically supported, even though the demo has been tested only on a couple of different 3D accelerators (ATI Radeon 9600).

Note:

The most important rule about the target platform is that if you want to sell a game on some specific platform, then you need to have the demo running on that same platform. According to a study by IGDA, most publishers list "demo on target platform" as their most important priority when evaluating game demos.

Memory Requirements

The demo should require a maximum of 128 MB of memory. This should be enough, since the "standard PC" we're targeting has at least 256 MB of memory.

In addition to system memory, the display adapter is recommended to have 128 MB of memory because we don't want to spend time optimizing textures at this stage of development.

Note:

Using 128 MB of memory might sound a bit high if you're thinking about consoles; however, it's a bit hard to compare console memory usage and PC memory usage directly. The biggest difference is texture memory. For example, on a PlayStation 2 game, it is likely that most of your textures are in 8-bit or 4-bit palette format. This alone reduces texture memory usage considerably. As you're aiming for a TV screen, you can also use smaller textures, which makes an even bigger difference. By halving the texture size, you save memory by a factor of 4!

Key Technical Features

The demo shows the following key features:

- Player character can move in a game level.

- Player character can aim and shoot with laser gun.

- Character animation system supports non-linear character movement speed.

- Interaction of world objects and character uses rigid body physics simulation; for example, a character can "kick" crates around.

- Camera follows the player character in third-person mode.

- Graphics rendering is done using normal mapping, colored lights, a combination of dynamic and static lighting, and various special effects like glow, fog, and particles.

Note:

We don't go into details here; this is only meant to provide the overview of the features.

3D Engine

The game demo was chosen to be implemented using the Ka3D engine. This saves time in development and provides a robust toolset that can be reused in the actual game. The 3D engine provides our demo the following features right from the start:

- Tool support
- Rendering engine
- Scripting
- Physics
- File system I/O and other utilities
- Performance profiling
- Unicode support

- Other commonly needed support functionality like linear algebra classes

Each of these features is discussed in more detail below.

Note:

When considering whether to use an external 3D engine or make your own, you should really consider whether you plan to create a game or technology. If you focus on technology, you might find yourself in a position where you don't have any time to spend making the actual game.

3D Content Creation Support Tools

The engine provides an exporter for saving game content from 3ds max to the game. It writes scene hierarchy, geometry and keyframed animations to a single scene file with an .hgr extension.

The exporter also takes care of optimizing the geometry for rendering. For example, it splits the exported character meshes based on bone/vertex constant limitations of the current generation of shader hardware. Exported 3D models and animations can be imported with a single line of code.

Viewing these 3D scenes and animations can be done before any game code is written, by using the external 3D file viewer provided with the engine.

The engine also supports flexible particle systems. The particle systems can be edited real-time using the same 3D file viewer.

The engine provides low-level support for writing/reading scene files used by the engine. Scene file input/output support can be used for user-defined file format conversions if needed in the actual game.

Graphics Rendering

Various features of the rendering engine are used in the game demo. Each of the features is introduced below.

The engine renders skinned characters using simultaneous diffuse texture mapping, normal mapping, glow mapping and specular level mapping, and colored lights.

Level rendering is done using combined static and dynamic lighting of the level based on normal mapping.

Various special effects are used to provide mood in the game, like fogged environment, particles, and post-processing effects like glow.

The rendering engine supports the latest DirectX features like the HLSL shading language, yet the abstraction level is much higher than plain DirectX usage.

The engine comes with a library of ready-to-use shaders, including normal mapping and per-texel variable specular highlights, which also work in 3ds max 6 in a WYSIWYG manner to assist artists in their game content creation.

The engine also supports text rendering using the familiar printf style format, and drawing textures as 2D images. 2D rendering is used for HUD, UI, and debug information.

The engine provides abstraction of transformation hierarchy, meshes, camera, lights, particle systems, and other traditional scene graph related objects.

Multiple simultaneous rendering pipelines are supported, which enables fog and glow to be rendered separately from the default scene.

Support is also included for render-to-texture-based post-processing effects like glow, negation, and motion blur.

To assist in such things as collision debugging, the rendering engine supports simple 3D line drawing.

Scripting Support Library

The purpose of the scripting support library is to provide a much higher level interface to Lua than using plain Lua directly:

- The wrapper gives the user the ability to use the one-line C++ method of registration and one-line Lua function calls.

- The wrapper also supports object-oriented programming in Lua.

The library consists of LuaState, LuaTable, and LuaObject classes. LuaState represents the state of the Lua script running environment. LuaTable is a handle class to Lua's associative array. (See Chapter 13, "Making Your Game Scriptable," for more information.) LuaObject is the base class for C++ objects, which are extended by Lua scripts. It provides functionality for mapping C++ methods to Lua.

Rigid Body Physics Support

A small wrapper library is currently an *open layer* above the Open Dynamics Engine (ODE). This means that you will also need to use ODE itself when using the wrapper, but on the other hand you will have all the features ODE provides, plus some of them are just much more convenient to use with the wrapper.

So why wrap ODE functionality at all?

- Better resource management (RAII idiom; Resource Acquisition is Initialization)

- Easy interface to create rigid bodies from 3D engine meshes

- Maps transformations between simulated rigid bodies and 3D engine meshes (it's not always straightforward, though, due to things like scaling, hierarchies, and different pivot point transformations)

Hides repetitive setup tasks and avoids the need to copy and paste code

Provides ODE function wrappers, which take 3D engine vector (float3, etc.) and matrix classes (odex.h) for convenience

Even though the wrapper currently has limited functionality, it makes various tasks easier when you are using ODE. For example, you don't need any callbacks, lengthy triangle meshes, or transformation setups to get a simulation up and running, even when the geometry comes from a 3ds max scene. For a usage example see the tutorials\physics_simulation folder.

Integration of physics is handled by describing physics properties as 3ds max object *user properties*. This is a way to pass text information to the application from 3ds max. The following properties are supported:

Physics=x, where x is a box or sphere, enables rigid body physics for the object. Body size is computed automatically from the object bounding box. See also Mass and Density below.

Mass=x sets the total mass for the object when Physics=x is used. Note that Mass and Density are mutually exclusive.

Density=x sets a size-relative mass for the object when Physics=$<x>$ is used. Note that Mass and Density are mutually exclusive.

Collision Checking

Collisions are handled indirectly by using various collision geometry objects supported by the ODE. The following collision geometry objects are used to represent game objects:

The character is simulated as a moving capsule.

Bullets are simulated as points.

The camera is simulated as a moving sphere.

Triggers are simulated as oriented boxes.

Sounds are simulated as spheres.

Level geometry is simulated as a single triangle mesh.

In addition, two 3ds max object user-defined properties can be used to toggle collisions on and off for level objects:

The collision=only user-defined object property can be used to add static level collision objects that are not visible in the level.

The collision=none user-defined object property can be used to add level objects that are not collided against at all but are still visible. All objects that can never be collided against should be tagged this way.

Mathematics Support Library

The main feature of the library is to provide support for various linear algebra classes like float2, float3, float4, float3x3, float3x4, float4x4, and quaternion.

The library also provides interpolation support with end-behavior specifications, which are useful while animating characters.

Random numbers are frequently used to assist special effects like particles and non-deterministic behavior of AI. The library also supports various random variables, like a randomizing point inside a sphere, provided by the RandomUtil class.

C++ Language Support and File System Abstraction

To provide better support for Unicode and to avoid excessive compile-time dependencies, a custom low-level language support library is used rather than C++ STL. The library uses only standard C functions in its implementation to provide maximum portability. The library has been successfully ported even to Symbian OS.

I/O library consists of input/output stream classes, PathName class for file and directory name string manipulation, and FindFile for finding files or directories.

In the final game, all files used by the game will be *archived* and sorted according to their usage pattern. This provides maximum performance when reading the files from CD, DVD, or other media.

Music and Sounds

Ogg Vorbis will be used for music. Ogg Vorbis is an open source replacement for MP3. Sound playback will be done with DirectSound.

Game Demo Controls

The demo starts right in the game. No menu navigation is needed to get into the game. The character is controlled with the keyboard and mouse:

W	Walk forward
A	Step left
D	Step right
Mouse	Turn Left/Right/Up/Down
Spacebar	Jump up
Up Arrow+Spacebar	Jump out
Left mouse button	Aim/fire weapon
Backspace	Drop weapon

Other functional keys in the demo:

F4	Toggle slow motion (10%)
Shift+F4	Toggle fast forward (3x)
F5	Restart
F7	Toggle debug info
F8	Next debug info mode
Shift+F8	Previous debug info mode
F11	Toggle default rendering pass on/off
F12	Toggle fog rendering pass on/off

Shift +F11	Toggle sprite rendering pass on/off
Shift+F12	Toggle glow rendering pass on/off

Note:

Leaving out menus is not intended to save demo development time, but rather to let the viewer know that this is not a finished product. It's better to look a bit unpolished in this sense, because having complete menus would raise questions like "Isn't there anything else to improve so they made menus?"

Game Character Animation System

There were three main goals while designing the character animation system:

- New animations and movements must be easy to add to the game.

- The character must be able to move with non-linear speeds inside a single movement. When the character starts a jump, for example, it first crouches a bit to gain strength, and only then jumps in the air. Character movement must reflect this accurately.

- While aiming, the gun must point to the actual target point.

These three goals ended up being a bit dependent on each other. It turns out that one major pain while adding new movements is how to specify the movement speed. This leads to the second issue: Because of an incorrect movement speed the feet slip. The same applies to the last item.

The first two problems were solved by using character animation data to define basic character movement speed. The speed of the character is automatically extracted from animations, so no manual tweaking is needed and new animations can be imported to the game easily.

In addition to automatic character movement speed extraction, the system provides automatic directing of animations. Rotating whole animations inside an animation package might be cumbersome, so we rotate the animations at load time in the game. This is a very low-overhead operation and provides additional flexibility in development.

Aiming/shooting is handled by having three sets of upper body animations: Up, Front, and Down. These are blended according to the character's pitch rotation. After this, the weapon of the character is rotated to match the real target direction in world space.

In the game demo, the character animation system is encapsulated inside the GameCharacter class. The relationship of this and other classes are shown in Figure 15-1.

Game Enemy AI

Game enemy artificial intelligence will be implemented by using finite state machines

(FSMs) and triggers. All AI parameters are scriptable to provide level designers the ability to customize the behavior by location-specific needs.

There are two levels in the FSM architecture: the behavioral level, which takes care of the high-level decisions, and the controller level, which performs more specific tasks such as fights against the player or navigation along a patrol path.

Finite state machines are selected by using various triggers. These include gunshot, damage, and area triggers and signals from other AI characters.

Game Framework Class Architecture

See Figure 15-1 in the previous chapter for an illustration of the high-level class hierarchy of the game framework. The class diagram has been drawn using UML class diagram notation.

Additional Reading

Tim Ryan, "The Anatomy of a Design Document, Part 2: Documentation Guidelines for the Functional and Technical Specifications," Gamasutra web site (http://www.gamasutra.com/features/19991217/ryan_01.htm), December 17, 1999.

Afterword

So, there you have it. I end this with a rousing and encouraging letter of hope for you during the late-night hours of game creation in the months and years ahead.

The world of video games is often thought of as the best of both worlds — the world of entertainment and the world of science — combined together to create an artistic expression and form that typifies the unity and success between diversity. I'm certain in times past that each field had growing pains, opposition, and struggles. From the work and dedication of those pioneers came many advances and better ways of doing things. Having that focus, that goal, and the opportunity to further our futures, they set up for us an environment unique to any other. Because of the commitment and this book you hold in your hands we are all that much closer to realizing our dreams.

My last thanks are for the criticism and feedback to come. We can all learn from one another to help further our skills and knowledge of creating games so that we will all be one step closer to perfecting this great form of expression.

Final Note and Reminder:

We have been given a present, a gift of sorts, that comes with a price tag. The price is our willingness and our time. I leave you with this: How willing, how motivated, how driven are you to become a game developer? I know you have it in you to create some of the greatest work and stories of our generation, but will you be the one to share it with the world and have gamers attached to and captivated by your storylines, your characters, and universes?

Good luck with all your endeavors and may God bless you in all you put your hands to.

Index

Looking for more?

Check out Wordware's market-leading Graphic Library featuring the following titles.

LightWave 3D 8 Cartoon Character Creation
Volume 1: Modeling & Texturing
1-55622-253-X • $49.95
6 x 9 • 496 pp.

LightWave 3D 8 Cartoon Character Creation
Volume 2: Rigging & Animation
1-55622-254-8 • $49.95
6 x 9 • 440 pp.

LightWave 3D 8: 1001 Tips & Tricks
1-55622-090-1 • $39.95
6 x 9 • 648 pp.

Essential LightWave 3D 8
1-55622-082-0 • $44.95
6 x 9 • 624 pp.

Modeling a Character in 3ds max (2nd Ed.)
1-55622-088-X • $44.95
6 x 9 • 600 pp.

3ds max Lighting
1-55622-401-X • $49.95
6 x 9 • 432 pp.

LightWave 3D 8 Character Animation
1-55622-099-5 • $49.95
6 x 9 • 496 pp.

LightWave 3D 8 Lighting
1-55622-094-4 • $54.95
6 x 9 • 536 pp.

LightWave 3D 8 Texturing
1-55622-285-8 • $49.95
6 x 9 • 504 pp.

CGI Filmmaking: The Creation of Ghost Warrior
1-55622-227-0 • $49.95
9 x 7 • 344 pp.

Advanced Lighting and Materials with Shaders
1-55622-292-0 • $44.95
9 x 7 • 360 pp.

Coming Soon:

Fundamentals of Character Animation
1-55622-248-3 • $49.95
9 x 7 • 400 pp.

Design First for 3D Animators
1-55622-085-5 • $49.95
9 x 7 • 300 pp.

Visit us online at www.wordware.com for more information.
Use the following coupon code for online specials: **demo0480**

About the CD-ROM

The companion CD-ROM contains everything needed to complete the tutorials presented in the chapters, the Zax demo, and extra examples. The directories are organized as follows:

- **Images:** All the images from the book in full color.
- **Software:** Demo software and company links.
- **Templates:** A set of blank templates for setting up a directory structure to keep your project organized.
- **Tools:** All supplementary max script files, and normal map tools for 3ds max and Adobe Photoshop.
- **Tutorials:** All the files necessary to complete each 3D tutorial in the book, along with additional files and examples.
- **Ka3d Install:** An installation executable that will install all the appropriate files for the programming tutorials and Zax game demo.

Warning: By opening the CD package, you accept the terms and conditions of the CD/Source Code Usage License Agreement. Additionally, opening the CD package makes this book nonreturnable.

CD/Source Code Usage License Agreement

Please read the following CD/Source Code usage license agreement before opening the CD and using the contents therein:

1. By opening the accompanying software package, you are indicating that you have read and agree to be bound by all terms and conditions of this CD/Source Code usage license agreement.

2. The compilation of code and utilities contained on the CD and in the book are copyrighted and protected by both U.S. copyright law and international copyright treaties, and is owned by Wordware Publishing, Inc. Individual source code, example programs, help files, freeware, shareware, utilities, and evaluation packages, including their copyrights, are owned by the respective authors.

3. No part of the enclosed CD or this book, including all source code, help files, shareware, freeware, utilities, example programs, or evaluation programs, may be made available on a public forum (such as a World Wide Web page, FTP site, bulletin board, or Internet news group) without the express written permission of Wordware Publishing, Inc. or the author of the respective source code, help files, shareware, freeware, utilities, example programs, or evaluation programs.

4. You may not decompile, reverse engineer, disassemble, create a derivative work, or otherwise use the enclosed programs, help files, freeware, shareware, utilities, or evaluation programs except as stated in this agreement.

5. The software, contained on the CD and/or as source code in this book, is sold without warranty of any kind. Wordware Publishing, Inc. and the authors specifically disclaim all other warranties, express or implied, including but not limited to implied warranties of merchantability and fitness for a particular purpose with respect to defects in the disk, the program, source code, sample files, help files, freeware, shareware, utilities, and evaluation programs contained therein, and/or the techniques described in the book and implemented in the example programs. In no event shall Wordware Publishing, Inc., its dealers, its distributors, or the authors be liable or held responsible for any loss of profit or any other alleged or actual private or commercial damage, including but not limited to special, incidental, consequential, or other damages.

6. One (1) copy of the CD or any source code therein may be created for backup purposes. The CD and all accompanying source code, sample files, help files, freeware, shareware, utilities, and evaluation programs may be copied to your hard drive. With the exception of freeware and shareware programs, at no time can any part of the contents of this CD reside on more than one computer at one time. The contents of the CD can be copied to another computer, as long as the contents of the CD contained on the original computer are deleted.

7. You may not include any part of the CD contents, including all source code, example programs, shareware, freeware, help files, utilities, or evaluation programs in any compilation of source code, utilities, help files, example programs, freeware, shareware, or evaluation programs on any media, including but not limited to CD, disk, or Internet distribution, without the express written permission of Wordware Publishing, Inc. or the owner of the individual source code, utilities, help files, example programs, freeware, shareware, or evaluation programs.

8. You may use the source code, techniques, and example programs in your own commercial or private applications unless otherwise noted by additional usage agreements as found on the CD.

Warning: By opening the CD package, you accept the terms and conditions of the CD/Source Code Usage License Agreement. Additionally, opening the CD package makes this book nonreturnable.